CHICAGO QUARTERLY REVIEW

Volume 29
FALL 2019

The Chicago Quarterly Review is published by The Chicago Quarterly Review 501(c)3 in Evanston, Illinois. Unsolicited submissions are welcome through our submissions manager at Submittable. To find out more about us, please visit www.chicagoquarterlyreview.com.

PROUD MEMBER

[clmp]

COMMUNITY OF LITERARY MAGAZINES & PRESSES
W W W . C L M P . O R G

TABLE OF CONTENTS

NONFICTION

POETRY

ART

EDITORS' NOTE

Twenty-five years ago, the first editors of *Chicago Quarterly Review*, Syed Afzal Haider, Debi Morris, and Brian Skinner, solicited work from local authors of our acquaintance, from fellow members of the Monadnock writers group, and from one another to fill our premiere issue. We stood at Kinko's copy machines for hours and had a collating party at the house with the large oval dining table. From such humble origins, we have grown into a literary magazine receiving many hundreds of submissions a month from all over the world. We regularly present special issues, such as our South Asian American issue of 2018 and our upcoming Australian issue due out in 2020. And we have been honored recently by inclusion in *Best American Short Stories, Best American Essays,* the *Pushcart Prize Anthology* and the *O. Henry Prize Stories.*

We've pressed a lot of ink since Volume 1, Issue 1. We are humble but not ordinary, and fully independent, all accomplished due to the kindness, courtesy and devotion of our editorial staff, a slew of hard-working writers and editors. We remain committed to offering our readers new voices as well as the voices of old friends. As in our premier issue, we once again proudly present the work of our fellow editors alongside the work of veteran contributors and a cohort of new writers. We keep on as a magazine for writers by writers, here for your reading pleasure. Humble and proud, we remain matchmakers between good writing and avid readers. That's a pretty high calling in our humble opinion.

Yes, we try to put a new spin on our mission and commitment, but twenty-five years ago we launched the *CQR* with the same commitment and dedication that has remained a constant on our staff. Comrades in writing we were, are, and will remain. It has been, and continues to be, a fabulous, magical ride.

[Syed's note: I guess of the old gang I'm the last man standing . . . I wonder where in the world is Debi. I think of her.]

We hope you will enjoy the show.

CONTRIBUTORS TO
THE *CHICAGO QUARTERLY REVIEW*,
1994–PRESENT

Abe Aamidor, Liz Abraham, D.M. Aderibigbe, Cindy Adrian, Vidhu Aggarwal, Leslie Marie Aguilar, Michael Alenyikov, Ronald Alexander, Farah Ali, Kazim Ali, Meher Ali, Kenneth G. Allen, Jr., Greg Allendorf, Judith Aller, Howard Altmann, William L. Alton, Cristina Alziati, Christopher Todd Anderson, Greg Anderson, Saskia Anderson, Traci Andrighetti, Mir Anis, Andy Austin, Tiffany Auxier, Kathleen de Azevedo, Jody Azzouni, Paul Michel Baepler, Wallace Baine, Billy Baites, Ann Voorhees Baker, Neelanjana Banerjee, Jennifer Bannan, Robin Barber, Samuel Rafael Barber, Joseph A. Barda, Lois Barliant, Aliki Barnstone, Sharon Barrett, Paul Kaidy Barrows, Mary Bartek, Ruth Bavetta, Michael Bazzett, Deni Ellis Béchard, Andrew Beckner, Andrew W.M. Beierle, J.E. Bennett, C. Wade Bentley, Richard N. Bentley, Roy Bentley, Marsha Lee Berkman, Bryce Berkowitz, J. A. Bernstein, Max Berwald, Jill Birdsall, Amy Bitterman, John Blades, Michael Blades, James Blair, Jacob Blakesley, Christopher Yohmei Blasdel, Ryan Bloom, Lisa Bloomfield, Randy Blythe, Carrie D. Boettcher, Alexander Boldizar, J.E. Boles, David Booth, Harold Bordwell, Heather Bowlan, Renée Branum, Jackson Onose Braun, Thomas Brian, June Rachuy Brindel, Michelle Brooks, Margaret Brose, F. Douglas Brown, M.L. Brown, Mark W. Brown, Randall Brown, Robert Brown, Rosellen Brown, Tim W. Brown, J. Scott Brownlee, Michael H. Brownstein, Craig Buchner, Claudia Buckholts, Christopher Buckley, Beverly Burch, Peyton Burgess, Mark Burke, Brett Busang, Harmony Button, John Byrne, Danny Calegari, Kevin Callaway, Rossana Campo, Lucas Carpenter, Steven Carrelli, Jane Carter, Susan Howard Case, Mauro Casiraghi, Mauro Castellani, Patrizia Cavalli, Marcia Cavell, Luis Cernuda, John Chandler, Nadia Chaney, James Charlton, Sean Chen-Haider, Glen Chestnut, Alan Cheuse, Yoon Choi, Hamida Banu Chopra, Dounia Choukri, George Choundas, Margaret Chula, Mara Cini, Curt Clapper, Kevin Clark, Stephen Cloud, Garnett Kilberg Cohen, Douglas Cole, Colette, Michael Collier, Casey Comstock, Wayne Conti, Thomas Cook, Tyler Corbridge, Jordan J. Coriza, Nick Courtright, Heather Cousins, Timothy Crandle, Diana Crane, Elizabeth Crane, Barbara Cranford, Gerardo Sámano Córdova, Bonnie Costello, Mark Crimmins, James Crizer, Emily Culliton, Robin Curtiss, Johnny Damm, Sayantani Dasgupta, Shelley Davidow, Corey Davidson, Deborah Davies, Michael Davis, Geffrey Davis, William Virgil Davis, Michael Day, Darren DeFrain, Laura Deily, Kathryn Delancellotti, Marcy Dermansky, Philippe Desportes, Doug Dibbern,

Fred Dings, Regina DiPerna, celeste doaks, Noah Dobin-Bernstein, Thomas Dodson, Olga Domchenko, John Domini, Paul Donahue, Fabio Donalisio, Toby Donovan, Tara Dorabji, Jennifer Dorner, David Downie, Ken Drexler, Christina Drill, Joe Ducato, Rudi Dundas, Iris Jamahl Dunkle, Jason Economus, Carol Edelstein, Chidelia Edochie, Malon Edwards, Temma Ehrenfeld, William Eisner, Adam Elgar, Kyle Ellingson, Donna Emerson, Patricia Engel, Myron Ernst, Robin Estrin, Ali Eteraz, Donald G. Evans, Andrew Fague, Donka Farkas, Kimberly Farrar, Saadia Faruqi, Shawn Fawson, Robert Fay, Anthony Feggans, Peter Ferry, Michael Fessler, Mauricio Montiel Figueiras, Jennifer Firestone, Julie Esther Fisher, David Fleming, Sherrie Flick, Victor Florence, David Flynn, Robert Long Foreman, Christopher Fountain, Graham Foust, Randy Fowler, Arthur Fox, Biancamaria Frabotta, Gina Frangello, Joan Frank, David Frankel, Suzanne Franklin, Janet Freeman, Adria Frizzi, Jack Fuller, Pepper Furey, Mala Gaonkar, Jared Garland, Edward Garner, Sciltian Gastaldi, Guy Gauthier, Bill Gaythwaite, Tracy Miller Geary, Pamela Morneault Gemme, Madhushree Ghosh, Panio Gianopoulos, Molly Giles, Georgia Emma Gili, Jessica Gilliam, Bob Glassman, Jennifer Esther Glickstein, RL Goldberg, Sharon Goldberg, Benjamin E. Golden, (Corinne) Renny Golden, Sierra Golden, Spencer Golub, Eva Sage Gordon, Ruth Goring, Deborah Gorlin, Toni Graham, Don De Grazia, Daniel Green, John S. Green, Leona Green, Emily Greenberg, Michael Griffith, Amy Groshek, Deborah Guerra, Aliete Guerrero, Ro Gunetilleke, Stephen D. Gutierrez, Yen Ha, Katharine Haake, Charles Haddox, Mark Hage, Robert Hahn, Syed Afzal Haider, Syed Ishaq Haider, Minal Hajratwala, Erika Hall, Rich Hallstrom, Colin Hamilton, Barbara Hammer, David Hancock, Paul Hansom, Erik Hanson, Rumi Hara, Jared Harel, Amy Harke-Moore, John Harn, Benjamin Harnett, Natalie S. Harnett, David Harrell, Alison Harris, Karl Harshbarger, Craig Hartglass, Risa Hazel, Caitlyn He, Richard Hedderman, Laura Heffington, Katherine Heiny, B.F. Helman, Vanessa Hemingway, Liam Heneghan, Jim Henry, Jan Herman, Lucien Hervé, Rage Hezekiah, David William Hill, Julianne Hill, Catherine Abbey Hodges, Carlie Hoffman, Coby Hoffman, Charles Holdefer, J.B. Hollander, Andy Holt, Joseph Holt, Florence Homolka, Bryn Homuth, Charles Hood, Stanley Horowitz, Gary Houston, Patty Houston, Matthew Huff, Richard Huffman, Michael Hutchison, Harry Hutson, Alta Ifland, Hugh Iglarsh, Ryuta Imafuku, Margaret B. Ingraham, Romana Iorga, Muhammad Iqbal, Cheryl Collins Isaac, Nathan Isaksson, Lowell Jaeger, Greg Jenkins, Charles Johnson, John Philip Johnson, Ryan Michael Johnson, Laura Jok, Henry L. Jones, Mary Jones, Paul Nicholas Jones, David Joseph, Jr., Mary Lou Judy, Jon Paul Jurasas, Soniah Kamal, G.S. Kaplan, Kirun

Kapur, Karen Kates, Elizabeth Kay, David Kear, David James Keaton, Kathryn Kefauver, L.M. Kell, James Kelly, Sharon Kennedy-Nolle, Trilby Kent, Tim Keppel, Robert Kerwin, Stephen Kessler, David Kherdian, Maya Khosla, Swati Khurana, Waqas Khwaja, Samantha Killmeyer, David Kinsbourne, Michael Kirylo, Christine Kitano, Jen Knox, Peter Joseph Koch, Richard Kostelanetz, Chuck Kramer, Carolyn Kraus, Jim Kudrick, Anu Kumar, Marianne Kunkel, Yumiko Kurahashi, D.E. Laczi, Shane Lake, Grace Lane, Richard M. Lange, Guillermo Lanza, Dorianne Laux, Alessandra Lavagnino, Michael Lavers, Jane Lawless, Jane Lawrence, Hank Lawson, Robert Lax, Louise LeBourgeois, William L. Lederer, Eric Lee, Thomas Lee, Laura Legge, David Lehman, Christine Lehner, C. Benton Lenz, Micki Lesueur, Ben Levaton, Suzanne Jill Levine, Trudy Lewis, Ilya Leybovich, Joan Li, Margit Liesche, Erin Lillo, Bronte Lim, Christopher Linforth, Ernesto Livorni, Nancy Lord, Diana López, Donna Luff, Paul Luikart, Aditi Machado, Valerio Magrelli, Amit Majmudar, Shikha Malaviya, Matt Maldre, Zafar Malik, Andrea Malin, Julia Malye, Gotham Mamik, Halcyon Mancuso, Osip Mandelstam, Annam Manthiram, Nicola Manuppelli, Catherine Mao, Louise Marburg, Lara Markstein, Lynn Martin, Pamela Martin, Michela Martini, Ben Masaoka, Silvana Mastrolia, Susan Mathison, Mary Beth Leymaster Matteo, Cathleen Maza, Taylor Mazer, Jane McClellan, Nancy McCoy, Sjohnna McCray, Kathleen McGookey, Elizabeth McKenzie, Sarah McKinstry-Brown, Michael P. McManus, Cortwright McMeel, Martin McMullen, Kelly McNamara, Karen McPherson, Kat Meads, Susie Mee, Margarita Meklina, Todd Melicker, Lynn Melnick, Joao Melo, Isidra Mencos, Joe Meno, Vikas Menon, Carrie Messenger, William E. Meyer, Jim Mezzanotte, Jen Michalski, Massimo Migliorati, John Milas, Michael Milburn, Joseph Millar, Errol Miller, Faith Miller, Gary Miller, Karen T. Miller, Linda Downing Miller, Rebecca S. Mills, Michael Miner, Evan E. Mingle, Faisal Mohyuddin, Luigi Monteferrante, Roberta Montgomery, Megan Moodie, Rod Val Moore, Dan Moreau, Deborah Morris, Peter Morris, Guido Morselli, Erica Mosley, Rose Rappoport Moss, Rachel Eve Moulton, Daniel Mueller, Dipika Mukherjee, Somnath Mukherji, Carrie Mullins, Andrew Mulvania, Naomi Munaweera, Devin Murphy, Teresa Burns Murphy, Gregg Murray, Franca Di Muzio, Scott Nadelson, Shabnam Nadiya, Dustin Nakao-Haider, Jan Nakao, Shivani Narang, Ifti Nasim, Sophia Naz, Maria Nazos, Eireene Nealand, Toni Nealie, Natalia Nebel, Ellen Nerenberg, Jacob Newberry, Jack Nicholls, Idra Novey, Naomi Shihab Nye, James O'Brien, J.E. Ogle, Naomi O'Hara, Rita O'Hara, Robert Michael O'Hearn, Willer de Oliveira, RCA O'Neal, Chika Onyenezi, Anthony Opal, Claire Harlan Orsi, W.P. Osborn, Robert Savino

Oventile, Chris Gordon Owen, John Stanford Owen, Clarke W. Owens, Aldo Palazzeschi, Katia Pansa, James Paradiso, Frances Park, Youmi Park, Juan Parra, Charles Parsons, Cassandra Passarelli, Laura Wine Paster, Stuart Patterson, Ed Pavlic, Gabriele Pedulla, Rebecca Pelky, Jonathan Andrew Perez, Micah Perks, Harry Mark Petrakis, Elina Petrova, Andrew X. Pham, Gregory Phillan, Alice Phung, Giacomo Pilati, Cecillia Pinto, Zack Ploszay, Genevieve Plunkett, Nicolette Polek, Trenton Pollard, Andrew Porter, Jory Post, Glen Pourciau, Jacques Prévert, Alta L. Price, D'Arcy Ann Pryciak, Greg Przekwas, Carol M. Quinn, Liz Radford, Mahmud Rahman, Reema Rajbanshi, Frederika Randall, Richard Rapaport, Signe Ratcliff, Jane Ratcliffe, Jenene Ravesloot, Diana Reaves, Frank Reckitt, Robert Leonard Reid, James Reiss, C.R. Resetarits, Jake Ricafrente, Timothy Richard, Jim Ringley, Alyssa Ripley, Elizabeth Robinson, John Robinson, Susan Rochette-Crawley, Esteban Rodriguez, Zack Rogow, Brad Rohrer, Rosebud Rosabella, Charles Rose, Jonathan Rose, Chuck Rosenthal, Malcolm Rothman, Evie Rucker, Micah Ruelle, Mary Doria Russell, Roshni Rustomji-Kerns, Jack Ryan, Robert Sachs, Ryan Salazar, Dennis Saleh, Kevin Sampsell, Edoardo Sanguineti, Ingrid Satelmajer, R. Craig Sautter, Camillo Sbarbaro, Angela Scarparo, Sara Schaff, Jeff Schmidt, Michael R. Schrimper, Emily Schulten, Catherine Ennis Sears, Olivia E. Sears, Catherine Segurson, Chaitali Sen, Susan Sensemann, Eric Severn, Leona Sevick, Pete Shanks, Craig Shaw, Jay Shearer, Peter Sheehy, Moazzam Sheikh, Ashley Shelby, Ravibala Shenoy, Annis Shivani, Ranbir Singh Sidhu, M.E. Silverman, Richard B. Simon, Laura Sims, Theadora Siranian, Marjorie Skelly, Paul Skenazy, Nicola Skert, Don Skiles, Brian Allan Skinner, Seth D. Slater, George H. Smith, Irene Hoge Smith, Peter Moore Smith, Robert McClure Smith, Ryan Elliott Smith, Christine Sneed, Jennifer Snow, Octavio Solis, Natalie Solmer, Robert Solomon, Scott Solomon, Sharon Solwitz, Adriano Spatola, Eleanor Spiess-Ferris, Matthew J. Spireng, Randolph Splitter, James Stacey, Lucia Stacey, Patricia Stacey, Sofi Stambo, Renate Stendhal, Alice Stern, Samson Stillwell, Peter Stine, Janferie Stone, Dorothy Stroud, Doc Suds, Adam Sullivan, Pireeni Sundaralingam, Moez Surani, Hema Surendranathan, Alison Carb Sussman, Barbara Sutton, Jim Swierzynski, Najm Hosain Syed, Patrick Sylvain, Lisa Taddeo, Goro Takano, Sandy Tanaka, Jason Tandon, Kenny Tanemura, Barbara Tannenbaum, Yukiko Terazawa, Clark Theriot, Jackie Thomas-Kennedy, Ronald Tobias, Jay Todd, Yukiko Tominaga, Umberto Tosi, Alison Touster-Reed, Sean Towey, Emanuele Trevi, Steve Trumpeter, Jake Tuck, Rebecca Turkewitz, John Twohey, Daniel Uncapher, Mitchell Untch, Sadia Uqaili, Melanie VanBeck, Bradley VanDeventer, Alfredo Vea, Jon Veinberg, Paul Verlaine,

Francesco Verso, Patrizia Vicinelli, Vito Victor, Roy Villa, Patrizia Villani, Alvaro Villanueva, Melanie Villines, Katherine Vondy, Dwain Voorhis, Siamak Vossoughi, Sachin Waikar, Tanu Mehrotra Wakefield, Noreene Walsh, Josh Wardrip, Larry Watson, Thomas Wawzenek, Daniel Webre, Wang Wei, Joe Weil, Brent Weinbach, J. Weintraub, Ken Weisner, Paul Wellons, Luke Whisnant, Les White, Jerry Whitus, Helen Wickes, J. Rodolpho Wilcock, John Sibley Williams, Laura Williams, Paul A. Williams, John Wilmes, Ian Randall Wilson, Yumi Wilson, Tim Winchester, David Winner, Mark Wisniewski, Catherine Wong, Anne-E Wood, Stephen Woodhams, Russell Working, Rogers Worthington, Gail Wronsky, Qianyue Xu, Yanwen Xu, Gary Young, Jake Young, Christina Yu, Robert Yune, Ilona Yusuf, Alexi Zentner, Jim Zervanos, Fan Zhongyan, Richard Lee Zuras, Eric Zurita

SKIN
Max Berwald

I became lost driving from the airport. As I was driving, a hard wind picked up and blew the snow sideways as it fell. At first there were woods on either side of the road, but then only the plains. Every so often a factory peeked over a high fence or a low wall. Even on this broad grid scheme I became confused, and after so long seeing no one, I stopped to ask directions of the first pedestrian I came across. It was an old woman, dressed inadequately, but even when I had pulled to the side of the road, she didn't move a muscle. She was standing by a fence, a closed gate to a factory of some kind. I could see the factory several hundred meters behind her.

I got out of the car and went over to her. She was trembling from the cold, wearing only a battered blue ski jacket and loose trousers that snapped in the wind. She'd tied a kerchief over her head but there were holes in it where her hair came through, also snapping about in the wind and giving a deranged impression.

I asked her the way to Daqing, and she said she was going that way too. Before she could ask, I had offered to drive her. She agreed. When she smiled I saw that she was missing most of her teeth. We went off together in my rental.

The package for Mil was at her feet. As we pulled away, she picked it up. "Oh," I said. "Don't touch that." I couldn't tell if she'd understood. She looked at the package, touching the creases where the brown paper had been folded over. Her fingers were filthy. "It's a gift." She rested the package on her lap. I wanted to tell her again, but she wasn't really touching it anymore.

She had me make a variety of turns, although each one led us down a road that looked much like the last. They were long blocks, always with high fences and usually with some kind of industrial complex several hundred meters distant. I never once saw anyone coming or going. Some of the fences were topped with razor wire, and others with blinking red lights. Occasionally, one of the factories would also appear to be topped with blinking red lights. The wind came harder and harder out of the north, so that I had to compensate with my steering.

Back home, I had struggled to imagine how Mil could survive this kind of winter. Now that I was on the ground, seeing it for myself, I was dumfounded. Of course he had the resources to protect himself from the elements. But in picking out a coat for him, just like mine, I felt that I would make physical all of my worrying on his behalf. It was no small part of me—my concern for Mil. I noticed that even now, when I was closer to his new home than ever before, he still felt worlds away. The coat was long and black and fur-lined, the type a certain kind of MP wore in the movies.

Suddenly, while driving down a long straightaway, the old woman cried out for me to stop. I did, and noticed that her attention was directed to a high wire gate we had just passed. She clambered out of the rental and began to open this gate. I protested but she begged me to pass through it. I can remember her standing before the gate as if it were her duty to open and close it, waving me through with her hair flying about her head. Snowflakes broke on her wind-cracked face. I brought the car through and asked her what was the matter. At first she said the storm was getting worse, but then she admitted she had been unable to find this place for some time—that it was where her husband was now living. For the first time, it occurred to me that this woman might be homeless. It's strange that I followed her, and stranger to say that it wasn't out of curiosity. To be honest, the woman was so pitiful and this world so harsh that I felt I had a duty to follow her.

Once we were beyond the gate, which, I might add, she left open behind us, the old woman clambered back into the car. She directed me down the road, although there was only one possible way, and as we approached the factory I realized just how big it was. There was no sign of its being in use, although I assumed the workers would have gone home for the day anyway. We passed a rusty forklift, and then another, and then a tremendous stack of rotted pallets. That's when I began to sense that some time had passed for this factory. The longer we drove down that road, the factory just kept yawning taller and taller in front of us, until I could no longer see the top, and we had a ways to go yet. I felt bad for having scolded her over Mil's package, even though now, looking over, I saw that she was again fingering the creases.

When she finally directed me to stop, it was at an annex jutting like a tooth from the main building. I couldn't see the door at first. It was marked in chipped red paint. I got out of the car and pulled my jacket close around me, keeping my left arm on the inside. The wind was unbearable, and all the feeling immediately left my face. The red paint seemed to have once spelled something out, and as I came closer to the door I tried to read it. With each step I became more certain that it *was* text, or had been, but soon I had come right up to it, and try as I might there was no way to make it out.

Inside, the smell of chicken stock wafted from a makeshift kitchen.

A radio balanced on a stool. Hay covered the ground. The place was a squat, established at the edge of this annex. Other corners had been left untouched. Rusted metal implements frozen to rusted metal implements. The jaw of a tractor. It was the kind of place I could picture Mil's ancestors having lived. Even his parents really, before Mil's own career took off. Not that he'd lost touch with his roots: I had long suspected the squalor Mil's ancestors had endured was the cause of his being so sensitive to my own entitlements, jealousies . . . finally my basic selfishness. Even when we were sharing a condo in Midmarket and doing so apparently "well," there was a purity to his own success that mine lacked. Perhaps because I could see no further than a raise, while his eyes were set on something nameless, noble.

Looking back at the makeshift kitchen, I saw that a gas range was lit and a pot boiling. A talk show came from the radio, but it was hard to parse words from static. The old woman went and ladled something from the pot and brought it to me. I stood there holding the bowl in my hands until she brought me a stool. I sat down and saw that it was a thin soup, with only some silt at the bottom. I took a sip and tasted ginger. The old woman asked if she could have a look at my coat. I didn't want to give her my coat, although it was obvious she needed it more than I did. It was nearly as freezing inside as out, and I'd have to go back into the wind at some point, even if it was only to my car. Of course, there was the other coat, neatly folded and wrapped, but that was a gift . . . What had possessed me? To think a coat would be enough.

Enough to prove to him that I had seen the noble thing.

That I had transcended greed, and now saw quite outside myself.

Foolish.

I was still thinking along these lines when I saw that I was taking off my coat. She took it and nodded and smiling said to me, "You're a good man, obviously a good man. First you gave me a ride, then you let me take you on this detour, and now just look at you, taking off your coat in the middle of winter. I know it's not warm out here, not even indoors. I don't want you to go cold. I know you'll be cold, but if you insist, I'll really keep it. Thank you so much." I tried to open my mouth, to tell her that I hadn't offered. For a long time, I couldn't, but then my lips finally smacked apart and I heard myself saying, "That's all right, that's all right. I can see that you're cold." "That's right, and at my age, you really have to look out for yourself."

I reached for the bowl of soup, which I had set down in the hay, and brought it back to my lips. I reflected that what the woman had said was true. There was no one to look out for the elderly these days. What if one reached an age where one couldn't work anymore? That happened to all of us. And if one had no children to look after one? It was hard to imagine the cruelty of such a world. The last bastion seemed to be people just like me, who were ready and willing to turn off the road for the elderly, or to offer the coat off their own shoulders. The taste of the soup was improving and the steam felt good in my nose.

The woman asked if she could see my shirt, and I saw that I was setting the soup down in the hay again. Steam rose in a curl and vanished. I asked about her husband and she said, "Yes, it will be so good to see him again. At this point, it's hard to say the last time we were really together. Of course, you try to make do, but when you've been married such a very long time, there's no fooling yourself. Are you married? Speak up. Speak up. Oh, that's all right." I felt freezing. I sat down again, exhausted, on the stool. My buttocks froze to the surface. She was still talking but it was hard to concentrate on the words. When I looked up again, she was taking a toolbox from the cart under the gas range. She brought a short peeling knife from the toolbox and cleaned it in the flame. I thought that the knife would be getting very hot. She came over to me with the knife, saying something, and made an incision by my collarbone.

I could barely feel her going in against the cold, only a certain dull warmth. She made another incision at the opposite side of my chest, and then drew the knife from the first point to the second to create a flap. She was struggling because of her age, but I was impressed by how well she managed. There was a sureness to her movements that made me wonder where she had got her practice. She yanked at the corners of the flap until, finally, my skin began to give way. Little bits of fat and sinew fought her, but she gradually pulled the skin down from my chest. I thought of her fingers, at the edges of Mil's package, and then my own hands—how they had worked the buttons of my coat. I tried to tell her that I wanted to finish the soup but only managed to mumble something. A glob of spit tumbled from my mouth to the bare muscle about my sternum, where it began to freeze. Steam escaped my chest cavity—a surprising amount.

When she had most of the skin from my chest and abdomen, she carried those flaps over to the kitchen, and she pasted them onto thin air. It was only gradually that I began to discern the shape of her husband, and for reasons of her own she saved the face for last. Her husband was visibly anxious. With each new piece of skin, his new form trembled and shook in the air, whether from cold or the "newness" of form itself I couldn't say.

I was surprised that, when she worked the knife behind my eyes, and severed the nerves there, I did not cease to see. In fact, I felt that I maintained eye contact with her the entire time. When she was finished, I looked down at myself: a pile of entrails, drenched in blood, steaming on the hay floor. When it came right down to it, there wasn't much of me. The soup bowl, which had long given up its own heat, looked like a gloomy old oil painting. I thought I should be going, but I found myself looking back at the husband. As I drew myself up to perceive him, I felt happy for the old woman, and glad for myself: I hadn't done anything wrong. I'd behaved well. Mil's eyes would soon be upon me—and what fault could he now find? A few selfish intimations notwithstanding, I hadn't hesitated to give up my coat for an old woman in need. It was gratifying to see that her husband looked just like I had. ∎

LIQUID BOUNDARY
Louise LeBourgeois

I once found an orange floating in Lake Michigan. It was bobbing in the waves several hundred yards from shore, looking as if it had been waiting to be discovered. That bright burst of color in the boundless expanse of subdued green seemed a cheery mishap, so simple and so utterly unexpected. I placed it inside the front of my swimsuit, like a third breast, and swam to the rocks. Back on land, I pulled it out to show my friends. Grace, who exudes maternal energy (she occasionally buys us socks or skin lotion, and we call her our den mother), laughed and said, "Don't eat that!"

Eating the orange had not occurred to me. It looked edible, but who knew how long it had been out there, absorbing the lake's unfiltered water. I had been drawn to its optimism.

There were several of us wriggling out of our wet bathing suits and into our dry underwear, casual about what our towels, wrapped around us like makeshift cocoons, concealed or revealed in the process. We women had seen plenty of each other's bodies by then, dressing and undressing in the locker room during our cold-weather pool swims. We just didn't want to startle the early-morning joggers or run afoul of some city public decency code. We averted our eyes from the men we swam with, and they from us, as we all dried off and dressed ourselves. We climbed the rocks and left the water behind. As we walked through the park, I placed the orange on a bench so it would be seen again, as if to say: this orange has a story.

I once found a basketball floating in Lake Michigan. It was less startling than finding the orange because I could more easily imagine a basketball going wayward than somebody's orange. Still, it was an amusing find. It was too big to fit in my swimsuit. I threw it as far as I could while treading water. I swam to it, then threw it again, several times. I moved the basketball about fifty yards before I decided to stop. It reminded me of the few times I played water polo in high school, which always made me feel miserable and waterlogged in a way swimming never did. All that starting and stopping. All that rough body contact. A boy once palmed my head, swathed in a yellow swim cap, and thrust me underwater. When I came up, sputtering, I turned to glare at him with a *What the hell*??? expression on my face and he said, "Oh god, sorry, I really thought you were the ball." No, I've always preferred the predictable rhythm of swimming. I had about a quarter mile left to swim back to the rocks and I didn't want to do it in any way that reminded me of water polo. I left the basketball to the lake's whims.

For all I know it's still out there.

* * *

Promontory Point is a man-made peninsula jutting eastward into Lake Michigan from Fifty-Fifth Street on Chicago's South Side. The Point, as most people call it, was built in the 1930s, constructed with limestone blocks as a revetment to contain the peninsula's landmass, a tree-filled park with a spacious field at its center. The limestone blocks are large, about the size of small refrigerators. They create giant steps, each about two and a half feet high, four of them from top to bottom, leading from the park above to the water below.

For more than a decade, I've been swimming at the Point with an eclectic group of swimmers with a wide range of abilities, from those who paddle around for a few minutes to marathon swimmers who train for several miles at a time. Without this community, I would never have grown brave enough to swim the distances I do in open water. One of the swimmers recently said to me that the only requirement to be a part of our fluid group is a willingness to brave cold water. I realized this was exactly right, his succinct definition something I hadn't yet articulated for myself.

More than anything else I do in my life, this activity and this group of people tie me to Chicago, where I've lived for almost four decades, and where I have many friendships from different periods in my life. Over the years, I have lived in four different neighborhoods at eleven different addresses, and I have held more jobs than I can reliably count, somewhere around thirteen. I met my husband, Steve, in Evanston, a suburb just north of Chicago, when we were both students in Northwestern University's MFA program in painting. We've both built our careers as artists in Chicago, and our decision to remain has been driven by our desire to set down roots and our shared delight in the city we call home. It is not as if I lack a deep connection to this city.

What I mean to say is that swimming in the lake connects me to all parts of myself, most significantly to the part I thought I had lost when my family moved from South Carolina to Chicago in 1978, when I was fourteen. I spent most of my childhood in the undulating foothills of the Blue Ridge Mountains, textured with all kinds of trees growing out of bright-red dirt, threaded with flashing rivers and creeks. My affinity with the outdoors was as vivid as any of my relationships with people around me. Leaving my wooded South Carolina landscape for a land of endless asphalt and traffic, brick and steel buildings crowded together, was wrenching. I still occasionally feel a sensation of protest in my body, an impulse to shudder, to renegotiate my uneasy treaty with the city's tight spaces. Mostly though, I feel quite comfortable in Chicago as I go about my daily life. Over time, its ceaseless thrum has become as familiar as my own heartbeat, but I can, at moments, still experience the city from the perspective of my bewildered fourteen-year-old self. It's a subtle shift that might happen when I'm feeling nostalgic, frazzled, or vulnerable, and I begin to think, yet again, how strange, how alien, this city is, how its rough surfaces prickle my skin and overwhelm my senses, how its constant electric glow never allows me the deep quiet I sometimes crave. It's always up to me to create my own refuge of dark silence at night because Chicago will not, will never, do that for me.

That I drive seventeen miles from my home in Rogers Park, on the city's far North Side, to swim at the Point in Hyde Park, on the South Side, might seem excessive, since I can easily walk half a mile down my street, from our condo on Greenleaf Avenue (I smile at my sly determination to make my home among trees), to the beach in my neighborhood. But there's something about swimming in Hyde Park, the neighborhood where I first lived in Chicago, that feels necessary and healing.

I grew up in South Carolina with an incredible physical freedom to explore, limited only by the distance I could roam and still be home by dinner, at first in my own neighborhood, and as I grew older, in an expanding radius aided by the ten-speed bicycle I'd saved up for. I was too young to drive a car by the time we moved away, but old enough to want to get around without always having to asking my parents for a ride. I biked everywhere, often to my friend Ellen's house in, as she described it, the sticks, on a secluded road with a majestic view of the Blue Ridge Mountains. Her house was uphill from ours, an arduous forty-five-minute ride north of our town, more in the direction of the mountainous northwest tip of our state than where I lived. The return trip was always faster and easier. I had to be home by dark, a practicality as much as my parents' rule, because there were very few streetlights between our houses, and no one, least of all myself, wanted me biking alone in the pitch-black night. My freedom felt infinite as I coasted home on a long stretch of road with hardly any cars, a gentle downhill slope of about three miles flanked by skinny pines. I whooshed through a pale-violet evening with a blur of dark green on either side, warm wind in my face. I sometimes sat straight up in my bike seat, hands off the handlebars and resting on my thighs or maybe my hips. I veered to the left side of the road, and then towards the right, in long, lazy arcs. I was content in the timeless space between spending time with Ellen, who always made me laugh, and arriving home to eat dinner with my family. That space wasn't simply the physical distance between our two houses, or the time it took me to bike home. It was a temporary release from who I was in relation to other people: a friend, a daughter, a sister, a ninth grader, a teenaged girl. All of that belonged to another realm. In these moments, I was simply a conscious, physical being gliding through space on my big, round planet. There was always a point when I got nervous about my downhill momentum, and I leaned over to squeeze my brakes, just a little bit. I was thrilled by wind and motion, but never attracted to danger. I never fell, not once.

That sweeping sense of freedom came to an abrupt halt when we moved to Chicago. The change was as distressing as if I had actually fallen off my bike and slammed my body into hard asphalt. My father, a history professor at Clemson University, received a yearlong research fellowship at the University of Chicago, but we never did return to Clemson as we had planned to. After six months in Chicago, my parents decided they wanted to stay, lured by the stimulation of a big city and the diversity of views they found there. My dad finessed a career change, leaving his tenured position at Clemson for an administrative job at the University of Chicago and enrolling in its nighttime MBA program. It was not what I wanted. I wanted to go home to my friends, my school, and my woods.

I eventually forgave Chicago for its flatness, though it took me a long time to stop longing for my mountains. But it was more difficult for me to forgive Hyde Park for restricting me the way it did with its meticulous boundaries separating it from surrounding neighborhoods. There were no fences, no actual blockades, but the streets I was not supposed to venture beyond were well established: Forty-Seventh Street to the north; Cottage Grove Avenue to the west; the Midway, a mile-long grassy expanse between Fifty-Ninth and Sixtieth Streets, to the south; with Lake Michigan to the east. I can't remember who told me not to cross those lines or how I learned where the boundaries were, but it was such common knowledge, so much a part of the neighborhood lore, that it practically emitted its own odor. All I know was I understood quickly that the area I could walk or bike was confined to an area of less than two square miles. I learned soon enough how to take buses and trains downtown, but my own bodily sense of agency was thwarted. To leave my neighborhood meant that I had to submit myself to the Chicago Transit Authority, the Illinois Central, or my parents' car, even though I was perfectly capable of walking very long distances and biking even farther than that.

My childhood sense of volition was erased, replaced by fear. I was scared of where I lived, a feeling I had never had before. Our first night in Chicago, the sky was the muddy red color it sometimes becomes. Its lack of darkness baffled me. I thought I was immersed in a thick soup of pollution, not yet understanding that the red glow was created by the collective light of the city reflected downwards by a cloudy sky. I didn't trust the air I breathed, nor did I trust that I was physically safe, hearing stories about break-ins, assaults, muggings at gunpoint, and rapes in our neighborhood. I stayed within my neighborhood's boundaries, although it was confusing because these crimes occurred on both sides of the lines I wasn't supposed to cross. They didn't seem to make the neighborhood safe. So what were they for?

I resigned myself to studying the map of Chicago at our kitchen table or sprawled on the living room floor, wondering about the nearby places I couldn't go. A specific destination wasn't the point. I wanted to feel my body traversing the city for the sheer joy of feeling my muscles contract and relax, and seeing the sights, whatever they might be, move across my field of vision.

I fantasized about the entire population of Chicago leaving for a day so I could ride my bike wherever I wanted to, without the nuisance of speeding cars and buses, without the fear of being physically attacked. In my imagination, I gave myself permission to ramble the streets, learning with my own body how one neighborhood became another, fitting together like a jigsaw puzzle. A map, a flimsy piece of paper, could not do this for me. I wanted physical knowledge. I wanted to know what a storefront or a park a few miles away meant in the currency of my own sweat and effort. I wanted to know Chicago's potholes as well as I knew the sneaky tree roots, the ones that could trip you up on the wooded paths, back home. I wanted to feel the texture of the ground beneath my feet, and I wanted to know what it felt like to ride over it on my bike. I wanted to learn the oddities of this place. I wanted to create my own internal, kinesthetic map of this unknown corner of the world in which I now found myself. I was simply trying to figure out how to become comfortable again inside my own body, which was now confined to a tiny space etched by crisply defined lines. This was not the experience I craved. My new neighborhood demanded that I shrink. I churned in protest against what felt like an insult, a sharp rebuke, and this became my most vivid bodily memory of my arrival in Chicago.

A single day only. It didn't seem too much to ask. Of course, it was a lot to ask, for a few million people to interrupt their lives so that I, a fourteen-year-old girl, might explore. It did not occur to me at the time to ask what *wasn't* too much to ask: why couldn't I go where I wanted?

Hyde Park is, and was then, a racially integrated and economically diverse neighborhood. I found out right away that its residents take great pride in that fact. Yet Chicago's South Side is predominantly African American, and Hyde Park is surrounded on three sides by neighborhoods that are poorer and almost exclusively black. It took me well into my adulthood to appreciate the irony that the strict boundaries separating Hyde Park from the surrounding neighborhoods were harsher and more terrifying than anything I had ever personally experienced growing up in the South. Of course, segregation existed where I lived in South Carolina too, and I knew my town had black neighborhoods and white neighborhoods, even though we all attended the same schools and participated in the same Girl Scout troops. But as a white girl, I had never had the occasion to encounter the unforgiving separation of nearby groups of people, people who lived within easy walking distance from each other, the way I did in Chicago. It was hard for me to reconcile my new neighborhood's self-congratulatory pride about its diversity with my own feeling of entrapment. These boundaries, now scars in my memory, were the reflection of racial violence and class divisions yet to be healed, all of it emanating from a brutal history much older than my Chicago neighborhood, older than the United States, even older than South Carolina.

All of this, plus the attitude that all Southerners who move to the North soon encounter, both subtly and overtly, that the South is more backward and racist than the North, completed the tangle of messages I could not make sense of as a teenager, unable as I was then to tease apart their contradictions. No one around me talked about them. All I knew was that I was free to explore my environment in South Carolina but not in Chicago, and, as a teenaged girl, I felt physically safe in one place and not in the other. The silence surrounding my angry confusion distilled in me a permanent and visceral skepticism of any Northern claim of superiority.

Walking the three blocks to and from my school, it wasn't unusual for me to see two, three, four, five, six police cars, belonging to two separate police forces, the Chicago police and the University of Chicago police, roll by, patrolling, observing. I wasn't sure whether seeing so many police cars made me feel safe or unsafe, but it did make me feel like I lived inside a fortress when I ached for freedom. It was, and still is, difficult for me to swallow the idea of Hyde Park's specialness. What was so special about confinement? About fear?

I understood on some level that this police presence was meant to keep me, a white girl, safe, but I was unconvinced that this is what I needed. I knew it wasn't what I wanted. I couldn't articulate my distrust then, but I can now. The danger resided not with the people who lived beyond the boundaries I wasn't supposed to cross, but in the mind-set within these protected boundaries that created the false need for them in the first place, and with the people from all times and places who find it essential draw a line to keep others out and claim the best resources for themselves. It didn't make sense to me then, and it still doesn't, how one group of people can claim they are more enlightened than another group when they both practice exclusion and insist on its necessity.

But, just as individuals are complicated and contradictory, so are places. The mythology of place I was now exposed to, about Hyde Park's openness to people of all races and walks of life, which is certainly partially true, was not something I could believe or accept at the time because the boundaries around it seemed so absolute. The restrictive shape of my new neighborhood was a shock to my body, and the pain I experienced from it obscured for me what actually lay within. I knew the South, my South, to be much more complex and nuanced than the stereotypes I heard about it when I moved North. My arrival in Hyde Park, as difficult as it was, caused me for a very long time to experience it only as a neighborhood of incredibly rigid lines, so that its own complexity and nuance was lost on me.

I had no words for any of this as a teenager. I knew only that I felt uncomfortable and out of place. I felt the sharp pinch of the Northern stereotype of the South, a sting universal to all stereotypes, the infuriating sensation that my own experience contained much more intelligence and complexity than other people's cartoonish ideas allowed for. I intuited that my ideas and my anger, inchoate as they were, were in direct conflict with what the people around me believed, so the Southerner in me retreated into the recesses of my psyche as I settled into my school and set about creating a new life for myself.

At first, the lake, to Hyde Park's east, also seemed like a barrier. I was already a competitive swimmer at fourteen, but the vast open water of the lake confounded me in a way that a swimming pool did not. The pool's underwater lane lines and fat black crosses at the wall instructed me to swim in a straight line and told me when to flip, push off, and glide. I associated the pool's regulated chemistry and chlorine stench with hard work and euphoria. The lake, on the other hand, was murky and unbounded. It was colder than any water I'd swum in before and its immensity, so lacking in the froth and salt smells I knew from my family's trips to the Atlantic Ocean, puzzled me. Seeing the lake for the first time, my sister Anne said, "It's almost real," a statement my mother kept alive in our family lore. My sister meant, I think, that it looked like the ocean but wasn't, so what exactly was it? It was not quite real for me either, in that I wasn't immediately able to connect it to what I already loved: swimming, the outdoors, and open space.

Before we left South Carolina, I logged about ten to twelve miles a week on my swim team. Moving meant the sudden end of a spirited childhood of running around in the woods, building dams in the creek, climbing trees, biking up and down steep hills, and playing kickball in the street on summer nights. I constantly strained against my body's limits. My joyous anticipation of attending a high school in Chicago with a swim team was pricked by my sudden realization that its swim season was only a few fall and winter months long.

The body revels in habit. It is almost as challenging to quit vigorous activity as it is to start from zero. My body felt itchy, twitchy, agitated with unfocused nervous energy, hot prickles and bursts erupting inside me like popcorn. I wrestled with lethargy, caged in by the strange rules of a foreign place. I didn't know what to do with myself during those first summer weeks in Chicago. I can barely remember what I did. My body's awareness, extending far beyond the limits of my own skin, which had grown up to accommodate the soft humid landscape of the southern Appalachians, was now abraded by the gritty surfaces of the urban Midwest. I chafed. My swimming muscles, for which I'd worked so hard, of which I was so proud, softened with disuse. I had never been very girly, and what I adored about swimming, besides the sensation of moving through water, was the fact that it broadened my shoulders and gave me noticeable biceps and triceps at the same time I was growing into my adult body. Swimming was the best way I could figure out to moderate my appearance while growing into a woman's body, with all the subsequent restraints and restrictions I perceived coming my way. Swimming was my way to become strong and feel less vulnerable as a female. It was my identity.

That first summer, my family explored the city, the museums, parks, neighborhoods, and restaurants. These were pleasant enough excursions, but they didn't come close to satisfying what I wanted and needed, the freedom to explore the space I was in, to stumble into the rambling, unmediated experiences I so desired, to feel at home in my own body and safe in my neighborhood.

It became my lifelong quest to accommodate myself to Chicago in a way that created space for my quiet insistence as a teenager that my loss of my South Carolina landscape was real and palpable. The South Carolina I left behind was my very own, an internal sense of place arising from my childhood imagination combined with the tangible elements of my environment. The Chicago I needed to create for myself was a Chicago able to resonate with the South Carolina still alive in my mind, a Chicago that knew how to embrace a body containing such a memory.

* * *

The south side of the Point curves southwest to Fifty-Seventh Street Beach. The beach itself stretches south, ending with a long steel-and-concrete pier jutting eastward into the lake at Fifty-Ninth Street. Every spring the Chicago Park District anchors six or seven cylindrical orange-and-white buoys from the southeast tip of the Point to the end of the pier. These buoys mark a line past which boats and Jet Skis are forbidden, creating a safety zone for swimmers between the buoys and the beach, the Point and the pier. It is an enormous swimming hole, an area about a quarter mile wide by a half mile long, open to the lake's immense 22,300 square miles. I remember swimming at the Point during high school, sometimes with my father, who was also a competitive swimmer, and sometimes with my friends who were on the swim team with me. With a companion at my side, the lake's enormity seemed more manageable. I think the human mind is innately wary of swimming alone in such an open, unbounded expanse. Water is so deadly in excess. For a long time, I had to fight being spooked by its emptiness and power. Open-water swimming demands reckoning with fear.

Several years ago, long after I moved to the North Side from Hyde Park, my friend Deirdre asked me to take her to the Point. She'd heard it was a great place to swim, and she knew I used to swim there. The next time we went, I asked my friend Grace, whom I'd met through a group I swam with after I graduated from college. Over time, the three of us met and befriended other swimmers who had, each in their own way, found their way to the Point. When we first began swimming together, we'd proceed in a loose group, pausing at each buoy to account for each other, deciding together whether to continue to the next. As our confidence grew, we trusted our own and each other's abilities to bring us safely the mile round trip to the pier and back. We kept watch over each other, and we still do, but it is not always an easy task.

The water's fluctuating surface confounds the eye. It is a trickster, spinning illusions as perplexing as the fact that the perfectly visible horizon line is merely the apparition of an utterly nonexistent place. When you are in the water it is nearly impossible to know, beyond your immediate vicinity, which part of the water's visible surface is near, far, or very far away. The surface of open water both compresses and stretches space through reflected light and the motion of waves. When I swim, I'm able to see the large structures that surround me, the pier, the Point, the Museum of Science and Industry, and the water crib, a structure that takes in and supplies water for the city, about three miles offshore. But when I pause to look for swimmers in the lake, it's hard to find a focal point. Until my eye lands upon the motion of a freestyler's bent elbow or a breaststroker's head bobbing up and down, it remains restless in a field of shimmering light. Grace bought pink latex swim caps for the entire group, transforming us all into bright exclamation marks in the flickering water.

There is a metal railing bolted to the Point's limestone perimeter. Years ago, someone fastened two sturdy steel ladders to the railing on the Point's south side, making it easier to get in and out. Each time I enter the lake, I face trepidation, leaving solid ground for a fluctuating mass of cold and wet. The lake demands that your body accept its conditions, its temperature and its motion. Cold water, in the low fifties, causes my breath to become sharp gasps and tenses my body into a fierce knot in futile defense of a pain I've freely chosen. Pushing off into warm water, around seventy degrees, lets my breath expand to the outer reaches of my body. My arms and legs ease into motion as if I were luxuriating at a spa. Water is so malleable, its surface changeable. Jumping from a high dive, hitting the surface feels like a playful slap; falling from an airplane, I imagine it would be as brutal as concrete. Slipping into the lake from the ladder, its surface is as delicate as a soap bubble, yielding to whatever mass enters it. I like to believe that the lake and I have an agreement, which is that the lake wants me to stay on its surface. There's a truth about it because as I swim, I feel its density beneath me, the sheer incredible weight of all of that water supporting my body. All that surface tension keeps driftwood, aircraft carriers, and swimmers alike afloat. Any swimmer knows that moving forward through the water is all about turning liquid into a force of resistance, making it as dense as you possibly can.

But the truth is, the lake doesn't care about me in the least. It is what it is, a body of water. Whether a thing floats or sinks is not its concern. For us land animals, swimming is the art of negotiating the water's surface. I know my safety depends on my having enough skill and energy to respond to the lake's demands at any given moment. A few times my body has told me clearly: *Get out of the lake.* I always obey. I am not worried about going under in rough water. I've never exhausted myself to the point I felt I couldn't swim to land. I've never had hypothermia. I've never had the fear of sinking, water closing over me, obliterating the sunlight above. I've always trusted my strength and buoyancy, as well as my own common sense. It's where water meets land that I fear, when the waves are big. Getting in is easy. The water, like an immense outstretched hand, invites. But the rough lake is like a jealous lover. Leaving it requires cunning, precision, and a fine attunement to its rhythms and moods. Trying to get out of the water where there are rocks, like at the Point, a wave can slam you into an immovable surface with punishing force, or it can suck you away just when your hand is about to grasp the ladder. Timing is everything.

A wave can be dangerous but its velocity is transient. It arises, rolls, and breaks. Once I was bodysurfing at Oak Street Beach and mistimed my approach so that the crest of a breaking wave shoved me underwater with startling ferocity. I was awash in churning froth, my humanity no more significant to the lake's power than the particles of sand on its floor. The sand was as hard as cement as I slammed into it. It scraped my hands and forearms. A hot soup of pure animal fear radiated from my gut into my brain. And then, a clear blue bubble of calm rose to the surface of my awareness. A thought. *Hold your breath. It will pass.* My underwater turmoil couldn't have lasted more than about three seconds. Then I was on my feet, wading out of the water to dry off and bike home.

A few summers ago, I found myself separated from my swim partner, Ruth Anne, by mountains of water. We had planned to do a two-mile swim together that day. Ruth Anne was training for an Ironman triathlon with a swim distance of 2.4 miles. She was in her early twenties, about half my age, six feet tall, muscular, with an irrepressible personality. Grace nicknamed her "our real-life superhero," a name that stuck, somewhat, but not as well as the name she brought upon herself when she said once, during a pool swim, "My boulders hurt—I mean, my shoulders!" Boulders. I need not say more.

The day Ruth Anne and I first met, earlier that summer, she claimed me. "You," she said. "I want to swim with *you*." I felt I had been summoned by a force greater than myself, a command from the universe that I put my hard-earned skill and love of swimming to use by assisting someone else with a momentous goal. I could not refuse. I was energized by her quest so I plunged headlong into being her training partner for the swimming part of the Ironman.

The waves were large and lazy at the Point, but not daunting. They got bigger the farther out we swam, and I began to wonder whether we should swim all the way to the pier a single time, let alone twice. After a while, I realized I couldn't see any of the several people who had started out with us, isolated as I was by the height of the waves. I treaded water, my small self in that big lake, rising and plummeting in waves within waves, turning circles, looking for Ruth Anne. I noticed a bank of fog rolling in from the east, unusual because most weather passes in the opposite direction over Chicago. I noticed the fog thickening over Fifty-Seventh Street Beach and the Museum of Science and Industry to the west. Getting lost in fog was a very bad idea. I didn't trust my sense of direction in the water without seeing the landmarks I depended on. The waves were more than I'd bargained for, stronger than I'd ever experienced, and they were pushing me towards the rocks to the southwest, between the beach and the pier. Fear whirred in my gut, threatening to purée all my thoughts into terror. I resisted. I was conscious of the battle inside me between fear's venom and cool reason as the lake hoisted and dropped my body. I knew it simply would not do to panic. My mind exhibited a strength I never knew it had as it wrestled my fear into a small compartment of my consciousness and locked it there. I reassured myself that Ruth Anne was strong and smart and that she would be okay. I told myself that I wouldn't want her to remain in threatening water to look for me.

Even when we could see each other in the water, would we actually be able to help each other in moments of distress? Maybe we would. Maybe we wouldn't. The base of our trust in each other, built over time, is that we can rely on each other's ability to know when we've had enough and still have the energy to swim back to land. On that day, I wanted out. I trained my eye on the beach, on a single lifeguard stand, about three hundred yards away. I swam a determined breaststroke, not my strongest stroke, but the one that allowed me to keep my eyes on my target. I worried that the waves might thrash me onto the rocks. I thought if I got hurt that way, so be it. At least I'd be alive. Scraped up and bleeding, perhaps, but breathing, conscious, and mendable. I told myself, *If reaching the beach is the single thing I accomplish today, it is enough.*

Adrenaline propelled me forward. I focused solely on that lifeguard stand. I kicked as hard as I could, whipping my feet around in circles, using every ounce of strength in my thighs to drive my legs back together. My hands darted forward, pulling out, down, and around with force, my head and torso plunging underwater, then rising to breathe. Water, lifeguard stand, water, lifeguard stand, water, lifeguard stand. I swam until my hands touched bottom, until I reached the place where the waves became a transparent sheen spreading onto the beach, absorbed into the sand, then becoming nothing at all. I stood, shaken. I was wildly grateful to be on land. I still felt the waves' undulation in my body as I walked the quarter mile back to the Point, knowing, but not caring, that I looked ridiculous wearing my prescription goggles on land. No one was there to see me anyway. It was not a beach-going kind of day. I picked my way through the fog over the sand and rocks in my bare feet. I could see the rest of my friends, already out of the water and waiting, transform from ghostly silhouettes to fully fleshed humans as I walked towards them. I felt like Odysseus as they exclaimed over my safe return. We exchanged stories of how we got out. Ruth Anne, the last one of us to return, made it back about ten minutes after I did. Relief poured through every cell of my body when I saw her swimming through the fog. She climbed the ladder, laughing about how rough the water was, how dense the fog had become. She asked me if I wanted to get back in and complete the two miles we had planned on. All of us, mostly women and most of us old enough to be her mother, protested in unison. We were fierce in our opposition and unified in guarding our collective safety. No one was allowed back into the water until the fog cleared.

More often, the lake is benign. Sometimes the water is as flat as silver coins on a table. The lake quietly reflects the trees and buildings rimming its edges. Light bounces between sky and water. On mornings like this, the world and everything in it seems exactly right. When the dregs of winter have melted to oblivion, around May 1, we venture in. No one thinks of distance. The frigid water cuts like a knife. We get in. We get out. The cold is like millions of tiny needles injected directly into my muscles, and I fear that it will paralyze me if it reaches my core. Breath is short and quick. I fear lack of air. I fear that my body will constrict in shock. The place where my fear intersects the cold propels my body to its very limits, but it is also a place that allows reassurance to come flooding in, making the entire world seem roomier, friendlier. My body tenses, then eases into itself, tightens and releases, a pulsation like life itself. I eventually warm up in the water, or I don't. Sometimes it becomes clear that the only warmth I'll find that morning is in bundling up and lingering over eggs and coffee with my swimming friends. Either way, it is good.

The water temperature, while steadily climbing over the summer months, can also change ten or more degrees from one day to the next. It depends on the strength and direction of the wind. A strong gale from the west will blow the surface water, warmed by the sun, away from Chicago, allowing the colder water below to rise to the surface. A strong wind from the north or the east will do the opposite, blowing sun-heated surface water to Chicago's edge. I remember a mid-July swim in flat, frigid water, its temperature having plummeted several degrees over a day down to fifty-two degrees Fahrenheit, although the day promised to be sunny and well into the eighties. We swam a quiet breaststroke near the rocks. The water felt more solid than usual, like rubber syrup, and it resisted movement, although those words probably more accurately describe how my own body felt. The cold confuses. As penetrating as it is, it is sometimes hard to know what's inside or outside of your own skin. My memory of that day shows me slow, hushed ripples in flat black water with a pale-blue sky above, all of us swimmers as resolute as monastics beholden to a vow of silence.

Rarely does the water temperature reach eighty degrees. I am wary of swimming in water that is too warm, in the lake or pool. It feels unclean, like swimming in someone else's sweat. I do not know what unseen creatures might thrive in the water when it becomes too warm. In contrast, the cold awakens every cell of my body. Every synapse snaps to attention. Lethargy flees. My entire body feels readjusted in the way it is meant to be, calmly energetic.

On a summer morning, when I plan to meet my friends and swim, my alarm goes off at five on a weekday, six on a weekend. I roll over and curl myself into Steve's body. He is enveloped in warm sleep, just barely conscious enough to pull me close. I breathe him into my lungs. He radiates throughout my body. I can feel it in my fingertips resting on his back or bare chest. I do not want to move. Drifting in and out of sleep, our limbs draped one over another, is one of my favorite ways to be alive and human. At that hour, the only motion in our bed is the crosscurrent of our breathing, rising and falling within rippled sheets. The day's first light has barely begun to spill over the lake's horizon, washing away Chicago's mottled nighttime sky. I am still dreaming, a little bit, seduced by floating images and elusive sagas that will only ever exist in that moment, and this makes me want to sink more deeply into my mattress. Why move at all? I must choose between one fluid world or another. It's never easy for me to get up this early and I reluctantly peel myself out of bed. We have other mornings to sleep in together.

I climb down the ladder, following some swimmers into the water, others following me. I push off on my back, loosening my shoulders in a languid backstroke. I see, as I swim south to the pier, my right arm, rising and passing in my peripheral vision, in shadow: a flat blue gray. My left arm, rising and passing, in turn, illuminated by the newborn sun: aglow, pink orange. My arms become a whirling kaleidoscope. Blue gray, pink orange, blue gray, pink orange, blue gray, pink orange. The sky is blue and bright in my eyes. Swimming backstroke, I see wet hands rising, spraying cascades of droplets, round diamonds luminescent against the infinite sky, its magnificence so perfect and smooth and deep I imagine how pleasing it would be to plunge upwards. Falling jewels of water sparkle against the royal sky and fall back into the emerald green where they just were, perfectly content, undisturbed by a swimmer's desire. How fascinating that these clear droplets create the lake's deep green. This is important to know: the surface of the lake can become many different colors—blue, green, gray, white, red, orange, brown—depending on the chop and what's happening in the sky. But when your face is underwater and your eyes are open, the color of the deep water is always the same: green. Sometimes it is clear enough to see the bottom of the lake some six, eight, ten, fourteen feet below, sometimes not. Clear or cloudy, the green remains.

I flip onto my stomach and swim freestyle. I breathe every third stroke. When I breathe to the east, I often shut my eyes against the sun's glare. When I breathe to the west, I see the city. Every few strokes, I lift my head to look forward, making sure I am still aiming directly for the tip of the pier or the Point. My face straight down, I see nothing but green. I paint images of water and sky, always aiming to get the essence of the lake into my work. I think about how I'd mix my paint to get this color: phthalo green, a little mars black, a little cadmium red, a little yellow ochre. Some titanium white. I've tried it, mixing these colors, and these are the ones that will create the slightly opaque virescence I see underwater. Sometimes I feel frustrated as a painter because I believe I paint the water's appearance more accurately than I am able to paint what the water feels like. As I turn to breathe, I see the white lace of the water's broken surface as I move through it. I want a camera attached to my swim cap. I want the blurry edge of the water, as I fracture it, frozen into crisp frames so I can pore over it, memorize it. I want to see the exact shape of the water as I disturb it. It happens too quickly for my eye to see it the way I want to.

Swimming is an exercise of seeing. Painting is an exercise of remembering what swimming feels like. I speak only for myself. I won't make these claims for any other swimmer or painter. If the water is rough, the waves high, my entire body carries the sensation of the lake's energy into my painting studio. It's as if the cytoplasm of each one of my cells mimics the heft and the roll of Lake Michigan for hours after I dry off. It seems right that I spend much of my day with another liquid substance, the colors I spread onto my panels, the early-morning light still aglow in my brain. Lake algae under my toenails, oil paint underneath my fingernails. Dried lake water on my skin, in my hair. I spend my summer days not as clean as I could be. A shower after a morning swim seems superfluous. A long soak in the bath before bedtime, after a day of swimming and painting, is luxury.

Swimming in the lake is joy. We meet the unexpected. Jenifer, who grew up swimming in the Pacific Ocean, taught us how to swim butterfly into large, oncoming waves. If you time it just right, a hard dolphin kick will send your arms flying out surprisingly high over a wave's back side, your entire upper body suspended momentarily in air. You fall tumbling into the water when you are already in the water.

When days are still warm but the nights hint at autumn, the water is noticeably warmer than the early-morning air. When I swim freestyle, my arms become chilled as I thrust them forward, and I can't wait to plunge them back into the cozy lake. It feels upside down, as if the air itself has gone rogue. The skim layer of the water, the top two millimeters, matches the air's chill. As I swing my hand over the water, I let my fingers graze the surface. I delight in the fleeting cold on my fingertips, a sensation erased as soon as my hand plunges deep. Knowing about this feels like a luscious secret. It makes me wonder about what other rarified events like this exist in Chicago, minutiae that make other people smile to themselves. I know there must be many, perhaps as many as there are people in Chicago. I need not know what they are. It is enough that I have one for myself.

We swim to the pier. Some of us swim back, *fast*. I time myself. Thirteen minutes or so. Once, when the water was as still as a mirror, I swam it in twelve and a half. I reach the Point, breathless, muscles twitching, burning. Some of us paddle east along the rocks, slow and lazy, to cool down, ease our shoulders, and slow our breath. We pass the end of the Point so we can look at the downtown skyscrapers, a jagged mass about eight miles distant. This is how I love Chicago the most. I am southeast of downtown, far from its noise and traffic, immersed in ridges of undulating water, blue ridges maybe. As Deirdre says, the lake is our very own urban wilderness. I can name so many of the buildings downtown, and I can name several that have been built since I arrived from South Carolina. They sprouted like exuberant mushrooms from the complex economic life of the city I've chosen as my home. Its vibrancy has nurtured me as an artist my entire adult life. I paint the lake's eastern horizon because it is a perfect metaphor of yearning for the mountains I so sorely missed, and for all the things I want that I still cannot reach. Treading water in the lake, away from urban surfaces and urban strife, my senses soothed by the cool movement of water, I can feel, finally, how much I also yearn for Chicago. The silhouettes of the terraced Sears (no Chicagoan wants to call it by its new name, Willis) Tower and the narrow, flat-topped pyramid of the John Hancock Building define the skyline, as familiar to my eyes by now as my own swimmer's body. I tread water and face east, then west, each direction holding something I deeply desire. A morning swim in the lake is sometimes so exquisite it's hard to tolerate. Joy is so often a barely disguised ache.

For years after I moved away from Hyde Park, I couldn't return for a visit without feeling jittery and unnerved. The fear I learned upon my arrival as a fourteen-year-old, plus the contradictions I faced in the competing mythologies about place, still lived inside me, vibrating with their friction and inconsistencies. Whenever I swim in the lake in the neighborhood where I first encountered this confusion, I bring this bundle of complexities with me. It exists as a vague bodily discomfort, a slight churning in my gut and tightness in my shoulders. When I ease myself into the lake, as wide open as outer space itself, my tension starts to dissipate and my main sensation is of being held and rocked by the rhythms of the universe. The boundless water soothes the harsh lines of my scars.

But I do not want to get carried away—it's not as if my swimming in the lake resolves the divisions we human beings create. I still live in a city with segregation, growing income inequality, and gun violence, all of them disturbing truths I must reconcile inside myself every day. But as I float on the lake's surface, freely rolling waves lift and drop my body, and I think it's much healthier to hold this sensation in my bodily memory than one of blockades and differences. My swimming in the lake is not only practice at becoming a better swimmer, it's practice in sensing the free flow of energy.

In late summer, starting in mid-August, the sun rises after 6:00 a.m. We get in the water while the sky to the east is a pale gray and the sky to the west a deep blue, still holding remnants of the fading night. Often we see the moon, fully round or a thin crescent. We see a stripe of pink on the horizon. It is surprising how much daylight seeps into the visible world before the sun makes its appearance. Depending on the date and how close we are to the fall equinox, we see the sun rise while we are in the water, sometimes immediately after we enter, sometimes when we are close to the pier. Swimming freestyle, I turn my head to breathe towards the east every sixth stroke, about every eight or so seconds, an interval that allows me to notice the subtle changes in the light on the horizon, from pale pink to vermillion to dazzling orange. It doesn't matter where we are in the water when it is time to pause. Watching the sun peek over the horizon deserves notice. On a recent fall swim, Jenifer, who was swimming beside me, reached over and tapped my shoulder. I lifted my head and she pointed to the sun, its edge just emerging, shooting a long, brilliant line in both directions along the horizon. We treaded water together, watching the light change by the second. The others, varying distances from the two of us, also stopped to watch, most of us in our pink caps.

The sun, when it appears at the horizon, moves quickly, much more speedily than it ever appears to traverse the midday sky. Of course, the sun's movement is a misperception. Our eyes deceive us. Its position remains fixed. We are the ones, floating in a vast body of water, who inhabit the rotating earth. We are the ones circling the sun. We know this. But in this moment, I give my intellect a rest and I let wonder take over. I am in awe, watching Lake Michigan birth a fiery-orange, dripping-wet sun from her cold, green depths. ∎

WEIRD PIG MEETS OWEN FLYE
Robert Long Foreman

O wen Flye was unaccounted for. Farmer Dan had arranged for him to come to the farm through a temporary employment agency. He needed Flye to lend a hand with the season's harvest and earn his keep by the honest labor of his hands.

Flye arrived three days late, Weird Pig watching as he stepped from the cab of a red pickup. He waved his thanks to the driver, who pulled away. Not being a shy pig, Weird Pig approached and asked, Are you Owen? Are you the man Owen Flye?

Flye took Weird Pig in for the duration of a pregnant silence that passed between them as he lit a cigarette and sucked at it as if relieved to have it there.

That's right, Flye said at last. There is a man at this farm I am meant to meet.

You mean Farmer Dan, said Weird Pig. That's not me. I'm Weird Pig.

I see that, he said, scanning the farmhouse before him and the farm that unfurled behind it.

Dan's out at the fields with the other men, said Weird Pig. I'm sure they'll be glad to see you. They need all the help they can get.

I suppose, then, said Flye, I should make myself comfortable. And he strode without another word past Weird Pig into the farmhouse through the front door.

Weird Pig didn't follow. He never went into the house without Farmer Dan. It was forbidden. He thought Flye ought not to go in, either, but he didn't speak up. He didn't know why. Something in the man's demeanor suggested he should not.

He heard noises coming from inside the house. They weren't noises he had heard before. He hadn't heard them because Dan had never used his electric juicer. It was a gift, from some birthday long before. Flye had found it. He was making a glass of fresh orange juice.

Weird Pig bounded out to the field to find Farmer Dan and deliver the news of Flye's arrival.

He's here? Dan asked. Why hasn't he come out to help us?

Weird Pig tried to explain, but it was plain Dan didn't really care what Owen's reason was. His temper had risen. He could not abandon the work in progress, however, so it had to wait.

It waited until the sun was going down over the farm and the men went ambling back to the house to eat potato chips and watch *Law & Order*. They liked to gather and do this at Dan's before they retired to the bunkhouse to rest up for the next day's labor. But when they entered Dan's living room they found a stranger with his feet up on Dan's ottoman, with four empty bags of potato chips on the floor beside him and crumbs down his shirt and on his pants. He didn't even look up when they came in.

Having a good time in here? asked Dan. Weird Pig stood beside him in the doorway.

Owen Flye said not a word. He wiped his greasy hands on the arms of the recliner and stood. Farmer Dan made a fist.

You're outta potato chips, said Flye.

And you're outta line, said Dan. Way out.

And what's gonna happen to me now? Huh? What passes for justice on this chickenshit farm?

One of the other men spoke up. Justice Basement, he said. It was Field Hand Rick.

What? said Flye. Speak up.

Justice Basement, said Rick again, louder this time. You got a problem with somebody here, you take it down to the Justice Basement.

And to the basement they went, all five of them, with Weird Pig close behind.

Weird Pig had heard of the Justice Basement. He knew that men went there to settle disputes. That was all he knew.

What he didn't know was that in the Justice Basement, which was Dan's basement whenever justice was carried out there, two men would meet and tie their right wrists together. They would thrash each other with their fists until one man gave up, or was dead or unconscious.

This form of justice wasn't condoned by any outside authority, and whether or not it really constituted justice was not something Dan gave much thought to. The Justice Basement was something he had made up, years before, when he'd grown tired of his field hands going to the police when they witnessed a murder or had something stolen from them. Often it was Dan himself who resolved a problem in the Justice Basement. It was he who had decided the men's right hands should be tied together, not their left hands. Dan was left-handed, unlike normal people, and so he had a great advantage in these arbitration hearings.

Owen Flye was left-handed, though, too. And as soon as his right wrist was tied to Dan's, he punched Dan in the throat, which brought him choking to his knees, and blinded him with his fingers. He choked Dan, and punched him more times than Weird Pig could count. Dan fell to the ground, bleeding from all of his face.

The men untied and separated them. Dan was a mess. He couldn't see. He had blood all down his shirt. Two of the field hands carried him to his truck to drive him to the hospital. They had not seen such a thing happen before in any basement.

Weird Pig stayed behind with the other man, Field Hand Clive, who told Owen Flye, This is your farm now. That is the rule Dan made. It's his farm by law, but until he returns it's yours to rule as you see fit.

Clive didn't ask Owen Flye what he was going to do with Dan Farm. He did not want to know. He would find out soon enough.

* * *

Owen Flye had seized the farm at exactly the wrong time, at least in terms of Weird Pig's life cycle. It was different in profound ways from those of other pigs. Early on, he had reached and surpassed pig puberty, but that was but the first in a series of steps on the way to full maturity for Weird Pig. It meant that Weird Pig was impressionable for more years than most creatures were, and that he enjoyed multiple coming-of-age episodes that stood out for their influence on his character.

One of those episodes began with the sight of Farmer Dan so soundly beaten at a fight he had invented. The maturation episode continued through what followed it.

The morning after his fight with Dan, Owen Flye called his men on Dan's house phone. Forty minutes later, the men arrived: skinny guys in jeans and hoodies with holes in their shoes and nothing at all to read behind their glassy eyes.

They must have been waiting nearby for the phone call, which meant Owen must have planned to ascend to his current position. Which was not reassuring to Weird Pig.

Owen yanked the phone out of the wall and set himself up in Farmer Dan's living room, by the window, where he sat with Dan's shotgun in his lap and ordered his men to bring forth, to the window, each of the farm's animal species.

Flye ordered Weird Pig to stand beside him. I will, he said, introduce myself to every animal and evaluate its usefulness. You are my right-hand pig. Pay attention. Learn from this what you can.

Flye interviewed the horses, first, summoning the three of them together. He asked them how much grain they ate in a day and how many apples. He wrote their answers down and asked what work they did. He wrote that down as well. He seemed to do some math, then, judging by the look of concentration on his face.

He dismissed them without disclosing what he had concluded. As they departed, he turned to Weird Pig and said, All three of those horses are the same horse. That's basically it. For all intensive purposes, that's how it is.

Weird Pig knew he shouldn't correct Owen Flye, who had said that last thing wrong. He resisted the urge to do it.

Next came the cow. Owen asked how much milk she produced, and she gave an honest answer, which satisfied him as he took a big drink of milk from the glass in his hand. The cow watched Owen as he took another long drink of milk, before dismissing her.

Owen turned to Weird Pig and said, with a milk moustache, Cows don't like it when they can see you drinking their milk. That's why I let her see me drinking her milk. I wanted her to know I could control her. What do you think?

Weird Pig thought this was unnecessary. Cows aren't hard to control, he thought.

That wasn't what he said, though. What he said was, Sounds great. Awesome.

Owen then called all the geese forward. Watch carefully, he said to Weird Pig, as the eight of them gathered before the window.

Geese, said Owen Flye. You are geese.

The geese looked around and looked back at him. They didn't seem to know what to do, which wasn't a surprise.

You have been addressed, said Flye. Now answer.

You are correct, said one of the males. We are geese.

All of us surely are geese, said a female.

They were silent for a moment, then, animals and human.

What, asked Owen, do you contribute to the farm?

They looked confused. No one, said the female, has asked us this before.

I am asking you now.

We keep watch, said another male. A few others honked in agreement.

It's true, said Weird Pig to Owen. They make better guard dogs than dogs.

Okay, said Owen. I have one more question. It's a rhetorical question, but humor me, please. Why do I need geese to keep watch over this farm when the farm has a closed-circuit surveillance system?

And with that, he lifted the shotgun, cocked it, and blasted to pieces the male who had only just addressed him.

He exploded into meat and feathers. Weird Pig's ears rang and the other geese scattered and attempted and failed to fly away. Owen cocked the shotgun again and aimed again but didn't shoot. He fell back in his chair, laughing.

When he was done laughing, he declared, Any creature that lives on this farm and eats and shits and does nothing more than that will be dealt with similarly.

He stood. The interviews have ended, he said. The example has been made. The work animals need not worry, but you may, he told Weird Pig, want to warn the rabbits and cats. If they want a place on this farm, they'll have to carve it out for themselves.

Owen sent Field Hand Clive to go out and buy more potato chips. He turned on the television, the shotgun in his lap, and for a while he watched CNN. There was a war on.

* * *

Weird Pig had nothing to worry about. Flye had assigned him the role of right-hand pig. He was essential. But he had to warn the nonessential creatures.

He found the cat and her kittens under the porch. She was nursing them and licking them.

I heard a blast, said Cat Mandu. What mischief is Farmer Dan making now?

It's not Farmer Dan, said Weird Pig. Not even close. It's a new field hand.

A new hand? I didn't know they needed one.

They did. But now Dan's in the hospital. The new man's taken over. Owen Flye is our ruler now.

Owen Flye, you say?

That's right. Blond gentleman. Likes potato chips.

This is the end of us, said Mandu. This is the end of the farm.

What do you mean? Have you heard of Owen Flye?

I've more than heard of him, she sighed, pulling her kittens closer. I didn't always live here, you realize. I grew up on a farm at least ten miles from here.

A farm like this one?

Not like this one. A boy and a girl lived there, and the man of the farm had a woman to go with him. It was better there. It was quiet. It was, at least, until Owen Flye emerged from the rest of the world.

Where did he come from?

It wasn't clear. A cat's not privy to official business.

Weird Pig didn't know what the word *privy* meant. But now was not the time to ask. Instead he said, What did Owen Flye do at your old farm?

You mean, what *didn't* he do? First there was trouble with the farmer's young daughter, something I did not at the time understand. An argument followed, between Flye and the farmer.

Oh no.

Oh no is right. Owen lost a finger on his right hand, and the farmer lost his life. For six days thereafter he acted as the farm's master. In those six days the farm was made a dead shadow of itself.

He ordered the deaths of all unnecessary creatures and kept the farmer's family chained in what had been the master bedroom. From there, he knew they would see what he did to their land.

He ordered all of the grass killed. He wanted no color on the earth.

He burned the trees at night and watched them burn, laughing and cheering as the flames rose higher. It seemed he wanted everything to die and would not rest until it was gone.

The police came, eventually. By then, the animals had all been killed, even the useful ones. He didn't even eat them. The house was ash, and Owen Flye was nowhere.

They never found him?

They never did.

How did you survive? You said all the animals died.

They *nearly* all died. I was the lone survivor. I hid under the porch until he'd burned the first of the trees. Then I crept onto a charred branch while he slept. I waited him out. I knew he wouldn't last forever there. Nothing lasts forever.

I'm frightened, said Weird Pig. What do we do?

There isn't much I can see to do, said Mandu. My old strategy won't serve me again. I've got kittens to look after. I'll not leave them to Flye. I will attempt an escape. I think the better question is, what will you do? Take your orders? Try to save the other animals?

I guess, said Weird Pig, it sounds like that might not work.

Smart pig. It's only a matter of time.

Oh dear, said Weird Pig. Oh my.

Let me worry about myself and my kittens, said Mandu. You worry about yourself. Do what you must do, Weird Pig. Be bold. Remember that death awaits you on the other side of Owen Flye, and you will know what to do when the time comes.

Weird Pig turned and stepped uncertainly from under the porch.

* * *

There was no one outside. Weird Pig heard the sound of CNN turned up loud—Flye, he thought, must still be checking out the goings-on elsewhere in the world.

Weird Pig had to think. He had to go to his thinking place: a tree he liked to stand under while thinking.

He went there but came up with nothing. He felt the bark of the tree with his hooves. He kept getting distracted. There was an airplane streaking across the sky. It was a sight that tended to empty out his mind and leave him enthralled to the distant vehicle. It always had done that.

He returned to the farm twenty minutes after he had left it, to see the sheep lined up in front of the house. Owen Flye stood before them with his shotgun as his two men took turns slashing the throat of every next sheep in line. Weird Pig watched them work, stunned by the sight of the corpses of the half dozen sheep who had been disposed of. They'd been rolled down the hill at the front of the house all bloody.

What is this about? asked Weird Pig. The sheep are useful. They provide wool.

Owen didn't turn to look at him. We won't be here long enough to need wool, he said.

Weird Pig was about to ask how long they planned, then, to stay, when one of Flye's men emerged from under the porch. His arms were full of the kittens, and from one hand hung the corpse of Mandu the cat. Her neck was broken.

I thought I saw the pig come out of there, he said. And I found these.

Some feline friends, said Flye, without expression.

The man threw Mandu onto the pile of dead sheep. He left with the kittens. Weird Pig didn't know where he was going.

The six living sheep had their eyes on Weird Pig. He couldn't tell if they looked thankful that he had returned, or if they seemed angry that he'd left for so long.

Weird Pig would have made an excuse to go inside and call the police, but Owen had trashed the phone. And he knew the police would not respond to an animal emergency. They would ignore him, because what Flye was doing was not illegal. Weird Pig closed his eyes for a moment and thought hard, as he heard the sound of another of the sheep choking on her own blood and trying to say *baa*.

Weird Pig stepped forward and said, Justice Basement.

Owen turned to him, surprised. What's that? he said.

I said, Justice Basement.

Owen laughed. His men laughed, too. Weird Pig was a pig, and the thought of a spry man like Flye fighting a pig was funny to them.

Weird Pig was still at a point in his life where he didn't like outsiders to know that he preferred to walk on his hind legs. Ever since Owen had arrived at Dan Farm, he had been on all fours, and so it didn't occur to the men that Weird Pig could stand and prove harmful to them. What, they thought, could the average pig do to a man if one of his legs was tied to that man's wrist?

The average pig would have been helpless. But Weird Pig was one in a million.

You're serious, said Owen. He wasn't laughing anymore.

I am, said Weird Pig.

You're sure?

Weird Pig was silent. He looked at Flye, at the sheep, and at the men. He made his way into the house.

All right, then, said Flye. Shit. All right. He propped the shotgun on his shoulder and ordered one man inside. He told the other to wait with the sheep. This won't take long, he said.

Down in the Justice Basement, Flye ate a few handfuls of potato chips and then let his man tie his right wrist to Weird Pig's front-right hoof. The man was laughing. This is fucked up, he said. He kept shaking his head in disbelief.

They had arranged for Weird Pig to stand on Dan's mahjong table, so that Flye wouldn't have to bend down to punch him. Flye thought he'd go easy on the pig. He didn't want to kill him, not yet. There were probably more useless animals on the farm he could trick the pig into ferreting out. He would rough Weird Pig up and get him back in line, but that didn't work because as soon as Weird Pig's hoof was firmly tied to Flye's hand, he reared up on his hind legs, found his balance, and in a heartbeat sank his teeth into the man Flye's throat.

It is easy, for a man like Owen Flye, who likes to categorize animals as useless or not, to overlook the chomping power of a set of pig jaws. Pigs may not advertise their utility the way a horse does, but a pig can bite. A pig has some of the most incredible bite strength of all the animals on the farm.

Bite strength was something Weird Pig had been cultivating, ever since he had learned from other pigs on the slaughterhouse truck about the ancient entelodonts, the so-called terminator pigs. They were long extinct by the time he was born, but they could smash practically anything that got into their mouths.

Weird Pig's first bite was lethal. He rent the throat of Owen Flye and blood sprayed across the Justice Basement. Weird Pig bit again, and again, tearing the flesh off of Flye's face and taking the muscle off from above his collarbone. Flye's man screamed and fled, but Flye couldn't scream. He only jerked his arms as he fell to the concrete floor with a wet slap.

Weird Pig swallowed what he had bit off Flye's body. It is what a pig does with what's in his mouth. He couldn't help it. It was Weird Pig's first taste of human flesh, and while he didn't relish it, he understood as he chewed that he'd discovered a new line of defense for himself.

This was what he could resort to, if the perilous world of men turned against him. He would not let himself forget it.

Weird Pig didn't wait to watch his opponent choke to death on his blood and watch the blood drain out. He chewed the rope off his foreleg, climbed the stairs, and trudged through the house, leaving the man Flye dead on the basement floor. He emerged into the front way of the farmhouse with the blood of Owen Flye running down his face and body. He held Flye's shotgun in his hooves and stood on two feet. He bellowed so that the whole farm would hear him and know what they had heard. He emptied the shotgun into the sky as Flye's men scrambled into Flye's Trans Am and sped away.

Weird Pig wept, there in the yard, for the kittens and sheep who had been butchered long before their times had rightly come.

* * *

Farmer Dan returned to Dan Farm with his two farmhands to a sight he could hardly fathom. Weird Pig was crying with a shotgun in his lap. A half dozen sheep's bloodied bodies were strewn across the slope of the front yard. There were dead kittens he'd never seen before, and he saw the dead cat, too. He didn't mind so much that she was dead; he had been trying to poison her for a month. She had often sat under the porch and meowed and kept him up at night.

Dan was bandaged up. He'd been given OxyContin for the pain, which made the sight he returned home to that much more surreal.

Weird Pig, he said, standing in the yard by the dead sheep. Uh. What's up, buddy?

Where could Weird Pig begin?

Where do I even start? he asked Dan.

How about the beginning, Dan suggested. Or, I mean, just when I left for the hospital. That was, like, what? Two hours ago?

I guess, said Weird Pig, sniffling. Give or take, he added.

Actually, said Field Hand Gary. Maybe you could start by saying whose blood that is, that's on your body. Then you can work your way back. Or whatever.

The shotgun, too, said Dan. It's unsettling that you have that.

Oh, said Weird Pig. It's empty. See? And he pointed it at Dan and pulled the trigger. He cocked it and pulled the trigger again.

Oh woah! said Dan. Okay. So, now, what happened?

Owen Flye. He took over the farm. Started rounding up animals he didn't like.

Really.

He did. He sent Clive out for potato chips. When he got back he ate a bunch of them and all this happened.

Okay, said Dan. And you put a stop to it immediately? As soon as you could?

Uh, said Weird Pig. Yeah. He looked at the sheep, who glared at him. I mean, I did when I figured out exactly what he was up to. And then left to think, and came back. About ninety minutes in, I think, was when I took action.

Okay. And, so, the blood?

It's Owen Flye's.

And where is he?

He's in the Justice Basement. I had to hurt him. I had to stop him.

You did? You couldn't wait until I returned here to do it myself? Without further bloodshed?

I didn't know when you were coming back.

I said two hours. I said I'd be back in two hours.

No you didn't.

Weird Pig, I did. I said that, and I asked if you heard me, like, right after I said it. You said yes.

Oh.

Goddamnit, Weird Pig.

All right, Dan, fine. I forget things. And I don't always pay close attention. I guess I'm the only one who's like that. You're perfect and I am the pig that isn't perfect.

I didn't say that. Come on, now.

No, you come on. All right? I just ate a guy's neck and face to save your farm and the animals. I didn't do it for me. How's that for a fucking sacrifice?

Dan looked up to see the other field hand he'd returned with emerge from the house, his face ashen. He nodded, to confirm Weird Pig's story.

Oh boy, said Farmer Dan.

What do we do, Dan? asked Field Hand Rick.

About what?

About the body in the basement. And the pig.

You mean Weird Pig? Nothing. He's fine.

Yeah?

Oh yeah. He'll snap out of this. What he needs is to take a nice long bath, get the blood off, and go sink in the mud for a few hours.

And the body? Won't the police take an interest in that?

Sure they will. And we'll tell them the truth. Owen Flye was an asshole, and he tied his wrist to a pig. The pig ate his body until he died.

They won't think that's unusual?

This is a *farm*, Rick. We're in the middle of *nowhere*. There are pigs that roam the countryside. We'll say one of them did it.

Oh. Okay. Shoot.

They'll pump Weird Pig's stomach for pieces of Owen, so we'll just make sure he's digested and processed, you know, before we make the call.

Well, all right.

And you were worried! Now let's go get that body, and put it on the field out there. That's probably best. Weird Pig, you know what to do.

He knew exactly what to do. Soon he would get to sink again into the cold, soft mud. And he would begin to feel a whole lot better.

* * *

The police never bothered asking Weird Pig about Owen Flye. They saw no reason to second-guess Farmer Dan's story about the rogue pig eating Flye's throat after being tied to him for no particular reason. Dan had done the smart thing and called the regular police, not the farm police, who would have asked better, more agrarian questions. They might have even searched Twitter for mentions of pigs and fighting, which would have led them to see that one of Flye's men had posted a Twitter thread about taking over the farm.

They didn't do that, though, and most of the time it didn't register with Weird Pig that a change had taken place in him. When he was alone, in the mud or elsewhere, he felt no different from how he'd always felt, all the time.

It was when Weird Pig joined the company of others that it felt different, that what he had done seemed to matter. At first, when he was up at Dan's house with the field hands, and when he was in the barn at night with the animals before returning to his shed, he thought everyone's attitude toward him had changed. He thought the others looked at him like he was a different pig, like they could see something in him that he couldn't feel, like he wore the skin of another pig and couldn't take it off.

As the months wore on, Weird Pig realized he had indeed changed. He had impulses, now, where there had not been impulses before. When he stood in the yard and stared into the sun, he saw visions of fire and mass murder.

With Mandu gone, there was no one on the farm to whom he could confide these things.

Cats, however, abhor a vacuum, and so Mandu's place was soon filled by a tiger tomcat who never gave his name. No one knew exactly when he arrived. He emerged from the rafters of the barn one morning, where it seemed he was now living. He fast became Weird Pig's confidante, his feline confessor.

Weird Pig told him that wherever he looked, he seemed to see fodder for the god of ruin. He felt, he said, like he was the agent of a nation not yet born, one that was opposed to all good things.

The tiger tomcat listened.

Where Mandu might have advised, though, that Weird Pig seek counseling, or religion, or whatever, the tiger tomcat said things like, That's really interesting. Wow. That's really remarkable.

The best idea that the tiger tomcat had was that Weird Pig ought to use his as-yet-unexpressed aggression for good. Why not maintain order here? he said. Keep everyone in line.

I guess I could do that, said Weird Pig. I'll give it some thought.

And Weird Pig did think about it. He thought about it a long time, as he sank into the cool, smooth mud. He had a dream that he was the chief of police, demanding tribute from every shop owner and homeowner in town. He ran strangers out of town for wearing their hair too long, or too short, and when he murdered he did it in cold blood.

When he woke from his mud nap he had forgotten all about this. Again he was Weird Pig—one in a million, if there ever was a million. ■

HIS LOVE
Naomi Shihab Nye

Gene Wesley Elder
leaving his life
wrapping household goods
kitchen cups
spoons
tiny tablecloths
grandma's china plates
in rumpled wrapping paper
snagged with ribbons
brown grocery bags
distributed to friends
ordering no memorials
give your money to an artist
who needs it
give my money to artists
just call my lawyer
get the money
take time
arrange things under trees
sit with them
make constellations of
cast-offs
till beauty rises
no I'm not scared
I'm just doing what we all do
sooner or later
lucky I had time to savor
think about what I lived
parcel things out
I wanted the windows and doors
left open
long last days
quiet filters
a few opera songs
deleted my emails
after writing a final one

THE END IS NEAR
ARTIST GOING UNDERGROUND
remember me   but even more
remember you

THE HOLY FAMILY
Yumiko Kurahashi

—translated from the Japanese by Michael Day

I think that maybe our father and mother are aliens. No, not just maybe, says my brother—they are aliens, no doubt about it. Anyway, he says, the two creatures we saw that night were not humans. I cannot deny that the scene was a big shock to me, too.

There was a small earthquake in the middle of the night. I think it was close to 1:00 a.m. Frightened and fascinated by the science fiction I was reading, I could not get to sleep, and as I lay stiff in bed, raptly turning page after page, without warning the ground began to shake. The frozen air cracked like glass, and I felt fragments shower my face.

Before long the earth stopped quaking, but I could not get back to sleep by myself. I crawled through the secret door beneath the desk and made my way to my brother's room. My brother (I call him Otooto, "younger brother," though in fact we are twins) was staring at the ceiling, eyes open wide.

"That was quite a quake."

"Yes, it was. But before the earthquake I felt a strange sensation, as if the air was shaking."

"What could it have been?" I wondered as I crawled into bed beside him. Like a corpse in a coffin, I folded my hands atop my chest, sensing something strange in the air, just as my brother had said. Our senses are especially sharp, and we can perceive vibrations in the air that ordinary people cannot hear, taking in the sound through our skin. Before long we sensed a vibration separate from that of the earthquake.

"There it is," my brother softly shouted.

It felt to me as if the air was jiggling like jelly or soft meat, sniveling tearfully as it shook. In any case something extremely unusual was occurring. Perhaps some otherworldly creature was spying on us. In the end, all I can say is, it was odd. In my brother's opinion, ground zero was our parents' bedroom.

"It could be a home invasion."

"What's that?"

"You know, a robbery."

My opinion differed, but what my brother said was not out of the question, so we stepped out onto the balcony to look into the rooms.

The first room you come to from ours is our father's. It was pitch-dark and absolutely silent. Skin drawn taut, we strained our senses to perceive the slightest sound, but there was no one inside, we were certain of it. The next room we arrived at was our mother's. Here a thin light seeped from the window. There was a gap in the curtains. We pressed our faces to the window glass, one above the other, and peered into the room. It was then that we witnessed that shocking scene.

To begin with, we had no idea what was occurring. We saw our parents (or shall I say, the naked creatures we assumed to be our parents). Our mother's face was visible, so we imagined the other figure must be our father. We could not see our father's face, so this is a guess. At first the disturbing thought that it might not be our father flashed through our minds. Our father and our mother were embracing. We knew husbands and wives did such things, but knowing and seeing are very different. The idea of a naked man and woman embracing may not sound so strange, but the position they were in was inexplicably odd, like a white, monstrous spider with eight limbs or maybe more. The arms and legs of this big white spider formed a complicated tangle as it squirmed.

Just then, from this jumbled mass, our father's face emerged. We were now certain it was him. Eyes open (for some reason our mother's eyes were closed, a pained look on her face), he looked our direction and seemed to see us. I grabbed my brother's arm, giving a sign. Suppressing screams of horror, we returned to the room in a daze.

We turned out the light and embraced, catching our breath. Fortunately, there was no sign our father was pursuing us. Then, as we had always done (or, to be precise, as we had learned to do in middle school), we fused together and exchanged opinions about the scene we had witnessed. My brother expressed grave concern. "Those things are not human at all. They must be aliens," he insisted. Even as a science fiction fan, I could not accept this explanation. What shocked me the most was to see that a man and a woman take on an inhuman, otherworldly form when they make love.

"Surely you do not really believe that," said my brother. "Even two crazy people still have eight limbs. I counted ten."

"Then you counted wrong," I said for the sake of saying it, but I felt as if the blood had drained from my body.

From then on, we have looked at our mother and father differently, always conscious that they could be aliens. They too seem to know something about us, and we see something strange in their gaze. They look at us like aliens who know their subterfuge has been seen through.

There is nothing more sorrowful or more frightening than knowing your parents are not human. We suspect they may soon find some way to get rid of us.

* * *

Since the recent earthquake, the children have been behaving oddly. They stare at us as one would stare at a strange animal. I am convinced they saw into our room that evening.

Several days later I attended a college reunion, where I encountered a classmate named Fukuda, who now works as a psychologist. I told him the following: "I am fairly certain they saw us. The kids, I mean."

"A case of the primal scene?"

"What is that?"

"That's when children catch sight of adults, their parents in particular, in the midst of pleasure. Freud calls it 'the primal scene.'"

"It must be a significant shock to the children. Perhaps that is why they have been acting so strangely. What should I do?"

"Nothing," said Fukuda, his expression again turning serious. "In any case that's my view. It's best to let time heal the wound."

That day we parted without discussing the matter further. My wife, still more disturbed than I, seemed to be taking pains to avoid the children.

"The children are up late every night, having secret talks," my wife said nervously.

Determined to find out just what the two of them were up to at night, in spite of some opposition from my wife, I secretly installed a security camera in the children's room. Thanks to my occupation, I am adept at such technical tasks.

The results could hardly have been more shocking. I still have not breathed a word of it to my wife. I believe, in fact, it may be best to stay silent. How, for instance, do you tell your wife that her children are having an incestuous relationship? Yet the truth is that what I saw was not so simple. You could perhaps call it incest, but it is beyond my ability to describe the extraordinary form that act took.

Their two bodies had undergone a total transformation (I could see what seemed to be their faces, so it was clear who they were), suggesting the shape of a sea cucumber. Ken was inside Yuuko like a sword in a sheath—or perhaps a more apt analogy would be that of a half-peeled banana. Their limbs were shrunken like fish's fins.

Those things were not humans. Perhaps the word *monster* is not appropriate. If so, I must refer to them as aliens. I recalled the fact that we had adopted the children, and I felt a chill. They were twins, the products of an artificial womb fertilized in vitro at a university hospital. What were they really? In the worst case, I might have to consider disposing of them myself.

Setting aside the problem, that night, for the first time in a long while, I went to my wife's bedroom. My wife bears no responsibility for the fact that the children are abominations. We discussed everything and concluded that we would have to devise corrective measures. At this I found myself feeling calmer.

Before we talked, my wife moved on me with unusual forthrightness, and I accepted her advances. Of course, so as not to be seen a second time, we took every possible precaution.

From the beginning my wife was aroused, and her response was quick. Following her, I too rode wave after wave of pleasure to the heights of ecstasy. My body sprouted many more pseudopodia than normal, more than sixteen, if I am not mistaken. For my wife's part, sixteen nectar-drenched cavities opened in response to the caresses of my pseudopodia.

When it was over, I started thinking. All men and women engage in essentially the same act. Being seen doing it should cause no great concern. The problem is that the children are unknowable creatures whose form of love differs entirely from ours . . . ∎

BIG TWIST
Gregg Murray

Then, because his wound was deep,
The bold Sir Bedivere uplifted him,
And bore him to a chapel nigh the field,
A broken chancel with a broken cross,
That stood on a dark strait of barren land:
On one side lay the Ocean, and on one
Lay a great water, and the moon was full.

—*from* The Idylls of the King, *Alfred, Lord Tennyson*

This is how it is with the artist who believes in his craft. He makes a study of the figure, countless sketches to understand, say, how the curve of a calf muscle is like the belly of a horse. He learns Latin. He rereads aloud passages of Homer to understand the meter of his verse.

* * *

You made rabbits out of napkins and smiled when you surprised us with them jumping up your arm.

* * *

Advanced tennis players swing as hard on their second serve as they do on their first. The difference is that they add spin to the second, allowing them, ironically, more control over where it lands.

* * *

A Rube Goldberg machine is actually the opposite of a machine. It is designed to do something very simple in the most complicated possible way.

* * *

The level of decorum that your wife, my grandmother, requires for anything that is or was ever formal is extremely inconvenient to you. You grit your teeth and do exactly what she wants you to do. You rarely falter. You did, one ordinary morning, actually put on a tuxedo for breakfast when she commented that your undershirt was "uncouth." This act of defiance was more motivated by humorous intent than any kind of resistance.

* * *

It is a rare combination to lead by giving way to others. To properly understand the importance of playfulness when conducting the most serious of rituals. When a leader is well loved, people are occasionally concerned that the leader is weak. This is because they think leading is the same as ruling.

* * *

As an engineer, your day job was to design and build machines and structures. You used words like efficiency and structural integrity to explain them to me. A machine is, technically, anything that helps us do work.

* * *

"When I consider how my light is spent," John Milton writes elegantly of his craft, "Ere half my days in this dark world and wide, / And that one talent which is death to hide / Lodg'd with me useless." He humbly realized his amazing talent for poetry, but his body would not cooperate. His eyesight would go. Milton also understood that he would not live forever, that eventually his light would go out.

* * *

You helped me with my necktie. You called it a choke rag! Later, when church had started, you whispered to me, "I used to wish I could sing. Now I wish you could."

* * *

In a one of their debates, Stephen Douglas called Lincoln "two-faced." Not known for his looks, Lincoln is said to have quipped, "If I had another face, do you think I would wear this one?" Like Lincoln, you were strong enough to deal with criticism. Told that a hat you'd bought made you look sickly, you said, "Good, because I bought two of them. One to shit in, and one to cover it up with."

* * *

You put so much spin on your second serve we all called it Big Twist. As I got older, and you got older too, Big Twist was no longer challenging for me to return. I'd learned from the master and had some spin of my own.

* * *

You never stopped telling your stories, and so they will never pass. As the Bard writes, "So long lives this, and this gives life to thee."

* * *

You once put ChapStick on a wound because it's "all the same stuff." I don't know if that's accurate, but both of your children became health professionals. Come to think of it, you rigged a LOT of things in the house. These inventions gave me more joy than the original objects could possibly contain.

* * *

Mark Twain's Tom Sawyer was always advising Huck that things didn't mean anything if they didn't have any style. And that's true. He'd say, "Why, Huck, you can't do it that away," and the ever-practical Huck would say, "Why not?" and Tom would say, "Because that ain't no kind of style."

* * *

When the Minneapolis bridge collapsed, I called you. Having overseen many bridge projects in your career, you explained to me the concept of structural integrity. In the United States, you estimated that as many as 70 percent of our bridges lacked this virtue.

* * *

You remember Japanese songs you learned during your service in World War II. Fifty, sixty years, seventy years later, you would sing them at the dinner table. We marveled at the power of your memory. Your voice, less so. I had to tell you, "I used to wish I could sing."

* * *

You memorized long passages of Tennyson. At my parents' wedding, you advised my father to take good care of my mother. "When I think about my love for my daughter," you explained, "I think about the words of Abraham Lincoln. When he talked about his love for his country. Lincoln said, 'I am loath to close.'"

* * *

"Virtually all of the top men's players use the kick serve as their second serve. Most right-handers use the American Twist, which bounces up and to the left of the receiver; when hit well, it is difficult to time on the return."[1]

* * *

You made me a functional clock out of marbles and a jumble of plastic ramps, an invention that, if we are perfectly honest, had no function. It did tell the time, even if it was slightly hard to understand WHAT time it said it was. You see, what you had made was not a clock at all, it was a toy, an object of wonder.

* * *

You were known by your fraternity brothers by the nickname Preacher. Because I am wary of this designation, I have the tendency to forget how accurately it describes your faithfulness. You were the preacher of our family, though not because of any sermons but because of the way you led the rituals of our family. At times, it's true, you could lead by remaining completely silent.

* * *

---

1   Geoff Macdonald, "The Art of the Kick Serve," *New York Times*, September 8, 2009

Travel had become difficult for you, but I found a way to take you with me to my dissertation defense. I wore a tuxedo.

* * *

Pete Sampras was battling dehydration during his famous match with Alex Corretja at the 1996 U.S. Open. At 7–7 in the tiebreaker of the fifth set, the crucial point in the match, Sampras missed his first serve badly. Noticing his weakness, Corretja moved in for the second serve. Sampras gathered himself and tricked him with a second-serve ace.

* * *

You said, "When I talk about the love I have for my daughter, I am loath to close."

* * *

At the end of his poem, Milton observes, "They also serve, who stand and wait."

* * *

Many of my memories are of performances of your great comic genius, the shaggy-dog stories you would tell, stories whose punch lines were actually disappointing when compared with their elaborate scaffolding. You were committed to the craft. You practiced your jokes. You told them again and again, never giving them short shrift. Or were they Rube Goldberg machines dutifully carrying their punch lines through a series of twists and turns?

* * *

You always seemed so healthy. As a kid I remember you carrying as many as twelve bags of garbage down our long driveway to the curb. How could we prepare for your body to fall apart?

* * *

In silence you live on, lead us. ■

HANDLING THE WIND
Emily Schulten

Before she was a mother, she took a job sewing sails
in a loft on Greene, near the harbor. This is how
her hands touched the wind.
                              In the quiet of dust,

she needled with small strokes the canvas
that would carry men across oceans.

Before knowing she would stay,
before her husband and her son,
                    she hemmed and patched
each broad piece with an affection for adventure
that permeated the fabric
that would manipulate the air,

pushing ships away from the Gulf,
maybe to come back, maybe not.

Perhaps she gave those ships
all of her wandering
there was to give.
Years later, she recalls,
with joy seldom replicated,
the work that's all but obsolete now.

Sail lofts have all closed, the work is done
by factories a hundred miles from the island—

there are fewer hands to guide the wind,
there is a greater divide between man and sky,
and there are so many ways to be trapped on an island.

ALL THAT MONEY
Christine Sneed

The more Sam repeated them, the more the words sounded like both an entreaty and a retort: *Who didn't want to be rich?*

Pooling their cash and buying four hundred lottery tickets was his idea, and eight people, Sam included, took the gamble. Four were his coworkers, the other three friends and family—each contributing a hundred dollars—and with a fat, wrinkled envelope stuffed with bills and a few loose quarters, some of the bills in singles, but most in tens and twenties, Sam drove to Bee & Dee's Liquor on Pine Street to buy the tickets after he clocked out for the day on Thursday afternoon. It was a few days after the Fourth of July, and the air was thick with humidity, a porous ceiling of gray rain clouds looming overhead.

He made his group's purchase the day before the drawing, the Mega Millions purse already soaring toward half a billion dollars, and as he'd expected, the liquor store was crowded, a line of ticket buyers snaking out the door, many of whom Sam knew or recognized. He was thirty, a father of two, and a foreman at the SurfMaster washer and dryer factory in Ryerson, Wisconsin, where he'd lived all his life.

Carrie, his wife, had grown up in Milwaukee and for years she'd been ready to move back—she insisted it had better schools and pediatricians and museums and countless parks, and the boys especially loved the zoo, and why wasn't Sam doing more to orchestrate their escape from Ryerson? Her contempt for what he thought of as their comfortable, mostly happy life in a town of seven thousand both perplexed and upset him, although he knew she didn't like her secretarial job in the foreign languages department at the small liberal arts college perched on a conifer-lined hilltop on the northwest side of town. She'd been there six years already and had no desire for it to become a career.

For an hour and a half, Sam waited in line with the other fools and rubes, doubts assailing him. He could hear his wife's voice in his head, her pitying laugh. As far as he knew, she'd never even been tempted to buy a scratch-off lottery ticket, nor did she purchase raffle tickets for the St. John's parish picnic in August or go to bingo with his mother, who sometimes went to the Elks Club on Tuesday nights. Carrie didn't know that he was spending a hundred dollars on what was probably the longest long shot of any of a million mundane gambles, money she'd have dutifully set aside for a new dishwasher. Theirs had been on the blink for several weeks—something had gone wrong with the wiring, and the repair bill would have cost almost as much as a new machine. They'd been hand-washing dishes since it broke down, Carrie unwilling to buy a new one on credit because they'd had to do that with the water heater over the winter and were still paying it off.

He did not expect to win, of course he didn't, but he'd dreamt earlier in the week that he did, and in the dream, it was the long-dead Johnny Carson, his grandfather's favorite talk show host, who called to tell Sam that he possessed the sole winning ticket. In the dreamscape's background, Sam could hear Ed McMahon laughing and a woman's answering laugh. "You've won, young man!" said Carson. "Who'll be the first person you tell?" "I'm not sure," said Sam. "My folks?" Carson laughed. "You'd better tell your wife first, or all hell will break loose." The day after the dream, it seemed suddenly as if everyone at work was talking about the jackpot too—for three weeks it had been climbing and climbing, no one in any of the Mega Millions states having yet managed to choose the right numbers. A sign, Sam was sure, that he should test his luck, that against the astronomical odds, he might somehow prevail.

Brian Rouse, in his early twenties and in need of a shave, was the Bee & Dee's employee in charge of operating the machine that spewed out the lottery tickets. His parents, Letty and Harold Rouse, owned the liquor store, and Brian and his older sister, Denise, were the Bee and Dee of the store's name, something Sam's own parents shook their heads over because what breed of idiots named a liquor store after their children?

"You want how many tickets? Four hundred? Each with the extra buck for the Megaplier?" asked Brian, staring dully at Sam when he'd at last made it to the front of the line. Brian had played football in high school and spent two years in Madison on a football scholarship at the state university before flunking out.

"Yes, four hundred with the Megaplier," said Sam, a little embarrassed. What a ridiculous word—Carrie's voice again in his head. "Can you guys handle that?" he asked.

Brian nodded his huge leonine head, his pale eyes fixed on Sam's. His cheeks and forehead were stippled with pockmarks and pimples.

"No problem," said Brian, flashing a rare smile, his eyes meeting Sam's again. What did Brian think about all of them, Sam wanted to ask. That every person in line was pathetic? Or maybe he too was excited. A half a billion dollars—it was an obscene amount of money, a portal that led, in a sense, to the top of the world. But what the hell did you do when you got there?

"Our lottery supplier knew it would be a big week," said Brian. "We're stocked up good." He reached for Sam's bulging envelope and dumped the bills onto the counter, two of the quarters flying onto the floor. It took him two attempts to count the money, Sam nearly snapping at him with impatience. He'd told Carrie before he left for work that he'd have to stay late to talk with his boss about some new quality controls for his department. Maybe she'd heard him, maybe not.

Either way, she hadn't yet texted to ask what he was doing. They were on summer hours at the college, and she was home by one on Thursdays and Fridays, Caleb and Eric picked up from the house of their sometime babysitter, Patty, on Carrie's way home. The boys would surely be keyed up on sugar—Patty loved to bake, molasses cookies especially, which on some days made Carrie grit her teeth, but Patty was reliable and patient with the boys; other sitters they'd tried in the last few years hadn't been nearly as good.

"You're going to let the machine pick them for you, right?" said Brian. He was sweating, the air-conditioning unable to keep up with the humid air streaming in through the door, which had likely been propped open for much of the day. "Because four hundred tickets—and the gang we got here—" He motioned with his head toward the line behind Sam.

"Yeah, I know," said Sam. "I've only got a couple that I picked myself and six others from the people going in with me. Birthdays, anniversaries, the date of the next full moon." He laughed. "Just kidding. But the birthdays and anniversaries, you know—the usual hocus pocus." He set the scraps of paper with the handpicked numbers on the counter.

"All right. No problem." Brian punched in the sequences, his thick fingers moving fast. When he was done with the custom picks, he passed the slips back to Sam. "Don't mix them up with the others or it'll take you all day to sort them out."

"Yeah, no kidding. Thanks." He watched Brian queue up the remaining 392 tickets, stuffing the personal picks into his back pocket. The other people in line were growing more restless; he could hear the heavyset woman directly behind him, a stranger, shifting her weight from foot to foot, the scent of coconut sunscreen wafting off her bare arms and neck.

For at least three of the people in Sam's lottery group, a hundred dollars was a week's worth of groceries. It was half a car payment, a dental checkup with X-rays, Cub Scouts dues or Little League fees for Caleb, his older son. He and Carrie could last a while longer without a new dishwasher, but Caleb would be kicked out of Cub Scouts soon if Sam didn't pay the Scoutmaster, Bill Streeter, whom a little while earlier Sam had spotted far ahead of him in line, waiting to buy his own golden ticket out of town or whatever it was he planned to do if he won.

What were the odds? One in a billion? Two billion? He didn't want to think about it; the dream with Johnny Carson, the euphoric feeling of suspense upon waking—they were why he was in line—gifts from his subconscious, and perverse or not, he knew he should try to enjoy them because later, when he lost, he'd be in trouble.

Carrie would be angry with him for a week if she found out what he was up to; she might already know and be on her way to try to stop him. Their next-door neighbor, Les Phelps, was a few people behind Bill Streeter in line, and he'd said hello to Sam on his way out of the store forty minutes earlier, waving his clutch of tickets and smiling goofily. He was already home, most likely, and might have told his wife that he'd run into Sam and offered him and Carrie some of the butter lettuce from their garden. Karen Phelps, in her knee-length shorts and bright, baggy T-shirt with a kitten or a sad-eyed dog on the front, her graying hair in a tight braid—Sam could picture her walking over to drop off the lettuce, freshly picked and rinsed, she innocently telling Carrie where he and Les had crossed paths.

If his wife didn't race over to Bee & Dee's to have it out with him in front of half the town, she might instead be packing suitcases for the boys and herself before taking them to her parents' house in Milwaukee. From there, she could just as easily file for divorce—more easily, probably, than in Ryerson. Milwaukee being, in Carrie's view, the source of all good things, it would doubtless be the place where the cures for leukemia and poverty and boredom were finally discovered, and, if the Second Coming ever did occur, Milwaukee would also be the first city Jesus visited.

Ninety-two minutes at Bee & Dee's, and he finally had the tickets. He sent a group text to six of the seven people who'd gone in on the purchase with him to let them know the buy was done. He'd have to call his father, who didn't want to be texted.

Lucia Cross, Curt Shukowski, and Annie Brinker worked in Sam's department at SurfMaster, and they each texted him back within seconds.

Hope we can all manage to sleep tonight! Thanks so much, Sam, replied Annie.

If we win, promise to remind me to pay off my credit cards b4 I do anything else, wrote Lucia.

Great! Going out now to buy my Porsche, was Curt's reply. A second later: *Just kidding.*

Gil Crandall, an old friend of his father's, texted an hour or so later. *Thanks, Sammy boy. Moving to Maui if we win. Taking my dog, but not sure yet about my wife. Ha!* A minute later he texted again. *Am I too old to learn how to surf?*

Sam's ex-girlfriend Ginger Jaworski, a secretary in the payroll office at SurfMaster, didn't respond. His good friend Owen Forrester didn't reply either, but he was probably at Four Corners Tavern, two or three beers in, his phone forgotten in the car, or else its battery was dead. Ginger, maybe, was with him. Owen had only had eighty-five dollars for the tickets and Sam had spotted him the remaining fifteen. If Owen were one of his employees instead of an unemployed car salesman, Sam wouldn't have done it, but Owen had agreed to host their group tomorrow night for the ten o'clock drawing.

Sam's house was empty when he came in through the garage, but he could hear his sons shrieking and laughing in the backyard. Carrie had turned on the sprinkler, Caleb and Eric squealing as they ran through the cold, rainbowed spray. She hadn't ever directly threatened him with divorce, and he didn't really believe she'd pack up and flee to Milwaukee without warning, but he was certain she'd thought about it.

When she saw him standing in the back doorway, silently watching their sons' horseplay, she got up from the sun-bleached green lawn chair she'd been sitting on, one of four that Sam's parents had given them after he and Carrie had moved into the house on Mill Street. The house had two bedrooms and was too small for the four of them, as it turned out, but it was well insulated and the garage was spacious. The basement didn't leak either, its foundation solid, uncracked cement.

His sons came charging toward him, grass clippings clinging to their bare feet. "Hey," yelled Sam, laughing. "You guys are going to get me all wet."

Eric charged into him, throwing his arms around Sam's waist, but Caleb, seven and more shy, hung back. Both boys were dark blond and long-legged like their mother, their faces pink with excitement, their hair standing up in wet quills.

"Hi, Dad," said Caleb. He was two years older than his brother but the leaner of the two boys, slender as a fawn, his brown eyes the same almond shape as his mother's. "Mom said we could have pizza tonight."

"Sounds good to me," said Sam. "Should we invite Grandma and Grandpa?"

"They have plans," said Carrie. "Your father called a little while ago."

"They do?" asked Sam. "That's a surprise." His parents rarely went out in the evenings. His dad was usually asleep in his chair in front of the TV by eight thirty, his two nightly cans of Coors empty on the oak lamp table beside his chair, its surface covered with scratches and water rings from years of sweating glasses and cans. Sam had made the table in his eighth-grade shop class, and his father refused to part with it.

"I think they're going to Oshkosh to have dinner with Shirley," said Carrie.

"Oh, that's right. Dad's supposed to fix her garbage disposal." Shirley was the older of his father's two siblings, never married, owner of an increasingly decrepit house that was too big for her and her two overweight poodles.

"How'd everything go today?" she asked, standing on her toes to kiss him. She had chocolate on her breath and the scent of talc on her skin.

He met her blue-green gaze, his conscience issuing warnings. Did she already know? Karen Phelps had probably come over with the lettuce and blown his cover. Or more likely, his father had when he'd called.

"With your boss," she said. "Didn't you have a meeting?"

He nodded, avoiding her eyes. "Yeah, it went fine. Thanks for asking."

"I got a raise today," she said. "My review went well." She smiled up at him, wanting him to be pleased too.

"That's great," he said. "I knew it would." He'd forgotten about the review. He'd meant to text to ask how it went, but instead was preoccupied with imagining how he'd spend the Mega Millions money. Owen had called twice too—once to offer to buy the tickets because he had nothing better to do, having been laid off from his job at the Ford dealership the previous week. The second time he'd called to say he was sorry, but Jennifer Lawrence had just called and asked him to be her sex slave. He didn't need any lottery tickets now.

Ginger had also pounced on Sam during his lunch break to say that she would blame him for getting her involved if they lost, poking him in the chest and giving him a look that Carrie wouldn't have liked at all. He hadn't asked her to go in with them on the tickets; she'd come to him about it, having caught wind of the plan from Owen, the two of them on-again, off-again for a few years now. Carrie couldn't tolerate Ginger—neither the sound of her name nor the sight of Ginger herself.

"I knew the review would go fine," said Carrie. "I keep the wheels from flying off the place, and they all know it too, but I wasn't sure about the raise because of the hiring freeze. You never know what else they're going to cut back on. It's only 3 percent, but I'll take it."

Eric let out a feral shriek as he chased Caleb through the spray, both boys giggling maniacally. Caleb's waterlogged red swim trunks were inching down his waist; he yanked them back up as he ran.

"Hey, you two, keep your voices down," Sam called after them. "You'll wake the dead. We don't need any zombies crashing our party."

"Sam! Don't say that," said Carrie. "You'll give them nightmares."

"Zombies are the undead, Dad," Caleb said.

Sam glanced at his wife. "They're not going to have any nightmares."

"Just remember that the next time one of them wakes up howling. You can go and sit with them until they fall back asleep."

His phone chirped in his pocket with another incoming text. He waited a few seconds before looking at it, conscious of Carrie's eyes on him.

Owen. *Can you bring over 2 4-pks of Guinness tomorrow?*

"I'm going out for a bit tomorrow night," said Sam. "Over to Owen's around eight for a couple of hours. Hope you don't mind."

Carrie looked at him. "Poker? Because I'd rather you didn't—"

"No, we're only going to hang out. He's still depressed about his job."

"Tell him to take up running. Cheaper than Prozac and he might lose his beer gut too."

Sam looked over at his sons. Their hair was getting long. Neither of them was a fan of haircuts or hair-washing. "Yeah, I'll tell him you said so," he said. "I'm sure he'll be all for it."

"Don't be a grouch, Sam."

"I'm not being a grouch." He wanted to say something harsher but held his tongue. "I'm going to take a shower," he said. He glanced again at his sons as they made another dash through the sprinkler before he turned toward the house.

"Pick your towel up off the floor when you're done," Carrie called after him.

Death by a thousand cuts, wasn't that the expression? He shook his head but said nothing.

He stopped in the kitchen for a glass of water, wanting a beer. "Should I order the pizzas now or wait until six?" he called through the open window over the sink.

She kept her back turned, pretending not to hear him.

"Carrie?" he called, raising his voice. "Do you want me to order the pizzas now?"

"No," she yelled, not bothering to face him. "I'll order them in a little while."

"Be sure to get pepperoni on one of them."

"Pepperoni!" Eric cried. "That's what I want too."

"I know, Eric," said Carrie. "Same as your father. It's what we always get. How could I forget?"

"I want cheese," said Caleb.

"I know," she said. "God, I know."

Overhead a plane left contrails on its way south, to Mitchell Field in Milwaukee or else O'Hare. Sam watched the boys crane their necks to look up at it, Eric pointing and yelling, "Aliens."

"Those aren't aliens," said Caleb. "They're cyborgs."

"They're people like you and me," said Carrie wearily. "Not cyborgs or aliens."

"That's boring," said Eric.

"Maybe so," said Carrie. "But that's what they are."

"Can't you lighten up a little?" Sam called through the window.

Again she ignored him. He stood staring at her back for a few more seconds before going into the bedroom, where he stripped off his work clothes and left them in a tangle on the floor by his side of the bed. The house was oppressively humid; they didn't have central air and relied on three window units, none of which were switched on. He flipped on the one in the bedroom before walking naked down the hall to the bathroom. Carrie hated this habit, but his father had done it while Sam was growing up, and as far as Sam could tell, there wasn't anything wrong with seeing your father naked. His sons should know what they'd look like when they were older, but Carrie worried they'd tell their friends that their father paraded around the house without his clothes, and then they'd tell their parents, who would think Sam was some kind of deviant.

For a big-city girl, he'd once said to her, she certainly had a small mind sometimes. "It's because of this place," she'd retorted. "I wasn't like this before I lived here."

* * *

He left the house to pick up the pizzas at six thirty, his sons begging to come along but they were still in their swim trunks, and he said no— they'd have to rinse off and change first, and by the time they were ready, the pizzas would be cold. He chose a route to Pizza Hut that took him past Bee & Dee's, its parking lot still full, but the line of lottery ticket buyers wasn't as long as earlier. No one was waiting outside the door.

While he was in line at Pizza Hut, Lucia Cross texted the group to say the jackpot was now more than half a billion dollars. The fat bundle of tickets was in his glove compartment. He couldn't remember if he'd locked the car doors and stepped out of line to run outside to check. He was sweating, his lungs squeezed by knifing surges of near panic. He didn't know what was wrong with him, why he couldn't make himself stop thinking about the drawing. It was something in the neighborhood of insanity, he was sure, to believe they had any kind of chance.

His car was locked, the tickets safe. He would sneak them into the house and put them in the closet inside the box that held his wedding shoes, a pair of black leather wingtips he'd only worn on that one unseasonably warm April Saturday, one of Carrie's bridesmaids, a chubby blonde with a high, whinnying laugh, nearly fainting from the heat and her too-tight strapless dress. Now there were six people ahead of him in line, and it was almost twenty minutes before he had the pizzas and was on the way home. By the time he pulled into the driveway, he knew Carrie would be fuming. He wished he'd thought to pick up a carton of chocolate ice cream and a bouquet at Pick 'n Save.

"Sorry," he said, setting the pizza boxes on the kitchen table. "There were so many people in line and I think the cashier was new."

She said nothing. The boys were already at the table, glasses of milk next to their plates. She opened one of the boxes and gave Eric a slice of pepperoni, Caleb a bigger slice of cheese.

"I want some pop," said Eric, looking at Sam.

"Did you ask your mom?"

"She said no," said Eric.

"Then that's your answer," said Sam.

"But we always get pop with pizza."

"We don't have any," said Carrie. "We need to go grocery shopping. I already told you that, sweetie."

"Why does Dad always have beer, but we don't have any pop?" asked Caleb.

Carrie's eyes flicked toward Sam. He could see she was trying not to smile. "You'll have to ask him," she said primly.

"Because I'm the boss," said Sam.

Carrie snorted. Sam looked at her but she didn't say anything.

"Dad's the boss," Eric shouted.

"Hey, inside voice," said Sam.

While he was on his second greasy slice of pepperoni, his wife gave him an unreadable look before announcing, "Your dad called again while you were gone. He wants to know what time you're going to Owen's tomorrow." She took a small bite of her slice of cheese, one she'd blotted the grease from with a paper towel. "Why is he going over there too?"

He reached for a napkin, avoiding her eyes. "We're not playing poker," he said. "If that's what you're wondering."

"You're sure?"

"Yes. We're going to watch the Brewers game and have a couple of beers."

"So you'll be home by ten?"

"Probably closer to ten thirty." The lottery drawing was at ten.

"Take the boys but try to be home by ten, ten fifteen at the latest."

"I want to go to Owen's too," said Eric.

"We'll see," said Sam. He couldn't take them without blowing his cover; he would have to tell her, but it seemed increasingly likely that she already knew. Most of it was his money anyway, pulled from the savings account he'd opened in high school, into which he'd once deposited part of his lawn-mowing and snow-shoveling earnings, money he'd supposedly squirreled away for college. The account had never climbed above $1,500. Now the balance was $42.18.

The boys were in the other room watching SpongeBob cartoons while he and Carrie cleaned up the kitchen. Her back was to him, one hand running a yellow dishrag over the counter, when she said, "Your dad let the cat out of the bag about the lottery."

Sam said nothing. He knew it would be pointless to pretend ignorance.

She turned to look at him. "Five tickets, all right, I could probably let that pass. Even ten, but fifty? Are you crazy, Sam? That's a hundred dollars down the drain."

"You don't know that," he said quietly.

She laughed in an angry burst. "Oh, yes, I think I do."

"I did buy fifty tickets, yes, but it's an investment. They're part of a pool of four hundred," he said. "Did my dad tell you he bought fifty tickets too?"

"Your dad can afford them. We can't."

Other than his mother, Sam had asked his father not to talk to anyone about the buy who wasn't a part of it, but he'd known his father was as likely as not to let it slip to someone. A year ago, he'd accidentally ruined the surprise of Sam's mother's sixtieth birthday party. And in previous years, in his childish enthusiasm for Christmas, he'd told Sam more than once what the wrapped boxes waiting for him under the tree contained.

"I wanted to try," he said. "This one time."

She gave him a stony look. "Don't ever do this again without asking me first, Sam. It's disrespectful." She shook her head and turned away. He stood looking at her, trying to think of something to say but couldn't. After another minute, she left the kitchen and he stayed at the sink and peered into the backyard. The lawn needed mowing again.

* * *

When he went to bed around ten thirty, Carrie was already there, wearing her lace-trimmed, bubblegum-pink nightgown, his favorite, but her back was to him, waves of aggrievement rolling off of her. They hadn't had sex in two weeks and Sam was tired of making overtures that were ignored or waved away. If it hadn't been for the lottery, she might have been in the mood for a change, her positive review at work and the raise good for domestic relations.

He lay sleepless until 2:00 a.m., when he got up and went into kitchen to look for a snack. On the top shelf of the cupboard next to the refrigerator, he found a package of iced oatmeal cookies. His wife had probably stashed them up there to keep them out of Caleb and Eric's reach.

Sam ate three cookies with a glass of tap water. He saved what little milk was left in the carton for the boys' morning cereal. The tickets were in the bedroom closet, and it amazed him a little that his father and Ginger and Owen and the others hadn't protested when Sam had said he would hold on to them. He knew he wouldn't have trusted anyone else to keep them until tomorrow night's drawing, though probably none of them believed they'd win anything, except if they managed to match four or five numbers; there'd be payouts for those matches too, but split eight ways, it wouldn't be much of a score.

He looked in on the boys, both of his sons asleep in their twin beds, Eric flat on his back, Caleb facing the wall where Carrie had painted a glossy jungle scene with smiling monkeys, a panther, and toucans, one of the many talents (piano playing, singing, and pastry making among them) that her enervating, dead-end job kept her from exercising as often as she'd like.

* * *

After everything changed, after they won all that money—their group the only one with a winning ticket—Sam would sometimes remember himself in the doorway, watching his sons sleep, their small bodies under thin white summer blankets, the monkeys grinning at him from the leafy mural. A car passed in the street, its headlights briefly illuminating the drawn blinds. As the light faded and the driver continued on his trajectory to somewhere else, Sam thought he could see, as if through a tear in the fabric of perception, the present receding to reveal his future. It was hard to recognize, but he knew what it was. He stood in the doorway for a few more seconds, waiting for his pulse to slow before going back down the hall to where Carrie was waiting for him, the red-shaded reading lamp on her side of the bed now on and casting its rosy light over her face and neck, a book about Michelangelo open on her chest.

"We're going to win," he said softly.

She looked at him with something closer to disappointment than anger. She shook her head. "No, we're not."

"We are," he said, hovering over her. "I'll bet you $75 million." This would be his cut if the jackpot reached the projected $600 million.

She offered her hand and he shook it. "It looks like I'm going to be a very rich woman soon," she said.

"You are," he said, climbing into bed next to her. "You'll see. I just hope you'll be happy." He could feel her eyes on him, but she said nothing, and in the moment before he drifted off to sleep, he could hear her turning the page of her book with a quiet sigh. ∎

PENCIL WEREWOLF
Gerardo Sámano Córdova

"Tired of being yourself?" the poster asked, and showed an illustration of a meek man in shadow, much like myself, peeking behind a door where men of solid construction wore flannel shirts, laughed and clinked beers. I kept reading. "Change is a nibble away," the poster claimed, and then a telephone number. I didn't know what they meant by *a nibble* but I called anyway, and was asked to detail what I considered was wrong with me. That was easy, everything. I simply didn't want to be me: Craig. Not this Craig, at least. I wanted to be one of them, the big men in flannel who laughed and drank beer.

I got an interview. Men like me sat in the waiting room, wispy men who looked at each other in side glances and smiled out of nervousness rather than joy. I was given a questionnaire that asked my age—thirty-eight—and then instructed me to check one box or the other. Marital status: single or other. *Single.* Employed or unemployed. I was employed, a diligent tax accountant in a firm. I checked *unemployed.* I would quit, yes, as soon as I was done with this, and though I didn't know what *this* was—not exactly—I had an inkling the process would somehow transform me into one of those big men. Whatever this was, it was most assuredly a fresh start. Straightaway, a judder like pleasure struck me, and I tingled all over.

Sexual drive: strong or other. I hesitated. What exactly did *strong* mean? Did it mean I humped everything in sight? I didn't, not that I didn't want to sometimes, but those times I attributed to spring; something with birds' hormones saturating the air made me have constant and unpredictable erections, in the street, at work, on the subway, and because I carried a book for the purpose of hiding them, I found I read much more in the warmer months. Nevertheless, I checked *other*, fairly certain that if my sexual drive were indeed strong, I would've had sex at least once in the past few years. Appetite: ravenous or other. *Other.* Outdoor or indoor. *Outdoor.* I did enjoy an afternoon stroll under a warm sun or through a crisp autumn air. Dominant or submissive. *Oh my.* I stretched my neck, trying to sneak a glance at my peers' answers but I could see none of them. Surely, I was failing. I tried to erase what I'd checked, to revise my life as it revealed me in carefully ticked boxes, but I hadn't been given a pencil but a pen. I had sealed my life in this questionnaire.

I was measured, weighed and ushered to a seat in front of a small table where other men had been interviewed and rejected. The interviewer, a strong-jawed man, much younger than myself, looked me over and then glanced at my questionnaire and documents. "Old," he said.

"Is that good or bad?" I asked.

"For our purposes, good."

I exhaled, my nerves modestly soothed.

"How much do you want this?" the man asked.

"Very much, sir. Very much, indeed."

He lifted an eyebrow. "Do you even know what this is?"

"No, sir, not entirely," I admitted. "But I want it very much."

"Are you prone to want things without knowing what they are?"

Maybe. Possibly it was the curse of my whole existence. "Your poster. It caught my eye. You offer a remedy, don't you?"

"A remedy." I wasn't sure if the man was asking or asserting. He leaned back on his ergonomic chair. "Yes, I suppose this is a remedy. Do you know what this is a remedy for?"

"I suppose . . ." I struggled to find appropriate words.

The man brought his hands together, fingers entwined. "Go on."

"Well," I said, "the poster. It had a beautiful illustration. A man in shadow peering into a wonderful scene of camaraderie: men drinking beer, telling tales, laughing the way friends do. I want to be in that room, like those men, sir, very much so. Very much so, indeed."

"Are you lonely, Craig?"

"Yes. I must admit, quite."

"We're not a companionship service, do you understand that? We don't offer men to be your friends."

"Of course you don't."

"So what do you think we can remediate?"

"This," I said, looking down at myself: my wiry arms that required help lugging too-heavy things; my long, brittle fingers that should've played the piano or strummed a guitar but couldn't; my short legs that would never carry me far. I wanted a remedy for the nerves that made me cower, for the mocking mirrors, for a world where I was nothing, and nothing was mine. "This," I repeated. "I don't want to be this. Not this rehearsal I am. This first draft."

The man stamped the papers and sent me to another room.

* * *

The room shined fluorescent, and the vents overhead hummed and creaked as if a bird were stuck behind their grates. Two men, almost identical in khaki and muscles, took my stamped papers and told me to wait. I sat in one of two empty plastic foldable chairs and smiled at them but neither smiled back. Minutes passed and another man came in, a young, hairy lump of muscle you could throw a rock at and it'd bounce. He handed his papers, and when he sat next to me, the top of my head scarcely reached his shoulder. Undoubtedly, this man wasn't here for the same reasons as me, he already was the men in the illustration come to life.

A woman came in. "Harriet," she said and shook our hands. She wore a T-shirt with a howling wolf, cargo shorts and combat boots with orange socks peeking out. She dragged a chair and, with the chair's back to us, she straddled it, folded her arms over it and inspected us, her head darting back and forth between the man and me. She stretched her open palm toward the two khakied muscle men. They handed her our papers and she shooed them away.

"I'm a scientist." She waited for the man, or me, to react, but when we didn't she continued. "Do you know what a werewolf is?" I muttered an answer but she paid no attention, instead she went on. "A basic premise: human transforms to wolf. An inspiring myth. Two things in particular. One," she stuck a finger out, "malleability, the idea that a body can change shape quickly and dramatically. Two," she stuck another finger out, "the lycanthropic virus, the idea that mutation can be transmitted the same way a virus could. Now," she said and stood up, fists on hips. "This is why you're here today."

"We're to become werewolves?" I ventured.

"No," she said, "not precisely."

"We're here to hunt werewolves?"

"There are no werewolves, Craig. Werewolves are folklore." She waited for another answer but I had no more ideas.

Then, the man next to me, in a quick voice, unexpectedly honeyed given his bulk, said, "Is this some sort of body-switching experiment?"

"Ah!" Harriet said. "Not switching, exactly, but yes. What we want to do is have you, Earl," she pointed at the man with her palms together, "transmit your physical information to Craig here, and if all goes as planned, Craig's body will transform into a replica of yours. Simple, isn't it?"

"What do you mean *replica*?" I asked.

"Your bones will lengthen and strengthen according to Earl's composition. Your muscle tissue will grow and bulk up, mimicking Earl's structure in your body."

"Will my face change, too?"

"Everything, Craig. If the science holds, and it should, you should be Earl's exact twin by the time the transformation is complete. Well, almost, it is possible you may retain some minor bodily features. Perhaps a scar or the shape of your nostrils."

I touched my nostrils, long, way more oval than round, aristocratic. It was perhaps the first time I had noticed my nostrils, but if I was to retain something of myself, I was glad it could be them.

"Is the transformation reversible?" I asked.

"No, Craig. Your physical information will be lost as it is taken over by Earl's."

"Have you done this before?" Earl asked Harriet.

"We have, just not on humans. You'll be the first, and if I may say so, you're the perfect candidates." Harriet assessed me and then Earl. "If all goes well, it'll be such a dramatic change. Isn't that exciting?"

"Are you okay with this?" asked Earl, turning to me, but before I could answer, Harriet summoned the two men in khaki, who came in wheeling a table. A needle filled with glowing magenta goo sat on top, also a bottle of disinfectant, some gauze and cotton balls. Harriet put on blue latex gloves and grabbed the needle.

"Are we doing it now?" I asked.

"This is what you've signed up for, isn't it?" Harriet said.

"But now, really. I don't know. May I think about it?" Could it really be true that I could turn into Earl? A strapping man, if I ever saw one; his gray eyes, a thick neck covered in beard, tree arms that could lug anything, open anything—be it jar or door—and his legs, long and hefty legs that could walk miles and carry me somewhere, anywhere.

Earl said, "We don't have to do it if you don't want to."

"Well," said Harriet, "you've already signed the papers, so . . ."

"Are you really a doctor?" I asked.

"I am a scientist."

"Are you sure?"

"Am I sure I am what I say I am?"

"It's a valid question," said Earl, and I sat up taller. Having someone on my side was quite invigorating, I found out.

"Why do you doubt it?" Harriet asked.

"You're wearing cargo shorts."

"Would you be more comfortable if I wore a lab coat and slacks?"

"Yes," I said. "I would."

"Now, Craig, I'm not going to dress up for you. May we start the procedure?"

"Will I transform immediately?"

"I estimate the full transformation will take about a week, possibly even less than that."

"A week? Wow!" I didn't know if I was surprised because a week was a short or a long time. I didn't even know if I was surprised at all, or just nervous, perhaps terrified. "Earl," I said. We hadn't been properly introduced and I was soon to be his twin. "Are you sure you want to give me your body?" I stammered. "I don't mean your actual body . . . I mean, your physical traits . . . I . . ."

"I'm good," he said. "Are you?" I could tell by the way Earl frowned, his abundant eyebrows bent down, his mouth closed, his eyes firm on mine, that he was legitimately concerned about me. "If we don't go through with it, I still get paid, right?" he asked Harriet.

"Well, certainly not the full amount," Harriet said.

"But I get to keep the advance. By the way, I didn't get my advance yet."

"You will, Earl. Now, are we ready?"

Harriet and Earl stared at me, expectant. I was hurt Earl was doing this for money, though it made sense, of course. Why else would he have done it? Certainly not for me. He didn't even know me before today.

"Don't you mind some stranger will have your body?" I asked.

"Not really. You look like an okay dude, Craig. Hey, maybe it'll be fun to have a twin around, who knows. I never had a brother."

My heart leapt. The mere idea that I could be anything like him, and furthermore, that we'd be twins—bonded—was so fantastic, I squeaked in joy. Earl offered me his hand and I shook it.

"Now if there are no more objections, may we proceed?" Harriet said.

"Where will you stick that needle?" I asked.

"That needle is not for you, Craig, it's for Earl."

"Will the procedure be safe, for Earl, I mean?" Sometimes I folded so deeply inside myself I forgot about others, and I didn't want to forget about Earl. If we were to be twins, I had to learn to care for him.

"Yes. We're going to weaponize him, make his physical essence virulent, that is to say, transmittable."

"And then?"

"He bites you and we're done."

"How hard does he have to bite me?"

"Hard enough to draw blood."

"Don't worry, I won't bite too hard," said Earl and he patted me on the back, not a gesture of condescension but one of solidarity.

"We can anesthetize you if it will make it all easier," said Harriet.

"No. I can handle it."

* * *

Harriet injected Earl and he didn't even wince. He only said, "That's warm," as if commenting on the weather. We waited for a few minutes before Harriet instructed Earl to bite me.

"Do I bite his neck?" Earl seemed worried.

"Preferably."

"Isn't that dangerous? I could bite into an important vein or something."

I was glad Earl was concerned.

"Maybe I could bite his arm. Is that okay?"

Harriet said yes. One of the khakied men cleaned my upper arm with a cotton ball doused in rubbing alcohol. Earl placed his mouth on my arm, his breath hot and his lips moist, and his tongue, though he tried to fold it back, licked my flesh, tasting me. I giggled. Earl leaned back, his eyes wide, as if he had done something wrong.

"Go on," I said, feeling courageous. I trusted Earl wouldn't hurt me. "Bite me."

Without a second thought and with a low, rumbling growl, Earl dived on my arm and bit. Earl's teeth clamped firmly into my flesh, at first tentative, and then determined to rip out a chunk of me. I could not even yelp in pain, maybe because it hurt so much, or because Earl's teeth inside me felt so intimate, arousing. He held a chunk of my flesh inside his mouth, and he desired it so nakedly, I wanted him to take it. But Earl withdrew before he ripped part of my tricep, my blood wet around his mouth.

I wept. I tried to stop myself but I couldn't. Earl, stunned, repeated, "I'm sorry, I'm sorry," in his honey voice and wrapped his arm around my shoulders. I blubbered, "I'm okay," trying to smile reassuringly through my tears. Earl pulled me to him, and I rested on his chest until I stopped crying.

* * *

For a few hours nothing happened, but we sat, Earl and I, alone in the same room with the fluorescents and the singing vents. Harriet had asked us to wait six hours to gauge any reactions, after that, we'd be free to go back home. I would have to report every morning for them to check my status. Earl was only to report if he presented unusual side effects, although none were expected.

If this was a legitimate operation, it needed better facilities. Curiously and perhaps fatefully, only after the procedure had taken place did I notice the details of the room—its cracked electrical outlets, its two (out of four) nonfunctioning overhead lights, the sordid lack of furniture and extravagant amounts of flaked paint that covered more of the floor than the walls. The linoleum floor stuck to Earl's rubber sneaker soles and he played, walking like a moon man, sticking and unsticking his shoes. I nursed my upper arm, where Earl had bit a tad too vigorously and which now smarted to high heaven. I couldn't complain, the procedure was done, but I began to feel loopy, unbalanced, as if the world had fallen a bit askew. I held on to the flimsy plastic chair.

"Are you okay?" Earl asked, one foot midair.

"I'm a bit dizzy. I can't quite focus." I squinted at Earl, the edges of his nose throbbed in and out of focus, his gray eyes one moment sharp and another a mess of lashes and irises.

"One of your eyes changed color," he said.

"Are you sure?" I opened my eyes wide. "Check carefully, please, Earl." There were no mirrors in the room.

"Yup, one's gray."

"Which one?"

"The left one."

"My left? Or your left?"

"Your left."

I closed my right eye and the world blurred and softened, objects lost a crispness I was accustomed to. Then I closed my left and opened my right, and the world dialed back into sharpness. "The new eye is out of focus," I said. "Do you think it'll adjust?"

"I dunno, you're probably gonna be shortsighted like me."

"But you don't wear glasses."

"Contacts."

"But I have twenty-twenty vision."

"Not anymore, I guess. Sorry about that."

"It's so dizzying," I said, and Earl steadied me by holding my forearm.

"Keep one eye shut, until they both change."

"Which one?"

"The bad one," he said.

* * *

After some time, one of the khakied men came in with juice and cookies. Earl asked for coffee but the man said it wasn't good to drink coffee now. Our bodies needed rest, he told us and left. I ate a cookie and leaned back on my chair, sliding my legs forward, and closed my eyes. A nap was in order, but as I tried to lure sleep, my left foot cramped, first sharp and tight, then pulsating as if it was bloated. I tried to take my shoe off—

a newly polished Bostonian—but it was stuck and I could feel my foot grow bent and gnarled inside. Earl pulled on the shoe, and I pulled on my leg, until the shoe came off. I stripped the sock from my foot. My toes were longer, rounder. I bared my right foot and compared; definitely longer, wider and a bit hairier. Earl looked at my feet in amazement. He slipped his left sneaker off, white sock and all, and pushed his foot next to my new one. They were almost identical except for my pinky toe, which had remained smaller.

"Wow," Earl said. "This is so cool."

"Cool, indeed." We stared at our feet, both of us transfixed. I wiggled my toes and he wiggled his. I tilted my foot to the left and he to the right, we bumped them and laughed.

* * *

"You taste good," Earl said and then shook his head as if he had just woken up. I had been drifting in and out of light slumber. There were still two hours to go. "Sorry. That's a strange thing to say. I don't know why I said it." He blushed.

"I'll take it as a compliment," I said.

"You're just so savory," he said. "Like really good beef." His smile transformed from one of embarrassment to one of lust. His stare was exciting. I certainly had never been looked at with such desire. It was also a tad terrifying. His eyes glittered, his teeth bared. "You're so yummy."

"I'm flattered, quite flattered, in fact," I said. "You know, you see, I . . ." I didn't know what I was saying, but I felt giddy, and my words didn't register, so full of passion was he that it was as if I might not have said anything at all. I let my words dissipate, there was nothing I wanted to say, really, I only wanted him to keep looking at me. He licked his lips and put his hand behind my neck. My whole body quivered, to be touched at all produced such a delightful effect. I smiled at him, unsure if I had to, perhaps, return his touch. But then he snarled, his eyes fire, and he clenched his hand tighter around my neck. My neck hurt and I tried to wrench my head out of his hand but he gripped me tighter still. I wriggled, bewildered, and when he didn't let go, I pushed him hard, so hard that I fell off my chair. He walked to me, sinuous and doggish. I said, "Sirs, sirs, I think something is wrong," but my voice didn't carry beyond my lips. I clenched my buttocks like a nutcracker and screamed, "Sirs," louder now, frantic. "Harriet. Someone. Please!"

The khakied men rushed in and Earl turned, his hands furled like claws, his teeth white and large like menacing Chiclets. He growled, a deep noise that came all the way from his sneakers, picking up a rumble inside his stomach, and finally out of his mouth like thunder. "Calm down," said one of the men, his palm open. Earl cackled, a supernatural sound that made the remaining flakes of paint—the ones still clinging to the wall—flutter away for their lives.

Earl lunged, knocking one of the men back, his mouth instantly clutched on the man's neck. The other man froze, but when the first spritz of blood spurted out of his companion, he blanched and dashed out of the room. I pushed myself on my feet, but almost at once, I lay sprawled on the floor again. My left leg was now considerably longer and I could not find balance. I had to drag myself to where Earl ripped the khakied man's flesh. A pool of red all around.

"Earl," I said, listening to myself speak but quite unbelieving it was I who spoke. Why didn't I crawl to safety? Why, instead, was I pushing myself toward Earl? "Earl," I said. "It's fine. Earl, relax. Earl, for the love of all that is good, don't eat that man." Earl stopped ripping into the man and looked at me. His ferocity turned into fear. I crawled to him. Next to me crawled an armadillo bug. Fast, the bug whirled its thin legs, not letting the blood stop its rush. The bug bypassed chunks of the khakied man and climbed others, the smaller ones, but when it reached Earl, the bug folded into a ball so fast, it rolled away by pure momentum.

"Earl," I said. I held my hand to him, and as he grabbed it, his body slackened, as if comforted. But then, Earl looked down at the savaged man and retreated in terror to a corner of the room. Earl mumbled words I could not hear. I managed to drag myself to where he had scampered, slipping through blood and chunks of man.

"What happened?" he asked.

"You ate him. A bit."

Earl's body shook so violently I held him, and he let himself fall on my lap, where we remained, he trembling and I swaying, hoping comfort would come.

Harriet burst in, the surviving khakied man behind her. "What the fuck?" she said, her face red, the man green. She threw her eyes at us.

"Side effect, I think." I said.

She inhaled deep, her face still contorted but struggling to rearrange itself into a semblance of control. "Right," she exhaled. "I was afraid this would happen." She reached to the back of her shorts but before she could snap her arm back, Earl, on all fours, leapt and knocked her down. A pistol skittered away, clanking through the room. As Harriet attempted to push herself upright, Earl scooped me up, and we fled.

* * *

We're in a motel now, Earl and I, in a peach-colored room with two twin beds, a TV and a bathroom. I assume they'll be looking for us and so we're lying low. Earl stares at himself in the mirror, and though less feral, he still snarls from time to time, like a dog who yips in its sleep. Earl wears a towel and drips. His clothes are a bloody heap on the floor, but he's showered now.

"Look at this," says Earl, opening his mouth wide. His incisors protrude, long and sharp. "They're not going down, Craig. Do you think they'll stay like this forever?"

"I don't know."

"We have to go back and get that woman Harriet to fix me."

"Earl, you kind of ate her assistant. I believe we're beyond their help."

"But we need help. Both of us. Look at you, Craig. You look all twisted."

It's true. I'm a little wonky. I'm still about three quarters me and a quarter Earl. The part that is me sags down, the part that is Earl props it up. "I'm sure I'll grow into it."

"Maybe we should go to the police."

"And say what?"

"We gotta do something, right? I mean, what if I stay like this forever. Will I . . . you know."

"Eat other people?"

He nods.

"You may, but we'll manage."

"What if I eat you?"

"You won't." I believe this is true. I trust Earl won't eat me. "Rest now."

Earl pricks his right index finger with his fang. "Ow," he says, and then crawls himself to bed. "I'm sorry."

"What for?"

"I ate that man . . . I really didn't mean to, I mean, I kind of did, not me, but . . . it was like I was possessed. He tasted really good . . ."

"Earl, eating that man was not your fault. It was a side effect." My voice is a pitchy croak, between my own raspiness and Earl's sweetness. "Tomorrow it'll all be better."

Earl turns to his side and bends his knees up to his chest. "How do you know?"

"Because you're not alone, we're in this together. We look out for each other."

Earl shakes, he is crying. From time to time he wipes his face with the sheets. I sit on the bed next to him and place a hand on his shoulder.

"You won't leave me, right?" he asks.

"Of course not, Earl. We're going to be twins, remember?"

I rub Earl's back until I can't feel him shake anymore. A framed print of a willow in fog hangs above him. I know motel art is supposed to be ugly and cheap, but this photograph is beautiful. The sun glimmers through the tree's branches, which droop majestically. One lonely blackbird sits perched in the middle. Earl goes to sleep. He snores a low rumble.

I turn the lights off, lie on top of my bed and, before sleep takes me, I make a mental note to go to the supermarket and buy Earl some raw beef, once my legs are the same size and I can walk without tripping. ∎

SONAR
Luke Geddes

WINTERHUNT
Luke Geddes

CAVE BOY PARTY
Luke Geddes

RONAN AND LIADAIN, THE OTTER: A FAIRY TALE
Liam Heneghan

Sadb did not remember her mother, Eithniu, and her father, Ronan, never spoke of her. She had heard variously that Eithniu had died of an infection the year after her birth, and, alternatively, that she had run off with another warrior and, from an aunt on her father's side, she heard that her mother was a fairy woman and that fairy women can be wed to human mates for only seven years. Sadb being the seventh child had been her mother's last, and when she weaned the girl, she returned to live among the Sidhe.

This aunt had told Sadb the following story of her mother:

One day Ronan went down to the river to fish. He had just returned from a raid in Scotland and was sated by his spoils. He now wanted time away from the company of men and so returned to the lands of his childhood, for these were the lands that he knew best. It was time, besides, that he chose a first wife. A woman known to his people seemed the wisest choice. This decision rested heavily upon him for Ronan felt unprepared for the burden of family. He had too many memories of battle, and there remained too much of war in him. Ronan went down to the River Boyne with an unsettled mind.

It was late afternoon in midsummer. The sun shone warmly on the river and its waters were clear. So deep was that river that even when its waters ran clear and the skies were clear overhead, its deepest holes remained shrouded in darkness. A small breeze troubled the surface of the water that evening, and little white waves ran from ripples in the center of the river out to the banks. Ronan walked on the west bank of the river among the reeds up to his ankles in the water. So bright the setting sun, so tall and dense the reeds, that even attentive fish would surely not notice him.

Ronan cast his net a first time but caught nothing. He cast again, and drew his net in. Again, he caught nothing. A third time he tried without success. Thinking that there might be easier dinners to find elsewhere—perhaps a rabbit had slipped into one of the snares he set earlier that evening—he was about to give up. Just then, he noticed that a she-otter was also fishing the same stretch of water. She would descend beneath the river-waves making a small silver plash and then would emerge at some point, either more distant, or closer by Ronan, with a trout or a salmon in her mouth. Each time she glided through the water on her back, reveling in her catch which she held fast in her mouth. She floated, gamboled, and headed for the shore where she stored her evening's catch.

Ronan cast his net again, this time close to where the she-otter dived. He spotted a salmon rise to eat an insect on the water's surface, and the fish swam over his net. He had merely to pull tight the net and this prize would be his. He lingered to see where the she-otter would rise. Perhaps this time she would be the one to come up short; this time it would be she that saw him catch the fish. A measure of pride swelled in him in anticipation. But the otter did not rise. By now, Ronan's salmon had plopped back into the water, and yet the she-otter still did not rise. He had but one moment to act before the salmon retreated to the deep pools of the river. He must gather in his net; and yet still he waited. All of a sudden, there was a mild clamor right in front of him. A dart of brown, a splash of foamy water, a glimmer of the light and Ronan saw the she-otter take his fish. He pulled in his net, but it was too late. The she-otter was gone. The fish was gone. His net was empty. Ronan kicked at the water. The otter took the fish and swimming on her back, she made to shore. He could, had he wished to, simply have walked the bank to steal the fish. However, he felt acutely shamed before the she-otter. No, he would not steal the fish, he resolved. Instead, he would catch the she-otter.

By way of a ruse, he continued to cast his net on the water. He did so in a seemingly desultory way. She had stopped fishing, and darted in and out of the reeds yards away from him. She watched him with a lively interest. Ronan was slowly casting his net in the waters closest to her store of fish. As he got closer, she seemed alert, now swimming a short distance away from the reeds, as if keen to be able to react to the thief. Finally, Ronan cast the net and let it drift alongside the bank where the fishes lay. The otter, now roused to action, disappeared beneath the surface. Ronan, suspected that she would swim toward the cache, but he now realized that she would leave the water and run the bank to rescue her supper. He scanned the bank for the wily animal. As he looked, he suddenly felt a pull on his net. He now looked toward his net—disappointed in some undefinable way: was the animal less canny than he had assumed her to be?—and saw that she was tangled in his net. He pulled it towards him. She was his.

As he pulled the net towards him to claim her, he thought, "Perhaps, I will let her go. She must surely know now which of the two of us is the more able hunter!" On the other hand, he thought, perhaps I will club her and sell her pelt. As he considered his options, he became aware of the resistance from the netted animal. She was swimming this way and that.

One moment away from him, one moment towards and even around him. She was an animal fighting for her life. He dug his heels into the soft mud of the river bottom the better to overcome her exertion. Nevertheless, try as he might, he was inch by oozing inch losing this match.

"What am I fighting for?" he asked himself aloud.

He had come to the river, he realized, to cleanse himself of war; to rid himself of battle, but he was now locked in obscure combat with this being: glorious and wild, who just a half-hour before he had so admired.

He relented. But as he loosened his grip on the net he realized that as she had swam within his net the she-otter had bound his feet together. With a tug, she gathered up the loose line and had upended him. He was fully immersed in the water when he realized that it was not he who had caught the she-otter, it was the she-otter who had caught him. He was being dragged to the center of the river where the currents were swiftest, and then he was pulled beneath the surface. He must surely drown.

Down, down, they went. The warrior held his breath as best he could. Down, down further they went. Down to the deepest of the Boyne pools. As he was passed out, he acquiesced before death. His fading thoughts registered the thought that he, Ronan, who had been the dispatcher, the hunter, the maimer, the life destroyer, would not marry, nor would he father children nor see these children grow. His life, which so recently had judged to be heroic: his arm so strong in pitching of the spear, his judgment so clear and measured on the battlefield, now seemed less valuable to him. Why, he wondered, had family seemed a burden to him, when now, its absence seemed crushing? It is said that the best deeds of one's past come to mind in death, yet Ronan found that what was left undone—what he had not before now suspected he would delight in—was what swarmed his ebbing thoughts.

Ronan finally allowed his disappointed mind to drift off, but as he did it vaguely occurred to him that he had a larger reserve of breath than he knew. Perhaps he was not so fatigued after all; bit by bit, the clouding of his mind lifted. He felt a growing sharpness of thought and a new alacrity of spirit come over him. He cast his eyes around him. Where before it had all been darkness in the depths of the pool, the water was now infused with blue light. He saw an old salmon wriggle in the slime—it warily looked back at him, but did not move. Looking down at his body, he saw that he had become an otter.

* * *

Ronan lived as an otter in the Boyne for seven years. He fished its lengths, he delighted in its waters, and he rolled on its banks. Most of all in those years he loved his bride, the she-otter Liadain. They fished together; they sprinted together along on the dry earth near the river. What they loved best was when their bodies tumbled one over the other in the secrecy of their holt. He loved the glossiness of her pelt, and the way a layer of air clung to her body like a thin silver coat when she dived. He had never seen something so beautiful. He exulted in the sharpness of her teeth when she nipped him as they made love. He loved the scent of the river on her sleek body, the smell of brine on her breath. He loved too her skill in fishing, her hunter's instincts. He loved her as she floated down the Boyne at sunset: often on her back looking up through overhanging boughs at the moon.

They had seven otter cubs together. Each cub had a special skill in the catching of each of seven fishes: trout, salmon, pike, perch, tench, carp, bream, roach, and eel. Each of the pups grew and became kings and queens of different reaches of the Boyne, though two of them moved and became the great scourges of salmon in the River Barrow. Ronan and Liadain missed them when they left, but they were proud of their family.

By then they were old. Liadain remained sleek on land and in the water, but some white hair mingled in her pelt. Ronan brought her fish in the holt for she tired now and became less able in the hunt. When he knew she must die, Ronan led her from their home and swam with her one last time. He held her body close to his as they cavorted in the water. They dived together towards the deep hollow where first Ronan had become an otter. There Liadain died with her body clinging to her husband's body. As he finally sensed the breath leaving the body that he had loved, a great sadness descended on Ronan and he became short of breath. He rose to the surface, Liadain's body in his arms. He had become a man again, and she had become a young woman. Eithniu breathed her first human breath. ∎

"P" CLUB
Jory Post

Our CPA has prostate cancer and Parkinson's disease. I have pancreatic cancer. Michelle's husband has polio. We're looking for others who might round out our 'P' club: someone with psoriasis, pelvic inflammatory disease, pink eye, pneumonia. We'll only meet at parks and we'll eat pastries, pies, pizza, peanuts, pears, and passionfruit. We will piss and moan, procrastinate, prevaricate, and pontificate. When one of us is cured, or dies, we'll throw a party.

MISSING
Jory Post

My grandpa Wes operated heavy equipment in the '60s to knock down trees to carve a highway through Northern California. One fell sideways and crushed his arm which was later amputated above the elbow. For the rest of his life, he swore he could feel an itch on the hand no longer there. Sometimes I'll run a brush across my scalp through missing hair. Will you roll over in bed in the middle of the night and reach to cuddle a body that's no longer there?

BURN, BABY, BURN
Jory Post

When I was young I didn't know who killed God or why. I didn't know how to interpret empty holes in the photograph albums. At age fifteen I brought a girlfriend, Kathy, home to meet my parents. I had never seen them so strange, quiet. I asked them later what was going on, and that's when I learned I had a sister who died of crib death, whose name was Kathy, who would have been the same age as the Kathy I had brought home. It was my aunt who told me twenty years later about the night it happened, about how my mom found her, about how my dad went through the house gathering everything related to Kathy, piled it on the front lawn, poured gasoline on it, and set it ablaze. "That's when God died, for all of us," Aunt Bev said. In my philosophy of religion class I learned otherwise. It was Friedrich Nietzsche who killed God nearly 100 years earlier, long before Kathy died, before my dad lit the match.

DIVERS' PARADISE: Making Peace with SOP on Tawi-Tawi

Hugh Iglarsh

—for Bob, much missed

Thinking about a brief stay years ago in the southern Philippine island of Tawi-Tawi, and about a minor but at the time maddening decision made by Madame and our other hosts, I see things differently than I did then. The rise since that time of President Rodrigo Duterte, the murderous, trash-talking demagogue whose power base is in the South, underscores just how thin are that nation's U.S.-modeled institutions and how little allegiance they command. The police and paramilitary goon squads who roam the archipelago, targeting hapless drug addicts as though they were the cause and not the symptom of dysfunction, are themselves expressions of a corrupt neocolonial state at permanent war with the society it purports to protect. In view of this Dirty Harry philosophy of governance, and the underlying abyss of violence and chaos it both propagates and reveals, it is hard not to accept Madame's point of view altogether.

No one knew the lay of the land, the frictions and booby traps, the catch-22s and Standard Operating Procedure, better than Madame.

Having personally established whatever harmony and regularity existed in an unsettled place, she was keenly aware of her own limitations. Still, her edict, gently rendered, not to permit my friend and me to visit the isle of Sitangkai left a bitter taste, for by this time that dot on the ocean, known (however accurately, in this land of slightly mocking tourist slogans) as the Venice of the Philippines, had become our Atlantis. And like Atlantis, it has remained a myth, its misty enticement underscoring the harder realities of our Tawi-Tawi sojourn.

Forgive me; I get ahead of myself. Tawi-Tawi is a remote place—the island's name is said to be a corruption of the Malay word *jaui*, meaning "far"—in more ways than one. The trip returns to me as a welter of impressions and images, reflecting my sense at the time of never being quite plugged in, and I must mentally squint to bring these memories back into order and focus. Let me begin again, this time nearer the beginning.

* * *

It became clear soon after our arrival on Tawi-Tawi that a climb up Mount Bongao was not in the cards. Our hosts offered a variety of shifting and imaginative reasons for repeatedly postponing our little expedition; I suspect it came down to fear of who or what might be creeping around in the hillside jungle—such as the powerful *saitan*, or nature spirit, said to reside on the mountain's peak—combined with the indignity of playing sherpa to a pair of rubbernecking tourists. We went so far once as to buy bundles of bananas for the monkeys who live on the slopes and have apparently developed a tetchy and resentful dependence on foreign aid. Standard Operating Procedure, we were told. If the fruit deal with the primates went sour, we had our four heavily armed Philippine marine bodyguards—another manifestation of SOP—to cover our retreat.

Despite these extreme precautions, the ascent of Bongao, always imminent, never happened. The volcanic peak, with its allegedly breathtaking views of the island-flecked Sulu Sea, loomed mockingly against the balmy tropical sky, close enough almost to taste, but not to touch.

Tawi-Tawi was "Divers' Paradise," according to the T-shirts in the hotel's dusty display case. But it was a BYO, DIY sort of paradise, as there did not seem to be a single dive shop or rentable tank or compressor in the entire province. We had come here to film the rituals and lifestyle of the resident Badjao people, the so-called Sea Gypsies of the Sulu archipelago and nearby Borneo, as part of a larger documentary project on the aquatic cultures of Southeast Asia. The lack of amenities, the intrusive marines, the failed climb—all served to remind us that the relative familiarity of Manila was a world away, and we were on our own in an area where basic questions of governance, loyalty and security were subject to a disturbingly wide range of answers.

To live in an interesting part of the globe like Tawi-Tawi means waking up every morning unsure of where the borders of one's community lie that day, and if one is within or without. There were shadows within shadows. Madame, our supremely generous and gracious hostess, was a force within the Autonomous Region in Muslim Mindanao, which included Tawi-Tawi and four other provinces in the far southern region of the Philippines. The ARMM was a vague entity subject to so many factional compromises and constraints that it recalled the story of the blind men and the elephant. Was it a quasi-government? A post–civil war demilitarized zone? A notoriously leaky bucket for oil-state philanthropy? A concession to the *datus*, or chieftains, of the Muslim South, and a social welfare agency for everyone else? Or perhaps, from the majority Catholic view, a reservation for an unloved religious minority?

Such a Rorschach blot arrangement could fully satisfy no one, and so the Autonomous Region's paltry and diluted existence egged on die-hard Moro (i.e., Muslim) separatists (i.e., "terrorists"). Accounts of these groups' origins, numbers, intentions, location, alliances and ongoing existence were as changeable as the moon, and more than once I wondered uncharitably if the "terrorists" of Tawi-Tawi were an extension of the monkeys of Bongao, an all-purpose alibi trotted out to avoid strenuous activity in a humid climate. Certainly the Tawi-Tawi I experienced was an almost morbidly placid and quiet little place, its tone set by the Badjao, whose level of aggression did not appear appreciably higher than that of the agar-agar seaweed they spent their days harvesting. The real issues in Tawi-Tawi, as in the Philippines as a whole, were grinding deprivation and the imperatives of survival, and a certain amiable sharpness was an understandable result.

Beyond the "terrorists" there were the ethnic divides among the Moros themselves—Tausug, Maranao, Yakan, Samal and many more—all with significantly different histories and outlooks, none with great esteem for the others, as I would discover. And more: the clan rivalries within the tribes and the *redus*, or blood feuds, between families. (Mediating these quarrels was a major responsibility of Madame, a *Bae a Labi* or chosen queen of her people, who would use her own considerable pearl-farm-based fortune to purchase temporary respite.) Then there were the competing territorial claims of the hard-pressed tribal peoples of the mountains and forests, and the guerrillas of the New People's Army hunkered down in Mindanao and elsewhere, who sought a Maoist, bayonet-edged solution to the Gordian knot of Philippine history.

Like the hypnotic native Kulintang music, the strife in the South has neither beginning nor end. All forces are centripetal, and any element added to the mix simply accelerates the rate of spin. Philippine politics have more than a touch of the tragic, and the overall sense of hopelessness is confirmed by the fact that nobody ever talks about them. The legendary gregariousness and joie de vivre of Filipinos are delightful to behold, but who knows what graveyards are being whistled past.

And who knows what story my friend had told—or rather, what his listeners had heard—to obtain this level of attention from Tawi-Tawi officialdom. I didn't inquire; I would have felt implicated in the masquerade, which, like a Gogol story, took on a momentum of its own. Because, without our asking, we had been given the bodyguard and retinue treatment, we were assumed by everyone—and sometimes, in moments of grandiosity, by ourselves—to be somehow worth kidnapping, and hence in need of all this security. On Tawi-Tawi, we learned, you can have status or you can have freedom, but it is unreasonable to expect both. Our unearned celebrity delivered us into the swaddling embrace of our detail of soldiers and staff, which kept us not only from harm, but also from most volitional movement.

Once upon a time, the Peace Corps had been present in Tawi-Tawi, teaching literacy to the chronically underserved Badjao. It was considered something of a golden age thereabouts, by those who still remembered. But the last volunteer had left a generation ago, pushed out by the horrific violence of the Marcos-era civil war in Mindanao and Sulu, which left tens of thousands dead. Since then the island has been on no one's radar screen, and after so many years of neglect and oblivion, the provincial authorities were willing to pin their hopes on anyone who showed the slightest interest in the place. How could we *not* be some combination of Claude Lévi-Strauss, Robert Flaherty, Joseph Conrad and the Ford Foundation? How else explain the presence of the affable, San Miguel–quaffing marines, the unctuous majordomo soon dubbed Vick the Tick, and the swarm of attendants and hangers-on, which waxed at mealtime and waned whenever the threat of activity loomed?

It was a tango of mutual disappointment, as our lack of funds rubbed against our hosts' equal and opposing shortage of initiative. Neither side had a clear idea what the other wanted or expected, and by the time we arrived on the island, it was too late to ask. Madame's standard answer to questions about the arrangement was a shrug and a reference to SOP, which, like the will of Allah, could be neither explained nor denied.

At least we had a name for our creeping sense of passive befuddlement: SOP. It was SOP that prevented the ascent of Mount Bongao; SOP that generated the esurient multitude at dinnertime, eating cheap Vietnamese rice charged to us at ten times market price; and a higher-level SOP that would halt our trip to the isle of Sitangkai, a half-submerged atoll where the Badjao, so we had heard, performed their nocturnal rites—the juicy, filmable mystery that had drawn us here. It was SOP that had transformed us from curious but not altogether focused backpackers and wannabe documentarians into minor celebrities, complete with a stilted interview on Tawi-Tawi's radio station, and it was SOP that would keep us from cashing in on that short-lived fame in any meaningful way.

And of course it was nobody's fault, least of all Madame's. She had consistently gone to bat for us in what we began to realize was not completely friendly territory even for her, a monarch among her own people up at Lake Lanao in Mindanao. Here she was only the wife of the frequently absent provincial governor, responsible only for . . . everything, including the care and maintenance of droves of dependents, who would otherwise go wanting in this hungry place.

One afternoon, we stepped into the eerie stillness of the Tawi-Tawi tourism office, startling the crowded room into a frenzied facsimile of industry—no easy task, considering the facility's lack of computers or other visible office equipment. Our request for a map or listing of local attractions produced a lengthy but futile search and a regretful response—it seemed that owing to continuing high demand, it was difficult to keep the requested material in stock. But showing the Filipino genius for improvisation, the tourist staff transformed itself in a blink into a tourist attraction, wheeling out gamelan-like gongs and other instruments, donning traditional garb and presenting a charming program of Samal folk culture featuring a supernally poised and beautiful child dancer—after which we left the artistes a generous tip. We were getting the hang of this. SOP.

The delicacy of Madame's position—politically and personally—became apparent to us not long into our stay, when we decided we could no longer feed half the provincial capital on a nightly basis, at least not at the prices charged us by the proprietors of the island's sole, Spartan hotel. As diplomatically as we could, we told Madame our story and made clear our resolve. Reddening and throwing up her hands, she blurted out, "I cannot do anything with these people! They are another *culture!*" It was a moment of commonality and shared suffering. We bonded.

From that moment on, we were promoted to Madame's mealtime guests and confidants. We were accepted into the warm bosom of this small seaside kingdom, fed royally by Madame's gifted and eager-to-please chef on meltingly tender lapu-lapu fillet and agar-agar salad, set straight on Moro history and politics, protected from the voracity of our protectors and assimilated into palace life. This involved meeting an array of in-laws and other adornments of Madame's court, including an impish Chinese transvestite whose existence was never acknowledged or clarified. Once, he cornered me leaving the royal bathroom and, with a mad gleam in his eye, began stroking my thrillingly hairy Western arm.

Despite this Caliban encounter and other moments of courtly fun at our expense—including a bucking, high-anxiety speedboat ride to Simunul, site of the oldest mosque in the Philippines and the nine-foot-long grave of Sheikh Karimal Makhdum, the big-boned Arab missionary who brought Islam to the islands six centuries ago—our days at the palace would be the highlight of our Tawi-Tawi stay. As Madame opened up to us, so did the society, and our vague and unsponsored project seemed kissed by fortune.

We made the acquaintance of the island-dwelling Badjao, although our staff-heavy, marine-accompanied trips to their stilt-house beach villages must have seemed to them more like invasions than friendly visits. There we took photos, purchased their fine woven mats and other craft items and distributed treats to the wide-eyed, impossibly patient and polite children. Once, the Badjao had spent their entire lives plying the western Pacific islands in their tiny houseboats, coming ashore only for rituals and burial. They had been pressured by conflict and need away from their aquatic subsistence lifestyle and into crowded waterside settlements and the cash economy of the seafood merchants on Chinese Pier. Still, they retained a dreamlike otherness and lent Tawi-Tawi such magic as it had. The image I carry with me is of a young mermaid with dark, dancing eyes and sea-hennaed hair, flashing a smile mixing pride and mischief as she held up to us a large, fresh-caught and very dead squid. Not a lei, perhaps, but not unfriendly.

Despite such prizes, in the southern Philippines, even the sea is something of a bad neighborhood. After many years of dynamite and cyanide fishing, Tawi-Tawi lacked a living reef—another chink in the "Divers' Paradise" concept. The only relatively healthy coral, we learned, lay just off the Tawi-Tawi Air Force Base, a military installation whose existence, here at the edge of the world and within the Muslim Autonomous Region, came as a surprise to us. And so, eager to accomplish one shamelessly touristy thing during our stay, or at least pass the time, we asked to visit the base.

Some obscure, possibly weather-related SOP prevented us from actually exploring this last remnant of the Tawi-Tawi reef. But the visit was nevertheless fascinating, as we kibitzed with the rummy-playing, undershirt-clad soldiery and came to understand their concerns. These consisted of golf and, to a lesser extent, Freemasonry. The true nature of the base was revealed to us over the course of a wide-ranging conversation with the genial commander, who graciously continued talking to us even after it became apparent that we were neither golfers nor Masons, and thus could not fully appreciate his life's work. This involved converting his lonely fortress into a romantic seaside getaway apparently for the use of well-connected Manila insiders and their temporary companions, complete with thatched, Gilligan's Island–style cabanas, an ever-growing and improving golf course, and military discretion. The machine-gun tower on the waterfront served as a reminder that what happened in Tawi-Tawi stayed in Tawi-Tawi, far from the eyes of wives and reporters.

The only out-of-bounds subject was combat. Judging by the colonel's sheepish expression, this reticence was less about security concerns than embarrassment at his limited non-golfing arsenal. There was the gun on the beach, used to scare off the poison and dynamite fishermen, who posed a threat to the aesthetics of his enterprise. But that seemed to be about it in terms of armament. If there were any planes on this air force base, they must have been of the extreme stealth variety, as I saw no trace of even an airstrip. Whenever the conversation strayed onto the subject of war or terrorism, the colonel skillfully brought it back to his pride and joy, the links that allowed Tawi-Tawians of all faiths, parties, ethnicities, genders and Masonic attainments to get in their eighteen holes without having to take the ferry to Zamboanga, the nearest real city. In his own eyes, he had done nothing less than bring civilization and amity to this benighted backwater, and no mere feat of arms could heighten his glory. Indeed, conflict could only be bad for business, and that would be bad—very bad—for his true constituents, the golfers of Tawi-Tawi and the on-the-razzle VIPs and cronies of Manila.

At the time, contemplating this garrisoned country club, I thought I must have gone down the rabbit hole with Alice and emerged in the Sulu Sea. In retrospect, the colonel's position—like Madame's—makes more sense to me. In a place like the southern Philippines, the best one can hope for is a shaky stasis; any positive action threatens a tsunami-like recoil. A wise officer in an unloved army engaged in perpetual low-level conflict with its own people, led by an oligarchical government signally lacking in social purpose and legitimacy, fighting an unwinnable "war on terror" at the instigation of reckless, domineering and clueless foreigners, would therefore tend to become very circumspect in his approach to the "enemy." Underneath the factional disputes and political maneuvering were social fault lines that could gape wide at any moment, swallowing up everything—a prospect that pleased neither Manila officials nor Muslim elites. An aggressive offensive launched by either side could trigger that cataclysmic social war.

Hence the performative nature of the army-"terrorist" struggle in the South, rife with whispers of divvied-up ransoms and protracted gun battles with no casualties on either side, except perhaps for the occasional strained neck caused by firing in the air. In particular, the fight against the dreaded Abu Sayyaf gang is reminiscent of Snoopy's endless battle against the Red Baron, with much impassioned cursing but little actual damage, at least when American advisors are not present. Each side needs the other: the army invokes the threat of "terrorism" to justify its hefty Yankee subsidy, while the "terrorists" depend on the army's heavy-handed presence to recruit members and retain relevance. Neither side is pure; both live off the land, one way or another, leading to a certain mutual understanding and a grudging respect for each other's turf. The logic of the situation points unambiguously toward stalemate.

No wonder the colonel—a man of optimism and drive—focused his attention on smoothing his greens and protecting his reef. History offers few examples of a committed golfer turned terrorist. The course was his contribution to world peace, the still-living coral his environmental statement. The rest was pantomime and SOP.

Soon after, the word came down that we could not go to Sitangkai to view the Badjao rituals, as "terrorists" had been spotted there. Very likely the marine bodyguards were the decisive voice. Accompanying two feckless Americans into reputed Abu Sayyaf territory in order to indulge their obscure fascination with the water-based indigenous shamanic religious ceremonies of the region was beyond their pay grade and, no matter how appreciative they were of the many six-packs we had bought them, definitely not SOP. It was impossible to guess how a militarized visit with such an unlikely premise would be perceived by the island's inhabitants. As fishy, I suppose, as militants of the Moro Islamic Liberation Front appearing at the Tawi-Tawi Air Force Base, asking to work on their putting skills.

What struck us then was that the presence of "terrorists" on flea-speck Sitangkai, where they had nowhere to hide, was seen as a military *problem* rather than an opportunity. Now I realize it was the extreme weakness of the Abu Sayyaf position that rendered the situation dangerous, by making contact all but inevitable, no matter how hard the two sides tried not to notice each other. However the consequences of that encounter played out, they were sure to be unpleasant for the marines, for Madame, for the colonel, for the greater golfing public of Tawi-Tawi . . . and maybe for the whole house of cards known as the Republic of the Philippines.

If we had read the signs right, we would have known from the start we were as likely to see the Badjao dance as we were the leprechauns; the remarkable thing is that we were given such access to their lives as we were. Sitangkai had loomed larger to us as the possibilities on Tawi-Tawi had narrowed, exactly because the little half-drowned islet with its full-moon rites represented an escape from the ubiquitous SOP. But for outsiders in the South, there is no escape from SOP. Once contracted, it sticks like bad karma.

My view of SOP, the culture of Filipino officialdom, has evolved over the passing years. Now that I am no longer in its grip, I see that behind SOP's passive-aggressive disingenuousness, its preference for slogan over action, is a sophisticated and at times elegant shared logic. It is the expression of a heightened sensitivity to the ramifications of change and conflict in a society marked by trauma and always lurching toward crisis. If one begins with the historically justifiable assumption that the world consists of an uncombable tangle of insoluble problems—and yet to retain one's sanity and self-esteem, one must act and make decisions as though this were not the case—then the natural result is the polite, well-intentioned paralysis that is SOP.

The hard truth is that violence and vendetta lurk under the surface of the South like depth charges, and the least pressure—a contested local election, perhaps, or even an unannounced visit—can set them off. SOP is the attempt to maintain some boundaries and at least the illusion of order by turning authority and social relations into a kind of semirealist theater. It defines the manners and mores of those who live on a tightrope, and those who do not live so precariously are in no position to pass judgment. To come to terms with SOP is to cease being a tourist and to start being a considerate guest, one who understands the limits of one's welcome and leaves no messes behind for the hosts to clean up.

These musings came much later. At the time, we were preoccupied with the problem of arranging our exit from Tawi-Tawi. This had become something of a challenge due to the enormous size of our hotel bill, reflecting the nightly family reunions of Madame's people that we had unwittingly catered. It would have bankrupted us. Somehow a compromise was negotiated, involving a partial IOU on our part and possibly some serious backstage arm-twisting on Madame's, who had reverted to her mediator role. But it was not a firm or happy agreement, and the signals we picked up from hotel personnel were not reassuring. We passed a bad quarter of an hour wondering whether we would be allowed to board the ferry back to Zamboanga, or shaken down for the full, outrageous sum. It came down to the marines' loyalty, which, after the Sitangkai disappointment, was uncertain.

We awaited our fate in a park near the pier, seeking as best we could to blend into the woodwork prior to sailing. It was not to be. The space must have served a particular demographic, for we found ourselves surrounded by a gaggle of girlish youth, as soft and fragile as sea-foam, who fluttered groupie-like around us. It was as though Tawi-Tawi itself wished to provide us with an accurate parting impression—not one of Abu Sayyaf "terrorists," entrepreneurial army officers and greedy innkeepers, but rather of an older and gentler layer of the culture, which we had glimpsed earlier in the Badjao settlements on the beach.

For once, SOP swung in our favor; the decision was made to allow our departure. After all, visitors to Tawi-Tawi do not grow on trees, and a noisy dispute about extortionate hotel rates would not have added luster to the Divers' Paradise. We boarded our vessel with a sigh of relief and said our farewells to our marine escorts, to Madame and to her staff, none of us entirely unrelieved to see the others' backs.

We had visited a place not quite ready for visitors and had encountered a dance of hospitality and hindrance, openness and opacity, as interesting and revealing perhaps as a Badjao sacred dance under the bright equatorial moon. Our hosts gave us all they had to offer, which was their world, their history and their truth. All I can offer in return are these words, and a long-delayed gratitude and understanding. It is not much, but it is the best that can be arranged under the circumstances. SOP. ■

GUAPA
Patricia Engel

Y ou would never know by looking at me that I used to be more than double my current weight. The loss isn't enough to get me featured in a magazine or on a news program, but it was a lot for me, this small frame, fat pockets I'd been carrying for decades since I had no father and my mother thought the best compensation was food. I was one of those round babies who could barely move, who would topple over when placed atop a bed and need help sitting back up. I blamed my mother for deforming my body practically from birth, but she was the first one to tell me I was predisposed for largeness and also: what nature gives, art can fix. I was a teenager before I understood she meant surgery.

In the factory, everyone still calls me la gorda, even though I'm now thin, my once-wide thighs narrowed to pegs. My ass went so flat with all the dieting and pills that I had to get it refilled with injections of fat from my other parts. The same with my breasts. They're new, imported from France, and when I lie down, they hover above me, as if saluting the sun. I haven't touched my face yet, but it's in next year's budget. Everyone thinks I fly home to Colombia for two weeks every year to spend time with my mother but it's really for my surgeries. I'm still recovering from my fourth aggressive liposuction, which was more of a sculpting, to carve out my waist, the soft pads over my pelvis, so I can have a prettier vagina. Every summer my friends from the factory go to Rockaway Beach but I always claim to be sick or busy. This summer they will see me in a bathing suit I bought on my last trip to home. I tried it on the day after the operation over my compression garment, even though I was sore and swollen and blue everywhere the needle had dug and sucked.

Edgar is the only one who never calls me gorda. He calls me guapa instead, just like he calls all the other ladies sweet names like hermosa, preciosa, linda, or belleza. Lorena, who works on the packing line beside me, says guapa is the least desired of all the names Edgar gives to the women of the fábrica, but I don't mind. I see how he looks at me when he delivers the pallet of boxes to the end of my line so I can pack them full of tiny ceramic penguins or ballerinas, bottoms proudly stamped with MADE IN USA. I see him look my way as he drives his forklift along the corridor toward the warehouse. At lunch, he always finds me outside by the food truck and sometimes even pays Don Pepe for my croquetas. He doesn't know this is the only time I allow myself such decadence. In the mornings, I eat only fruit. In the evening, only vegetables. On weekends, I eat almost nothing at all. I am so hungry but it's the only way I can sustain this new body.

Sometimes he brings me mangos he buys on the street near his home in Washington Heights. He takes the 172nd Street guagua with the other Dominicans in the morning and back in the evening. I ride the guagua from Dover with the Colombians and a few Puerto Ricans. When I'm through paying for my surgeries, I will buy a car and this way I will be able to offer Edgar rides home.

He's ten years younger than I am but he told me once, as we stood in the parking lot smoking a cigarette together, that he likes older women. His first affair was with a young friend of his mother's, who taught him to make love when he was fifteen. This was in Santo Domingo, where his mother still lives in a house he paid for with his money from the fábrica. The first years in New York, he thought, just like we all do when we arrive, that he would eventually go back once he had something saved, but now he's been here long enough to know there is no returning—once you cross over that ocean, those borders, they cross over you.

I know he's had relations with other women in the fábrica. There was Mayda, who works in receiving, young like him, and he might have loved her until one day they were no longer speaking and soon she was pregnant with Rolando from dispatch's baby. They both work at a factory in Newark now, and Edgar moved on to Leidy and Prisca, who are both old like me. But those relationships didn't last either. In those days, they were more beautiful than me, but I have made myself into something far superior now. My neck may still droop, but if I wear my hair down, nobody can notice. I'm dotted with holes, I've got some indentations, and my breasts are lined with scars, but it's nothing that would catch your eye in bedroom lighting.

We kissed once. It was fast but forceful, out in the parking lot during one of our breaks, which we always take together. He'd stopped smoking but he would still join me outside, even in winter, and on that afternoon, the bruised and moldy sky ready to break with rain and all the others already back inside, he pushed his lips against mine, our teeth clanked, our tongues slipped into each other's mouths, and then, like lighting, it was over, and he said something only young men say, something like *I wanted this*, or *I was waiting for this*, or maybe it was *You wanted this*, guapa. To tell you the truth, I can't remember.

* * *

My mother named me Indiana after what she said was the most beautifully named state of North America. This was in Cali, where all the girls of my generation were named María or Ximena. My name, my mother said, would be my destiny. She's still alive, in the house that belonged to her mother and father. When I left, I was twenty and my mother took me up to the church of San Antonio on the hill facing the three crosses shining over the valley, protecting the city from the demon Buziraco. She said some people were born to stay and others were born to leave. She was sure a better life waited for me on the other side of the Americas. When I arrived, a friend of a friend met me at the airport and took me to her house in Dover. It wasn't really her house but one she shared with seventeen other people, mostly Colombians like me, who didn't yet have social security numbers or enough cash to pay rent anywhere else. We lived five or six to a room, slept on floors or mattresses if there was one available. I cried through my first winter from the lack of sun, the cloak of snow, and the wet chill that filled the house as we slept. But those people comforted me, fed me, dressed me. *The tears will pass,* they said, *and soon you won't even remember how to cry.* I don't know if this was true for them, or words they told themselves to endure the distance building between them and their own countries and families, but I listened. And then it was as they said. In a year, maybe three or five, I stopped crying and decided this was home.

The same woman who brought me to that house brought me to the fábrica. She said the owner was a good man who hired Colombians without hesitation, who employed half of Washington Heights, and who paid fair. They started me cleaning bathrooms. I didn't mind. I cleaned offices and beauty salons back in Cali and I knew how to do things fast. Then they moved me to the cafeteria. I was to keep it clean, especially after the lunch rush, when the men left their garbage all over the place. If I were better with computers, which is to say, if I had ever used one in my life, maybe they would have moved me into one of the more administrative positions, like Mayda. But I wasn't good for that. So they put me to packing boxes. I like the rhythm of it, especially when the speakers overhead blast a song I like. Luckily Mauricio, the plant manager, is in charge of the radio station and likes salsa and merengue just like us. The classics. Grupo Niche and Joe Arroyo. Sometimes it feels like the whole factory is singing along with those songs we grew up dancing to with our cousins and our first loves. I had a first love, though you might never have guessed it, since in those days I was at my absolute fattest and hardly left the house because everyone in the barrio called me la cerda. He was a neighbor. A boy who could be with almost any flaca he wanted and still, he chose to come over to my house when my mother was out to be with me.

I told him I loved him and asked if he loved me and he said yes, of course, otherwise he wouldn't sleep with me just like that. There has to be some kind of love there, he said. He told me I was a good girl and said I could even be beautiful with some effort. Not quite a reina de belleza but maybe like one of the telenovela actresses or bikini girls like Natalia París, who was short like me. "I know you have it in you, Indi," he said. "You just have to try."

He died in a motorcycle accident. The beautiful thing was that his family donated his organs to science and then we heard there was another man his age walking around with one of his kidneys, and another man somewhere who got his heart. I had dreams for a while that I would be so sick that I'd need a transplant of some kind and they would operate and give me a part of him, maybe a lung, his spleen, liver, whatever. I knew from an early age that I would never be able to have children. A malformed uterus and only one ovary. But I thought if I could find myself close to death, maybe one of his organs would save me, and it would be better than giving birth to his child, because he would be the one living in me.

* * *

I share an apartment with my friend Soraya, who works at a bakery on Blackwell Street. She has been trying to convince me to come work full time with her. She says I won't have to do the hour-long guagua commute to the fábrica every morning and night, but I wouldn't give it up for anything. I spend each ride sitting in the front row of the van, planning things I will say to Edgar during our breaks, during lunch, practicing the way I will smile at him when he brings the pallet with the empty cartons or takes my packed boxes away on his forklift. And when the guagua driver pulls into the parking lot and I see Edgar standing along the brick wall by the back entrance with some of the others, waiting for me—la gorda!—to descend, I tell myself and my mother in my mind, and even the demon Buziraco if he will listen, there is no other place I would rather be.

From the way I talk about him, you probably imagine a guy with movie-star looks, some kind of prince, moneyed and polished. Edgar is all those things, or maybe none of those things. It doesn't really matter. I can tell you about his eyes and lashes and canela skin and broad shoulders that make everything hang off him like drapery. I can tell you about the way he smiles, his front tooth angled outward, his crooked walk, the way he swallows half his syllables and makes fun of my singsong Spanish, and you would still not understand his beauty, his brilliance even though he can't write more than a few words, much less read. I know this because he confessed it and yes, that's something that always makes a man more attractive to a woman, especially one like me: being made a confidant, a secret keeper.

No matter that Edgar is thirty and I am forty. In the fábrica, under summer heat that blows through the vents like fire, where we stand in front of the rusted metal fans unashamed about the sweat dripping down our collarbones, dampening the seats of our jeans; or in winter, when the icy humidity of the Hudson penetrates the concrete and cinder block, when we work in our warmest coats, gloves on with the fingertips cut off so we can still pack our boxes and load our pallets; here, we are the same: two bodies, a woman and a man, and I think only of another kiss waiting for me in the parking lot, hot and wet and hungry just like the last. In the apartment I share with Soraya, carved out of the basement of a house owned by an Iraqi family, I dream of a life with Edgar, not in his country or in mine, but in this one; a life new for both of us.

* * *

Everyone is talking about the Christmas party. The boss booked an entire restaurant on Dyckman, with a dance floor and everything. Normally our Christmas parties are here in the fábrica, with food served on foil trays, and all our dancing happens between the cafeteria tables. But this year business was good, productivity above average, and there were no lawsuits or union disputes, so we deserve to be rewarded. All the Dominicanas are planning to wear gowns normally reserved for weddings and quinceañeras, with salon hairdos and their best joyas de fantasía. The men will wear their funeral suits. The Colombianas don't want to look underdressed in comparison and many have bought new dresses or borrowed ones from friends. I have a dress I bought with some extra hours I worked at Soraya's bakery packing holiday cakes. It's royal blue with a cascade of beads along the chest and down the back. Satin that fits like skin. Secondhand but you would never know.

Soraya is twice divorced and thinks it's odd I haven't been divorced even once, as is normal for a woman my age. I didn't have to marry for papers. My green card came clean and easy, and everyone said I was so lucky but I thought it was the least God could do for me. I don't want you to think I've been celibate all these years in New Jersey. I've had plenty of lovers in my days as both a gorda and a flaca. I had a Syrian lover for a very long time, even in the first months that Edgar came to work at the fábrica. Perhaps I would still be with him but he couldn't take the homesickness and returned to his country. Not even a war could keep him away.

Edgar worked in other factories in the area before he came to ours. The worst, he said, was a brewery in Queens where the boss locked them in from dawn to dusk. There were monthly raids, in which someone always got carted off due to false papers or stolen social security numbers.

"It's always sad when you see a compatriot taken away," he told me. I nodded.

He touched my hand. "We are the lucky ones."

This was back when I used to clean the cafeteria and Edgar would find me there sweeping and float around the tables while I worked. Sometimes Gilmer, Pinto, or one of the other guys would stick their head in and make a whistling sound or start singing a love song and we'd both roll our eyes, as if the idea of the two of us as sweethearts was beyond the possibilities of this world.

The summer of the blackout, when the factory went dark as outer space, Edgar found me by my packing line, took my elbow, and led me to the one of the emergency doors—not the one everyone else was rushing toward, but another one, on the far side of the building, where we found ourselves completely alone in a patch of parking lot, warmed by peach afternoon light.

"Why did you come looking for me?" I asked.

"Because you're my guapa," he said and embraced me in the way of two lovers who have been together a very long time, resting our arms around one another's torsos with ease and familiarity. He held me close. I was still wearing the compression garment from one of my liposuctions and hoped the pressure of our bodies wouldn't make my wounds ooze blood through the bandages.

* * *

I gave up smoking a few months ago. It was my last vice to go after ice cream and chocolate bars. I was used to stopping temporarily in preparation for each of my surgeries but I always took cigarettes back up because I found them to be great company in the solitude of my life in this country. I can tell you how poisonous and deadly they are, information you can get anywhere else, without denying my Parliaments brought Edgar and me together those first days. But now that we are both healthier people, now that we've both tasted each other's lips, we don't need them as excuses to come together.

Now, in the mornings, Edgar waits for me outside the fábrica with a cup of coffee from Don Pepe's truck. It's bitter and oversugared but I drink it even as it singes my insides because it came from Edgar. He always arrives to the fábrica first, since his guagua only has to make that short trip over the George Washington Bridge. The Dover guagua ride is eternal, along the Christopher Columbus Highway, where there is always traffic, but on most days we manage to arrive just before it's time to clock in.

Edgar greets me every day with a kiss on the cheek. He's not even shy about it. If you were to ask anyone in the fábrica who Edgar's girl is these days, they would tell you, without hesitation, it's la gorda. Maybe they would say they don't really know or understand what our story is, being that we live far apart and only see each other for bits of our shift on weekdays, but those moments are loaded with promise, and if there is a romance brewing in this ancient building, it doesn't involve one of the pregnant machine operators or one of the line mechanics with three or four novias. No, it's between Edgar and Indiana. What we have, anyone would tell you, is true.

* * *

On this morning, my guagua arrives at the factory first. The workers who came on the St. Nicholas Avenue guagua say that right after they crossed the bridge, a tractor trailer turned over on the upper level and there you go, un trancón del carajo, traffic like it's the end of the world. Edgar's guagua got stuck behind it.

A streak of springlike days has hit New Jersey. It's no longer frigid as a morgue. The grass in the lot next to the factory grounds has resurrected in a bright and fluffy green; even the birds and squirrels have emerged, hyper and shameless. A group of ladies gathered by the fábrica entrance brag to one another about their dresses for the party. I'll show them. They'll see la gorda dressed like Miss Universe, with hair extensions and fake lashes I've already bought at the beauty supply, all my surgery swelling down, my body starved and deflated and contoured to perfection. Mami was right. *What nature gives, art can fix.* On my next trip home, I'm going to bring my surgeon a gift to show my gratitude to him for my new life.

I ask Don Pepe for two coffees, one for me and one for Edgar. He lives with a cousin and his family on 167th Street. He's told me he sleeps on a sofa in the living room. He has the money for something better, at least for his own room somewhere, but he sends most of what he earns back to his mother. One day I asked if he wants to have his own family someday and he shrugged.

"I'm not like most men. I don't care if I am never a father."

He's doesn't spend weekends like some of the other fábrica guys, drinking, dancing, putiando all over the West Side. Edgar prefers to stay in and watch television or play computer games with his cousin's kids. If the weather is nice, he might go play soccer with friends at one of the fields nearby. If he's seeing a lady, maybe he will take her for walks in the park or to a party. From what I've told you about his other factory novias, you might think Edgar some kind of mujeriego, but it's just the opposite. No woman has been good enough for him, his pure heart.

One of the women who lived in my first residence in Dover, the house that turned over tenants like the Port Authority, has her own botánica in Paterson now and when I'm feeling desperate, usually before a surgery, I pay her a visit for a little spiritual cleansing and white magic trabajo for good luck. She's a casual hechicera. Not like those brujas and magos who make you pay hundreds of dollars for all sorts of initiations. This one is more about service. She just wants her community to be happy. I told her about Edgar and she said she would take care of it for me, and I wouldn't even have to do something pathetic like slip drops of period blood into his coffee to make him love me. All I had to do, she said, was light a white seven-day candle and burn the petals of a single rose each night until they became ash. And then I was to collect that ash in a sachet of silk and bury it in the backyard. I had to wait until the Iraqis upstairs were sleeping in order to do this, because the wife is very protective of her flower beds.

Don Pepe hands me the coffees and I return to the brick wall by the fábrica entrance. Everyone is waiting until the last second before the morning bell rings to go inside. There are no windows where we work. The fábrica is a long charcoal tube, like a subway platform, and in the winter, with overtime, we can spend the whole day in there without seeing the sun rise or set. My mother, the one who wanted me to come here so badly, often asks me why I stay. It's been twenty years, she says, and my life has not drastically improved since my arrival. Other immigrants do far better—start their own businesses, marry, have children who will be educated and able to provide for them in their old age. I have none of that. "Maybe it's time you return home," she says. "You can take care of your mamita. We can be old ladies together." I understand her impulse. I am her only child. But I tell her, "No, Mamá. It's not yet time."

* * *

The morning bell rings and most of the parking lot crowd drifts into the building for work. The last thing you want is Mauricio to see you're not yet at your station when the production lines kick in. You never know his mood. Sometimes he will let it go without writing you up, or, you might later hear your name called over the intercom system and find yourself sitting in human resources begging to keep your job. You might think this is just a fábrica, and why would anyone beg to keep working here, but the fact is there is a waiting list of people just dying to be employed by the big boss. For every line worker, there is another handful of cousins or neighbors or newly arrived friends who've heard about this place and are looking to get in. There are people who've worked here twenty, thirty years. Parents, children, even three generations of a family all on the same production line.

I want to wait for Edgar. I want to be the one to hand him his coffee when his guagua arrives, before he goes inside to work, so I hang around outside while the others disappear. My friend Rosa, who works the same line as me, sticks her head out the door. "You'd better get in soon, Indi. Mauricio's making rounds."

I tell her I'll be right in. Besides, Mauricio can't go hard when there's an entire guagua of workers late for their shift for reasons beyond their control. Mauricio is Costa Rican and thinks he's better than us because he has some kind of degree in who knows what. "You could have Mauricio's job someday," I once told Edgar. "You're smarter than him. All he does is babysit us like we're in a daycare."

"You think so?"

"You're the smartest guy in this whole place," I said. I could tell it was what he needed to hear. Everyone needs positive affirmations. I heard a woman on TV say that once.

I hear the guagua's old engine before I see it tear into the lot. Rusty is driving. His only job in life is to deliver people over the bridge and back at the start and end of the factory's three shifts and he's usually as careful as a surgeon. But today, no doubt with his passengers complaining they might have time deducted from their checks for being late, he rips across the pavement toward the back of the building, where I lean against the brick factory wall, holding Edgar's coffee.

I search past the tinted windows for Edgar's face. I know he sees me. The van comes closer and closer and I approach to meet it, but it doesn't stop; it keeps rolling and rushing as if delivering its passengers straight through to the other side of the wall, and I am pinned, the bumper pressing my thighs, the grill and hood cracking my ribs against the brick. I feel nothing, only hear the crash, the skidding, and then screams.

* * *

My legs were severed. Well, they were still attached by something. Tendons or ligaments or fibers, I don't really know for sure. Only that they were unusable. My pelvis, shattered. A few ribs too. My organs appear to be intact. They keep saying I am very lucky.

Many years ago, when Colombia played in the World Cup here in the United States, before the famous autogol that eliminated them and cost poor Andrés Escobar his life, the country was celebrating the national team's defeat of Romania. I'd watched the match at a cousin's house and, in the hours after, walked home alone wearing my yellow jersey, the streets packed with cars waving national flags from the windows, horns honking, joyful victory howls, and already fireworks overhead. I was crossing a jammed intersection, inching between two cars stopped one behind the other at a red light, when I felt one car roll forward and push me against the one ahead. It was less than a second, this awareness that I would be stuck there, my legs cut as if by a blade, but I felt something lift me, carry me out of danger, and place me on the sidewalk. I was shaken and told my mother the story when I got home. She had no doubt angels had saved me. Nobody else would have been able to lift a gorda like me like a bird carrying thread. It was a miracle if you believe in miracles. Or just an unexplained mystery if you don't. But it happened. I'm still here. All of this is to tell you that I'm not surprised I wasn't so lucky the second time. This time Buziraco got his way when he said, "Gorda, your legs now belong to me."

* * *

My friends from the fábrica brought me on oversized card that everybody signed wishing me a quick recovery. *Recovery.* Such a funny word. As if my legs have only been misplaced and might still be found. I picture them walking around the factory, waiting for my return. *This is what you get for being late to work,* they will tell me when we are reunited. But no, they took those scraps of flesh and bone wherever they take detached body parts. I wonder, now that I have time to think about such things, whose job it is to pick up those human pieces, to discard them in the hospital trash.

Edgar signed the card near the bottom. He only wrote his first name, in letters of uneven sizing. I remember little about the crash. They tell me I was on the ground for a long time before the ambulance and police came, before they assessed the mess of my body and decided what to do with me. I bled so much they thought I would die. But my system has always been good at clotting. I know this from all my surgeries.

I remember Edgar kneeling on the concrete beside me. His face close to mine. I don't think I was crying, just dazed from the shock, heat shooting through my bones. I remember asking what happened and Edgar said, "Hold on, Indi. You're going to be okay. Just keep talking to me." I felt very sleepy then very cold, and I sensed the wall of people standing nearby watching and crying. I heard the big boss's voice. I heard the medical workers. Then I was no longer there.

They determined it was an accident. The brake on Rusty's van malfunctioned. It wasn't his fault and there will be no criminal charges. He may be able to sue the car manufacturer or the garage where he had his last tune-up. I don't feel the need to blame. I know these things happen. Bad fortune is as certain yet unpredictable as the weather.

I lie in bed and feel my phantom limbs, kick them into the air, practice the steps I was planning to try when Edgar asked me to dance at the Christmas party. These were moves I'd rehearsed with Soraya in our basement on many nights, the music turned low so the family above wouldn't complain. "He's going to fall in love if he hasn't already," Soraya told me. This Soraya was full of hope for my future. Soraya today only looks at me with wet eyes, shaking her head. "I knew you should have come to work with me at the bakery," she says. It's too late for such thoughts but I forgive her. I forgive everyone.

* * *

A guagua full of my Dominican friends from the fábrica comes to see me at the hospital. Edgar is among them but he hangs back. They've reduced my pain medications, sewn my stumps with thick black socklike seams at what used to be my thighs. I keep them covered when guests come because I realize most people can't handle the sight of my nubs, and still, their eyes drift to the flatness under the white hospital sheet. They take turns coming to my bedside and holding my hand. "We love you, gorda," they say. "We miss you so much on the packing line."

The Christmas party has already passed and they have the kindness not to mention it to me. Their faces are sad and I feel I must be the one to make them feel better.

"I'm not dead," I say. "They'll give me new legs and I'll be back on the line soon. I know it."

When Edgar comes to my side, the others clear the room so we can be alone.

"Indiana. I don't know what to say."

He holds my hand, or rather, I hold his. He is the one more in need of comforting. I hear the others whispering in the hall. It's not their fault they can't gauge their own volume. *It's such a tragedy*, someone says. *All that work she did to her body, and now this.*

My mother has already suggested this was some sort of punishment or retribution for the ways I've gone against nature to change my appearance. I was cheating God's design for me, she said, becoming vain, and I needed to be humbled.

My mind flashes with images of Edgar pushing me in my wheelchair, helping me stand on my new legs that actually make me taller, like a model or a beauty queen. I see us dancing together, me in my blue dress, Edgar shaved and glowing in a dark suit.

I tell Edgar a few lawyers have come to see me. They heard about my case and say I might be entitled to compensation. The factory's insurance company will surely want to settle because there should have been a safety rail or something protecting the entrance from incoming cars. One lawyer says I could get millions.

"We can take my new robot legs and travel the world," I tell Edgar.

He smiles. *I* would call it a smile, not counting the tears in his eyes.

"I have to go, Indi. They're all waiting for me. We have to get back over the bridge before rush hour. I'll come see you again on my own. I'll figure out which bus to take and come soon."

He kisses my forehead and I'm embarrassed because I know I've got the hospital stink even though the nurses bathed me in bed this morning and helped me brush my hair nice so it covers my shoulders. I would hug him, but my pelvis is in a cast and I can't shift my weight.

* * *

Arrangements have already been made for my mother to take me back to Cali with her once the doctors decide my body can handle the journey. The only thing we know so far is that there is nobody to care for me here, to help me with all the necessary things, the ugly things, going to the bathroom, learning to walk. I would have to go live in a special residential facility. Years of therapy await. A psychiatrist told me nightmares will come when it settles in that half of me is missing. But I will adapt, they say. All humans do.

They warn me not to get fat again because it will make it harder to walk on my new legs. Little did I know that by losing all that weight, I was getting myself into optimal condition for life as an amputee.

My mother says I should consider myself blessed. Not because I didn't die under the guagua, but because I might get some money out of the whole endeavor. "Just think how all those people back home who've had their limbs blown to bits by land mines have no such luck. Maybe you'll make friends with some of them," she says. "There are support groups for people like that. I saw it on the news."

This is her first time in this country. She has seen only the airport, the hospital, and the basement where Soraya takes her to sleep each night in my bed, pushed along the window near the good radiator. When she comes to the hospital to see me each morning, she says, without fail, she's almost grateful this accident happened because it's going to bring me back to Colombia with her.

She sits on a chair, thumbing the pages of a magazine she bought in the gift shop downstairs. She says she doesn't understand how I endured so many grim winters or what kept me here year after year. It's not the future she hoped for me. So many people come to this country with much less and accomplish so much more than I have with my little factory job. Why, for such a life, she wonders, did I try so hard to be beautiful?

I don't argue or try to explain. I want to save my words for Edgar. Maybe he will come see me tomorrow or the day after. I want to think of a funny joke or story to tell him so that when he looks at me his first thought is not tragedy. But my mind is tired. The doctors warned I would feel this way for a while due to the trauma on my body, the loss of blood. My mother asks if I can hear her. *Indiana, Indiana*, over and over. But I only roll my head toward the window. Through the glass, only brick in place of sky. ∎

THE IMAGE OF A DAY
Dipika Mukherjee

The sun is relentlessly hot all day under the blue skies of Andalusia, but the wind is cool, sifting through the stunted almond groves in the shadow of the mountains. The poplars tower over Nina's head, the sharp breeze through the leaves startling with a sound like clapping hands.

This is harsh country, with spiky flowers and the soil white under sharp cactus leaves. Nina pauses at the crest of the hill, where a pine shades enough of the ground to lay her rug. She takes a sip from the can of beer and looks up, checking for a processionary moth nest over this particular tree, something that she might inadvertently shake, releasing a mist to instantly blind her and asphyxiate her lungs.

This landscape looks benign, but needs constant vigilance.

The homestead shimmers white in the far distance, the only human dwelling in view. She is here for two weeks of uninterrupted thinking and writing and painting, which will, presumably, finally lead to something amazing. She published her last book on art history six years ago. Every day, she passes young people engrossed in work—the trio gathering wood shavings for an outdoor installation, the young woman coloring her canvas more detailed every day—and Nina thinks her own creativity has dried to a crust. All her inspiration is mired in the petty administrative emails she answers, careful not to give offence.

Once, Nina had dreamt of greatness. She had won fellowships and awards and travelled farther than any of her family, certainly farther than the men had gone. But all that was past glory, from a long time ago. So far, at this elite retreat, it has been nights of collegial dinners over red wine and piscatory meals. There is the constant commingling of ideas, yes, the cross-pollination of fertile minds, but Nina has abandoned one sketch and produced nothing new at all.

* * *

On her third night here, she sits under the stars with Ur from Amsterdam. Ur, who speaks halting English, is a professional photographer who could easily be on the other side of the camera for the advertorials she shoots to make the rent. Now in her early thirties, Ur wants to do something more meaningful. She is working on a project about women supporting other women . . . in intimate platonic settings . . . through the ages—she explains herself in a staccato burst of words, her thoughts as scrambled as her syntax.

Nina leans back, listening. She has never seen the sky lit up like this, as if someone perforated a blue bedspread with tiny needle points and is shining a torch down. She shakes empty the second bottle of wine and watches a star fall.

"I have never seen a falling star before."

"You will see more." Gently, Ur draws Nina's finger down. "We do not point at stars. I'm not sure, but something bad happens."

Nina feels wine coursing in her blood, warming the hand held by this beautiful stranger. Ur's blonde hair glows silver in the night.

"See that Ursa Major there? The upside down question mark? That's the only one I recognize. My father's favorite, he taught me for navigation. The top right star in the rectangle, see? That, it always points north."

Nina peers into the sky. "My people also navigated by the stars."

Ur sinks farther down on her seat. "It is beautiful, no? I am glad I come here, to this residency. To meet people like you who critic of my work, I mean, I don't just hear, *Well done, this is SO good!*"

Nina wonders whether she was open to criticism in her early thirties. In a small government college nestled in the foothills of the Himalayas then, she had such fantastic ideas every day, more ideas than the time to execute them. She painted the series *Unbowed*, a triptych of such importance that the National Gallery of Art had displayed it. She remembers the endless parties in Delhi, the asking and giving of favors.

Has she ever been open to criticism? She certainly is not open to it now, although she frequently dishes it out in her column on art.

She feels herself spiraling into sleepiness as Ur talks. "The male gaze . . . is a problem, yes, these women, and hierarchies of women, even in intimate settings, I am glad you said that, my work . . . the gaze . . . I was wondering . . ."

"That sounds awful! All I said, Ur, is that if you photograph young and beautiful women getting dressed or groomed and they are showing a lot of bare skin, it *could seem* voyeuristic. I mean, it could seem that way."

"Yes. But women also make women feel beautiful, no? We make other women beautiful in the way we see, sometimes notice small things that make a woman . . . special?"

"Of course. I just meant it'd be good to have a variety in your models. Ages, looks."

"I know! People want pay for me to shoot an advertorial on clothes, food. But no one—no one!—wants to give money to art project like this, no famous people here. So I ask my friends. Easy to get young models, shoot in exchange for pictures, for portfolio, you know? And the free pictures are young, really beautiful girls, they think they have a chance, only need portfolio. No older models. Not any—how you say it?—imperfect? So who, who will pose for my project?"

"Well," said Nina, "see what you can do when you are back in Amsterdam. Dutch women—all that biking around—you'll find someone real to shoot."

But Ur was looking at her steadily.

"How about you, Nina? You pose for me?"

"Me?"

"Why not? I do an aristocracy, like queen, at her bath, with maid. You are so tall, you have lovely skin, the hair, the eyes . . . I see you the first day and I think, she is a goddess."

"Hahaha! No!"

"Why not?

"I've never posed before!"

"That is the point? I want to show women at toilette, not like models, real women, with hair on legs and everything, with other women. You are perfect. Why not?"

And under the circumstances, Nina agrees. *Why not?*

* * *

Within these towering Andalusian mountains, in the ruins of an old Moorish castle nearby, there remains the remnant of a hammam. And it is here that Nina and Ur and the residency artists all gather the next day.

All nine of them.

The resident dog ambles along. The two other resident photographers act as light men and crew. Ur makes this into a lecture demonstration of her project and the young British lad from London is clearly smitten by it all.

Natalie, an artist from New Zealand, poses as the servant girl. She will wash Nina's hair. The portion of the hammam that is relatively intact is lit up and the tiles look less grey in the blinding light. A wooden chair is staged with a wooden bucket next to it, as well as a loofah and a bar of soap. Ur shifts pots of ferns to cover broken bricks and crumbling walls, then spreads a colorful sheet on the floor as a carpet at Nina's feet.

Everything is arranged and rearranged again, until it is just so.

Nina has worn a light white shift with spaghetti straps so that she can let down the top easily. The thought of being topless in this milieu starts to unnerve her (she had assumed that the only one seeing her topless would be Ur, who'd be behind the lens anyway). But now it is too late to back out; even the residency director is taking notes for his blog.

In this all-European cohort, her squeamishness at partial nudity seems ridiculous. They are all artists here, that's all.

Nina settles into the chair. She can hear Natalie asking questions about how long she needs to lather the hair before washing it, should the head massage be sensual, can she move around or should she stand at a precise photographic angle? Nina clutches at her bodice.

And then—inescapably—Ur gives the signal. She lets her bodice fall.

All the lights come on as Nina feels the cool air on her naked breasts. She leans far back and closes her eyes, not looking at her audience, and tries to relax, slopes her shoulders deliberately back, but all she can feel are her breasts rising.

She thinks of the frescoes at the Art Institute, where she now works. Those heavy-hipped women of temple art, with round breasts and firm nipples.

Then she feels Natalie gently pour the first mug of water, which cascades down her crown. There is the gentle pressure of warm fingers on her scalp, the smell of lavender soap, and Natalie's fingers playing a soft arpeggio though her head. She smells lemon and a whiff of mint. Natalie's fingers work their way to her neck and her head falls farther back.

She stops hearing the clicks of the camera or the soft shuffle of Ur's shoes or the swish of the other cameraman moving to different angles.

Natalie's fingers are magic. The thumbs are near her ears now, turning in little whorls of delight, while her other fingers scrape gently at her crown.

She is falling into a trance. Perhaps she will fall asleep.

Then, it is all over, too soon. Nina finds herself damp haired and cold. A robe is gently draped around her wet shoulders, covering her breasts again. Ur, in the opposite corner, gestures through a talk on the interstices of gender studies and art history. Everyone claps. They congratulate the trio on a fine performance, and people tell Nina she was fabulous.

Nina straightens the straps on her shoulder again and draws her arms around her torso.

* * *

Two days later, sitting on a mat in the stark sunlight, Nina is not so sure anymore. She opens the file to the pictures again. An immediate sense of pride—she really does look fabulous, especially at her age—

is followed by remorse. Her full breasts with the dark-brown areolas, her face reflecting that moment of uninhibited pleasure; how would people view these photos?

Her students? Her department?

Her family?

She wonders whether she can ask Ur to withdraw these pictures.

These beautiful, gorgeous pictures. They remind her of the iconic black-and-white pictures of naked men, work that she teaches.

The ancient hammam looks like a monument preserved in time, and the two women timeless. A slight smile lights up Natalie's face in shadow; she is worshipful. They are incandescent in the bright lights reflecting off the glittering tiles.

Ur had wanted to capture a powerful and mature woman in the prime of her life, like someone beloved of the caliph of this Moorish castle. Nina looks every inch the part.

Nina thinks of the women in the small town where she was born, her friends who cover their heads after marriage. Her friends who holiday in the South of France, but won't post their bikini-clad bodies on Facebook. She thinks about her teenage years, the times her mother clucked while tucking in a bra strap that was barely showing, or the way her sister would softly chant that her Sunday was longer than Monday if her slip was visible . . . the relentless ways her family signaled their discomfort with her female body.

So many ways in which she has been told to cover up—especially by other women. It is never enough. Her body can still be claimed by men in a street whistle, like a dog brought to heel.

She smiles at the pictures. She sees herself through Ur's eyes. There is a subtle artistry in the presentation of the pictures so that they are triptychs of repletion, a mature blossoming.

The sun crests into the mountains, streaking the sky with the palette of another glorious sunset. It is time to go. Nina looks at the pictures one more time, then puts them away.

There is no reason to change anything. ∎

CYCLIST BRAKING FOR TWO FOXES CROSSING A COUNTRY ROAD IN EARLY MORNING
Michael Collier

One first dashing, right to left, looking over its shoulder
then disappearing into a muddy farm yard.
The other following at an interval, dashing as well
but holding a creature in its mouth, like a black sock.
The world begins and the world ends.
The tube gorging the mouth of a friend in ICU is an umbilicus.
Her good arm and hand restrained.
The fox drops what it carried at the edge of the road.
It doesn't look back at the body whose wings
shouldered with bright red and yellow, unfold.
The bird's dead but the foxes crossed safely.
Dead space in the airway. We can hardly breathe
for what our mouths hold.

ORANGE
Cheryl Collins Isaac

In the peace of night, full of so much enduring
And of books I've read

> —*Fernando Pessoa, April 1934*
> *translated by Richard Zenith*

In the evenings, when the sky is a silvery blue, I sit at the Caneca de Prata, the Portuguese café below my Airbnb apartment, where they know me as "The American." I do not know their language, yet they bend their words to match mine. I no longer have to say "coffee with milk" in order to get a cup of *meia de leite* or a glass of *galão* placed before me. Today the waiter and owner ask me if tonight will be the night I will sleep well, or maybe go out with the group of American writers I came with. As usual, I shrug and smile. They laugh and walk to serve other guests, leaving me to my favorite table, where I will sit reading, drinking several cups of coffee, smoking, until they tell me that it is time to close shop.

Lisbon is a city that embodies an ordered disorder. Hail a cab from Rua da Prata and beware, the driver may come to a sudden stop in the middle of the street, just in front of the looming bus. The grocery store in the Chiado district may have decent prices, but the grocer charges ten cents for the grocery bag. The atmosphere in Lisbon is festive, the wine sweet and chilled, the sounds of violins from street artists pleasant—however, pickpockets linger with the crowd.

But in this tiny corner of wood-decorated chairs and benches, accessorized with blue-and-white Portuguese art, the smell of meat and coffee and beer interspersed, I have found some form of serenity.

* * *

Three generations of women in my family were forced to leave their homeland, and yet I do not come to terms with this until I am in Lisbon, immersed in the poetry of Fernando Pessoa.

It is as if the intensity of Lisbon is a pathway out of the tunnel of myself and into the openness of actualization. Lisbon places my life into context.

My Liberian American great-grandmother, Bertha Long Corbin, was forcibly exiled because, as editor of a Liberian newspaper, she dared report the truth about the former Liberian president and dictator William V. S. Tubman. After having lived more than twenty years in Liberia, she sought political refuge in America, the country of her birth.

Decades later, during the First Liberian Civil War, my Liberian mother was rescued by an international agency when she sought political asylum from the warlord who had taken her hostage. She became an exile in America.

I was nine years old when I was separated from my mother while she was held captive, and from my father while he (a member of the disgraced president's team) fled underground. I was hidden at a war shelter for children and displaced people at our church. When the international rescue agency finally helped my mother and me escape to America, I was a teenager seeking asylum from war, the daughter of political refugees (my father also a former diplomat for two dictators: Samuel Kanyon Doe and Charles Ghankay Taylor). I survived six years of war and now, I too am an exile.

I wander the streets of Lisbon alone at dusk, the most beautiful time of day, when the sky is a blanket of pale blue and silver hues, and my mind is a slate of the Portuguese poet Fernando Pessoa's verses from *A Little Larger Than the Entire Universe*, translated by Richard Zenith:

> And my peaceful, mean little home
> Sank with me into a deep silence . . .

My brand-new American passport secured within my waistband, I cope with the occasional bursts of cranial nerve pain by trying to think like Pessoa, in different versions of myself. This is the first time, since leaving war-torn Liberia, I have fought to quell anxiety and have gained enough courage to leave America, fly across the ocean alone to attend a conference for *disquiet* writers. I had been reading Pessoa for months, leaning into the feeling of his words, when my writing mentor told me about the conference that centers on Pessoa. I knew I had to find my way here. I carry Pessoa's books with me—all translated by Richard Zenith—*The Selected Prose* of Fernando Pessoa, *The Book of Disquiet*, and *A Little Larger Than the Entire Universe*.

In Lisbon, I am an entranced, disquieted exile. The feeling is novel. The feeling is profoundly painful, yet exhilarating.

* * *

After a morning of workshops and seminars, I visit the plaza merchants in the evening. The jewelry maker's table is set on the corner of Rua da Conceição, across the street from the river plaza. She calls me closer when she notices me viewing her pieces.

"Speak English?" she asks.

"Yes," I answer.

"Your eyes," she says, and then pauses to think of a description in English, "good eyes."

I smile. "Thank you."

"Every day. You write?" she asks, motioning to the notepad I carry. "I see you walk there," she nods towards the river.

I nod. We begin to chat.

I am here for the Disquiet International Literary Program, a conference that brings together eminent scholars and artists, emerging writers, Portuguese and American writers, and a blend of some of the most intriguing, free-spirited, and brilliant thinkers.

Writing poetry next to the river in the plaza is one of my favorite Lisbon pastimes, especially on the unusual day when the tide from the ocean is so high, the river flows over the borders, up the stairs, and settles around my feet.

In fragmented spurts of Portuguese intermingled with English, the seller offers to make me jewelry, telling me that orange will be a good color for me, something about a good omen for artists. I watch her steadied hands as she creates a gorgeous piece of jewelry from aluminum, and we both laugh when she advises me to clean it with baby wipes. While she twists the aluminum into intricate shapes and adds elegant stones of orange, she tells me that she is a cleaning woman during the day and an "artist only on weekends and holidays." She has a casual boldness that is intriguing. She smiles contently when she places the necklace on my neck.

The next evening I trace Fernando Pessoa's steps. I stroll next to a boutique on Rua Garrett, the street that runs next to Café A Brasileira, one of the cafés Pessoa frequented. When I stop to admire a dress, the seller immediately beckons. At first I shake my head no, immediately feigning disinterest, until I'm persuaded by the familiar expression on her face: a smile laden with sorrow, bright eyes seemingly joyful, quietly desperate.

She tells me that the dress on the mannequin looks like it suits me and the sales tactic makes me hesitate. Yet when she pulls the dress off the mannequin for me to try on, it fits perfectly. The bodice of the dress is cream-colored lace stitching, the bottom an orange-and-green fabric.

The dress has streaks of orange. The necklace from the previous seller is orange. Orange is citrus: bitter or sweet. Orange is the main fruit in Liberia. Orange is a river that flows through southern Africa. Orange is a color that becomes my accent in Portugal; a color that years later will have its dominant place in my home, work, and attire.

I do not know what to do with the elegant sundress, and I'm wondering about the price and if it is even my taste, when the owner starts to yell obscenities at the seller. Her words are a mixture of Portuguese and English, her immaculate makeup, pronounced jewelry, pencil skirt suit and chignon hairdo indications of classic, upper-echelon Portugal. But the words "fucking" and "fuck, fuck, fuck" are universal. The credit card machine is not operational and the owner-designer blames the "idiot" seller for this mishap. The woman, who looks to be my age (midthirties), explains that this is only her second day and she hasn't even been trained. The absurdity of it all makes me buy the dress from her. When she glances at the book I've just bought, *Raised from the Ground*, by José Saramago, the woman's smile widens. "Make sure you read *Death at Intervals* too," she whispers as she hands me the dress.

I picked up the book because of its political angle; because I have been reading and researching everything about Portugal's strained political past; because in order to come to terms with something my family refuses to speak about, I have to go outward.

Around 1955, my great-grandmother Bertha Long Corbin was editor in chief of the Liberian newspaper *The Independent* when it reported unfair election practices of the Liberian President William V. S. Tubman. She was jailed. Under the Tubman regime, journalists were frequently jailed and thrown into cells unfit for humans.

Bertha spent five months in a Liberian jail cell. I cringe each time I try to imagine what they could have done to her during that time. Fortunately, she was still an American citizen. The United States State Department intervened on her behalf. Left with no other choice, President Tubman had her deported to America with a warning: *Do not return.*

Her story seems to have paused there. In fact, whenever her name is brought up in family discussions, it is as if her existence also paused once she was exiled to America.

Bertha lived in American-influenced Liberia for over twenty-five years with her Liberian-born husband, my great-grandfather William A. Corbin. She was known for her razor-sharp rhetoric. As a writer, journalist, and frequent lecturer, great-grandma Bertha was a staunch defender of free speech, an advocate of the written word. And according to family, she was "mouthy."

What I know of her I have learned from Liberian and American archived newspapers, from whispered family discussions, through the history of the high school she cofounded in Liberia, now called the St. Augustine Episcopal Senior High School.

In my despondency I am drawn to her courage, her life of possibilities despite setbacks.

* * *

Next to my bed, Pessoa's *Book of Disquiet* is propped open so that occasionally, I glance over to find comfort in these words: "My soul is a secret orchestra, but I don't know what instruments—strings, harps, cymbals, drums—strum and bang inside me. I only know myself as the symphony."

Years ago, while recovering from war in America, I was diagnosed with trigeminal neuralgia, a chronic pain condition that affects the trigeminal nerve, which carries sensation from the face to the brain. The condition sends electric shocks of pain to the jaw, face, neck, forehead, and back of the head—everywhere connected to the trigeminal nerve. The disease is likely the psychological offspring of war trauma. The jolts resemble the rumble of war, when bombs would explode nearby and everything, even the very insides of a person, would turn to shards as darkness descended. Anxiety exacerbates the pain. Nightmares of war, of the dead people I saw, exacerbate the pain.

I understand Pessoa's use of heteronyms perhaps because I understand the significance of existing through heteronyms. This night I imagine my heteronym is a Maya or Alia, someone lofty, someone exalted, someone who is free-spirited because she is naïve about the tyranny of war, and certainly someone not to be messed with. She is someone who says "fuck off" so naturally the *k* flows into the *o* and forms a syllabic chant: *fuckoff.*

Fernando Pessoa writes with valorous and even slightly contemptuous heteronyms, or alter egos, because how else does one keep the world at arm's length? What better way to say fuck off? I like to think that he lived inwardly, viewing everything on a microscopic level that some call eccentric. His heteronym Alberto Caeiro is my favorite, not only because he writes with a Whitmanian flow, but because he views the world simplistically, and by doing so, he makes life's complex travails seem simple, as in this excerpt from XXI:

> What matters is to be natural and calm
> In happiness and in unhappiness…

When one sees things as they are, without reasoning, one avoids cataclysmic ruminations. Even when the inner self is emotional chaos, Pessoa believed that an even-keeled mannerism should always prevail.

* * *

In Portugal I feel a strange serenity as I discover Pessoa's city through poetry, as if my disquiet has been relegated to allow me the perspective I need to write these words. The wave of panic settling into the dungeon of me slowly dissipates with the turning of each page.

Fernando Pessoa is the writer you love because you understand him or you hate because you cannot grasp his eccentric undertones. His cosmos is an abstruse one, one I immediately found relatable the moment I encountered *The Book of Disquiet*.

Pessoa did not belong and he did not seem to mind.

Pessoa's early years of childhood in Lisbon were marked with death and abandonment. At five years old, he lost his father and brother. Shortly after, his mother left him with relatives when she moved to South Africa to remarry. He was around seven years old when he joined his mother and stepfather in South Africa, where he came of age. At age seventeen, he found himself back in Lisbon. It is possible he never recovered from this involuntary estrangement of place that sometimes causes a person to live a multidimensional existence, wherein self becomes elusive, because wherever one goes, one is never good enough to fit in. From his work, it is evident that Pessoa wrote to discover himself, to create his own world and identity.

Subconsciously, I've chosen the evenings to study his work: Pessoa and I daily, next to the river that runs by Lisbon's Story Centre; Pessoa and I, dinner dates at restaurants along Rua da Prata, the street where Pessoa, a disheartened employee, worked and wrote *The Book of Disquiet*; Pessoa on me, the pages of his *Disquiet* resting on my breasts as I sleep to the opened-window sounds of Lisbon's nightlife. I read him constantly, three books stuffed into my backpack as I walk around, thousands of words glued to my brain.

Those words bandage the neuralgia that torments me. When the shock-like waves of pain start, my head becomes that once-darkened Liberian city called Monrovia, lit only by flashes of light when bombs land; my teeth grind and grate like war tanks on cement, my face is hammered by gunfire, and my skull feels as if it is being blasted by bazookas. I carry the burden of an entire city in my head. Since I cannot speak and can barely swallow, I disappear into agony explained in black and white—*The Book of Disquiet*.

After she was exiled, my great-grandmother was a sought-after speaker in America. In an article written by her in *The Warren County Observer*, published on August 22, 1961, she'd hoped that America, which helped found Liberia, would learn the true story about the "sorry mess" in Liberia and intervene—she was referring to the dictatorships that were forming. Liberia was the "key to the present situation in Africa," she said, and the one place the "United States has both the opportunity and obligation to exert its influence constructively." Without American intervention, there would be wars or a coup in Liberia, she warned, even insinuating that a Liberian war would set a flame of wars in Africa. She was right. The African wars that followed the Liberian Civil War of the 1990s were cataclysmic and would affect two generations of women in her family.

* * *

One of my favorite Pessoa poems is "Un Soir à Lima," one I enjoy reading outdoors to the hums of cicadas. It is a simple, melancholic song of a lost place and time:

> Nostalgia for what was—
> It all lives in me

The country of my birth was uprooted and transformed and in Lisbon, I have decided that this is not a good or bad thing. It just is. Nostalgia for the childhood I had before war lives and always will live in me. But in Portugal I soon realize that those good childhood memories are pure enough to disinfect the painful memories of war.

Bertha Long Corbin never returned to Liberia alive, but she asked that her remains be buried there. I'm not sure Pessoa ever returned to South Africa, where he spent his formative years. And as I write this, nineteen years after leaving the land of my birth, I wonder when I will return.

Could Pessoa have written in heteronyms because somehow he struggled with the displacement he'd encountered as a child? I ask something like this of Richard Zenith, Pessoa's eminent scholar, as he discusses his translations during one of the conference's seminar at Casa Fernando Pessoa, Portugal's elite literary club. I watch him read and lecture, observing his relaxed posture, that of an elegant, articulate thinker, and I wonder how he would have fared, meeting Pessoa in person. Would they have been good friends?

Zenith does not have an answer for Pessoa's psyche. No one really does. Somehow, this is a relief, this lack of an explanation for the oddity of the psyche—all one can truly know of a person is what he or she leaves on the page. And some stories, some thoughts, some truths, *should* be left on the page.

In Lisbon, I fall asleep to these words from *The Book of Disquiet*: "I am, in large measure, the selfsame prose I write. I unroll myself in sentences and paragraphs, I punctuate myself."

Calmness has taken residence in me. The room soothes with bursts of orange: an orange throw, orange jewelry, orange shirt and dress, books with orange covers, orange sandals. Orange replaces the pain in my cheeks and skull.

Instead of nightmares, I dream of my great-grandmother Bertha Long Corbin. She is sitting comfortably in a white dress. There is a book in her hand; it has an orange cover. She is smiling. I sense assurance; I sense she wants me to write to find my truth, to find my family's truth.

And when I wake the next morning, Pessoa's words linger:

I punctuate myself. ■

LIBERTÉ
Scott Nadelson

In order to devote herself wholly to art, Louise Nevelson—born Leah Berliawsky—has left her marriage of thirteen years. She's been drawing and painting since childhood, but at thirty-four she's hardly more than a novice. She has never had a show of her work, has not yet discovered her medium. It will be many years before she's famous for her massive monochromatic assemblages, considered a queen of modern sculpture. Famous, too, for her bold style—colorful headscarves and enormous fake eyelashes—and brash, uninhibited speech. When asked, in her late sixties, how she's maintained such vitality for so long, she'll reply, Why, lots of fucking, of course.

In the early summer of 1933, however, she's both unknown and relatively inexperienced with men. Since separating from her husband, Charles, a shipping executive whose family has oppressed her since their wedding—wealthy and cultured Jews who cherish art and music but laugh at those who dream of making it—she's had only one affair. Her lover was another American businessman, whom she met on her first crossing to Europe a year ago, her first, that is, since emigrating from Russia at six years old. And though the newness of the affair excited her, as well as its illicit charge—the businessman was married, his wife joining him in several weeks—she found sleeping with him largely dispiriting. Like Charles, he was overly solicitous, asking constantly after her comfort. With both she has just barely glimpsed what she guesses to be the dark and thrilling possibilities of sex, the struggle and near violence of it, terror and triumph outweighing simple pleasure.

She found her three months in Berlin, chaste while studying with Hans Hofmann, far more rewarding than those hours naked in a stranger's cabin. And so now she decides to make another trip, this time planning to spend several months in Paris to learn contemporary technique. So at least she has told herself, though a part of her knows she may never return to New York. She will do whatever she must to become the artist she has long believed herself capable of becoming, no matter the sacrifices.

* * *

About leaving Charles, she feels little remorse. She was always honest with him, and he knew what she wanted when they married. If he didn't believe her when she confessed her ambition, that is his fault, not hers. He acquiesced to the separation with little argument, though she knows he is hoping she will soon come to her senses and return to him. Or more likely, that she will find it too difficult to survive on her own, that his money, if not his love and loyalty, will draw her back. But unlike her shipboard lover, whose manufacturing interests were only mildly affected by the crash, Charles may not have money for long. His family's business has suffered enormous losses over the past four years and is now on the verge of collapse. More than her own survival, she fears for his. What will Charles do with himself if he can no longer spend his time tracking shipments and accounts? What purpose will guide his days?

Any discomfort caused by deserting her husband, however, is minor compared to the guilt she carries over abandoning her son. Myron—who prefers to be called Mike—is nine years old and bewildered by the changes thrust upon him. Last summer she sent him to stay with her parents in Maine, and though she tried to tell herself he'd be perfectly happy there, her mother spoiling him with her baking, her father, a builder, teaching him to how to frame a house, she nevertheless imagined him smothered by the same boredom that had driven her to marry the first wealthy man she met, when she wasn't yet twenty-one. At the time, Charles lived on the twelfth floor of a building on Riverside Drive, and she believed it was the city she was marrying as much as the man, the opportunities such a move would afford her. If she'd known he would soon pack her off to the suburbs, to be surrounded by his brothers and sisters-in-law and cousins, who would judge every word she spoke, she would have refused his offer instantly, or so at least she tells herself now.

She agonizes over Mike, and yet the thought of her own suffocation were she to stay overwhelms all others. She books her passage and sends her son back to Maine.

* * *

The ship, a single-class steamer bound for Le Havre, is called *Liberté*. A fitting name, she thinks, though worries about Mike's unhappiness keep her from feeling terribly free until the second evening out from New York, when she meets a handsome Frenchman, a doctor named Destouches. Louis Ferdinand Destouches. He says the name as if she might recognize it, and when she doesn't, shrugs to confirm she couldn't possibly.

This takes place in the ship's narrow dining room. When she enters, most tables are already occupied by families and large parties of young people traveling together. Those few passengers on their own wander the edges, looking for friendly faces. She finds herself seated with five strangers, all men. More Americans on business, two disembarking in Portsmouth, another traveling on to Frankfurt. The remaining two are heading to Paris, and before the entrée is served, both have offered to take her to dinner there, or to a show. All five laugh at her jokes, and the two closest to her pour wine into her glass as soon as she empties it. They smile feral smiles as she unwraps her stole to reveal athletic shoulders— she was captain of her high school basketball team, as well as its sole Jew—and a long neck. The most attractive of them has bits of bread stuck between his teeth, the tallest unappealingly bushy eyebrows. One of the others—she can't tell which—smells ripely of sweat.

The Frenchman approaches just as the meal ends. When she stands, he takes her hand lightly and releases it before introducing himself. His accent is so thick she has a hard time understanding what he says. But she thinks he tells her she has the appearance of an artist, the only one on the entire ship. He is sloppily dressed but fierce looking, with a large head, dark hair combed back from a widow's peak, prominent cheekbones, dazzling blue eyes. He's an inch or two shorter than all the other men, but the low tones of his voice and his way of leaning forward as he speaks diminishes them. He is bold yet nervous, fidgeting with his tie as if it chokes him, and after saying a few more words she can't make out, gives a nod, shuffles backward, and disappears into the crowd exiting the room.

One of her dinner companions suggests stepping outside to look at stars, but she excuses herself, says the wine has made her dizzy. In her cabin she studies a picture of Mike, dapper in a tuxedo, though dour, taken just before attending a concert with Charles's insufferable relatives. Later, when most people are asleep and the passageways are quiet, she does go out on deck. The stars are hidden behind clouds she can't see. Beyond the ship's lights, everything is black. She can't distinguish ocean from sky.

* * *

She spots the Frenchman again the next day, soon after lunch. He is seated in a cardroom in which the tables have all been moved to one side. A thin, stooped man stands next to him, handing out books to people waiting in line. The Frenchman, Destouches, signs them, hands them back with a little dip of his head, unsmiling. She learns from another passenger—a sharp-faced Parisian who looks at her with disdain, as if in not knowing already she is either ignorant or mad—that in addition to being a doctor, he is also a novelist whose first book was published to great acclaim some months earlier, called a masterpiece by many critics, herald of a new French literature, one more raw and honest and free than any previous. He writes under a pen name, Céline, in tribute to his grandmother. He is returning home after traveling to California in hopes of having the book made into a film. Will it be? Louise asks, but the woman shakes her head. Cowards, she says. Communists. The producers were warned before he arrived, alerted to his political leanings, and as a result they all declined. What those political leanings are, the woman doesn't say.

Céline. Once Louise hears the name she can't connect him with any other. She doesn't stand in line for a book and doesn't think he has seen her before she walks away. But when she arrives for dinner, he is waiting for her. His slender companion hands her two copies of the novel. In one is just his signature, he says, in the other a special inscription. The book is thick, at least five hundred pages, and heavy, and to hold two she must use both hands. The simplicity of its cover appeals to her. White, with red and black type, no image. She likes the sound of the title, too, but knows enough French only to decipher *voyage* and *de la nuit*. A voyage of the night strikes her as both mysterious and enticing. The meaning of *au bout* she will have to do without.

The slender companion vanishes, and Louise joins Céline at his table. He speaks quickly, with vehement gestures, and again she misses many of his words. He jumps from topic to topic, but always follows a central thread: the essential corruption of humanity, the yearning for filth even among the most so-called refined of society—he mutters this while jutting his chin at a well-dressed couple across the table—which itself is a cesspool, needing to be emptied and scoured. Everything he says is bitter and morose, and yet there's a charm in his passionate insistence, a relief after so many years of listening to Charles and his relatives speak with mild disinterest about even those things they claim to value most. He stares at her as if he will soon pounce and clamp his jaws around her neck. She wants to hear him say more about how he recognized her as an artist just by looking at her, but for now he talks only about himself, about his family, his mother who traveled house to house selling liniments and herbal remedies so he could study legitimate medicine.

I'm peasant stock, he tells her. Last of a line. When you have a head like mine, you know you've reached the end.

After the meal, she expects him to invite her for a drink, maybe at one of the ship's several bars or maybe in his cabin. And she is prepared to accompany him to either. Instead he delivers his nervous bow, tells her how much he has enjoyed their conversation, asks if they might continue to talk tomorrow. His companion has reappeared, bony and silent, and the two of them hasten below deck. In her cabin, she flips through his novel, unable to read any of it. Like the text, the inscription is in French, the handwriting loose and rumpled like his suit, and she can make out only a handful of simple words: *bien* and *au* and *courage*. Another looks like *ravissant*, but she can't be sure. The image of Charles comes to her for no reason she can imagine, taking off his trousers and carefully folding them before joining her in bed. She has a headache but cannot sleep. She goes upstairs, finds a bar, orders a whiskey on ice, and interrogates the bartender about which cocktails he enjoys mixing most and why.

* * *

The crossing takes seven days, and a part of four she spends with Céline. At times they sit on deck, enjoying sun and a light breeze. On a stormy day, both are mildly seasick and huddle on velvet sofas in a deserted lounge, where Céline smokes to calm his stomach and Louise drinks to settle hers. He still asks nothing about her life, why she's traveling to Paris, what sort of art she hopes to produce, but she takes his silences as opportunities to tell him about her failed marriage, her previous work with Hofmann, her plans for the summer. If I like it, perhaps I'll stay, she says. She does not mention Mike, though almost immediately a vision of him springs to mind, standing on the shore of Rockland, staring out over the ocean into which his mother has disappeared. Céline, brooding or nauseated, says nothing.

Later, when the sea has calmed and they have returned to the deck, he tells her that Paris is a toilet, full of nothing but thieves and con artists, and yet compared to America it's an oasis, a place where you can speak your opinions freely and not fear reprisal. She recalls what the woman said about Hollywood producers and wonders what opinions scared them off. It's the only place to live, he goes on, a disgusting city but an honest one, where all depravity is on display. He has seen it firsthand, patients coming to him with wounds from scuffles, with horrifying sexual diseases, everything left to fester because all have been contaminated by the pestilence of contemporary life.

Every time he mentions his work as a doctor, she is surprised anew. Afterward she quickly forgets how he makes his living. It's as if the information won't stick in her mind, crowded out by the heft of his novel. Or maybe it's because she can't imagine going to him for medical attention. With those harsh, inward-focused eyes and large hands with blunt fingers, how could he possibly ease someone's suffering?

As if she has spoken the question aloud, he says, waving a hand, It's mostly pointless, this whole, how you say, enterprise. He heals those he can, but soon enough they are ground up again by the machinery of decadence, of the world going to rot. In times like these, he goes on, who should rise to the surface, like shit floating on a flooded river? Yes, the Jew, the bottom-feeder, thriving on the foulness and decay of a poisoned culture, poisoning it further, until those few left with dignity must burn everything down and plant new seeds in the ashes.

His face is flushed as he speaks, flecks of spittle at the edges of his lips, and yet his voice remains calm, with the lilt of amusement. When he finishes, he smiles and apologizes, not for his sentiments, but for his mixed metaphors. Louise tries not to reveal anything by her expression, though she can't help leaning away. Surely he knows what she is, if not from her features, then from her name. And yet he keeps staring at her with the same hunger, the same ferocious need. Only now he is finally ready to act on it. He moves toward her, sweeps an arm across her shoulders, bends to kiss her. She turns away, swivels out of his grasp, hurries inside without looking back.

But for the rest of the day she is less horrified than fascinated. It's an important discovery, she thinks, a profound one: that someone can detest what he desires or desire what he detests. Which comes first, the wanting or the loathing, she doesn't know.

* * *

On the last day of the voyage, she takes her meals in her cabin and does not encounter Céline again before the ship docks for the last time. She doesn't see him on the train from Le Havre and learns from the sharp-faced woman that he disembarked at Cherbourg. She assumes that will be the end, she won't hear from him again. But he soon contacts her in Paris, sends a note to her hotel, invites her to lunch. He does not apologize for what he has said, nor for trying to kiss her afterward, does not acknowledge their last meeting in any way. His note is brief and self-deprecating. *Dear Miss Nevelson*, he writes in English. *By now you must have been married over and over again. What passion will be left for me?* During the summer she sees him once, and though he flatters her with compliments, he is otherwise distracted and distant, avoiding all serious topics. She finds herself both relieved and dejected when they part. He kisses both her cheeks lightly, the smell of tobacco lingering until she is well down the street.

Later, she learns from an acquaintance that she is not Céline's first American infatuation. He once lived with a girl from California, with similarly strong shoulders and elegant neck. Not long ago, this girl returned to the States and married, leaving Céline heartbroken. To find that she served as someone's replacement is less insulting to Louise than sad. She pictures Céline entering the ship's dining room, scanning the tables for a passable likeness. She imagines Charles similarly scouting for someone new in the lobby of a theater or the reception hall of his synagogue, someone who will both remind him of what he has lost and help him forget.

Her time in Paris is, on the whole, disappointing. She sees much artwork that moves her, attends parties, has many flirtations. But the mood is generally bleak. Too many people are out of work. There are fears of more antiparliamentarist demonstrations like the one in February that left fifteen dead. She considers returning to Berlin, where she was so much happier last summer, but she meets a number of German artists and musicians and writers who have fled since Hitler became chancellor, all of whom warn her to stay away. Hofmann, she learns, has left, too, emigrated to New York. So why has she come at all?

Mostly, though, her disappointment is personal rather than political. Her friendships feel shallow. The prospect of establishing a career in Europe seems more daunting the longer she stays and the more she sees. Here the tree of modern art is massive, with many limbs, thick and healthy and intimidating. She could be no more than a small leaf, clinging desperately to a twig. But at home, in the country Céline described as a swamp of naiveté and repression, she might grow to be a branch, or perhaps, with enough effort, a part of the trunk.

She visits Chartres, Versailles. Depressed, she travels to the Riviera, sleeps with a sailor in Nice, and boards a ship home from Genoa. She arrives just as summer ends, when Mike is due back in school, and pretends this has been her plan all along.

* * *

To her surprise, Céline writes to her in New York. They begin an extended correspondence, the strangest of her life, part seduction, part debasement. He invites her to come live with him in Italy, or perhaps he will move to America, even if it is a reeking bog, filled with the dregs of the earth—though now that Germany is being purged, he writes, France, too, is overrun with slime. Why she puts up with these letters she doesn't know, except that they captivate her, so many contradictions on display. Or perhaps she is simply lonely, longing for any interest to distract her from the sight of her empty bed.

By then she has settled into an apartment on Fifteenth Street and Third Avenue. It's a large space though spartan, with a bedroom for Mike and a studio for herself. While Mike is in school, she spends her mornings painting. She takes classes at the Art Students League, with

Hofmann again, and George Grosz, both of whom are shaken by their flight from the darkness that has so quickly consumed their home country. She wishes she could offer them some comfort, but their distress puts her off, makes her keep her distance. She wants only to admire them, see them as great men, full of wisdom and fortitude they can pass on to her. She tells neither about her exchanges with Céline.

When Diego Rivera comes to New York to work on several commissions, she is enlisted to help paint one of his murals, not the monumental *Man at the Crossroads* at Rockefeller Center, but a smaller one called *The Workers*, close to her apartment. She is in awe of Diego, approves of his appetites. His second wife, Lupe, shows up at one of the many parties he throws, kisses everyone, dances with her eyes closed. She is beautiful, though less mesmerizing than his current wife, Frida, still in her twenties and shy, though with a calm poise that makes Louise forget she's almost a decade older. Both women smell faintly of semen when they hug her goodbye. She doesn't think Diego loves them so much as he feeds on them. They set flame to his passions, stoke his painting. If she weren't afraid of draining what little fuel she has for her own work, she might offer up her heat to him as well.

Instead she begins to experiment with sculpture, plaster figures painted in primary colors. They don't satisfy her, except that she can feel herself searching for form, knows for the first time that she will eventually find it. She shows pieces in group exhibitions, but galleries turn her away. She occasionally considers throwing herself out a window, but her studio is on the first floor, the sidewalk only ten feet below the sill.

* * *

Céline's letters increasingly confuse her. After Hindenburg's death and Hitler's ultimate ascent to power, he writes sincere condolences, saying he hopes any friends or relatives she has in Germany have managed to escape—and if not, that he may be able to help with arrangements. But then he castigates the French government for accepting refugees, whose stink pervades the air whenever he walks through the streets. Sometimes she doesn't respond for months, and then he pleads with her not to abandon their friendship: it is too important to him, he writes, she is the only woman in his life who is both beautiful and intelligent, and knowing such a possibility exists has been crucial to maintaining any hope for a world so deeply mired in excrement.

And then he visits her in New York. When he calls, Mike is in school, and she doesn't hesitate to invite him to her apartment. She gives him coffee, and he sits across from her, smoking, smiling a pained smile. She wears a loose dress, with a low neckline and no sleeves. She has downed a tumbler of whiskey and left the door to her bedroom open. She thinks, I am free to do whatever I please. She can gratify herself or harm herself as she chooses. There is no one to stop her, no one to judge. Céline leans forward, elbows on knees. His voice is low, desperate. How would you like to marry me? he asks.

She thinks she ought to laugh but doesn't. She knows he is serious. She pictures Charles again, when he proposed at her parents' house in Rockland, when she was just a girl yearning for the promise of city life. She thinks of the brutality of that sailor in Nice, the hammering of his huge body that both unnerved and enthralled her. She sees shit floating in a swollen river. Which is worse, she wonders, the fanatic who wants what he hates or the one who wants what hates her?

After the war she will read about him in *LIFE* magazine. Collaborator. Nazi spy, propagandist. She will learn about the vile pamphlets he has authored, calling for the extermination of all Jews in France. She will tell those friends who knew of their correspondence that she is appalled, disgusted. She will give away the books he inscribed for her, toss his letters into the fireplace. She will regret doing so, not right away, but later, after Mike has grown up and moved out, while working on the first of the many walls of black boxes for which she will become known around the world, filled with arrangements of found wooden blocks and cylinders that suggest the messy intricacies of mind and heart. She will think he was one of the few who understood her, because, like her, nothing could ever appease him. And she'll think, I wasn't ready then.

You know, dear, she says now. You would be worth more dead than alive to me.

She isn't quite sure what she means by it. But he doesn't object, just nods, shows his woeful smile, finishes his coffee and cigarette. At the door, he tells her not to worry, she has all the strength she needs to thrive, he glimpsed it in their very first encounter. But then he asks, as he steps into the hall, Is this a world worth thriving in?

Before she can answer, he's gone. ∎

THE HEALER
Harry Mark Petrakis

W hen I was twelve years old, illness shattered my life.
There had been ominous signs for months that something was wrong with me. After school, when other youths were playing, I needed to rest. On weekends, when other boys and girls were eager to begin their days of leisure, I remained in bed until early afternoon.

There were other symptoms. My appetite declined and I lost weight. Fatigue made it difficult for me to concentrate, and my schoolwork suffered. At the end of the school year, I failed to advance to the next grade.

My mother took me to our family physician. Dr. Javaras was a skinny figure in his ill-fitting white coat, his stethoscope dangling from his hairy ears as he listened intently to my chest. He ordered X-rays, which revealed ugly lesions the size of silver dollars on both my lungs.

The doctor's gloomy face and somber voice explaining my condition to my mother did not augur well for my survival. He urged that I be sent for a minimum of a year to a sanitarium in the mountains of Colorado.

My father worked eighteen hours a day, struggling to survive on the meager earnings from his lunchroom. A sanitarium was an expense he could not afford.

The alternative, Dr. Javaras cautioned my parents, with a fifty-fifty chance I might not survive, was total bed rest for an indeterminate period of time in hopes the lesions might heal.

I received the doctor's prescription with glee. I would be spared the tedious hours at school, liberated from doing chores at home and freed from attending church on Sundays.

After a few weeks of being bedridden, however, my days and nights in bed bred boredom and a growing hopelessness.

During those days I had spent in school, my mother had worked as a waitress in my father's lunchroom. My confinement required she remain at home to take care of me. My father had to hire a waitress to work in my mother's place, further reducing the meager income the lunchroom provided. I was aware my illness was causing my family financial hardship and that added to my wretchedness.

For the first few months of my confinement, friends of my mother volunteered to help look after me. After a while they wearied of my growing irritability and their unpaid labor and gave up. Once again, my mother had to leave her work at the restaurant to stay at home.

At the beginning of my second year of confinement, a social worker visiting my parents informed them about a program whereby seventeen- and eighteen-year-old girls living in a city orphanage could be granted leave to live with a family. In return for receiving food, shelter and clothing, the girls would be expected to provide the family some assistance. My parents applied, and the orphanage approved a girl moving in with us to look after me.

For the following year, I was tended by a series of girls who lived with us and cared for me during those hours my mother worked in the lunchroom. A cot was placed at the foot of my bed, so the girls could also attend my needs during the night.

There was Celestina, who was small and petite and who had a gentle touch. She was also frail and lasted only a few weeks.

For a four-month period there was Mary Louise, a plump blond girl, soft fleshed and pretty, who smelled of assorted powders and colognes. Mary pampered me and for the first time I felt the proddings of early love.

There was Crystal, a shrewish girl with a sharp temper. For a minor infraction on my part, she slapped me, and when I wet my bed, she whipped my buttocks with a clothes hanger. Afterwards, she warned me of a more severe beating if I told my parents. Fear kept me silent until an evening when my mother, changing my pajamas, discovered the welts on my buttocks. My mother angrily berated Crystal and dismissed her.

Then, at the beginning of my second year of confinement in bed, Olga came to live with us. She was nineteen, a year or two older than the other girls.

Olga was an unattractive girl, her cheeks pocked from early smallpox. She had short, stringy hair. Her bulky body and big, strong hands belonged more to a man than a girl.

As if her ungainly body and homely face were not burden enough, Olga also had a clubfoot, a misshapen appendage that knotted her toes and twisted her ankle so far sideways, she seemed to be treading on her own foot.

As a consequence of her deformity, in place of walking, Olga lurched forward and back, her breathing labored and hoarse.

The first time my mother saw Olga, she was repelled. Olga was aware of her reaction.

"Give me a chance, missus," Olga pleaded. "Don't send me back to that place! See how strong I am!" Olga clasped me around the waist and, holding me in one arm, effortlessly swung me off the floor.

"Missus, give me a chance!"

My mother was a compassionate woman and that evening I heard her tell my father, "I could hardly look at the poor soul, but I felt sorry for her too, so I felt we should give her a chance."

In the weeks that followed, I was fascinated by Olga's strength. She picked me up and put me down as easily as if I were an infant. When she held me in her arms, I was excited by my total helplessness. I watched in admiration at how her big hands and muscled arms effortlessly flipped my mattress. I was also soothed by how tenderly Olga treated me. She stroked my cheek, rubbed my arms and fondled my back. Sitting on the side of my bed, she would pull me onto her lap, holding me so tightly I could feel the pounding of both our hearts.

"You are going to grow up to be a handsome man," she said quietly. "You'll have many girls chasing you."

"Will you chase me, Olga?"

"I'll be an old woman by then," Olga sighed.

During the next few weeks, I looked forward each night to Olga's massage. I would lie naked on the bed while she applied lotion to my shoulders, thighs and legs. I savored her strong hands dominating my body.

As time went on, Olga's hands began to linger on parts of my body, and the massage for me became more of a caress. I lay still, fearful of saying or doing anything that would make Olga stop.

One afternoon, Olga gave me a long massage, her hands moving slowly across my stripped body. I felt tense and excited. When she finished the massage, I did not put my pajamas back on but climbed naked under my blanket. I stared silently at Olga.

"Why are you looking at me like that?" she asked.

"Come into bed with me," I said.

"Don't be naughty or you'll get a spanking!"

"Please, Olga," I pleaded. "Just for a little while."

Olga looked at me for several minutes in silence. She seemed to be struggling, and then stiffly and awkwardly she began undressing. When she had stripped down to her cotton panties and brassiere, she hesitated.

"That's enough," she said.

"Take everything off, please, Olga, so you'll be naked like me!" My voice held a plea.

Olga stared down at me for a moment, her cheeks flushed. She reached back slowly and unhooked her brassiere. For the first time I saw her naked breasts, pale and shapely, her nipples like big, dark grapes. I realized her breasts were the only part of her body that was beautiful.

"Please, Olga . . . please."

She stared at me nervously for a moment and then tugged down her panties. I saw the smooth flesh of her belly sloping down to a patch of hair between her legs.

Totally naked, she scrambled under the blankets beside me. As our naked bodies huddled against one another, both of us giggled like children playing a wicked game.

In the next few weeks, every afternoon when my mother was at the restaurant, Olga and I would lie naked together in the bed. In the beginning, our caresses were timid. As we both grew bolder, I rubbed her thighs, stroked her legs, felt the ridge of her abdomen . . . my fingers fumbling at the wisp of hair between her legs.

Olga stroked my arms, shoulders and chest . . . at times gently, at other times roughly. She led my hands to her breasts, pressing her nipples into my palms. We became familiar with every hill and cranny of our bodies. When Olga fondled my genitals for the first time, I felt my body burn like fire.

We kissed often, at times her lips gentle, our tongues tasting one another. At other times, Olga seemed to become angry, her mouth so rough against my mouth, her teeth biting my lip, and I tasted blood.

For the duration of that summer Olga and I played our game. When I first opened my eyes to daylight, my thoughts were of Olga and the delight ahead. We caressed during the day while my parents were at work and late at night when my parents were asleep. Both of us naked, we'd lie side by side. I delighted simply looking at her as well as touching her. I came to know which caress pleased her the most. She became familiar with those caresses that pleased me. Even after I slept, in my dreams we continued to make love, our bodies pressed so tightly together, our limbs seemed to fuse into a single body.

And then in the fulsome joy of our loving, I woke late one morning, and Olga was gone. My frantic questions to my mother went unanswered. For weeks I dreamt of Olga and cried in my sleep.

To this day I don't know if my mother found out and drove her away or whether some prodding of guilt about loving a child prompted Olga to leave.

A lifetime has passed since my boyhood. I am an old man now.

I have been married four times and divorced the same number. Our unions have produced nine children, seventeen grandchildren and twenty-one great-grandchildren. Our family gatherings are crowded and festive, my grandchildren and great-grandchildren sitting on my lap and at my feet. I love them all.

None of my divorces were the fault of my wives, but of my own erratic and restless nature. In all these years, I have had few days or nights when I felt fully at peace.

Looking back across the long span of my years, no memory remains with me as vividly as those nights in my childhood when I nestled beside Olga. Her homeliness, her misshapen club foot and her masculine body meant nothing. I thought her beautiful. Even as a child, I understood that all the love she hungered for and couldn't have, she lavished upon my young body.

I know that in the times we live now, Olga would be labeled a pedophile, a child molester, someone to be jailed for her abuse of a child. That is not how I remember her.

After all these decades, I can still feel the warmth of her powerful arms embracing me, her hands caressing my shoulders, my chest, arms and thighs, her fingers fondling that most intimate part of me.

Bearing the magical power of a nymph born of myth, Olga brought to my boyhood the powerful emotions of desire and love. ∎

SUPERSTAR
Christopher Todd Anderson

July evenings, waves of fireflies drifted across childhood, floating
over my backyard and Mr. Krebbs's hay field, seeking mates.
They flickered like star-sparkle on night's humid black ocean.

The neighbor boys, Ricky and Hunter Smith, Jared Leominster,
Kevin Keeley and a few others, bored by twilight too dark
for Wiffle ball, smashed lightning bugs with plastic bats:

blobs of bioluminescence smeared the barrels and kids rubbed it,
that amber glimmer, onto cheeks and foreheads like war paint,
where it glowed a few minutes, then dimmed and disappeared.

The shy kid, the bookish one, I felt sad for the fireflies, sad
for living beauty walloped into oblivion for boredom, for nothing,
for an adolescent buzz of power. I didn't say anything, just moped

and watched the older boys take their bats to moths and junebugs
and each other, then went inside early for TV or whatever. Truth is,
I'm ashamed to admit, I too thumped fireflies dead with a blue

Little Slugger. Alone in the dark, I daubed their soft yellow afterlight
onto my lips and eyelids and chin, imagining, I guess, that I was
angel or starman or Icarus in drag, some glowworm superstar
who could rise like moonlight over lonely Indiana nights.

JACK AND ROSE IN SAN MIGUEL
Christina Drill

I thought I saw Pleiades when I first opened the door to Sophie's flat in San Miguel, a beam of light or small-boned thing darting around the corner diagonal to the door and out onto the terrace. After I napped and regained a moral understanding of the mess I'd made at home, I walked around the border of the apartment with my finger on the lip of some cat food, and I started to worry. What if Pleiades had fallen off the limestone wall that distanced the house from the street and, having already moved on to its second life, walked into town to make a family?

I had really outrun myself this time. Three hours before my flight, up north, I was doing my hair in the mutely lit morning when my boyfriend, Tom, picked my phone up and saw my texts with Jack Dawson. To him, the sexts look really bad. Unforgivable, almost.

"Please," I begged for him to understand, "Jack and I existed together way before *us*. The fact that we found each other again after so many years is—"

"My ass," Tom said, helping himself to my open luggage, hurling my shoe at the window and my purple caftan like a Crimsonette ribbon up in the air. "The fact that you've found each other again is . . . my ass!"

"Tom, *listuhnnn*," I pleaded, half my hair wet and clamped in a clip, the other half styled and blond. I cupped Tom's face in both my hands. He averted my eyes by rolling his around, like his head had just been decapitated. I had been looking forward to this solitary trip for weeks.

"Jack and I died together on the *Ti-tan-ic*," I whispered. "Have some respect?"

Tom wrestled his head out of my arms. He pulled on the blond side of my hair, kicked my Samsonite, ripped off his shirt and tore it in half. "You are Jekyll and Hyde!" he said. He was capable of anger. "Delusional. I hope you never come back."

* * *

It is a thing I have always known, that I am Rose DeWitt Bukater. From the first time I saw the movie, when I was nine in the theater, my mother's hand stuck in front of my face to shield me from the breasts—Mom,

I know those boobs, I said. They're mine. And the charcoal sketch. I gasped when I saw it, when Gloria Stuart saw it. That was me. I had not seen myself in lifetimes. I thought I had died upon the ship. No, you lived, Mom said, see? You lived to be a woman, you died old in your bed. But I don't remember that part of it. I only remember Jack.

Tom, forget it. I can't bother. Anytime I mention who I used to be, he groans, throws his big body on our plaid couch, and says, "Can't you save this for story time at work?" I work at a shipyard museum. I take care of kids in a big blue room, and the answer is no—because this isn't just a story.

* * *

So I had made it to San Miguel de Allende. I was at Sophie's. Sophie was in London visiting her sister and Sophie, I should mention, is a narcissist. The only thing she loves is this cat, the cat I have mentioned, Pleiades, and cats are narcissists too. Sophie is the kind of person who absorbs everything. Everything becomes her, for better or for worse. She is lucky she's smart, which makes her a good artist. If she were dumb, she'd just be a sponge. Her apartment in San Miguel is a gallery for her own paintings, colorful gouache canvasses she calls "American abstractions of Mexican landscape." She is half Mixtec, half Bostonian. I know she loves this cat, so I decided to walk into town to find it.

* * *

One time, in California, I recognized a poet on Venice Beach. I'd met her at a reading in New York just three weeks before. At her reading she'd mentioned her move to Southern California, how it would be better for her sick husband. Her poems were about relationships in which the "I" always gives away more of itself than the "he" and the "she." When I locked eyes with the poet—she was propped up on a traffic blockade like a teenager would be, her legs skinny and her hair so long—we recognized each other in an abstract sense. I do not think she recognized me as someone she'd met recently. I like to know survivors are out there.

I knew she had died on the ship, too.

* * *

In Old Greek the word for "cat" is *ailouros*: "thing with the moving tail." I felt curious as I locked the big granite door of Sophie's condo, and effervescent as I walked out onto the street. There was a feeling in the air around me. I had a feeling I'd find someone.

I walked the uphill road leading to the middle of San Miguel de Allende, which is a revived ghost town. After an influenza epidemic killed many residents or ran the healthy out of town, postwar foreigners moved in and opened art schools like Bellas Artes. They maintained all the baroque architecture. San Miguel first became an art town, and then a tourist town. The public now seemed wildly white, many Canadians and Europeans—everywhere I looked I saw well-to-do couples in sundresses and hats, carrying wine wrapped in embroidered cloths on their way to early dinners. I reached the beginning of the center of town, which began at the foot of the landmark Rosewood hotel, where two teens kissed fondly on a park bench. I stopped to admire them as if they were a painting in a museum, the kind of Renaissance composition where the light of God directly floods them from above. They touched each other like neither could believe the other was real. I sighed at the integrity of it. Then Jack appeared beside me, wearing what he always wore.

"This is what it feels like, kissing you," Jack said casually, pointing a thumb at the teenagers. The teenagers were dressed in orange, and Jack in brown suspenders. He didn't look directly at me at first, so I thought he was a ghost. "Oh my god, you found me," I said, grabbing his arm tightly and forcing him to turn the corner. Now the road steeped downward, towards the square. I told Jack I wasn't expecting the person I ran into to be him. "I have a lot to say to you," I said, over and over again. I wanted to tell him about Eleanor, my short cousin who was in this horrible dirt-bike accident that had paralyzed her and killed her boyfriend. How two years later, she'd died in a fire of smoke inhalation—how at the funeral my aunt kept saying "broken heart, broken heart"—as she breathed in and out, almost impossibly.

"Why are you telling me this right now?" Jack asked me. He leaned into my neck, like a vampire.

"Because I've lost Sophie's cat," I said, pushing his face away. I grabbed my neck like it might fall off. We had finally arrived at the large town square. Balloon vendors lugged carts with their merchandise floating slightly above the barrow on hundreds of strings, creating the illusion that this was a place of no gravity. A mariachi band played a pop song from inside an open gazebo. Lovers and companions danced. A gigantic church was pink, and the sky was, too. "I'm sorry, Jack," I said. This was the most romantic place in the world, and I was worried about finding the cat.

* * *

Jack helped me split the town square into six search parties as we orchestrated a frantic hunt for Pleiades. Those who did not trust us scattered towards the spider roads that led to other smaller plazas, but many people stayed to help. We instructed those who remained to tear up the patio and frisk all the cypress trees. In the end, Pleiades was nowhere to be found, but the organized chaos of the cat hunt reminded me of the last time Jack and I had been a part of something so grand and tragic. "Jack," I said, caressing a street cat that was more or less the same color as Pleiades but was not a purebred Russian Blue at all. Volunteers lay exhausted on the rubble of cobblestones. One group had climbed the pink church and sent the stone angels carved on the spire crumbling to the ground. The mariachi band still played, but it was a slow, dreadful song.

"Jack," I whispered. "This is where we first met."

* * *

I brought Jack back to Sophie's apartment immediately because I was so turned on by what we had made happen at the square. We only made it to the sofa, where he was inside me before I realized, and right before he came I told him he should scream "Sophie" in order to keep the feng shui of the apartment. In the wake of the missing cat.

"We should probably talk about the cat," I said, after Jack removed his hand from my throat.

"We should probably talk about Tom?" Jack said.

"Who's Tom?" I asked, coughing. "I'm talking about Pleiades."

"She's right there, dumdum," Jack said, pointing across the coffee table. Oh my god, Pleiades was sitting in the armchair directly across from us, and she was not healthy. She looked like death itself.

"Throw me something," I said, snapping my fingers at Jack. He threw me a knit throw from the other side of the sofa. I wrapped myself in it and tiptoed over to the cat. It was huge, with big sculpted ears. You could see in its face it was losing life.

"Hey, cat," I said to the cat, really softly. "Are you okay?"

The cat meowed in this dismal way. I tried to pet it but it shuddered against the back of the chair.

"Did we kill the cat?" I asked Jack.

"Maybe you killed the cat?"

"I kill everything," I said. I went into the guest room to find my cell phone.

"What are you doing?"

"Killing Tom."

The phone rang once before going to voicemail. I tried six more times.

"He probably won't pick up," Jack said.

"Why don't you call him then, Jack? Ask him what I should do."

I watched Jack try to feed Pleiades his pinky finger. What would Sophie say? There was hardly any blue left in the cat's fur.

* * *

There was this young woman on the ship I was friendly with who sat at our table during supper. She was the daughter of a countess, like I was, except she was happy with her life. She was married to an Ismay and spent hours pressing her hair in the evenings because it was dense and curly but by the time I saw her, in the afternoons, it was always trapped in a sleek chignon.

"The key is to always seem French," the girl said, and she had been French, I think, or something like it. Part of being French, she said, was to either become happy with your unhappiness and use it to your advantage, or throw it all to the wind and live alone. She was a disciple of the former. I can't remember her first name, but she must have survived the sinking because she had access to the Ismay lifeboat. She sailed away—easy for her to say.

Tom wasn't on the Titanic. Tom, dependable and successful, angry only when he deserved something. If Tom had been on the Titanic with me, maybe I'd've had the architecture to save myself.

* * *

"So we *shouldn't* give her a hot bath," Jack said as I cradled the thing in my arms, three days later. We had not left Sophie's place since we'd found Pleiades in the flat. The poor thing had stopped using the litter box two days ago and had stopped eating today.

The animals on our earth have parallel-incarnation species that live in water, except for cats and foxes. Cats and foxes are, actually, land-bound animals through and through.

"Are you serious?" I seethed. "A bath won't do shit." The cat moaned, then jumped to the floor to slink under the couch. I still had not called Sophie.

"Running out of ideas here," Jack said. "Just call your friend?"

"I don't know," I thought. I imagined what Sophie might be doing while Jack and I sat here, both not showered, fretting over the cat. "Right now she is probably riding the London Eye."

"Oh. That means she can see us," Jack said.

Jack knew exactly what to say to stave me from pitch-dark dread for small moments at a time.

"Ha," I said, smiling.

"Here's your golden ticket," Jack said. "A veterinarian. How's your Spanish?"

"It's amazing," I said. "So is my French."

"I forgot," Jack grinned.

I ran to a phone book on the counter and called the first veterinarian listed.

* * *

"The reason why cats like to be alone when they die is because they don't want to be seen in a vulnerable state out in the open. We forget that in the wild, small cats are both predator and prey," Dr. Abhishek told us in the white hole of the examination room.

"So nothing can be done?" I asked.

"*O sea*, no," Dr. Abhishek said.

"Oh my god," I said. I wanted to cry on Jack's shoulder but after a few days of this misery he looked so cold and disturbed I was a little bit scared to. His blond mushroom cut was fucked up, his roots really oily.

"Do you want to put her to sleep now?" Dr. Abhishek asked.

"No way," I said. I wanted Pleiades to have a dignified death.

It was a slow, low-cost clinic, and we had spent most of the day there in the waiting room. The sky was a heated pink when we left around dinnertime. I carried Pleiades back to Sophie's in the same blanket sheet I'd used on the way to the vet. Older couples passed us, their wine bottles wrapped in similar cloth, and they smiled at us, thinking we were also walking with our wine to dinner. Or if not wine—the cat was bigger than a bottle of wine—a newborn baby. I recognized all these smiles—people give you these smiles when you remind them of themselves and a time they thought was happier.

* * *

"Jack," I said after we'd gotten back to Sophie's. The second we got home, Pleiades jumped from my arms and went to hide in Sophie's bedroom. It was heartbreaking to watch her do that. Did she think I was going to kill her?

"What is it?" Jack said. He held his head in his hands, but he was barely there anymore. The suspenders he used to keep up his pants were missing, like he was a drawing that was getting erased. His T-shirt was yellowing out from his armpits.

"I feel like you need to go," I said. I could not be responsible for two dying things at once.

"But I'm not dying," he said. "Just tired. You're tiring! You were tiring in the first lifetime and you're tiring again."

"I'm dying again?"

"No, *tiring*."

"I don't understand."

"You really don't," Jack said. He flipped open his leather portfolio, which I actually had not seen him carry in this new iteration of our romance. He began sketching with a piece of charcoal from 1912.

"Don't draw me," I said. "Serious. I'm not showered."

He didn't answer. He just looked from me to the canvas and back. All I could see of his face were his blue eyes moving, like that one shot in the movie when he sees me naked for the first time. I wanted to get up and look for the cat.

"Don't move," Jack said.

Lucky for Jack, when he looks at me I paralyze.

* * *

"Hey, I'm ready for you to take me back, so just let me know," I said to Tom's voicemail the next day while standing in Sophie's kitchen. I guess he was still ignoring me. Pleiades had remained in Sophie's room all night and now was emitting these low animal moans that were making me regret taking her home from the vet alive.

"What?" Jack said, coming out of bathroom in a bath towel. "Are you for real?"

"Shhh," I said, putting my phone down. "It's not going to work if he knows you're here."

"The shower feels really good," Jack said. He was combing his hair in the mirror. "Best I ever took."

"Oh yeah?" I said. Then I turned to him.

"Hey, Jack. Do you remember my French friend from the ship?"

"Not really," he said.

"Cora?"

"Huh? That's her name?"

"I think that was her name. Cora or something."

Jack rubbed aftershave on his jawline and shrugged.

"I wonder, in the end, if she was happy she survived? Or like, bummed she didn't die. I read an interview with a survivor who, after he got old and depressed, said it would've been better if he'd gone down with the ship when he was a kid, because then he wouldn't have ever felt the loneliness and the despair he felt being old and alone. "

"I don't get what you're saying," Jack said. "You lived too."

"I'm sorry?" I was confused.

"You lived, I died," Jack said. "I let you float on the door."

"I'm not sure that's what happened," I said. The cat's moaning was getting louder and more desperate. I shut the door to Sophie's room.

"It did. I told you to keep on living without me, so you did," Jack said. He was clearly bored. "I said, 'You're gonna die an old lady warm in her bed.'"

"Oh."

That was upsetting news to me. I couldn't remember a single thing from my Titanic lifetime that didn't include Jack. You don't really see it in the movie.

"This all sounds unfair. I wish I'd died with you."

"Why?" Jack took his razor and put it in the outside pocket of his canvas bag. He looked around to make sure he had everything. He looked good again, like the ideal love interest of all my lifetimes, and I immediately regretted telling him to leave.

"Okay. It's goodbye," he said.

"Maybe you should just stay?"

Jack walked over to me and tried to kiss me on the cheek. I moved his hand to my throat.

"Choke me so I never have to live without you."

"Sorry," Jack said, pulling his lifelike hand away swiftly. "You need to stay with Pleiades. And I have, like, thirty more appointments today."

"Appointments?"

"*Everybody* loves me," Jack said. "You're not the only one." And then he left me with the cat.

* * *

Pleiades took her last breath in my arms late that evening. Not for nothing—I really had to stretch myself under the bed to reach for her. She was, in her final moments, more grey than blue, more trusting but still dignified. I wanted to let her know I was here for her.

"Pleiades, in your next life, you're going to do *tons* of shit," I whispered. Then, her lizardy eyes dilated and she was gone.

She was still warm when I wrapped her tightly in the blue sheet and fastened it with safety pins. I went to the bathroom and considered shaving my eyebrows off—I knew it was customary mourning to do this in ancient Egypt when a house cat died. But I didn't because I knew I'd need all the confidence in the world in order to face the mess of my life.

* * *

San Miguel was beautiful and I was going to miss it. But I wished I'd been able to experience it more. I walked with dead Pleiades to the center of town, stopping at the Rosewood, disappointed that the teenage lovers were no longer there, continuing into the town square, which was empty, to my dismay, so late in the evening on a weekday, and destroyed, too, because of our search party. It did not bring me much nostalgia, though, not without Jack here, but I dug a shallow grave behind the crumbling church and kissed the cat into its next life.

Back at the apartment I planned to talk to Sophie and get in touch with Tom. I'd be landing back in New Orleans with the ghosts tomorrow. Was this what it had been like in my last lifetime? I still tried to remember how I'd gone on living without Jack after he'd died, and I couldn't really remember.

I read Sophie's London phone number off the fridge. She was scheduled to come home tomorrow so it felt a safe time to break the news. One thing I can do is I can see something to the death, I reminded myself. I can do it on a big scale and I can do it on a small scale and I can always do it again. The phone rang and as I sat down to prepare myself for another sinking ship, a Russian Blue rapped at the window of the terrace. It looked a lot like Pleiades, so I hung up the phone and let her in. ■

HILDA'S WORK CAMP
Billy Baites

Until I became a young adult, I lived a stark, black-and-white existence within my family. In our home, even the youngest child was given one—and only one—chance to do whatever he was charged with doing perfectly the first time. It wasn't until I left home that I learned there were actually gray areas in life and that it was perfectly acceptable to make mistakes and learn from them so I could grow as an individual.

My mother's family came to this country from Germany's Rhineland in the early 1750s and eventually settled in Burlington, North Carolina, in the heart of Alamance County. From the beginning, they were God-fearing, hardworking farming stock and their demanding perfectionism and Germanic approach to life survives to this day. In their minds, you were put on this earth to work and work hard, live modestly, and be thankful for anything you were given in life. One could expect nothing more than that.

My maternal grandparents lived off the land their entire lives. My mother, her three sisters, and her two brothers were expected to work on the farm alongside their parents after school and in the summers from dawn until dusk. She often told me how much she hated being in the country and that she could never live there again.

"It's so quiet there you can hear ants walking around," she used to say. "You look out the window and it looks like death and destruction . . . just nothing to see or hear or do."

Maybe that was what drove her to take a step that none of the others ever took—to marry someone from outside the immediate area and move into town with no intention of farming. That did not, however, deter her from adhering to her family's extreme work ethic, which has been passed down, undiluted, to a new generation: me, my sister, Joan, and my brother, Dana.

I keep a photograph on my desk that makes me laugh to myself every time I look at it. It was taken in front of the Christmas tree in our living room on Christmas Eve. Dana, Joan, and I are sitting cross-legged in our pajamas, each holding a wrapped gift in our lap. The wood floor beneath us has been waxed and buffed to a sheen that makes it look as if we are sitting on water, with our reflections shining back from the floor.

That gleaming floor was no accident. We grew up in a fairly typical 1950s ranch-style house in the suburbs, and my mother saw to it that our home was kept clean and orderly year-round. In my mother's mind, if you weren't working and productive every minute of every day except Sunday, which of course was spent in church, you were worthless.

So the floors in the house never got a *chance* to get dull and the windows were rarely dirty. My brother, my sister, and I waxed floors and cleaned windows as frequently as we took out the garbage. Every Saturday, unless we were assigned to a specific project, out came the Kenmore vacuum cleaner and we cleaned the house in the morning and then mowed and worked in the yard all afternoon. My mother would come behind us as we finished each room, running her hands and fingers over surfaces to check for dust that we might have missed.

"Billy, come back here. There's still some dust on the coffee table."

Usually in January or February—probably on the coldest day of the winter—we would get up on a Saturday and she would pounce on us.

"Today we're going to scrub this filthy house from top to bottom. I can't stand all of this dirt another day!" We would put on our winter coats and hats and clothes and she would open all of the windows while declaring, "It's time to air this place out. It stinks in here!"

Windows would fly open and blasts of arctic air would fill the house. The three of us would line up in the kitchen and Mama would give each of us a bucket of scalding hot water that contained Lysol, a scrub brush, and stack of dry towels.

"We are going to start in the corner bedroom," she said, and off we went. Daddy and Mama would move all of the furniture out from against the wall and we got down on our hands and knees to scrub down the backs and undersides of the furniture and the baseboards. After a while my hands would start to get numb from the cold and I would say, "Mama, my hands are freezing and I need to warm them up!" Without missing a beat, she would shoot back, "If your hands are freezing then you need to move faster to stay warm. The faster you three work, the sooner we will be done!"

When summer would come, I was shipped out to the country to stay with cousins and work in the tobacco fields, hoeing and weeding and doing whatever slave labor my aunts and uncles had in store for me. Back home, while my brother and sister and I certainly weren't working in the fields, we still worked. And if we couldn't behave properly, we got the daylights spanked out of us and were put to work, either cleaning the house or working in the yard or any other kind of hard labor my parents could dish up for us. While my father was somewhat easygoing, my mother put the *p* in perfectionist. If one looks up the German meaning of the name Hilda, one will see it translates as "Maid of Battle."

* * *

For twenty-seven years, my father bought appliances for Sears, Roebuck and Co. After my parents were married in June 1946, they moved to Atlanta, where he trained at the big Sears building on Ponce de Leon Avenue and took a streetcar back and forth from West End, where they rented a house. When he finished his training, they moved to Greensboro and he went to work at the big Sears distribution center on Lawndale Drive, just about a mile from where we lived.

In those days, everything we owned came from Sears. If Sears had made cars we would have had one. Because my father bought appliances for Sears, he got a discount on personal purchases and access to scratched and dented models at reduced prices, but that did not mean we had all of the modern conveniences at home. My mother simply would not hear of it. During her entire life, she never owned an automatic dishwasher, despite the fact that, in later years, my brother and sister and I tried to give her one for birthdays and at Christmas. She would emphatically state, "People who own dishwashers are lazy! You never know if your dishes are clean unless you wash them yourself!"

Every night after supper we followed the same drill. I washed, Joan rinsed and put the dishes in the drying rack, and Dana dried them and put them away while my mother looked over our shoulders and supervised our work. She demanded the soapy dishwater and the water in the sink used for rinsing be absolutely scalding. I had to wear two pairs of rubber gloves in order to put my hands down in the dishwater. My sister had to use tongs to dip the plates in the blistering rinse water and place them in the drying rack. My mother would peer between the two of us and examine every single piece I handed over to my sister to be rinsed. Every now and then her eagle eyes would bring the process to a halt.

"Stop! I see a speck of something on the bottom of that plate, Billy. Put it back in the dishwater and scrub it some more!"

Likewise, despite my father's attempts to get a clothes dryer for my mother, she refused to have one.

"I'm not having one of those things in my house. Clothes dried in a machine like that smell sour," she said. "Besides, I have a perfectly good and usable clothesline and there is no reason to clutter up this house with another appliance."

She meant every word of it. With the exception of days on which rain was in the picture, clothes were hung on that clothesline year-round. I remember my brother, my sister, and I taking clothes off the line during the aftermath of an ice storm. Towels that were so thin because Mama refused to spend money on new ones could stand up against the wall by themselves like sheets of plywood. Let me tell you—you haven't lived until you have dried off after a bath with one of those towels.

* * *

Our household was one with rules, rules, rules and structure, structure, structure. There was a time of day to do everything. The television could only be turned on after dinner so my father could see the evening news, and then we were allowed to watch several television programs. We were to take our bath or shower either in the evening or first thing in the morning, never in the middle of the day, when we were supposed to be working. Leisure time was extremely limited. If you had time to sit around, then you had time to work!

As soon as my brother, my sister, and I were tall enough to reach the handles of a lawnmower, we were put to work mowing the neighbors' yards for pocket change. There was one particular yard that seemed like acres to me at the time, but I got ten dollars every time I mowed it, which I considered a small fortune.

Once I turned sixteen, my mother became obsessed with me having a demanding summer job after each school year finished. She would start in around the end of March, circling summer jobs in the classifieds section of the local newspaper and leaving it on my dresser.

Because my father worked for Sears, he was able to help me get summer jobs there after the tenth and eleventh grades. The first year, I worked as a packer in the department that filled mail orders, and the second year, I worked in the same department actually sorting and distributing the orders as they arrived by mail. After I graduated from high school, though, my luck had run out. It was 1972 and the economy was in the toilet. There were almost no jobs of any sort to be found for summer employment. As the end of the school year approached, my mother became more and more frantic as I had no employment lined up for the summer. Finally, on a Friday a few days before graduation, I came in from school and she followed me down the hall, shaking the classifieds at me, in a state of near delirium.

"Billy, you stop and listen to me right now! In today's paper there is an ad for a part-time busboy at the Albert Pick Motor Inn near Kernersville! I want you to get up first thing tomorrow morning and drive out there and apply for it!"

Now Kernersville was a good twenty minutes or so outside of Greensboro and, in my mind, to drive that distance for a part-time job that was probably below minimum wage made no sense at all.

"Mama, that's crazy. I am not driving to Kernersville every day to work as a part-time busboy!"

"Well I want to know what you think you're going to do this summer! You're not sitting in this house doing nothing all summer, little man. You're gonna work. I'm telling you, you are going out there and applying for that job tomorrow!"

"Mama, I would burn up what little I earned in gas just driving to and from work. That makes no sense at all!"

"That's not the point! You need to get this job so you will be working instead of sitting around like somebody sorry! You are going, do you understand me?"

I didn't say anything else. The next morning, she burst into the room just as the sun was starting to come up, stomped over to the windows, threw back the drapes, and announced, "You've laid in that bed long enough! Get up. Your breakfast is ready and you need to eat and get cleaned up so you can get out to Albert Pick Motor Inn and apply for that job."

Then she marched over to the AC window unit and flipped it off.

"And turn this thing off! Sealed up in this freezing room! Lord, it's cold enough in here to hang meat. Get up, I'm not going to tell you again or I'll go get the belt!"

I showered, dressed, and sat down at the kitchen table. As Mama set my breakfast down in front of me, she began raining instructions.

"You tell them you can start the day after graduation. You say, 'Yes, sir,' if it's a man and, 'Yes ma'am,' if it's a woman. Whatever they tell you they will pay you, you accept it and say, 'Thank you.' Tell them you like to work hard and for them to give you as much work as they like. Are you listening to me, Billy?"

"Yes, Mama."

I finished breakfast and went to the bathroom to brush my teeth. She followed me.

"You need to hurry up and get out there! There will probably be a lot of people applying for this job since there are so few others in town. Hurry up, Billy!"

I choked on my mouthwash, said goodbye, and headed out the back door. I had made up my mind that there was no way in hell I was going to apply for that job, much less drive to Kernersville and back all summer for a part-time bussing position. She was out of her mind.

So, I just drove around for a couple of hours and then came back to the house.

As soon as I stepped in the back door, she was on top of me.

"Did you apply for the job? What did they say? Did you get hired?"

She was on my heels all the way to my bedroom. "Did you get it, did you get it?!"

In my frustration, I wheeled around and shouted out at her, "I am sick and tired of listening to you hound me about a damn summer job!"

I had just taken my shirt off and in two steps she crossed the room and smacked me so hard on my back that she almost knocked me down.

"What a filthy mouth!!! Where did you learn such filth as that?! I better not ever hear you utter another word like that in this house!!! Do you understand me? I don't know who you think you are but if you keep on showing yourself you're going to get your legs torn up with a switch. And if you open that smart-aleck mouth to me again like that, I'll smash it flat! Just try me! You mark my words, mister, you are not sitting in this house all summer!"

She spun on her heel and stomped back up the hall to the kitchen. I changed clothes and walked through the kitchen and out the back door without saying a word to her. She followed me out on the back porch. I jumped in the car, cranked the engine, and, as I started backing down the driveway, she shouted out loud enough for the neighbors at the end of the street to hear, "You better be headed to Albert Pick Motor Inn to apply for that job! And if not, you better be headed somewhere to apply for a job!" I sped off down the street, watching her in my rearview mirror shaking her index finger at me, her mouth still going.

Somehow the gods looked down kindly on me that day. I drove over to a friend's house to see her and catch up. As soon as she saw me she knew something was wrong.

"Oh Karen, my mother is driving me crazy about finding a summer job and there's just nothing out there worthwhile."

"Billy, you know what, my father is looking for a pianist for the dinner hour in his restaurant. He's right in the den. Let's go talk to him."

Karen's father owned the Nosherie Restaurant on West Market Street. Mr. Whitney knew I was about to enter college as a piano major and had known me long enough to feel comfortable hiring me on the spot. I was to start a week after graduation, playing from 5:00 p.m. to 9:00 p.m., Tuesday through Saturday. I was thrilled!

I thanked him and Karen, ran a few errands, and then headed home. As soon as I walked into the kitchen, my mother said, "Where have you been? Did you go apply for a job?"

"Mama, I have some good news. I have gotten a job. Mr. Whitney, Karen's father, has hired me to play the piano in his restaurant during the dinner hour each week."

She got a horrified look on her face.

"Well, what kind of job is that?! That can't amount to much and it surely can't last very long! What do you think you are going to do during the day before you go to work?! Well I can tell you right now what you're going to do. You are going to work in this house, painting, waxing floors, cleaning windows, cleaning out the attic, and a lot of other things that need to be done!"

So went the summer. I spent my days doing hard manual labor and my evenings playing Broadway selections with sore hands and raw fingertips. Some Sundays, I was given time off for good behavior.

One Saturday, a close friend was visiting and we were sitting at the kitchen table talking to Mama. "Well, Jimmy, what kind of job are you working at this summer? It's good to keep busy and not waste your time. As we know, an idle mind is the devil's workshop." Jimmy replied, "Well, Mrs. Baites, my parents don't want me to work in the summer. They want me to relax and enjoy myself." My mother looked like someone had just held up the tip of a rifle to the space between her eyes.

"I've never heard of such a thing in my entire life. I can tell you right now the three in this house aren't going to slouch around all summer. I don't know if I'd go around announcing that you're not working to just anybody."

* * *

As I got older and moved away to pursue a career, I would still make trips home where I would walk in the back door and my list of to-dos was waiting on the kitchen table. By the time I was living in Atlanta, I was renovating a Victorian house and my mother got wind of all of the things I had learned to do such as drywalling, wood stripping, plaster patching, and so forth. She was eager to use my free services. She would start calling me in the spring at my office in Atlanta to find out when I would be taking a week of vacation to come home and work around the place. I never thought much about it at the time. I thought everybody else did the same thing for their parents. My mother would call and tell me what she wanted done on a particular trip home.

"This time, I want you to take up all of that old wall-to-wall carpeting in the dining room, living room, and hallway and refinish the wood floors."

"When you come home this time, I want you to plaster all of the cracks in the dining room, living room, and hallway and paint."

Heil Hilda! Your wish is my command!

When I returned full-time to Greensboro in 2005, my mother was beside herself because that meant her elder son would be living just across town. Of equal importance, he would again be available to attend the camp and provide free manual labor in addition to a cavalcade of services only a phone call away. Honestly, as Mama was getting older and had developed some health issues, I was happy to do what I could.

All that said, she was still as fierce as ever. One afternoon she called me. "I am absolutely furious with the dryer repairman who was just here and I want you to see if you can do something about it," she preached into the phone.

"Mama, what is going on?"

"Well, the Kenmore dryer stopped working several days ago so I called the Sears repair people and this man came out this morning. He figured out what was wrong and called to try to get the part. He told me they don't make that part anymore and I would have to replace the dryer. That is ridiculous! I told him I had never heard of such a thing and there is no good reason why he couldn't find that part somewhere. He looked at me as if I had just threatened him with his life and responded, 'Mrs. Baites, that's the absolute truth and there's nothing more I can do here. Here is my bill.' Lord have mercy, you can't repair my dryer and you're going to charge me for it?" she said incredulously.

In frustration, the repairman loaded his kit, left the bill on the kitchen table, and quickly left, shaking his head all the way out the back door. I tried to bring her around.

"Mama, do you remember what year Daddy bought that dryer?" There was silence on the other end. "He bought it in 1969. It's time to replace it."

"I don't care when he bought it. There's no reason it can't be fixed."

I ordered a new dryer, not telling her a thing about it, and one day when she was at Gate City Beauty College getting her hair fixed I had them swapped out. She called me as soon as she walked in the back door and saw the new dryer.

"I guess you think you are real smart, little man." And then she hung up on me.

I had taken over handling my mother's finances and monthly bills as I found it made my life simpler as she wasn't calling me and wringing her hands with every fifty cents that was spent from her checking account. I had hired a lawn service to keep up the yard at her house and every time they came to do the weekly lawn maintenance, she called me.

"I see dollar bills flying out the window when they show up over here. How much am I paying them each time they show up?"

I learned to just let her talk and then I always answered her with the same remark, "It's within your monthly budget." That usually worked.

Occasionally, I would go over and mow the yard for her myself, which pleased her no end. One particular Saturday in the summer, I had just finished mowing the yard and come in the house. My mother walked into the kitchen holding her hand up to her throat with a wild look in her eyes.

"Something's wrong with the gas. The pilot on the water heater is low."

Only Mama could find something that quickly. I called Piedmont Natural Gas and they sent someone out. Unbeknownst to me, the blade on the lawn mower had accidentally hit the gas valve switch on the exterior meter and turned down the flow of gas. The repairman found it and corrected it quickly and then, as he prepared to leave out the front door, he casually mentioned to my mother that the call would cost fifty dollars because it was on the weekend and not during regular working hours. Mama threw her hands up in the hair and shouted, "Fifty dollars! Are you kidding me? That's highway robbery. You haven't been here thirty minutes!"

She followed him down the front steps and all the way down sidewalk, wagging her finger at him. I stepped out on the porch to watch the festivities.

"I am a poor widow and barely scrape by. I've had to raise three children on my own since my husband died and do my best to make ends meet and you want to charge me fifty dollars?"

The poor man could not get a word in edgewise. Finally, as he climbed into his car, he turned to her and said, "Okay, just forget it. You won't be charged."

My mother turned, put her hands on her hips, and with a big smile on her face she marched back up the sidewalk and as we walked in the house she said, "Now, Billy, let that be a lesson to you. The squeaky wheel gets the grease. I'm not putting up with such stuff as that!"

The years passed and with them Mama, like all elderly parents, began to show her age. By 2007 I started seeing a frailty and weakness in her that broke my heart. She became fearful of everything and the powerhouse of a southern woman she once was had faded away. She began spending most of her day sitting on the sofa because she was afraid of moving around and falling. Every time I left the house I was in tears because I loved her deeply and had an abiding respect for her accomplishments in life. When my father died suddenly in 1973, she had to go to work and take care of all three of us and she did just that beautifully. My mother rarely showed favoritism among us but I caught her talking to a friend once when I was younger about me. She didn't know I had heard her. "The oldest child is always the special one and there is a bond with the mother that, in life or death, cannot be broken." Mama passed away in 2009 but she would be happy to know that the habits I learned from her as a child continue to live on in many ways. I feel her with me in a thousand ways in my daily life and I laugh to myself at those memories every time. As I remove the dishes from the dishwasher, finding one speck of food remaining on a dinner plate can send me into a tailspin. I will stop in the middle of whatever I am doing if I spot a stain on the carpet and will find myself scrubbing it out mercilessly until it is gone. Yes, the apple did not fall far from the tree. At Christmastime, I find myself browbeating myself if my gifts for others are not wrapped perfectly. I sweat over my social skills and manners as if my life depended on it in a day and time when so little of that seems to matter anymore. When I cook, and I love to cook, I do my best to prepare the dishes perfectly, especially if I'm having guests. Anything that does not turn out with a grade of A+ doesn't go on the table. Like both my parents, I respect family traditions and try to honor them and keep them with me. I carry over two hundred years' worth of them with me and for the sake of those I have loved and are no longer here, I try to preserve them and share them with others.

I hope wherever she is she is looking down on me . . . smiling and proud. She is still deeply missed in my heart with every day that passes. Hilda Perth Whitesell was a beautiful southern lady inside and out . . . a steel magnolia at its best. ∎

SELF-PORTRAIT AS HOUSE CENTIPEDE
Alyssa Ripley

one hundred thin limbs / cling / to shag carpet / pluck me
an orange blossom / from off-white baseboards / carry me
out like a child / to bed for rest / their hands / my hands
clasped around safe necks / lie me down
in the grass / I am here / still / asking / for a goodnight kiss
asking / to be tucked in / still / asking / for forgiveness

OKAY, CUPID
Roberta Montgomery

Feel peculiar since yesterday. Six hundred calories, mostly vinegar. Hope my kidneys don't shut down. Having failed at every diet, I look to literature for a plan and discover Lord Byron was not only a great Romantic poet but also the first celebrity dieter. Sometimes he fasted, other times he gorged himself and drank vinegar to stay slim. Also, being a sex maniac probably helped. Adding vinegar to lose weight sounds easier than subtracting food, so I give it a try. And like the poet, I, Amanda Murphy, am mad, bad, and dangerous to know.

I titrate two ounces of ACV into a shot glass. My nose tingles. I dive in, chugging a mouthful, surprised at how easy this is until the sour liquid catches fire on its way down my esophagus. Agonizing! My gut seizes from the bayonet thrust of the acid and I double over, vowing I will never eat again. Hey, seems Byron was on to something, this might work! I've always identified with the poet, sexy and a little bit fat. He had a passionate relationship to food and would sometimes eat several lobsters or an entire goose at a meal. Other times he'd starve, dining on a single raisin. His vegan friend P. B. Shelley was indifferent to the pleasures of the table and depended on his wife, Mary, to remind him to eat, but Byron battled his lusty appetite his whole life.

I check the clock. In less than an hour I'm to meet a guy from OkCupid. This is my first date since signing up with the website and I'm nervous. We exchanged texts and agreed to coffee at the French café near my house. I hope my stomach quiets down because right now it's in a shouting match with the vinegar. Should I call his attention to the noise and explain I don't have some terrible chronic condition? Don't know much about him, except he works in media promotion and we both like cheese. Is that enough to build a relationship? I'm hopeful. With my hair brushed and makeup colored in between the lines, I run down my front stoop and head toward Doheny Drive and La Conversation café. The scent of orange blossoms from my neighbor's tree makes me crave something sweet, a pain au chocolat or slice of tarte tatin, but I will order only black coffee, like I have a dainty appetite. When I reach the park along Santa Monica Boulevard, the honeyed air gives way to the smell of a urine-soaked sidewalk. Beverly Hills is home to a small tribe of homeless people and they congregate in the park near my house. There's the guy on roller blades. All day he skates in circles, warning of the Rapture. And the woman I call Granny, with clumpy hair and men's loafers as big as clown shoes. The garbage cans around here have many treasures. She's the one I usually give money to. In general the street people leave you alone. But there's a new guy on the scene, in his early twenties. He belongs on a college campus, not hustling strangers for cash. Of all the vagrants in the park, I find him the most unsettling. Not because he's dirty or has crazy Charles Manson eyes, but because he's kind of hot. Being attracted to a homeless person is not as disturbing as finding Ted Cruz sexy, but almost. I think of my mentor, Lord Byron. He wasn't squeamish; he pursued carnal relations with all types—family members, street beggars. Today this young, handsome homeless man falls right in step with me as I race to my date.

"Hi, I'm Eric," he says. I try to outwalk him but he's fitter than I am. "You got a name?"

"Amanda." Damn, couldn't I come up with an alias?

"Hey, Amanda. Nice to meet you. You live near here?"

"No," I wise up and lie.

Eric continues to walk alongside me, measuring his pace to mine. Is he going to follow me all the way to the café? He launches into a spiel about his First Amendment rights, like we are on *The Rachel Maddow Show*. "Are you aware that the Beverly Hills City Council passed an ordinance against begging? And do you know that my right to panhandle is protected by the Constitution?"

I nod to show I'm not a plutocrat oppressor. "So Beverly Hills is a tough place to be homeless?"

"The super rich are super stingy."

"I'm not surprised," I commiserate. I feel around the bottom of my bag. I'm on a tight budget so I can only spare a bit of change.

"If not for tourists, I'd have nothing to eat."

I tip my bag and shake it, beginning to identify with his plight. "This town can be brutal on your self-esteem," I say. "You think you'd do better in the Valley? Like Reseda or Canoga Park? You know, where people relate to being down on your luck?" His hair isn't greasy or matted, but gold where the sun hits it.

"Down on my luck? Did I say I'm down on my luck? I'm Mister Luck. And the Beverly Hills cops are relatively tolerant." *Relatively tolerant?* That's some fancy diction for a bum.

"I'm in a hurry," I say. "Got a date." I hand him all my coins. Has to be two or three dollars' worth. While he stops to count his good fortune, I hightail it.

When I arrive at the café, I find all the sidewalk tables taken so go inside to nab a spot. I scan the room. Looks like Doug hasn't arrived yet. A strong Scottish name, Doug.

A rapping on the window snaps me out of my sexy Highlander fantasy. A tubby man in a green cap waves at me through the glass. He points and mouths what must be my name. We shoot each other question marks. Give him a chance, I mumble to myself as I join him outside. Oops, hope he's not a lip-reader.

I pull out the wire café chair at the cute Parisian table that he dwarfs. "You been here long?" I ask.

"I like to scout an escape route." He laughs and his belly shakes. If I were casting Falstaff, he'd get the part.

I laugh along with him to disguise how I'm hatching a plan to bail.

He leans back, drinking me in. "Glad we jumped right to it. Didn't play that game where I text you and you text me, and it goes on for weeks. Waste of time."

"Yeah," I say, thinking the opposite.

His eyes shift from me to the menu. "What do you recommend at this joint? That better be a magic cup of coffee for five bucks."

"It's French press. You get your own pot."

"I'd split one," he says. There's a groaning from his chair as he redistributes his weight. This may not end well.

I change my original plan. "Think I'll have tea," I say. He isn't feeling queasy like I am. He's used to himself. But I must not rush to judgment. I point to his cap with its crayon-colored embroidery. "What's King Parrot?"

"Australian band."

"Would I know any songs?"

"You a fan of grindcore?"

"Probably not."

"Then you wouldn't. Anyway, it's merch from a job."

"Nice. Free stuff." Now that the meaning of the hat has been explained, I move on to his tee shirt, which is a baby smoking a stogie. I decide not to inquire. I look around for the waiter but he seems to have vanished.

"As a nurse, you must get lots of perks. Any good drugs?" he says.

"Oh, I'm not a nurse. I do medical transcription."

"Meaning what?" He leans forward, to show interest, but his eyes dart away.

"I type patient notes for a group of cosmetic surgeons."

"If a lady comes in for a boob job you write up her story? I'd enjoy reading that." He grins and his eyes dart away again.

I follow his gaze to the next table. Two teenage girls in school uniforms. I look around but still see no waiter. Why prolong this? To protect his feelings? He's more into the fourteen-year-olds than me. He'll recover. It would be an easy escape, just make any excuse and take off down the sidewalk.

I launch in. "Doug, I'm not feeling well. I've been on a diet where I have to drink vinegar and my stomach's a mess and I've got this sour taste in my mouth." I clutch myself to emphasize what a dire situation I'm in.

His eyes narrow. "Well thanks a lot."

"Oh no! It's not you. It's me." I stand and grab my bag.

"That's it?"

"I'm sorry."

"You could at least leave a buck for the tip, for taking up the table."

"Sure." I look through my wallet and only find a twenty. I gave all my change to the homeless guy. I drop the bill on the table, getting off cheap.

"Good luck with the diet," he says, grabbing the money and shoving it in his pocket. "You could stand to lose a few lubs."

I walk home, telling myself I'm not superficial, that it wasn't his appearance that turned me off. Hey, I'd date Benjamin Franklin in a heartbeat.

Before I make it through the front door, my phone chirps. Oh no, he's texting me.

"Shit date but get it on anyway? I have a big dong." I hold the phone closer. Yup, he's sent me a dick pic. It looks like a liter bottle of coke. Block him!

"You could lose a few lubs," he says to me. He's the one testing the solder joints on the chair. I live in Beverly Hills and recognize I'm considered fat as a consequence of my place and time. Would I be drinking pints of vinegar if I lived in Vermeer's Delft? Or Renoir's Paris? No way! But since I can't time travel to a more voluptuous era, I want to lose a few pounds to increase my value on the dating market. I have not kissed a man in two years, not since my ex boyfriend, the unemployed tequila connoisseur Jeffrey, left me for a cocktail waitress.

So now, to end this period of celibacy, I'm swilling apple cider vinegar and online dating. I ask you, would Charlotte Brontë have said, "The trouble is not that I am single and likely to stay single, but that I am lonely and likely to stay lonely," if she'd had a Tinder account?

Maybe I need a new profile picture. Me riding a donkey may not be attracting the right kind of guy.

Ping!

Cool. OkCupid again. Hope springs eternal . . . "Hey beautiful!"

"Hi there!"

"You're hot."

"How'd you guess? Just got back from long walk. Must be a hundred degrees. Lol."

"I like."

"Really?"

"Is your hot body sweating?"

"I'm perspiring. Ladies perspire, right?" Who is this guy? Not promising.

"I like big tits. You like big dicks?"

Another record-breaking penis? "Sorry. Not the girl for you," I type.

"Come on! You make my dick hard. You're so hot you make my dog's dick hard."

His dog? Indeed. Now he's being silly. Must not give him the satisfaction. It would take more than bestiality to rattle Lord Byron. While he was at Cambridge, dogs were not allowed on campus, so he got around the rule by keeping a bear in his rooms. He walked it on a chain and tried to enroll it in classes. He encouraged the rumors of zoophilia.

I type away: "You fool. I'm an awesome woman, why do you want to revolt me?"

Oh . . . Looks like he's gone. Scared that one off. Online dating is the end of civilization. ■

ON THE BEACH
Luke Geddes

VIDEO GAMES
Luke Geddes

DINERLAND
Luke Geddes

PORTRAIT OF THE ARTIST AS A YOUNG WOMAN
OR
HOW JUSTINE DE JONGH CAME TO POSSESS THE FORTY-NINTH KNOWN COPY OF THE GUTENBERG BIBLE

Peter Ferry

In my mind's eye, Justine De Jongh as a girl was always on tiptoes as if she were full of helium and being pulled toward heaven; she gave the impression of lightness like one of those titanium bikes you can lift with a single finger. She *was* thin like a blade of beach grass, but it was more than that. Her ideas also seemed to be light and lacy and her spirit ethereal, although you might not have known those things about her at first because she was passive and observant. She lingered over life; she did not hurry past it, and she didn't always engage with it. She often just watched it.

It was for this reason that few people really knew her, even her parents. When she was in third grade, they had been summoned to the school to meet with her teacher, Sister Mary Pascal. They were already feeling guilty before they got there. What had they done wrong? They had neglected her, they knew, which was easy to do in their great brood of children because she not only didn't need attention, she didn't want it, and this would be true her whole life and may be the reason the world gave her so much of it. At the age of eight, all she wanted was to be left alone. She sometimes took a book and a flashlight and climbed up to the top shelf of the linen closet and read or drew pictures of giraffes until she was finally missed and people started calling her name. "Justine? Has anyone seen Justine?"

So in the car on the way to the school, her mother told her father and her father told her mother that they would be better with her, they would work with her, tutor her themselves, hire a private tutor if need be. Then they told all of this to Sister Mary Pascal. "I don't think you understand," the nun finally said, hands folded atop her desk. "The reason I asked you to come in is not because Justine is behind. It's because she is ahead. In third grade she is reading at the ninth-grade level. Justine is a gifted child."

"Justine?" they each thought.

Her high school art teacher saw her talent. He told her to come to the art room anytime she wanted and gave her passes out of study hall and lunch and sometimes other classes as well. She became known as the class artist, and she was treated with the curiosity and deference with which artists are often treated; she was drafted to work on the student newspaper and to make whimsical drawings for the yearbook and to paint theater sets for plays. She didn't mind. Eventually the art teacher created a space for her, a corner set apart by file cabinets and bookshelves, a bright, quiet corner against the windows. "There," he said, "your own little studio. 'A room of one's own.'"

"Virginia Woolf," she said.

"How did you know that?" he asked.

She knew it because the school librarian had handed her the book one day. "I think you might like this." People did this kind of thing for her often: clipped an article, played a song, wrote her a little poem. One boy even drew a picture of her. She was looking down as if at her work her hair falling across one eye, her brow frowning in concentration, her lips pursed. She kept it for many years.

* * *

Justine was a virgin when she got to the university. She should not have been. She should have had sex with the high school boy who drew her picture although she might not have kept his drawing all those years if she had. Instead she first had sex with her freshman art instructor, who was forty and had five children. They often did it in his studio with the lights turned off and the door locked, sometimes on the little raised platform where the model sat, sometimes bent over a tall stool, never on the couch in the professor's office because, she came to realize, that would be too conventional. Jelly Talbot had had some early success drawing vaguely Blakean figures intertwined in erotic ways, but by the time Justine encountered him, a lack of convention was most of what was left of his art. She once followed him all the way across the campus, watching his thick, layered hair that was long on top and chopped off radically behind so that it bounced as he walked. Her intention when she first recognized him ahead of her was to catch up with him and tap him on the shoulder. "Hi, Jelly!" Instead she realized step by step that he was rising unnaturally on the balls of his feet so his hair *would* bounce, that he probably knew that someone was watching him, and that he was a fraud.

* * *

These were the things that she was thinking about on the Wednesday night she passed the Blue Note Tap, heard the music and went upstairs to sit in the corner and watch Spinoza Jones play the piano, and realized that she was done with Jelly Talbot. She didn't fall in love that night. She wasn't even attracted to this guy whose name she didn't yet know, and she wasn't thinking of him the next day when she broke it off with Jelly. In fact she didn't see Spinoza Jones for some weeks after that night, although for a while she did walk by the bar hoping to hear his music.

When she did see him, he looked different. His hair was shorter, his face fuller, his cheeks rosier, his eyes less sunken. In fact she wasn't sure it was he at all, so she asked him: "Aren't you the guy who plays upstairs at the Blue Note?"

"Yes."

"You haven't been playing lately."

"I've been away."

All of this happened as they were both reaching for the last Dreamsicle in the carton in the ice cream freezer of the 7-Eleven on Court Street. He backed off. "All yours," he said. "Please."

"No, no," she said. "You take it."

Now, I cannot tell you if what he said next was the kind of thing he said often, but I can tell you that what she said next was not. He said, "Shall we share it?"

And she said, "Yes." And what they both said was to change their lives, as such simple questions and answers sometimes do.

That night they shared the Dreamsicle, they sat on a bus stop bench to do so and passed the ice cream back and forth. There was something intimate, almost a little sexual, about putting the thing in their mouths one after the other. They sat there long after the Dreamsicle was gone, and it was only the stick they were handing back and forth. In that time they told each other things they didn't ordinarily tell other people. Spinoza told Justine about how he thought in music and that songs played in his head much of the time.

"Is it happening right now?"

"Yes," he said.

"May I hear?"

And he sang some bars for her while he tapped the bus stop bench with his fingers. She thought as she listened how easily this could all be bullshit and how certain she was that it was not. This was in part because when she asked where he'd been away to, he said, "I was in the hospital," without further explanation.

She told him about the giraffes, and that she was one of them. She'd never admitted this to anyone before and was pleased that he did not say,

"Oh, you don't look like a giraffe at all." She told him about *her* artwork, and he listened but did not say that he'd like to see it. She wondered later if she had been trying to impress him, had been saying, "See, I too am an artist," but she did not think so. She had done that kind of thing with Jelly Talbot, and he had done it with her too, had talked of his "agent" and vaguely of a trip to New York to meet with gallery owners. She had never believed him even in the beginning, and their relationship had never gotten beyond bullshit and pretense.

So she told Spinoza Jones about Jelly, too, and it was not to impress him or to flirt with him or to mark her territory. No, it was something else, and she would not know what that something else was for quite a while, but whatever it was, he had it too, so that finally when the next bus (he had already let three or four pass) was only a couple blocks away, and he said, "I better catch this one. May I have your phone number?" she gave it to him.

And when he was just about to step onto the bus, and she was still sitting on the bench watching him, she had a sudden fear and said, "You're never going to call me, are you?"

And he said, "Of course I am. You and I are going to have a baby together."

Some men say things like that. Some men try to be provocative or outrageous, but not Spinoza Jones; he had a feeling about this girl he had just met, and if he didn't know that they were "going to have a baby together," he did not know that they were not.

* * *

And did he call? Well not before that next Wednesday night, when she came around the corner and heard the *plink plink plink* of piano keys, not before she climbed the stairs in the Blue Note Tap and sat in front of him, not before he smiled up at her from the piano and sang a song called "Dreamsicle," not before they went back to her place and sat in the open window despite the chill and talked until dawn, not until she rolled a joint and handed it to him and he said, "No thanks; I can't," not until they had slept together that first time and not until she realized that all the talk and cigarettes and cups of coffee had not been foreplay, not until she showed him her drawings. That happened the next day. He sat on a stool with her sketchbook on his knees, turning the pages without comment, and she sat beside him, wanting very much not to feel the need for approval that she was feeling. Then he lit a cigarette and drank his coffee and turned through them all again and said, "You need something serious to draw."

"What do you mean by that?" she said.

"Your subject matter."

"My subject matter is irrelevant," she said, making the argument that it is not what you draw but how you draw that matters, which sounded puerile to her even as she was saying it.

"Read poetry," he said. "Try Wallace Stevens. Try Sylvia Plath. Try Emily Dickinson, Adrienne Rich."

"How about Blake?"

"No, he's done all the work for you. Find your own vision."

* * *

So he had passed both the William Blake test and the Jelly Talbot test. She did not draw that week, not until the Tuesday before the Wednesday. Then she made a lone drawing that was very delicate. It consisted of dozens and then hundreds of very fine vertical lines of varying length that were concealing something she and anyone looking at it could only imagine but were somehow compelled to imagine. The more lines accrued, the harder it was to see through or beyond them but the more one was tempted to do so. Finally the figure was a nearly solid block, but one with frayed edges, and one could not help but see the lines that composed it even when one could not see them. Beneath the drawing, Justine wrote Wallace Stevens's words:

One must have a mind of winter
To regard the frost and the boughs
Of the pine-trees crusted with snow;

And have been cold a long time
To behold the junipers shagged with ice,
The spruces rough in the distant glitter

Of the January sun; and not to think
Of any misery in the sound of the wind…

Now when Justine looked at the drawing, it wasn't black at all. It was white. It occurred to her then that it might have been the first thing she'd ever really done, the first thing that wasn't somehow copying someone else.

And so it was that fall. Spinoza played, they sat in her open window until one night it was too cold so they closed it, she showed him her drawings, he smiled and suggested another poet to read. Then one night he said, "Try Ecclesiastes. King James."

"In the Bible?"

For the first time she read the wise, weary, ancient words of Solomon. "My God," she thought. That week she made a drawing of a man watching. He was sitting and watching, and although you couldn't see what he was watching, it was easy to imagine that it was a television. At least he had the posture and dull affect of a television viewer. This was at the time when people were questioning the value of television and calling it the "idiot box" and the "boob tube." Beneath her drawing Justine wrote, "Say not, 'Why were the former days better than these?' For it is not from wisdom that you ask this." The man in the drawing was her father, who was fond of telling her about the days of his youth when people left their doors unlocked and the keys in the ignition of their cars. "People had cars?" she finally asked one day.

"What do you mean?" her father said.

* * *

That Wednesday she went to the Blue Note and sat with her sketchbook in her lap, but Spinoza Jones didn't show up again, and he didn't show up the next week either, so she stopped going. He didn't come back for ten weeks. By the end of that time she had a whole series of drawings based on Ecclesiastes that she was now doing in pastels.

In early March she came up the stairs to her room to find Spinoza sitting on the top step. He said that he wanted to tell her that he'd be playing at the Blue Note on Friday and Saturday nights. "I need the bread," he said and smiled. His hair was clean and shorter. He had put on a little weight. He looked rested. She held her sketchbook across her chest and stood on a step a couple beneath the one on which he sat. "I've been away," he said.

"Well I know that," she said sarcastically.

"I'm an addict," he said. "I've been in treatment."

"In a hospital?"

"Sort of. They call it a rehabilitation facility. I call it a summer camp for fuckups."

After he left she went into her room. For a long time she looked out the window they used to look out together. "Addict," she thought. These were the days of marijuana and LSD. Jelly had taken speed, but an addict? Heroin?

That Friday Justine went by the Blue Note and stood at the back of the crowd, but he spotted her right away. He smiled at her. Then he played a song called "Woman in the Window." The next Saturday she stayed until the crowd had cleared and it was just the two of them and a waitress clearing the tables. "I have some drawings I'd like to show you," she said.

She laid them out across the bed and on the floor of her room. He put on glasses and studied them. She had never known that he wore glasses. "He looks like an old woman librarian," she thought. She realized how very little she knew about him, but also how very much.

"These are exquisite," he said not quite to her. He straightened up and smiled at her. "I want you to meet someone."

* * *

When they came down the corridor of offices and Spinoza turned a key and opened a door, Justine said, "Wait a minute." She had followed him here with some uncertainty, and now she felt more. "You have your own office?" she asked. She was still angry that he had allowed her to get so involved with him without telling her the most salient fact: "Oh by the way, I really ought to mention . . ."

"No, I don't have an office," he said. "It belongs to a friend of mine."

Just then the door opened and the friend came in. He was tall but narrow shouldered with red hair slicked down and combed hard against his head as if by a mother, and he had freckles everywhere. He looked like a large, old boy.

"Spinoza!" They embraced, and then Walter Willie took Justine's hand in both of his: "I feel as if I already know you," he said, and he seemed to mean it. "What do you know about me?" she thought. "What did Spinoza tell you? Did you know that I fell for this guy's bullshit? Did you know that I blew him and didn't like it? Did you know that I make silly drawings? And what a name: Walter Willie."

Now they were all sitting on the floor cross-legged, Walter Willie absurdly like the adult among children but somehow also like the child among adults in his huge, shiny shoes and tweed sports jacket. They were looking at Justine's drawings, turning them one by one. "Now this one . . ." Spinoza said.

And then Walter Willie was asking her questions. "Explain to me why you matched this verse with this image."

"Who is this guy?" she asked later with some insistence. "Is he a priest?" For there was something of the chinless BBC vicar about him.

"Walter's a scholar. He studies the Bible as literature. He's an objectivist."

"Does that make you a subjectivist?" Justine liked to think now that doubting Spinoza was a small act of defiance and did not like to think of it as a small act of punishment, but wasn't sure that it was not. She had been hurt.

Another thing she did was have sex with Jelly again but just once or not quite once, because in the middle of it she opened her eyes and pushed him off of her. "Hey!" he said. "What's wrong?" What was wrong was that Jelly wasn't Spinoza Jones, with whom she realized right in the middle of fucking Jelly she was really in love, goddamnit.

* * *

Then one day she saw Walter Willie at the library in the reading room with its tall ceiling and windows sitting at the end of a long table in front of a green shaded desk lamp, and he then saw her. "Justine." This was her favorite place to study, and she wasn't sure how she felt about the fact that he knew it, too.

"Dr. Willie."

"Hey, I have something for you," he said, searching through his pockets until he found the three-by-five card on which he'd written a verse from Ecclesiastes. "These lines made me think of you."

Justine carried that card around with her. It was Ecclesiastes 4:10–11: "Woe to him who falls when there is not another to lift him up. Furthermore, if two lie together, they are warm; but how can one be warm alone?" She was intimidated by it. What the hell did it mean? Was he mocking her?

For some days she didn't draw anything at all. When she finally did, something had changed. She very tentatively wrote the verse at the bottom of the sheet without realizing that this would become her trademark. Then she let her hands smooth and feel the paper. She did this for some time, then very deliberately she began to draw.

* * *

The first time she went alone to see Walter Willie, she didn't show him her drawing, although she had it with her in her portfolio. Instead she asked him questions. She perched on the edge of the chair beside his desk with her neat list and went down it with her forefinger. The next time she came alone, she did show him, if timidly.

"Oh my," he said. He guided her to another verse, and she illustrated that, too, and her drawing was better yet. Through that winter she showed up at his door every week or two, sometimes with Spinoza and sometimes alone, until one day in May it was the chair behind the desk that was empty. "Sit there," Walter Willie said. He sat beside the desk smiling, his legs crossed, his fingers interlaced behind his head as if he were the student. Finally he nodded toward a book open on the desk. "Take a look at that."

"What is this?" she asked. "This is very old. This is Latin. This is the Bible."

"It's open to Ecclesiastes."

"May I?" she asked.

"Of course." She turned the pages. "This can't be . . ." she said. "Is this . . . ?"

"It is."

"My God. May I . . ." she gestured.

"Sure."

She closed the cover and looked at the inscription. "It's Spanish."

"It was to be a gift to the Archdeacon of Sevilla from the merchants of the town."

"Was to be?"

"It was never given to him. The Inquisition got in the way. Look at the names."

"Yes. I'm not . . . what about the names?"

"They are Jewish names. The merchants were Jews. They were conversos, Jews who had converted."

"Why are you showing me this?"

* * *

The next time that Justine went to the Blue Note, she brought Spinoza Jones home with her. In truth, she wasn't sure that he'd come and somewhat to her chagrin was relieved when he did. Just as in the past, they sat up all night looking out the window, smoking, drinking coffee, talking, listening to Miles Davis and John Coltrane, but it wasn't as it had been in the past. Now they had no illusions. And in the dawn light when they made love, they were not doing things for or to the other person but with the other person. Justine would remember thinking later, "This is how it's supposed to be," but she would also remember the melancholy that settled upon her with the certain knowledge that life is dangerous, and love is risky, that in the end whatever else love is, it also hurts. Perhaps because the semester was ending, she wondered if they were ending, too.

* * *

And in the fall everything had changed and nothing had changed. Spinoza went up the hill and down the hill and played weekends at the

Blue Note and stayed over in her room on Saturdays, but now there were subtle differences. Walter Willie had sent one of Justine's folios to a friend, who published two prints in *Art and the Artist*, and the campus radio station had begun to broadcast Spinoza live on Saturday nights and had picked up some chords of his to use as a signature.

* * *

And Justine was pregnant. She did not know it at first because she had taken the pill religiously, but the second time she threw up, she said, "My God." She looked at her pill dispenser, and it was a day off. "Shit." Then she went to the student health center and found out.

Spinoza seemed to take it all in stride, but in fact he wasn't taking it at all, and she was to realize that that was what he did or really did not do with things he couldn't handle. He blocked them out. No song was written on this occasion.

For the first time Justine began to think that everything Spinoza did was pretense, but not like Jelly, not in the haughty sense of that word, but in a child's sense of it: make-believe. Spinoza was inventing himself as he went along, but he didn't really go along very far. He was a pianist, a composer, a freethinker, an original, maybe a genius, but, or maybe "and" is the better conjunction here, he was a dreamer, a dilettante, an avoider, an evader, an ignorer, and a drug addict.

And in the case of Justine, he did not recognize dilemma or crisis. He never brought it up, and when she did, he passed it off by saying that he'd deal with it without ever dealing with it. "It" was an abortion. She did not intend to have this baby, and abortion was still illegal in that time and place, so having one meant long-distance arrangements and going to New York and that meant money. Spinoza had no money. Saving was another thing he did not do well.

"Don't you understand consequence?" she asked him, but before the words were out of her mouth, she realized that he did not. The next Sunday morning she put a chair in front of the door and sat in it. When he woke up, she asked, "What are we going to do about this?"

"I'll get some money," he said.

"How?" There followed a seesaw discussion about whose responsibility or fault the whole thing was (not his), which seemed to Justine beside the point at best, childish at worst. "I'm not asking you to fix this thing. I'm asking you to help me figure out what to do. Okay?"

Well, it wasn't okay. He did not have any ideas at all, so she began to list off possibilities. Her parents? No. They would insist on knowing what the money was for and were steadfastly opposed to abortion. His mother? He hadn't spoken to her in over a year.

"Really?"

"How about Walter Willie?"

"Oh God, I'd hate to ask him," Spinoza said.

"Why? You know he has the dough, and he loves you."

"No," he said. "I can't do that."

So Justine did, and Walter Willie didn't hesitate. He took his checkbook out of his top desk drawer. "How much do you need?"

"I promise . . ."

"Hush," he said. "Take care of this. Worry about that later."

Spinoza went with her, although he might as well not have. They took the night bus so they would only have to pay for one night in a hotel. He slept all the way, and she slept none of it. It was midmorning by time they turned onto Forty-Second Street. Justine asked Spinoza to try to check into the hotel. He balked. Check-in time was four o'clock.

"Look, man, I gotta sleep."

To their surprise a room was ready. She fell asleep almost immediately. When she woke up there was afternoon light in the room. "Oh my God, Spinoza, what time is it?"

He was sitting at the foot of the bed, eyes in the heels of his hands, rocking back and forth. "Spinoza?"

"I really fucked up bad."

She looked at him. He did not look at her. He kept rocking. "I am so sorry, Justine."

Finally she picked up her backpack by its strap and left. She walked a long time. She asked directions twice. When she finally found the clinic, it was closed. She stood across the street looking at it. For the very first time she thought about the strange feeling in her stomach as a baby. She put her hand there. She began to cry. She stood there and cried herself out.

Then she walked to Grand Central Station and asked the price of a one-way ticket. She did not go to the bus station. She did not want to see Spinoza Jones, although she somehow doubted that he would be there.

There was a Western Union office in the train station, but it was closed until 7:00 a.m. She copied down its address and phone number. She called Walter Willie collect from a pay phone.

"Walter, I have a huge favor to ask you. Would you please wire me eighteen dollars at seven o'clock this morning to this address." She read if off. "And now I have another favor to ask you. Please don't ask me any questions. I give you my word that I will repay you the money forthwith."

She had never used the word "forthwith" before and wasn't even sure what it meant, but she was sure it was what she wanted to say.

The train station benches had wooden armrests every couple feet so you couldn't lie on them. She lay on the floor instead. She slept fitfully, using her backpack as a pillow. At 6:59 a.m. she was standing at the door of the Western Union office. At 7:00 a.m. she was standing at the cashier's window. The clerk was sorting through overnight cables. "No," he said, "nothing here for you I'm afraid."

"Are you sure?" In the thick glass of the cashier's window she saw Walter Willie's reflection as he came in the door. She turned. "What are you doing here?"

He held out an envelope full of money. She looked at it and plucked out one twenty-dollar bill. "That's all I want."

"But . . ."

"It's too late. I missed my appointment. It takes days. Besides, all I want to do is go home."

"Well," he said a little lamely, "I'm going that way."

"No thanks, Walter," she said forcefully. She slung the backpack over her shoulder. She started out the door but stopped. Without looking back, she said, "I'm not looking for a father, Walter."

"Well," he said, "I'm not looking for a daughter." ■

THE NEW PAST
David Lehman
—for Stacey

Subtract three letters
from paradise and
if you're lucky

you'll get Paris
in March or
April with you

dodging the drops
of dew and
horns of Gershwin

at Le Dôme
sipping coffee reading
the *Tribune* solving

the puzzle planning
a musical set
in Paris 1968

the signs on
the walls say
la lutte continue

with rue your
heart is laden
on rue Delambre

while citizens cross
the Blvd. Montparnasse
to join us

and escape into
the new past
we're keeping alive

A TOAST
David Lehman

"When the doctor breaks the news,

will you cry or sing the blues?"

"No way. I'll raise my glass,

take a sip, get off my ass,

and bounce my red rubber ball

against the rubble of the ghetto wall,

and catch it, feeling good,

catching it as a centerfielder would,

while a skirt walks by hoping I'll notice,

and five decades pass as swiftly as a kiss."

A STONE IN THE RIVER
Steven Carrelli

Teo stood in the parking lot, staring at the thin old man digging in the dumpster. The boy, who had been playing soccer alone in the lot behind the Catholic church, was walking home when he looked up from his feet and saw the man maybe ten yards away. Teo didn't have many words for what he saw. He thought of the cartoons he had watched on Saturday mornings, in which he had seen alley cats reaching with their paws into garbage cans to pull out whole fish skeletons for dinner.

The man, perhaps in his sixties, had close-cropped white hair, and his sunburnt face hadn't been shaven in about a week. His flattened jawline and strangely flaccid mouth stirred in the boy a combination of pity and discomfort. Teo had once seen his father remove his dentures and stick them into a glass on the bathroom sink. It had startled him to see his father's face suddenly become so soft and weak.

The man at the dumpster hadn't noticed the boy at all. He had simply walked up to the dumpster in front of the Lawson's dairy, pushed up the lid with one hand and thrust his head in as if peering into a freezer in a grocery store. It was midday, but he foraged through the garbage without any sign of shame, as if no one could see him.

At eleven years old, Teo was accustomed to being invisible. He liked it sometimes. It allowed him to watch and study his surroundings without drawing the embarrassing attention of adults, who almost always smiled indulgently at his answers to their questions. He watched people in their cars stopped at the light and imagined who they were and where they were going. He told himself stories about the fallen trees in the woods and the freight trains that passed behind the lumberyard every few hours.

Teo was not the name by which other people called him. His parents, both recent immigrants from Italy, had named him Matteo. At school everyone called him Matt, which irritated his father.

"Why Americans make everybody's name so short?" he would frequently say. "Bob, Tom, Pat, Matt. Pah, pah, pah. Like a gunshot."

Teo was what the boy called himself when he was alone. He went for walks in the small woods that separated his home from the local high school, and he particularly liked to sit next to the creek that flowed there. He had learned in school about the world's great rivers, the Nile and the Amazon, and how they supported vast and complex ecosystems. The creek was small and shallow, but he liked to watch the flowing of the water and observe the animals and plants that lived in it. He practiced skipping stones for hours, standing at the bend and throwing the flat stones sidearm downstream so they skipped across the crests in the water. He had once looked on a map to see where the stream joined with others to eventually feed the Ohio River, then the Mississippi, ending in the Gulf of Mexico. He wondered if any of his stones or the leaves that he placed on the water's surface would eventually make their way to the great delta at the mouth of the Mississippi.

But now Teo walked quickly along the shoulder of the Tuscarora Highway, the wide commercial strip of gas stations and car dealerships that ran past his house and divided his world into two halves. It was only three blocks from the dairy to his house. He crossed Erie Road and ran toward his back door, passing between the neighbor's house and the auto body shop behind it. He ran along the tall red fence that separated his backyard from the auto junkyard, and he sped up at the sound of the dog barking as it kept pace with him on the other side. He ran up the steps to his bedroom and pulled the four dollars out of the top drawer of his dresser. It was money that his godmother had given him recently. She visited nearly every week to talk with his mother, usually on weekday afternoons while his father was working. She always brought a little present for Teo and told him improbable stories with a loud voice and flamboyant gestures.

"Oh, Matteo! You know, one time I danced with the Pope," she had once told him, taking his hand in hers and kicking her feet. "Yeah. What you think? He is a man, too."

Teo loved her visits. He would laugh with complete abandon when she was around.

He carefully folded the bills and slid them into the right front pocket of his jeans. Then, quietly closing the back door behind him as he left, he walked quickly back toward the Lawson's parking lot. He arrived to find the man still standing at the dumpster, with his back to the highway and his head bent over the opening. Although Teo had hurried, he had half hoped the man would be gone, relieving him of the compulsion he felt to help. Teo walked cautiously toward the man, stopping a few feet behind him.

"Sir," said the boy, "do you need some money?"

The man, his mouth half-open, slowly turned his head, his unsteady eyes gradually focusing on the boy with a look of apprehension and surprise. In his left hand he held a windshield wiper that he had scavenged.

"Sure," replied the man, "I could use some." He said something more, but his raspy, breathless voice was difficult for Teo to decipher.

Teo then stretched out his arm toward the man, holding the four dollar bills and saying, "Here, you can have this."

Lowering the lid of the dumpster, the man stepped toward Teo, reached out and took the money. He paused for a moment, then thrust the windshield wiper into the boy's open palm.

"Here. It's new—still in the package."

Startled, Teo instinctively withdrew his hand, and the wiper fell on the ground between them.

"It's good," insisted the old man, almost pleading with the boy. "You should take it."

Teo had intended to give him something, not trade with him. Besides, what could he do with a windshield wiper—and one pulled out of the garbage, at that? But as Teo paused, the old man's trembling body grew more agitated.

"Take it! It's good. Still in the package!"

In a sudden, quick motion, Teo reached down and scooped the wiper up off the ground. "Thank you," he said, holding the wiper up for the man to see. "Thank you."

The man stared silently at the wiper, his head gently shaking. "Thanks," he said, slipping the bills into his pants pocket and turning back to the dumpster.

Teo walked back home along the highway, with the river of traffic rolling past him on his right. The windshield wiper dangled at his side. He knew he couldn't take it home without explaining it to his mother, but he figured no one would notice if he tossed it over the junkyard fence from his backyard. Spying a large round stone in front of him on the shoulder, he kicked it, swinging his leg out and striking the stone with his instep as if kicking a soccer ball. It rolled away from the street in a long, shallow arc, then curved back toward the center of the shoulder, stopping a few yards in front of him. He kicked it a second time and watched the graceful arc that it traced in the pebbles at the side of the road. Teo tried to imagine where the man would go next and how he would live. He kicked the rock again, this time with the outside of his foot to reverse its trajectory. But the stone rolled up the shoulder and into the street. Teo watched as it bounced across the pavement and came to a stop in the eastbound lanes. It was a small miscalculation, a tiny failure, but it made him stop walking and follow the stone with his gaze, as if his eyes could hold on to it. He wanted to run out and kick it back—to retrieve his soccer ball—but the constant flow of traffic didn't allow it.

Teo stood motionless, looking at the stone, it too standing still in the ceaseless river of traffic. To the boy, it looked like a tiny iceberg or a little rocky island, solitary and precarious, jutting up out of the asphalt's uniform surface. He imagined the road as a wide and fast-moving river, the cars propelled not by their own engines but by currents that, like the wind, were invisible except in their movement. He saw the rushing of the water cutting into its banks, breaking down rocks into dust, depositing new layers of silt at its delta. He saw that his stone, now a still point cutting into the surface of the river, would inevitably be carried away and its mineral hardness worn down to sand by the soft persistence of the current.

Had they been paying attention, the hundreds of drivers per minute navigating this stretch of highway might have wondered what this boy was staring at with his tractor-beam gaze. But as the traffic carried them toward their destinations, they were moving too quickly to follow his eyes. The stone was invisible to them, and the boy a small presence in their peripheral vision. ■

DEEP FREEZE
R. Craig Sautter

"And now it's *Weather-on-the-Sevens with Kevin.*" The mockingly joyous announcement by a female hip-hop drive-time DJ was heralded with pre-recorded, off-key trumpets.

"Thanks, Kim. Looks like another frigid night in Chicago. Temperatures are currently hovering at negative five degrees, dropping down to minus ten by midnight, and, baby, that's just the good news. Tomorrow morning the bottom sinks out of sight faster than the Titanic. We could see windchill diving to minus twenty by tomorrow night. And we won't get much relief after that. Another Arctic Attack is headed our way, so we could fall even further by the end of next week, and that's no jive. But what do you expect in Chicago in mid-January? So dress warmly, friends, and keep that fireplace burning like a '*Towering Inferno.*' Oh yeah, I forgot unless you're living up on the Gold Coast, you probably ain't got no fireplace. So wait for the groundhog, baby." He laughed with an exaggerated cackle. "Back to you, Kim."

Roosevelt Harvey hit a button to pull in some FM jazz. As long as it wasn't a blizzard engulfing his worn-out tires or an ice storm sending his dented, five-year-old Taurus spinning out of control, cold weather didn't bother him much. He just bundled up like any good Chicagoan. After all, this was just a light dusting of frozen crystals settling on his windshield, his gas tank was still a quarter full, and his car heater was pumping seventy-five-degree air streams onto his feet and chapped hands gripping his steering wheel. He'd get gas in the morning, like he did every Saturday. What he really worried about was getting home alive with all these crazy high-speed drivers weaving in and out on black ice that dotted the Dan Ryan Expressway. They all were headed south out of the Loop after a week of snowstorms. The eight-lane divided highway was one of the enduring monuments of Mayor Daley the First, who put it here to keep black neighborhoods separated from white ones like his beloved Bridgeport. That was before panic selling in the mid-to-late 1960s turned most of the South Side black. Over 300,000 cars and trucks traversed it every day in a mad rush. At least it was early evening and no one was taking potshots yet at their fellow commuters. That usually didn't happen until after midnight.

Roosevelt edged over into the right lane and followed the slower trail of red taillights ahead of him. He was moving steadily enough toward

Seventy-Ninth Street, where he'd get off before a final two-and-a-half mile sprint east toward his apartment building on Yates, about a half mile from Lake Michigan. He'd try to get a couple hours sleep before hopping off to the clubs for a hot Friday night, another damn week of work in the city's Housing Department over at last. He vaguely feared this cold snap might mean he'd get called up on emergency cold relief duty. He'd have to find shelter for some poor folk whose slum landlords refused to fix their heaters. But what he really was thinking of was how to convince Delilah to come home with him that night when the music ended, before the liquor wore off and she "came to her senses," as she would say. The very thought of her made him sweat. He brought his right hand up to his forehand, pushed it back across his full, bushy hairline, and blinked for a moment. "Oh baby, that would be sweet, so sweet."

When he opened his eyes, he had to blink again. The enormous streetlights overhead that normally flooded the expressway with a harsh salt-white winter wash had gone entirely dark in a flash. The road was midnight black except for high beams that shot out of cars headed in the opposite direction toward downtown and the red taillights in front of him that all lit up simultaneously. Everyone had thrown on their brakes trying to figure out what the hell was going on. The four-lane caravan of southbound trucks and cars uncharacteristically slowed a bit as a sudden uncertainty gripped them with calculations of escape. Some were headed to their modest south suburban retreats, many to cramped cubbyholes scattered across the South Side. Others were strapped in for the long haul up and over the Skyway to Indiana or straight to downstate Illinois. A few even headed way south to Kentucky. His radio blasted nothing but static.

"Their transmitter must have crashed too," Roosevelt grumbled. He pushed another button to scan channels. The blue digital selector ran all the way from 550 up to 1700 AM and repeated the whole cycle of stations without finding a clear signal. He flipped back to FM with the same result, then turned it off for a while, at least until he got back to street level, twenty feet above the dug-out expressway that cut like an bulging artery through the southern neighborhoods of the frozen city. Maybe he could pull in some distant signal up there. He was tempted to grab his phone to check for a news flash, but fear of rear-ending the Chevy Impala in front made him think twice. He'd pull over once he got up on Seventy-Ninth to find out what was going on. As his Taurus elevated up the exit ramp to street level, Roosevelt glanced left and caught sight of a stalled rush-hour CTA Red Line train halted in the center rail median between the eight lanes of traffic. He saw dark silhouettes of standing passengers. "Those suckers are stuck in the cold," he commiserated. "At least I got wheels and a heater."

He turned east off the off-ramp onto Seventy-Ninth. "Everything is down," he muttered in amazement as he surveyed the darkened rows of shops, blank neon signs, empty apartment house windows that lined both sides of the normally bustling street. Fast food joints, supermarkets, restaurants were all shutting down too. "Damn ComEd. I knew when they deregulated something like this might happen. Usually it crashes in summer from air conditioner overload, followed by blackouts, mini-riots, and a good old time in the streets, not on the coldest damn day of the year. Somebody didn't pay their damn bill. Now we're all paying."

He switched on his radio again. Static. He turned down the AM dial to 560, where he occasionally picked up Milwaukee Brewers or Bucks games. At street level, WTMJ came in weak, but clear. "Thanks for that special report for our commuters headed south," the DJ said. "To sum up, the power grid serving Chicago and sections of northern Illinois seems to have experienced a major disruption. Commonwealth Edison officials in Illinois aren't answering questions yet, and there is no way to say how long this blackout will last. Officials at Wisconsin Power and Light confirm the problem has not spread north. The WTMJ news team will . . ."

The station faded out as Roosevelt moved through a tunnel of mid-rise apartments, so he snapped his radio off again. He decided to check his phone, but before he picked it up from his passenger's seat, the familiar voices of the Staple Singers lit up with a few lines of "Respect Yourself." It was his ringer for Delilah. "Yeah, baby, you all right?"

"Rosy, this is scary. I'm headed home down Drexel. The lights are off. What's going on?" She lived on Forty-Fifth near Greenwood in a fourth-floor condo she'd recently bought with her mother.

"They're off everywhere, sugar. I just heard a report out of Milwaukee. Chicago's whole damn grid is down. You want to come to my place?"

"Maybe later. I got to get out of these straight clothes." She worked at a downtown law firm as an executive secretary. Good salary. Good benefits. Good parties with the bosses from time to time. But stiff, very stiff. She didn't particularly like it but was supporting her mother and treasured her financial independence. Roosevelt had known her since their days at King High School, when they sang together in choral group. She knew Roosevelt was sincere in his admiration and friendship, and he had a good, steady job. He knew she liked that in him. But he suspected she had something else going at work with one of the lawyers, who earned much, much more cash.

"Yeah, I got to change too. If this lasts, we better bundle up good."

"The streets are crazy, Rosy. No streetlights, cars coming from every which way. Stoplights are out. People are pounding on my hood when I slow down, trying to see if my doors are unlocked. I just swerved past a crash on Thirty-Fifth, but I don't see any cops directing intersections. Scary, very scary."

"You don't have that far to go. Just be careful. Don't stop for no one. And watch out, especially when you park."

"I got Betsy with me," she assured him. Betsy was her .22 snub nose.

"Keep her close. Look, I got to watch this damn traffic. I'll call when I get home. I guess if the lights stay down, the clubs will be closed." He didn't want this to disrupt his plans.

"Duh." She liked to zing him whenever he gave her an opening.

"Well, we can sit this one out together under some blankets at my place," he hesitated, "or yours. Your mother has her own room."

"Sounds romantic," she sarcastically quipped. "You bring the candles and we'll fry franks." They both laughed. "Seriously, I'm so hungry. Been up since six, worked through lunch. And the microwave won't be working."

"Have some ice cream."

"Very funny." She turned cold on him.

"Is it a date? You and me and the blankets?"

"I have to take care of Mama first." She paused. "We'll see." She clicked off.

"Damn." He shook his head. He had waited all week for another Friday night with her. Maybe he could still work something out. A long line of cars crept along Seventy-Ninth, and more seemed to be hitting the intersections from cross streets out of the neighborhoods, slowing things down even more, eating up gas. With stoplights out, it was one car at a time at every intersection, unless some jerk roared through with horn blaring.

"No heat in them damn buildings," he mused as he looked around when traffic halted at a corner. "Electric heat is out. Oil heaters won't work without power, blowers won't blow. Where are folks supposed to go to keep warm? I guess cars are the only place, as long as their gas lasts."

By the time he reached his pad on Yates, it was past seven. No lights lit his ten-story yellow brick apartment building next to a darkened hardware store. As temperatures fell, his car heater only blasted warm air. He pulled into a parking space behind his building and knew as soon as he shut off his engine he'd soon start feeling the cold seeping deep into his muscles and bones. He tried his radio once more before cutting his engine. This time he pulled in a weaker-than-usual all-news local station that must have been back on with an emergency transmitter.

Some reporters were shouting questions. "Mayor Hernandez, Mayor

Hernandez. When did ComEd promise power?"

"I already told you. They are doing all they can to hunt down the source of this shutdown. Emergency crews are rushing in from Indiana, Wisconsin, and downstate to repair the transformers that blew when the power surged."

"We've heard rumors that the grid was hacked and counter surges blew transformers all over the city. We've gotten reports of fires raging out of control at substations on the North, West, and South Sides."

"I can't confirm that." The mayor was testy, as usual. He was refined and dignified when he wasn't under pressure, but paranoid that the press was laying for him, which it was.

"Is the city being held up for ransom?" another reporter repeated.

"I can't tell you any more right now."

"Mr. Mayor, are you worried that with your reelection next month this could be your Bilandic moment?" Roosevelt laughed. The bungled snow removal job after a series of massive blizzards in December 1978 and January '79 had cost Mayor Michael Bilandic his job. He had been installed by "the machine" after Daley the First died of a heart attack. His failure to get the snow off the streets enraged voters and ushered in the city's first female mayor, Jane Byrne. That was before Roosevelt's time. But his father, who once worked as a precinct captain before he died, had told him all about it.

"Get this straight," the mayor shot back. "I don't give a damn about politics at a moment like this. My total attention is on getting the lights and heat back on as soon as we can. That's all for now." The reporters kept shouting questions as he retreated.

"Yeah, right," Roosevelt scoffed. "Everything in Chicago is about politics." He knew the mayor's ass was on the line. He would check news updates upstairs on his phone without wasting more gas. His gauge was hovering below a quarter tank.

He glanced up ten floors at the blackened rear windows that reflected a silver-blue winter night. Most of the curtains were drawn to hold in the remaining heat. He thought he saw Mrs. Hightower's second-floor shades move. She was always keeping watch on the parking lot and alley. A few cars had been broken into lately. He'd have to check in with her, she was old and must be plenty scared. He opened his car door. A rush of cold air bit his skin like an ice-cold morning shower. He felt the burning freeze corkscrew into his joints. Within thirty seconds he was inside the rear foyer and hiking up the stairs to his fifth-floor apartment. The elevator was out and the stairwell packed with teenagers running up and down. Voices ricocheted off the narrow walls. He felt people pushing, moving in closer to one another to retain the little heat.

Old Jordy Jones carried a flashlight as he crept up stair by stair and its beam bounced off the grey walls like shooting stars. Cell phones lit up in the hands of youngsters, who were laughing and joking. Someone stumbled and fell behind him at the third-floor exit. He heard a girl scream. The flow stopped when her friends yelled for help. She must have gotten up because the downward stream picked up speed again.

Up on five, Roosevelt groped his way down the hallway to his three rooms, unlocked the front door, and entered the pitch-black apartment. The lights on timers and stereo were out, of course. He stumbled over a stack of newspapers on his way to the kitchen, opened the top tool drawer, where he kept a flashlight. He hoped the batteries were still good. They were. He shined it around the living room. Everything was in place. What did he expect? Few robbers would be out in this dreadful cold. Then he directed the beam on an old barometer/thermometer on his kitchen wall. He'd picked it up at a yard sale two summers earlier.

The temperature inside had already dipped to forty-eight degrees. It was cold, but not brutal like outside. He dropped the venetian blinds on his front windows over the towels he had stuffed into the cracks to keep the wind out during the last snowstorm, retreated to his bedroom to put on long underwear, two more pairs of socks, a light sweater, and a heavy winter one over it. He threw his shiny brown work shoes into the closet and pulled on a pair of heavily lined snow boots. He scrounged around his closet for a second pair of gloves to fit over the thin leather ones he wore to work.

Before he hauled on his down coat and stocking hat, he sat down on his bed and pulled out his phone. He needed to call Delilah. He was worried about her, about them. But first he had to get some kind of news update so he could plot a strategy. He wasn't sure how long his phone battery would last and had no way to recharge it. He'd never gotten a car adaptor and had forgotten to energize it after lunch. He punched in the *Chicago Tribune* website, looking for headlines, but it still was offline. He pushed his CNN app. A female anchor was interviewing some IBEW rep from the electrical workers. The chyron said he was coming out of South Bend, some guy named Al Goddard.

"That's ninety miles away, probably as close as they could get an expert right now."

Goddard wore a closely cut grey beard, had lively blue eyes, rosy checks, and a sly smile that broadened as he listened to the anchor's insipid question. "That's nothing but company PR," he shot back at her. "The press should know better than swallow that old line. Management knows what's going on. Here's the truth and I have testified about it before the Chicago City Council Committee on Economic, Capital, and

Technology Development twice, and downstate Illinois before the General Assembly three times, warning about something like this. They're all in my region. I know how bad the company's equipment is."

"How bad is it?" the reporter countered.

"Very bad. It's old and decrepit in many places. Commonwealth Edison's management hints that someone might have hacked the system. That's possible. Foreign or domestic terrorists could have figured out how to shut it down or reverse energy flows in a way that caused this surge and crashed the grid. Heck, the computer system is so old a teenager could probably do it. But what's more likely is that old and overused equipment failed at one or more power stations in this cold, or that winter ice damaged electric transmission lines and caused a short circuit somewhere in the grid to cause an overload that damaged the entire system."

"Like in Cleveland a decade ago?"

"Except that was summer. This is January. And it's cold as Siberia. Unfortunately, it could take a day or more to repair. The equipment is barely able to handle a heavy load, summer or winter. Management has put profits first and failed to adequately invest in new apparatus, just like they don't pay fair wages to our workers, who have to patch it all up. What they've done is criminal."

"That's a serious charge," the anchor interjected.

"Damn serious. But whatever the cause," Goddard continued, "the result has been extensive damage to the infrastructure that will take time to repair, even with extra out-of-state crews. If it's as bad as I think, tens of thousands of people, maybe even hundreds of thousands, could suffer hypothermia, frostbite, or just plain freeze to death. And with stores shut down, where's the food going to come from? Forget all those foreign wars we're always spending billions on. This is a national emergency of the highest order. And it was all preventable!"

"Jesus," Roosevelt exclaimed. He felt numb. "Maybe I should just get in my car, go pick up Delilah and her mother, and head back across the border to Indiana. Evidently, power is unaffected there." He shook his head. "But do I have enough fuel to make it?" he said out loud. "And I wonder if everyone else is thinking the same thing and all the roads will get gridlocked?"

He stood up and put on his heavy winter coat. "If I can make it to Hammond or East Chicago, at least I can buy some gas and keep the car heater on. Then I can put Delilah and her mother in some motel and come back to help." He knew he might be on emergency call for the city. He hesitated. "Or would that be an act of cowardice? A dereliction of duty?" Roosevelt had done some rescue work during his two-year army stint in the Middle East before he went back and got his degree in business administration at Southern Illinois. He still had some army in him. He stood still in the darkness, thinking hard. He didn't know what to do. The cold was getting to him.

Before he could call Delilah, the dreaded ringer on his phone played a verse of "Clueless" by Usher, telling him a work call was coming in. He answered and heard his boss, Lynette Barclay, telling him to report to the Harold Ickes Homes back up at Twenty-Fifth and State Street to help transport elderly residents to the police station at Fifty-First and Wentworth, where a temporary gas generator was pumping out heat that might save their lives. They were gathering the seniors in a main lobby right now.

"I might not have enough gas to get there myself," he protested. "All the pumps at the stations around here are down, not to mention their cash registers."

"Can you get to Oakley and Fifty-Second?" She was annoyed at his insubordination. "Streets and Sanitation has a maintenance garage there, a generator, and a working gas pump for city workers. Show 'em your ID and you can fill up halfway. They're under orders from Emergency Management and Communications to fuel up city workers. Everyone is on call. Then report to Ickes as soon as you can. I'll assign you to other housing projects for rescues after that."

"I'll try." He hung up. "Damn. What am I going to do about Delilah?" He punched in her number and it rang five times before she picked up.

"Roosevelt?" Her voice was strained. He knew something was wrong.

"You home yet?" He spoke softly, afraid of what she might tell him.

"Been here for about ten minutes. But it's freezing, forty-two degrees in the living room according to my thermometer. I got to get Mama to one of those warming stations they're talking about, quick. She's weak, very weak. She hasn't eaten and I think she's getting sick from the cold. She has a bad heart anyway."

"Where can you take her?"

"Our battery-operated radio said the city's Extreme Weather Notification System posted a list. Hospitals, police stations, some libraries have gas generators running heat. I think we'll try the police station at Fifty-First and Wentworth. It's closest, but not that close."

Roosevelt perked up. "That's where I'm supposed to transport seniors from the Ickes Homes. Maybe we can meet there. You can keep warm, too, until I get done moving the seniors."

"I don't think so. The city says only the elderly and mothers with young children under five will be admitted because of limited space. I heard from Winston that all these places are filling up fast. I'm afraid they already may be overflowing."

Roosevelt blanched. Winston was one of the lawyers he was always hearing about. Why was she calling him first? "How much gas you got?" he softly asked.

"Over half a tank."

"That's way more than I have. Maybe wait in your car until I get there. It's got a heater. But if you can't get her into the police station, try for Indiana. Head out US 41 to US 12/20 over to Hammond or East Chicago. Power's still on there. Or drive as far as you can away from Chicago and get a hotel room. Then contact me. And why are you calling Winston?"

"Roosevelt. I think I'm losing you. My battery might be about to run out. I forgot to charge it at work."

"Just do it, baby. Those are your best choices. You hear me?"

He heard no answer. "Damn, double damn," he swore as he slammed his phone down on his bed.

He pulled on his hat and gloves and headed for his car, then remembered to check in on old Mrs. Hightower, who had been covered in blankets and sitting in her rocker before she let him in. He stayed just a few minutes, promising to check on her later. Her grandson was on his way to help. The rear parking lot was filled with idling cars packed with two, three, four people, each curled up inside, sitting under blankets with heaters blasting. Exhaust fumes twisted in the wind and crawled under their hoods, making them seem like their engines were smoking or on fire. He was afraid to think what would happen when their gas ran down.

His Taurus started right away, even in the bitter cold. He turned his heater on low to conserve fuel, but so as not to freeze. He checked Google Maps on his phone before he headed up north on Yates toward Seventy-Fifth, a busy crosstown street that could take him west to Parnell, then north a block to Seventy-Fourth, over several miles to Halsted, north a final eighteen blocks to Fifty-Second, and then west a short shot over to South Oakley and the Streets and Sanitation garage with its gas pump. That was a lot of territory, but he figured he could make it if traffic was moving steadily. If it wasn't, he didn't know what would happen. "I sure as hell can't walk it."

Roosevelt hadn't decided what he would do once he filled his tank. Maybe he should double back and pick up Delilah at Fifty-First and Wentworth. She could help with the seniors while her mother was taken care of at the police station. But if he missed her there, he'd waste a trip and maybe put some seniors in jeopardy? Maybe he could link up with her after he took the seniors to the station, if she was still there and not off somewhere with Winston, or headed for Indiana. And if the warming station was overflowing, what would he do with the seniors he picked up? Why wasn't the city's Housing Department sending a fleet of school buses? Or maybe they were, but still needed extra rides for the old folks? There had to be several thousand of them living in Ickes, and in housing projects all over the city. They all must be on the verge of panic, if not hypothermia. His mind was in turmoil as he ran through the scenarios.

"Oh, Delilah, why is it so hard for us. All I want to do is love you and have you love me."

He felt a new seriousness settle upon him as he backed out of his parking space and onto Yates. He tuned in his radio again. WBBM was transmitting a weak signal. He caught the middle of another press conference as he headed north up the residential street of darkened bungalows and snow-covered lawns. He barely listened to one of his favorite reporters, J. S. Logan, as she rattled off the list of still-available emergency warming stations. There were hardly enough to accommodate more than ten thousand out of the city's three million shivering citizens.

At the corner, he had to barge out onto Seventy-Fifth and turn left between cars that barely yielded. They laid on their horns. Traffic was heavy and slow, too slow. Every car seemed to be filled with people who he figured were just trying to keep warm or were joyriding, looking for an opportunity. On Seventy-Fifth, he got a better panoramic view of his South Side neighborhood unimpeded by the big trees that lined Yates. He was shocked to see a tall apartment building and several three-flats burning in the distance north and south of him. He figured people had been trying to heat their cribs with gas stoves and they just exploded, caught a curtain on fire, or something. "It happens every winter whenever the damn landlords cut their tenants' heat."

All the way across Seventy-Fifth he saw snowy vacant lots crowded with desperately cold people gathered around bonfires fueled by lumber torn off garages or the sides of buildings. In some alleys, they simply set fire to the garages and stood around the warming flames. Roosevelt was sure some of them would get injured by exploding gas tanks of the cars inside. He saw no fire engines or police cars anywhere. "Where the hell are they? They're usually crawling all over the damn place."

His radio droned on. He barely listened. He kept mulling his next steps, thinking of the woman he loved, worried about what she would do if they missed each other. "Is she all right? I wish she kept her damn phone charged. If I don't go get her and help with her mother as soon as I fill up, she may desert me for Winston for good." He paid attention when the mayor came on to announce a citywide state of emergency, effective immediately. Hernandez was ordering all but official cars off the main roads. He'd called up the National Guard. He said they'd be stationed around the city soon to enforce his order. "Hell, how's that going to keep people from frostbite or freezing to death?"

Fifteen minutes later, Roosevelt finally turned north onto Halsted, one of the city's main north/south streets. Fewer cars were on the road now. "Either they've run out of gas, are sticking to the side streets, or heeding the mayor's decree, if they even heard it." He glanced down at his gas gauge, dipping below the empty red line with over two miles to go. "Damn, damn, damn. What am I going to do?"

He looked up in time to catch the headlights of an old red SUV bearing down on him, a speeder running a darkened stoplight. He yanked his steering wheel hard right and avoided a collision. The SUV smashed into the old clunker behind him. Roosevelt's Ford came to an abrupt halt in a three-foot snowbank that at least stopped him from jumping the sidewalk and crashing into a darkened pizza joint. His seat belt and discharged air bag held him in place. But he was dazed and his face and neck ached from the impact.

"What the hell are you doing?" Roosevelt screamed. The SUV's horn was stuck, blaring away. He glanced back through his rearview mirror. The driver looked seriously injured, maybe even dead, his motionless head pressed against his cracked windshield, blood gushing from his forehead. A couple of following cars just sped by, the people inside gawking at the accident. No one was willing to stop or get out of their cars, risk a hijacking or brave the brutal cold wind whipping around them. "Good Samaritans," he spat.

Roosevelt sat stunned for a couple of moments, gradually felt the sore and bruised bones of his arms, shoulders, right leg, and neck. He was basically uninjured, except for head abrasions caused by the powerful punch of the air bag. He pushed it down into his lap, trying to deflate it like a popped balloon. His engine was still running, eating up precious gas. "That son of a bitch. If he weren't almost dead, I'd . . ." He took a deep breath, closed his eyes, tried to calm down. He didn't have time or energy to think about revenge and that wasn't his style anyway. He refocused on his mission, getting to Streets and Sanitation, getting gas so he could help the seniors and reunite with Delilah. He jammed his gear shift into reverse and accelerated. His tires just spun and the car moved a few feet back before it settled into a rut. He shifted into drive and rocked it forward, slamming further into the snowdrift. He threw it into reverse again and spun his tires once more. He heard them squeal and smelled rubber burning. This time the car jerked and dislodged from the snowbank, almost crashing into a rapidly passing car behind him. He hit his breaks in time to avoid a second wreck. He shifted into drive, then reverse, then forward and was clear.

He feared he'd used too much gas getting free. He stared in his rearview mirror. "Thank God someone is stopping to help the SUV survivor." That relieved him of the necessity of getting out to give emergency aid. He peeled away up Halsted, his gas tank almost dry. His right tire was bent from where he'd hit the curb. It wobbled so his Taurus hopped up and down like a jumping bean. His shocks squeaked and moaned. "I'll get 'em to change the damn tire at Streets and San, if I can make it. If I can only make it," he prayed. He was frazzled and fearful, but worked to stay focused. He knew how to operate under duress. At least this wasn't like the artillery fire he had dodged in Iraq.

At Sixty-Second Street his engine sputtered, stalled, shot forward in a final spurt, and died. His gas gauge fell way below the red empty mark and all he could do was roll the old broken junker to the curb, out of the flow of traffic. "Damn, not now. Oh please, I'm so close, so damn close." He pounded the steering wheel with his fist. If he hadn't been wearing two sets of gloves he would have broken his hand. He began to cry. He hardly ever cried. He thought of Delilah. All the tensions he was facing poured out. His body heaved and his warm tears flowed freely as he gritted his teeth. He watched dumbly as the few cars on Halsted rolled by without even slowing. He put his hands to his head and tried to gather himself. "I can't give up now. I won't. I won't." After all, he had carried sixty pounds on his back through 120-degree temps in the desert. Now he was facing a desert of white snow dunes stretching as far as he could see through the black South Side. He knew he was tough. He knew it. He wouldn't give up.

He unfastened his seat belt, shoved the deflated air bag onto the passenger's seat, and jerked open his side door with his sore shoulder. A brisk wind shot icy-cold bullets against his bruised face. He jumped out. Despite two stocking caps, his ears soon stung. The northwest wind was wicked and the bitter cold was even worse. His skin immediately tingled, then burned and stung. He gnashed his teeth. He drew his stocking caps down further over his ears, wrapped a brown scarf around his tender face, leaving only his eyes exposed. He began to limp the final blocks north to Fifty-Second. He was hungry, he was weak. His left leg, which had jammed against the steering column, ached like it had been hit with a baseball bat. He hobbled forward.

Ten blocks north, maybe five blocks west to go. He tried to flag down the next car. It was full of young faces that blankly stared at him as it passed without slowing. They didn't have any room any way. He forged forward, the wind and sub-zero cold ripping deep through his pants and long johns, icing his bones. He shivered almost uncontrollably as he staggered forward two blocks before he realized he had lost his phone, that it must have slid off the passenger's seat when he hit the snowbank. To turn back now would be fatal. He knew he couldn't do it. "Damn it," he barely had the strength to mutter. "Damn it to hell."

He tried to wave at each car that passed him. They were filled, some with anxious teenagers, some with serious men and their families, some with frightened women and their children, all bundled up, barely keeping warm. All of them seemed, in the quick glance he gave them, to be as desperate as he felt, not knowing where they were going or when they would be caught in the devastating cold like the poor homeless bum they thought they were passing. He turned ahead and walked, leaning forward to cut resistance to the churning wind, slipping every now and then on a patch of black ice or tripping on a pile of snow, catching himself as he fell, willing himself forward, then not even hearing the cars behind him until it was too late to turn as they sped past.

The inside of his scarf that covered his entire face was filled with the temporarily warm moisture of his breath, which soon turned to slivers of ice on his lips and tip of his nose. He wanted to hurl the scarf away so he could breathe freely, but the sharp slap of wind against his face would be even worse. His fingers were going numb. His feet felt like lead, like he was a prisoner in some chain gang. His leg muscles ached, tightened, and went stiff. He groaned with each step. Finally, his legs stopped moving. He stood up straight like he'd been hit with a Muhammad Ali uppercut, looked skyward at the deep darkness of the buildings on both sides of the street, then further up at the even darker sky, crystal clear in its infinity and biting cold in its emptiness. He groaned and fell sideways into the street. He couldn't even swear, couldn't even comprehend that he could go no farther. He closed his eyes and prayed, opened them again as he felt the snow stuffed against his face harden into ice. His eyes watered not with tears, but with the discharge of sparkling snow. He tried to lift his arm. He knew he was dying, that he hadn't made it, that he would never see Delilah again. He closed his eyes and thought of how his mother had tucked him into a warm bed on cold nights, how she had sung him sweet good-night lullabies. He lay there cold as an ice block.

He thought he heard a car idling, a door slam, felt two arms grab under his shoulders, lift him like a stiffened corpse, drag him up over the snow. His left hip and leg seemed to smash against the metal of a doorframe. He opened his eyes and saw a young, strong woman's smooth bronze face grimace with determination, her lively brown eyes blaze beneath her Bears stocking cap, and then other arms were grabbing him, pulling his numb body over their seated legs and knees into the blue blanket that covered them in the back seat, tugging him into a sanctuary of dull heat as their car sped off up Halsted. ■

AN EXCERPT FROM *FREUD IN MALIBU*

EVERYTHING YOU ALWAYS WANTED TO KNOW

Patricia Stacey

I opened my eyes and my mother was standing in my doorway, clicking her fingernails against the molding. She turned her lips up at the sides; I instinctively felt alarm. *It's that smirk.* She brought out what she was holding behind her back, a book, yellow with white writing with the word *SEX* in red with an asterisk next to it.

I recognized *Everything You Always Wanted to Know about Sex*, of course. How could I not? It had been splayed on the coffee table and on my mother's nightstand for weeks. I hated that particular book the minute it made its overimposing appearance in our house. I despised its Easter egg-colored vibrance. And what was the creepy asterisk about?

She came and sat on my bed, smiling sweetly, settling in to tell me something with that book, but there was a kind of edge to her voiceless whisper, as if she was relishing her words, her topic. *Please, Mom, go away*, I repeated again and again in my mind, but she wouldn't. And I fought within myself between wanting to show her I loved her company, fearful she would be hurt, and wanting to sink back under the covers to avoid the book. My heart sped up so quickly I thought I felt the bed jerk.

"You know," she said, "my mother never told me anything about this."

She was holding the book, looking at the cover now. "Do you know when I had my period, I stood in the middle of the bathroom thinking . . ."

"I remember . . . You were going to die." I finished in a hurry and looked away, with a studied air of casualness. She started chuckling at herself, but she stayed on the subject, drew a picture of her childhood. She had been premature, an ugly duckling. I looked at the shapely painted mouth, the country-club teeth, the glorious knobs of cheekbones and wondered if she was nuts. It seemed almost like some backward fairy story because there seemed to be a sense that she was trapped for no reason or trapped by beauty even. She held the book in front of me again, like it was going to be our lifeline. My lifeline.

The asterisk started spinning like a pinwheel, like some kind of hypnotist's tool.

"So you'll read the book?" she asked.

"Yes." I nodded and forced a yawn and closed my eyes, although my thrumming ribcage made my fingers tremble well after she left. I let the book fall off my bed and tumble half under my bed skirt, pushed it the rest of the way in.

She's trying to heal. And this has something to do with it?

* * *

I did not retrieve the book for several weeks. When I did, it was only at the suggestion of a girl at school named Marla. She had had a long conversation with her mother, who told her that sex was an expression of love.

"I asked my mom if she had sex with my dad," said Marla.

"What did she say?"

"She said it was none of my business."

I thought back to the conversations I'd had with my mother, remembered the strange carnival enthusiasm she had for the subject of sex. She always had an extra sparkle in her eye. "Listen," I said to Marla on our way walking home from school. "My mom gave me this book." I described it. "Meet me down at the park in a half hour. Bring some food and I will, too."

I took a blanket from the hall closet and wrapped the book deep inside, pulled out some graham crackers and apples and put it all into a large shopping bag, and left the house without telling anyone where I was going. Rushing to the park, feeling that the bag was on fire, that I was betraying some fundamental rule of the universe, I was certain that I was ruining my mother's honor, or betraying my love for her by reading such books, although I couldn't figure out exactly how. I sensed her fragility and felt somehow that for me to read the book could break her. I couldn't handle her thinking of me as sexual, even if she had given the book to me. Let her push it on me; my job would be to turn away and deny everything about it. I would have to protect her.

Never admit to having read it.

Down at the park a bunch of men were playing soccer on the field. I chose a place against the neighborhood fences as far from the players as possible, darted my eyes in either direction for Marla. From the houses on the ridge of the park, I heard a harsh synthetic sound—steel strings like corrupted lightning. A rogue electric guitar filled the sky. It could only mean pot to me and what my mother and father and Walter Cronkite and our politicians knew came with it—a slippery slope to heroin and LSD and serial killing. The Zodiac Killer was still on the loose and drugs could be the only sure reason for the killer's cynical connection to mystical forces and his entanglement with the occult and astrology. Drugs helped him cross into a world or dimension of pure evil with which innocence and love of mankind, familial bonds, hygiene, the stock market that my grandfather held dear, and the common sense of people like our President Nixon or Walt Disney could never coexist.

I pulled the book out of the blanket and quickly shoved it into the bag, looking around to make sure no one had seen. After waiting for what seemed a very long time—although it easily could have been five minutes—I pulled the bag over to myself and held it near my lap, and keeping everything inside hidden, unfolded the book, still covered by the bag, and began to peek inside at the index:

Impotence

Increase, size of,

Multiple partners

Oral sex

Penis-in-a-bottle

Pubic lice

Sex crimes

Sexually transmitted disease

As I read, the words became almost non-words, characters, mere filaments.

I flipped pages.

A penis could be artificially rendered out of a plastic so soft it was called *jelly plastic*. One should not let it grow cold. The woman would feel she was having sex on a frosty mountain peak way up there with "Big Foot."

What?

Flip the page.

One woman's vagina had apparently completely deteriorated or fallen out?

Ouch.

Flip.

A sex technique called "The Princeton Rub" involved two high school students pressing against one other in an act named "the dry hump," which would end when the boy ejaculated all over the girl. The doctor seemed more concerned that underwear was soiled than anything else. He even wondered if it was worth the benefit of the "satisfaction" compared to the ruined clothing.

Whose satisfaction did he mean?

One woman enjoyed when her husband, dressed up in a furry stuffed-animal-like costume, became extremely sexually excited and together they would take out yet another stuffed animal—this time a "white gorilla plushy." She seemed to be even more excited for sex now. She loved this stuffed-animal sex because it reminded of her of her childhood and she felt like "a little girl again."

Really? Wow. I have a teddy bear the size of a beanbag chair and I sit on him. I don't talk to doctors about it.

Flip again.

Women could be "unclean." One should not get near them during this time. They are "unapproachable." Sex would be wrong.

But what about the ejaculation? Wasn't that unclean?

Flip again.

Hookers were prostitutes who sold their services to "johns."

Surely he doesn't mean bathrooms.

"Hookers" seemed to be an angry bunch with "tricks" up their sleeves, particularly if one didn't pay. Example of a prostitute's stunt: She would pretend to be a maid from the hotel acting as if she thought the man's wife had left her dirty lingerie in the room by mistake. She would pour some oil onto her own underwear crotch and send the greasy apparel to the man's wife with an innocent note that she must have left it by accident in the room.

Prostitutes must be very busy at the post office.

Flip.

Spanish Fly.

I think it might be a drink my mother orders. I hope…

"Oh, you brought the book!" Marla startled me. My veins were humming by the time she sat down. I was so worked up it took me a moment to notice she was speaking in flat tones. "I talked to my mother about that book. I told her you had it. She said she didn't want me to read it." She dropped her bag on the blanket. Now I wasn't just betraying my mother; I was betraying Marla. I looked away to hide my cheeks, and tensed my fingers.

Why would my mother give me something Marla's mother needed to protect her from?

"I am so bummed out," said Marla, arranging her bag as a pillow. "Maybe I'll just ignore her—read that book anyway."

"Listen. You don't have to read it. I can. Do you want me to skim over it and tell you what it says?"

"Okay," she said. "Yeah."

I opened the book and began to read about sex positions and learned a lot of things that a woman can do to a man with her mouth.

When I told Marla, she told me she didn't want to hear any more. Still, I was curious and couldn't imagine putting the book down now.

"How about if I change to a different section?"

"Okay," she said. I flipped to a part about a woman lying dead in a bathroom, didn't even read that to her. God forbid "Mrs. Marla," as my mother called Marla's mom, would find out.

I flipped again, found a different section. "It says some people have sex with the same sex—like men with men. Did you know that?" She motioned eagerly for me to go on. I read about how men called "homosexual" had a special way of having sex. They would lie facing each other, one on the bottom. The man below would squeeze his legs together and the other one would use the tightened legs near the testicles for pushing the penis into. This was the way they had sex and it was called "interfemoral intercourse."

Marla seemed speechless. She stared out at a group of men playing soccer.

In the periphery of my vision I saw someone, turned my head slightly to note one of those Jesus figures coming up the path from the direction of the L.A. River, wearing holey jeans.

I slipped the book into the bag and my mouth immediately went dry. The lanky, mustached, long-haired blond with a bandana on his head was standing in front of us. He looked to be between twenty-five and thirty from where I sat on the blanket. I was frightened by his messy hair and the self-assertion in his dirty slouch. I had heard stories of guys grabbing girls, of disappearances, and my heart was doing double duty to keep from banging out of my chest. The Jesus figure had a strange smile on his face, part smirk and part something menacing and unrecognizable to me. I prayed he wouldn't expose himself as an old man had once done in front of me at the park.

"What are you readin'?" he asked, standing far too close to the blanket.

"Nothing."

He smiled and looked off, then back.

"Let me see."

"No, that's okay."

He moved closer. I had the strange sense that someone had poured Drano down my throat. *Go away. Please go away*, I thought. I looked at Marla. She was ashen and kept her head down.

"Do you girls like to read?" he asked with a huge smile on his face.

"Sort of."

"What have you got in the bag?" he asked, trying to keep himself from laughing.

"Apples. Food."

He tried to grab it. I held on tight.

"I think I know what you're reading," he said. "It's dirty."

He reached a second time. I pulled in again, couldn't bear to think of him reading those words in front of us. I didn't know if he would laugh and make fun or rape us then and there. I prayed and prayed, *Please, please leave*, while I rocked with the bag on my lap.

As for him, he just wouldn't go. He asked us questions. Marla was much better at not giving in to the pressure to talk; I worried about being rude, which I knew, even then, wasn't right. He asked about school and where we lived and I somehow steered him onto the subject of ballet. I could see his eye on the bag.

"Why are you holding that that way?" he asked. I rocked some more.

"You want an apple?" I finally asked.

"Sure." He sat down.

I stuck my hand into a small hole I made at the top and proffered the red globe. He bit in.

The ballet morphed into a discussion of the theater and soon he said, "Hey, girls, I have an idea. Want to go see *Hair* with me?"

I shook my head and looked off toward the San Gabriel Mountains, working to keep from seeming upset, trying to focus my mind on imagining the Sierra beyond.

I shook my head and let my hair fall in front of my face.

I knew more than a little about the play *Hair* and what this question meant. The show came to the stage in LA to seep into our lives and unearth them. In *Hair*, the greasy long-haireds sang songs about sex and protesting the war and might even burn a flag on stage. Clearly, the entire cast, who stood naked in front of the audience, must be an intentional affront to us. They professed peace, but this was the real war, a frontal assault. Seeing all the nakedness on stage would be less about us watching and more about asking us to face something I didn't want to see. My mother had been smiling her devious, slightly lascivious smile one day in fact when she asked us if we wanted to go see it.

"If someone is going to be a Victorian in this house, it will have to be myself, Mother," said Paula. "And I'll stay home with Patsy." She put a protective arm around me.

Leave, leave! I wished the man away and studied his hands.

"You going to let me read that book or not?"

The bag smoldered a hole in my stomach.

"Don't you have to go play soccer or something?" Marla said finally.

"No."

He continued to smirk at us for several more minutes and finally got up and left.

As he walked away he said, "And take some advice from your elder;

you two are too young for that shit."

* * *

That night, my mother made lobster on the hibachi and Marla slept over, as did Paula's friend Sybil.

I was aware, as were we all, that Sybil was in the process of a profound transformation in her life, metamorphosing from being a horse to believing she was a vampire. She watched a show called *Dark Shadows* constantly, uttered the name Barnabas with religious fervor, and was interested in black magic. While Sybil rarely deigned to speak to us kids, she often expressed herself in other ways. On this particular night, we had tried to hang out in the living room, but the blond, big-breasted vampire, wearing a black choker, held the hem of her cape just above her nose and pierced us with the evil eye. When that didn't scare us, she leveled a low, guttural horse's neigh, scratched her hooves on the carpet, dilated her nostrils, and chased us out of the living room.

Marla and I ran and collapsed on my twin bed.

"Open the book," she said, getting comfortable with a pillow. "Read the prostitute section," she whispered.

"I'll read it and translate for you."

"Just read it," she said. "It's a free country."

I read what it was that prostitutes do to men—most of it seemed like an awful lot of work with not much to recommend it. Dr. Reuben included the names of each of the activities. It sounded more to me like a list of stuff you'd buy at a hardware store. I wondered out loud how a respectable doctor would know so much about prostitutes.

"Maybe he's a pump," she said.

"*Pimp*, it says."

"Yeah."

Marla and I were soon aware that one could not read Dr. Reuben's book without noting that an awful lot of adult sexuality had to do with what you do with your tongue. He also noted that licking ice cream cones was a way a girl could prepare herself for a gratifying sex life. "Yuck." Marla stuck her tongue out. "Read something else." We skimmed the sections about geriatric sex, premature ejaculation and mildly argued about whether to investigate autoeroticism or aphrodisiacs. In the end, we soon admitted that neither of us knew what the words meant, which required going behind enemy lines to retrieve the massive *Webster's* my parents kept open like a prayer book in the living room. Back in the bedroom, better armed with definitions, we determined that autoeroticism was more intriguing than aphrodisiacs.

Now Marla was sitting on my bed reading over my shoulder. The faster reader, she impatiently tried to flip over the page before I was finished. I batted her hands away when she tried to turn too early. She sighed in frustration. When we were done, we looked at each other. She leaned back on a pillow.

"Want to try it?"

"What . . . you mean . . .?"

"Ye-es."

"Right now?"

"No, no. In the bathroom."

"Forget it."

"Go ahead. It's your house. You first." She pushed me.

I made my way cautiously but could hear my parents in the next room talking. I lifted my nightgown and followed the doctor's directions. Focusing was not easy, especially since I could tell that my parents were vaguely arguing.

In the end, I returned to the bedroom, a failure.

Marla urged me out the door. "Try it again. You didn't give it enough time."

I went back and found myself really concentrating this time, working hard—not quite as hard as a prostitute works, but I did give it my all. Within a minute, I began to feel something, an involuntary lifting feeling, the motion of my own body moving on its own, tilting, rising. I ran back to tell Marla.

"Did you feel anything?"

"Maybe."

"What?"

"You know that feeling you sometimes have when your foot goes numb and you try to get it to come back. Something like that."

"That's not right," she said. "You must have been doing it wrong." She buried her face in the book, looking for a description. "Anyway, I hear they say it's more like a sneeze."

Oh God, don't tell me I'm going to be bad at this too. "I didn't do anything like a sneeze."

"Well I'm going for the sneeze. It sounds better," said Marla.

She was gone for fifteen minutes.

But when she came back, she was smiling triumphantly.

"What happened?"

She wouldn't answer. And put her covers over her head.

"Come on." She shook her head under the bedspread.

I had my first inkling that sexuality wouldn't separate me from my mother alone. When I finally persuaded her to fess up, she peeked out of the covers, like little red riding hood, and whispered, "Not a sneeze. More like stars shooting out your fingers."

* * *

The next day we walked to the park, enshrouded in conspiracy, bonded by a sense of newfound awareness—this time without the book. Down by the soccer field, something was happening. Trailers scattered around the grass. At first it seemed that perhaps a carnival was coming to town, with no rides, and a small group of people were sitting on the grass not far from the trucks and trailers. Large power cables snaked through low-lying shrubs and zigzagged out into the soccer fields. We found a small band of women sitting in the shade of a little sapling casting the wimpiest bit of shade. A man in a brown jumpsuit came and handed them pills and urged them to swallow.

"What is that?" I asked.

"Salt tablets," said a brown-haired beauty.

"You take salt?"

"Yes," she said, and I noted that her cheekbones were so prominent they looked to me like elbows lodged in her face. She spoke in a sultry whisper, a little like Marilyn Monroe, breathy and gentle, and I was immediately struck with a sense of attraction even as I was repulsed by something I sensed false. "Oh, yes," she said. "It's very hot out here and we're working all day. We get sick," she more breathed-out than actually said.

"You work that hard? That you get sick?" I immediately thought about the prostitutes.

She moved her face from side to side in an almost musical manner, "Yes, darling, oh yes."

"What do you do?"

That moment another beauty in a bikini plunked herself down in the meager speckled shade and grabbed a thermos and pill. And in the moment, disorientation came over me that bordered on fear. I knew these people. "She wants to know what we do, Goldie," said the dark beauty.

The blond giggled frenetically and wiggled her head and said, "Ever heard 'Sock it to me'?"

A man wearing another jumpsuit came up and said, "Hey, kids, want to be on our show?"

Marla nudged me and called out, "Yes!"

"Come this way." The man took us to the far side of the trucks where about thirty oversized beach balls were strewn about the soccer field. "Run and jump on the balls," he directed. "That's all you have to do."

We did. We jumped and rolled and laughed while cameras rolled. Soon twenty spectacular women in bikinis came running down from the trailers. We knocked about with the beauties in bikinis for an hour.

I grabbed Marla on the way home. "Was that who I thought it was?"

"Man, we just met *Laugh-In*." The blond was the girly one who giggled a lot and danced in a cage. I couldn't think of her last name, but Marla remembered her name, Goldie Hawn. I was breathless and began to run. I could not get to my mother fast enough. All morning I had been feeling dirty. If I read the Dr. Reuben book, I was doing as my mother must have wished, being a good daughter. And yet I had done wrong, felt ugly, or the book's world was ugly. I couldn't help feeling that, even though she felt she was giving me the liberation of free knowledge, she was unwittingly binding me to something unsacred and vile, something like her attempts to meet men.

But today was different. We had finally been touched by something holy, dipped in a sacred river and come out clean.

I had been worrying all morning that I would never be close again to my mother, had perhaps become perverse and dirty, but now fame, or the proximity of it, had made us worthy.

"That brunette was famous too," said Marla, chasing after me, panting. "I recognized her from the show about the guy with the shoe-phone . . ."

"*Get Smart*." We rounded a corner and came across Paula and Sybil with three dogs, doing their dog-walking business. "They're filming *Rowan & Martin's Laugh-In* over there, guys. A man gave me a salt pill." I opened my palm.

"What do you want that for?" said Paula.

"It's hot out here. You could get heatstroke." I began to run again and called out, "We're going to tell Mom."

As we ran, I knew exactly what we would do; we'd fly in the door. My mother would be sitting there doing nothing, and we would enter and tell her and we would make her day. In return, she would make a party—cucumber sandwiches, olive and cream cheese, Ritz Crackers with cheddar, but not before we all went back to meet the stars. The hosts of the show were supposed to be coming and my favorite comedienne of all was supposedly on her way.

The closer to the house we came, the faster we ran. We gained the four suburban blocks and burst in the door to find my mother in the bathroom. When she came out, we pantingly told her what was happening. I begged her to come back to the park with us, to meet all the famous people. "Mom, you have to."

"And the woman who does the phone operator will be there, they said Lily Tomlin," added Marla. But my mother said she was tired and it was hot and she just disappeared into the bedroom.

By the time I grabbed my autograph book and we made it back to the park, the crew was just pulling up their thick electrical cables. We made the rounds and got signatures, met the hosts. On the way home, I was vibrating with the energy of my autograph book, with so much talent and fame held cold and fast inside the red leather binding. I knew I was changed and I remained consumed for days afterward with a sense of reflected importance. We mattered, somehow, just having been with all the stars.

And yet, a little vein of doubt crept into my thinking. I did not understand why my mother wouldn't go with us back to the park. She always said, "I'm growing up with you girls," but this was the best part of growing up, and she wouldn't come. ■

GRATITUDE PRACTICE
Kathleen McGookey

Thank you for the gray and fraying milkweed pods ready to release swirling clouds of silk, for the pumpkins, not yet rotten, for my children interrupting at mealtime, the greasy knife clattering to the floor, water pooling under our glasses; thank you for the thankless task of making dinner again, for the smudged and sticky kitchen floor, for the nights that come so early now, rain turned briefly to hail and back again; thank you for the phone call that the car went off the road but not into a tree; thank you for the chocolate cake though it's burned and I forgot the frosting, for the child who stood by my bed last night and whispered again and again until I jerked awake; thank you for eye rolling, for *I'll do it in a minute*, for *you wouldn't understand*, we have so little time together after all; thank you for my mother and father, absences we search for in the sky; thank you for the broken dishwasher, for the repairman who calls back but can't stop by today, and thank you for the yellow leaves shaped like teardrops drifting from the birch, which hover a little, then fall like falling is all they'll ever do—

ULTRASOUND AT FIFTY
Kathleen McGookey

Basil from the garden sprouts skeleton tendrils, curling inside a glass next to my sink. I just meant to save it for a day. I forgot that quiet, hidden force, wetly propagating. I forgot the ultrasound's underwater whoosh, valves ticking, spark of news, buzz-whir-click. Only my heartbeat this time. In the waiting room, I type my name into a computer and a woman says, *You're in the right place.* The technician checks the pulse behind my knee, then slides the wand over the teensy grief, size of a kidney bean, that sprang up overnight in my thigh. She doesn't invite me to view the screen.

HERE
Kathleen McGookey

While she was waking up after emergency surgery, my mother blinked and said in a bright slurred voice, *Here I am!* Like she had just burst out from her hiding place. Then she closed her eyes. A few minutes later, she lifted her head and said it again. She didn't yet know what they had done to her body to keep it temporarily in this world. And after she knew, she didn't complain. The visiting nurse didn't say the stoma looked like a rosebud. He taught us to look in our bathroom mirror and trace its shape on the adhesive of the colostomy bag. We tried our best but didn't always get it right. In the end, it hardly mattered.

NATURE IN THE MIDWEST
Charles Hood

1. Begin by flying west to east, landing in Chicago, driving north. Of
    course this is contrary to the grain of history, given that Wisconsin
    is a good place to be *from*. People who fled Wisconsin and never
    returned:

    1.a. John Muir.

    1.b. The man who owned Aldo Leopold's sand county farm right
    before Aldo Leopold bought it—the man went to California
    and never came back.

    1.c. Poet, scholar, critic, drag queen, and my primary poetry mentor,
    Robert Peters, a bear of a man who wrote forty-four books
    and who used to keep a glass-topped coffin in his living room,
    complete with papier-mâché occupant. He left Wisconsin for
    California and never came back.

    1.d. My first publisher and another poetry mentor, Clint Colby
    of SUN-Gemini Books. He went to California in the war but
    ended up in Tucson afterwards and said he would not go back
    to Wisconsin even if his mother was dying, Rock Hudson had
    moved there, and the state legislature paid him $1,000,000
    a minute.

    1.e. Every single relative on my mother's side—a mix of Germans,
    Swedes, Calvinist Presbyterians, Lithuanian Catholics, civil
    engineers, car salesmen, drifters, thugs, racists, and Holocaust
    deniers.

    1.f. John Clayton, Earl of Greystoke, better known as Tarzan of
    the Apes. How did he end up in Wisconsin? Read the first of
    the Tarzan books (1912, and a good companion to *Heart of
    Darkness*) and find out for yourself. I will tell you this, though:
    there is a forest fire, several secret identities, and a broken heart.
    Wisconsin causes Tarzan more pain than do all the wild beasts
    in the Congo.

2. No, we do not begin with Wisconsin, we begin with glaciers.

 2.a. There are seven kinds of glacier: the Ducati, the Royal Enfield, the Guernsey, the Lesser Ayrshire, the Greater Ayrshire, the Milking Shorthorn, and the Harley-Davidson. The last glacier in Wisconsin retreated ten thousand years ago, except it did not retreat, it just established a new strategic position. Before that, glaciers came and went across the tablelands of Wisconsin and Minnesota like too-hot blankets being shoved off and then hauled back up to the chin of a restless and gigantic sleeper, a sleeper whose sprawling hulk spread from Bob Dylan's hometown of Hibbing in the Iron Range to the other arm, scattering the Green Bay Packers, down to Madison, home of 106.7, The Resistance (long may it rock). Glaciers gave us kettle ponds like the one that was the central feature of John Muir's childhood homestead and gave us the stones now stacked as cairns of brown, gray, white, and purple rocks that mark field boundaries, and of course the fine, silty soil called loess, soft as corn silk.

 2.b. There were never any glaciers in Wisconsin, just a long, gray winter, a winter that lasted thousands of years, a winter with no singing and no birds, just steady *whap whap* of John Muir's father's leather belt beating young John Muir for not learning enough Bible verses that day.

 2.c. And afterwards, hands trembling, John Muir's father drank one cup of black coffee, no sugar, and went to bed. When he woke up, all the glaciers were gone.

3. But we do not begin with the day the last glaciers left, nor with the John Muir homestead, now a county park with a ballfield and mergansers and beaver-felled birches, nor with Aldo Leopold, who liked to make sourdough biscuits in a Dutch oven when camping and to shoot quail for lunch, nor with any of his friends who went with him on canoe trips to hunt ducks and bake bread and argue over the meaning of life. We do not begin in Dunbar, Scotland, where John Muir was born, nor with the flint-hard faith the Scots chiseled out of the face of glacier ice, one raw syllable at a time.

 3.a. That is because we begin with the lightning-harrowed burr oak that Aldo Leopold sawed into quarter sections for firewood, the one whose tree rings proved that in this year this thing happened and in that year that other thing happened, as the newly sharpened teeth draw the crosscut blade deeper into the rind of time. Cutting oak is hard work and as the joke says, you are warmed once in the cutting and a second time in the burning, and if you rake the sawdust out of the mud you can burn that too, maybe fortified with a splash of kerosene, kerosene that in Aldo Leopold's time came from Texas but in ours is fracked out of oil sand, and how you write about nature in the upper Midwest is you agree not to think about the sublime or floristic provinces but just to do it, so that if your notebook says, *Three hundred tundra swans in the ice-ringed lake, one kingfisher, and above it all, the clattering gobble of sandhill cranes,* then you have done it, you have started, and if your notebook later says, *So many dead raccoons, the berms swell with bodies,* then you are continuing on in steady, reliable form. Black-lacquered deer skulls on the wall in the redneck cafe and it is starting, it is happening, somebody wave to the glaciers to hang on, because here it comes. Who harmed you as a child, who still flinch-dreams your nights for you? Never mind: we will burn sage, purge them from the page of your memory. They never have to be part of your story ever again. Push the blade harder—cutting the good, dense wood and smelling the years rise up on a mix of pitch and hope, time and resin. Inside the tree, the grain is a kind of skin clock—here is when you were born. Here is the Black Hawk War, and this, by it, that is the circle when Henry Thoreau was sending turtles in alcohol to Spencer Baird at the Smithsonian. The farmers in Concord were puzzled by soil erosion; could it be related to cutting down so many trees? Shakespeare died on the same day as Cervantes—did the sky go just a little bit dark? This burl marks the Avignon Papacy; hippos have started to become rare in Egypt. This part is Jesus, when lions still occurred in Sicily. Tigers came to Rome from Asia Minor, not so far, not really. Somebody you're related to was alive then, your fingerprints quoting theirs like love letters from your parents' parents' parents.

3.b. This part of the tree looks like your elbows—here, take a picture.

3.c. *Once upon a time, there was a child just like you.* How much of my life has been spent listening for the end to that story? Let's just hope no wire grew into the tree, some lost fence line waiting to snap a tooth off the blade, jagged fang of metal spinning out and aimed at somebody's eye. Hemingway: after the Michigan years, another person born in Chicago who would not go back. He was a brilliant shot, Hemingway was, even at the end; most people don't know that. Could have shot professionally, or, earlier, been a market gunner thinning the sky of its plague of doughbirds and passenger pigeons. Market gunner: sometimes you used a small canon called a punt gun. All the guns in the Ketchum house were kept in a locked case, the key, small and light, hanging right next to it. Locked and yet not locked. You could touch them any time you wanted, rub the stocks with linseed oil, just hold them and sit quietly. Of the W. & C. Scott & Son full-choke Monte Carlo B with ivory sights, the gun that was the last gun Hemingway weighed with weary familiarity, the last thing he would have touched and thought about, the gun he had bought secondhand in Italy while staying with a count and first tried over the lagoons of Venice, after his death the stock of that gun was smashed and the mechanism was smashed and the long damascus barrels were shaved into curls with a welding torch and those pieces cut and cut again, and then all the pieces were buried at night in a field. Somebody's house rests, lightly, on top of that dirt now. If only we could bury all our fathers as cleanly and decisively. Hemingway's other guns, clean and bright, belong to the Nature Conservancy. Or Kurt Cobain's sunburst Hi-Flyers, the one with stickers and pink pickguard and the other guitar whose neck he cut down to hack onto a Greco Mustang? Both disappeared in 1988. Swap meets weep in hope, waiting. What color suit would you bury him in, our sad Mr. Cobain, if you had to pick? The body of this poet we have burned on the shore in the custom of our people, but we have saved a package of his cigarettes. A sash and medals: all that remains of the Ottoman Empire. Of the long and great Song Dynasty, barely a trace. Should we make an appointment to review the Aldo Leopold papers in person? Will it make any difference? One day everybody I have ever admired will be dead. We are like an immense pod of dolphins, leaping in and out of the water, bow riding, until one by one we each forget to come back to the surface. Who will quote any of us in an afternoon English class, looking out the window and smiling? Maybe the blinds will. Maybe the small, dead flies. The windows are trying so hard to remember, to take it all in. *Yes*, they say, *Robert Creeley, yes, okay. Isaac Babel, his book* Red Cavalry. *And* The Collected Poems of Charles Olson, *that one about all the kinds of snowflakes he can make out on his coat sleeve. Yes, okay.* Can we trust them to get it right? Maybe we should all live another hundred years, just to be sure. Lorine Niedecker—her red wood house has a bronze sign on a pole in front of it, but is it enough? Her middle name was Faith. I can tell how hard the windows are trying to help by how they shine my own face back at me, but from the future, a future-old-me face returned back to today to tell me something important, helped by the windows, come back to say, Remember this moment, press it into your hand like your first lost tooth, do not let it go. Hold it tight, because you need to understand, *you really need to understand*, how you will never get another one like it. ∎

RUNAWAY
Regina DiPerna

As a child I used to jump out
the window of the laundromat

just to hear my tennis shoes crunch
the gravel like a runaway's would.

It was only a single story,
just high enough to sound like a bone

splintering as I landed, like the static
of a comet's tail as I ran across

the parking lot with imagined urgency.
There were horses in the adjacent field.

I watched the muscular sheen
of their jaws, snouts, setting sun

silhouetting their eyelashes,
the wild plums and blacks of their eyes.

It's hard to define what *away* I wanted
to run to, what *this* I wanted to leave;

my father drank but I didn't understand
that yet, my mother hid her bruises,

my brother was still alive. Sometimes
we would feed the horses fruit.

An image I've always kept: my brother
holding a red apple out towards

a brown horse, his face full of freckles,
the horse's forehead smudged

with a white star. The produce bag
in his other hand like a thin apparition.

These were the things I imagined
tying up in a bandana, throwing over

my shoulder in the middle of some night,
the things I imagined leaving.

But I would always come back.
Run past the horses, loop through

the back door by the dryers, then escape
all over again. It was never about *after.*

It was about the moment you realize
you are free, the feeling of being tied

to nothing and bound for everything,
using each muscle under my skin

for its wild purpose.

ABANDONED HOME
Natalia Nebel

My aunt Cesarina and uncle Enrico live in a white stucco house with red shutters that overlooks the Adriatic Sea. They bought it years ago with money Cesarina had inherited from her family, before the town below them became a second-rate resort area, and their house a valuable property. Uncle Enrico is a doctor, but at heart he is a farmer, and in place of a lawn behind their home, he cultivates an extensive, completely practical garden of beans, peas, and squash; of fruit trees, lettuce, tomatoes, and rosemary. He spends hours in his garden digging, picking, weeding, and it's a source of great pride for him that any day of the week, at any meal, his table holds what he has if not created, then at least nurtured along to transitory, vegetable beauty.

My cousins, Daniella, Stefano, and Alessio all spent a good amount of their childhood working in the garden with their father. I remember them transporting dirt and fertilizer in wheelbarrows, running dutifully from one end of the garden to the other, and I remember the large buckets of water they dragged to fruit trees the hose wouldn't reach, and the baskets full of vegetables they picked. Uncle Enrico supervised their lives relentlessly, and when I visited them during the summer, the fear that I might never be able to leave the small colony always came over me, keeping me awake at night.

When I drove through the open iron gates and up their unpaved driveway for my first visit in several years (I had been working and studying for a master's degree in America), Uncle Enrico appeared out of nowhere to greet me, waving one of his arms broadly.

"Bella, oh-ho, you're back!" he shouted as I got out of my car. He hugged me and kissed me on each cheek. We were almost the same height, which shocked me. His black eyes, which had terrified me when I was young, seemed to have grayed, and he had grown a beard since I'd been gone, long with white scattered throughout.

"Well, well, well, I can hardly believe it. You decided to come back. How are you!"

He spoke loudly, and as he spoke his volubility came back to me, his temper, his drive and warmth.

"I'm fine," I said. "How are you?"

"Great! I've made tremendous strides with my garden. Tremendous.

I cut down that old pine tree because of its shade, an ugly tree anyway, but here, I'll show you."

He placed a hand on my upper arm, I could feel calluses through my shirtsleeve, and together we walked to the back of the house. He walked fast, and by the time we came to the corner of the house, we were practically jogging. When we turned the corner, he stopped abruptly. "Here we are!"

From the edge of the house to the stone wall that enclosed their plot of land, every square foot had been cultivated and at least three dozen different plants and trees were flowering in the July sun. Uncle Enrico set his hands on his waist, brought his elbows out, and breathed in deeply, his chest expanding and his beard pointing up.

"What do you think?"

"Incredible. Beautiful."

"It's all good, that's the thing. You've never tasted anything like my tomatoes here. I go into the garden, sprinkle one with salt, and eat it on the spot. That's all it needs, a little salt. I've got everything here: rhubarb, cayenne, sunflowers, I eat their seeds. I've even got poppies, I'm going to make opium one day!"

He threw his head back and laughed at this idea, the wrinkles around his eyes spreading downwards and deepening. I noticed the khaki pants he wore were pinned together, and his white tee shirt was almost transparent. I couldn't help smiling.

"What's he laughing about now?" Aunt Cesarina said behind me. I turned around. Aunt Cesarina was wiping her hands on the apron she wore over a baby-pink dress; she'd obviously just come from the kitchen. Cesarina's small features, her wide mouth that curved up naturally, her large blue eyes and round face gave her an air of innocence and youth even though she was almost sixty.

"It's so good to see you, you are beautiful as ever," I said. We hugged and I breathed in deeply because I liked her scent: basil, soap, a hint of mint and garlic. Uncle Enrico edged away from us and began poking at the ground around a plant.

"It's so nice to have you here, Bella. And you look wonderful. America agrees with you."

"I like it there," I said.

"You've been looking at Enrico's garden. Isn't it something?" She leaned closer to me and said softly into my ear, "He's so proud of it, it's an obsession now that he's retiring. I suppose there's no harm. There are worse things. On the other hand, I worry. He won't eat meat anymore. Everyone should eat meat sometimes."

"What's all the whispering?" Uncle said loudly, irritated, having finished with his plant. "What are you talking about?"

"Nothing, nothing," Aunt Cesarina said. She was practiced at filling in over her quick confidences.

"Our lunch today will be almost entirely from your uncle's garden, Bella."

"That's right," Enrico said, "everything except for the pasta. I could do without pasta, but your aunt insists. Well, what can you do? I don't eat meat anymore and soon I'll stop eating eggs too. I'll become completely self-sufficient. This is how we were meant to live." He made a sweeping gesture with an arm towards the garden.

"When I think of the waste in the world!" he continued. "Bella, did you know that America, where for some reason you see fit to live, accounts for four percent of the world's population and consumes—"

"Twenty-five percent of the world's resources," I finished for him.

"It's immoral."

"Do you think another people would do differently?"

"Yes. Americans invented consumerism, that's their contribution to humanity."

"Bella," Aunt Cesarina interrupted, "I'm going to go get the pasta ready."

"I'll help."

"No, please sit down. Relax. But you, Enrico, do go change your clothes; they're filthy."

"This is dirt, wife dear, from the earth. Nothing to be afraid of. The air we breathe, that's different. 'Enrico, change the air before we eat lunch,' you should ask me."

"Please, Enrico."

"No!" Enrico shouted.

Aunt Cesarina rolled her eyes discreetly.

"Lunch will be ready in ten minutes," she said.

"I'll go in with you and out the front door. I have to get my overnight bag from the car," I said, and I followed Aunt Cesarina into the house.

"I'm not changing!" Uncle Enrico shouted after us.

* * *

We ate lunch on their terrace in the shade surrounded by sun. A breeze tugged at the table linen and blew my hair into my eyes. I sat facing the sea, which from our height seemed obsequious, almost timid, its low waves collapsing weakly before they reached the shore.

Uncle Enrico opened a bottle of red wine and made a toast *to his favorite niece.* After all his protest, he came to the table in a clean button-down shirt and a pair of khaki pants that weren't missing buttons.

Tactfully, Aunt Cesarina didn't say a word about his change of heart and clothes.

We ate pasta with porcini mushrooms for the first course, the second course was breaded veal cutlets, green beans, a tomato and mozzarella salad. Only the tomatoes and beans were from the garden, but if Uncle was disappointed in the menu, he didn't say so, and he even ate a bit of veal, asking me questions about America between mouthfuls of food. When we finished the bottle of wine, Uncle got up and brought out another one. Cesarina drank, "Just one more glass, though my head is spinning," and then tears came to her eyes.

"You're so mature. You're all grown up," she said, looking at me from across the table where she sat. "My children are grown too, of course. I know it has to be, but it makes me sad all the same."

"We can do without the melodrama today," Uncle said.

Aunt Cesarina looked down to the table and picked up her fork. "All the same," she insisted softly to her fork.

"How is everyone?" I said. "I've been meaning to ask."

"Fine. Daniella is doing well. Her husband is a wonderful man," Cesarina said.

"What she means is that he has a good job," Uncle said.

"My only problem is that they live so far away."

"Three hours. You call that far?"

"And I have no place to stay in Rome. They have an extra room, but I'm an intruder, I sense that, and so I never stay long."

"They could come here more often," Uncle said.

"And Stefano? He must be done with school now," I said, ignoring Uncle's asides.

"This is his last year. He's very smart, Bella. I don't mean to brag but I don't know how my children became so smart."

"What did you expect? Imbeciles? Of course they're smart, I'm their father," Uncle Enrico said. I laughed, he spoke so spontaneously, and he even sounded hurt.

"And Alessio?" I asked, as casually as I could. I'd heard that they rarely spoke with him, even though he lived in town, and so I almost didn't ask. On the other hand, it would have seemed strange not to mention him, and I wanted to know. The truth was I was disappointed he hadn't joined us for lunch. Of my three cousins I liked Alessio, the middle one, the most, because he was generous and the only rebel in the family. He had sometimes refused to work with Uncle Enrico in the garden or would quit early; the fights between them then were loud, ending either with a spanking or Alessio dashing past the driveway's tall iron gates, escaping. He always ran to the same place, an abandoned house half a mile or so from their home. Only two of its outer stone walls were standing, its floors were covered with graffiti, not a single door or fixture remained in it, and what was left of the second floor was precarious, too dangerous to climb on. Uncle Enrico stopped dragging Alessio out of his hiding place because the walk there and back was tedious; however, as punishment, Alessio wasn't allowed to speak with anyone when he returned. Alessio's blue eyes never seemed more expressive to me than in his isolation, and I believed he had a thousand urgent things to say; I wanted to listen to him.

Alessio was also the only one of my cousins who spent his allowance rather than saving it. Uncle Enrico lectured him that his comic books, the packs of gum and candy, the squirt guns, and yo-yos he liked wouldn't last, but Alessio bought them anyway, and in Uncle's eyes his son was destined to become either a criminal or capitalist, in either case a moral failure.

"Alessio," Aunt Cesarina began, "is in one of those transitional moments that young people seem to go through these days. They don't know what they want from life, they don't know what to do."

She spoke apologetically, anxiously, as though I might not agree that was the case, these days.

"It's perfectly natural," I said.

Uncle Enrico slammed his fist down on the table, and the plates rattled ever so slightly.

"He's a bum!" he shouted as the plates shook.

Cesarina drew back in her chair. "He's finding himself, Enrico," she said.

"He's thirty years old—where has he been looking all this time? Hell. He's a bum and he's always been one. When he was a kid, he was the only one who didn't want to work with me. He barely scraped by in school, then he bought a motorcycle with his high school graduation money two minutes after he turned nineteen and moved out of the house when I wouldn't let him use it. He lasted at the university three months. Three months!"

Uncle's nostrils flared, and he leaned over the table, holding the edges with both hands like he might flip it over.

"He needs to talk to someone, someone who understands him," Cesarina said.

"He's spoiled. What he needs is someone to lay down the law with him, which is what I did, which is why he moved out. The crazy thing is, though, I'm being blamed for this. No, no, I won't have it!" Here Uncle Enrico turned to me. "My other kids know the meaning of work, Alessio is not my fault. You know what the problem is nowadays? Psychology.

All defects are psychological. He's troubled, people will say. In my day we had another word for troubled—lazy!"

"I'd like to see him," I said.

"Go ahead," Uncle Enrico said derisively.

"He'd love to see you. You two always got along well. You had a special understanding, it always seemed to me," Cesarina said. Tears filled her large eyes again.

Uncle Enrico let go of the table, sat back in his chair, turned away from us, and looked to the sea. His eyes closed, he opened them with effort, they closed again.

"You're tired, Enrico," Cesarina said gently.

"No, I'm not. I need to walk. It's this sitting down that will kill me one day."

Saying this, he pushed his chair back and threw his napkin on the table.

"Excuse me," he said, and he turned on his heels. We heard his footsteps on the driveway for a bit, and then silence. Cesarina sighed.

"This was literally the best meal I've had in years. Thank you, Auntie," I said.

"Oh, please, it was nothing."

"It was delicious."

"Thank you," she said, and then she looked at me and held my eye like she would a friend's, something she'd never done.

"Would you go visit Alessio? He needs someone to help him find direction. He's working in a hotel, at the front desk, you understand, it's not much of a job. And it won't last, I'm afraid. They never do. You've grown up so much. He'd listen to your advice."

"I'll go see him this afternoon," I said.

* * *

I called Alessio, and he suggested we meet at the beach where he went most Sunday afternoons after work. It was five o'clock when I left to join him. I had helped Aunt Cesarina with the dishes, then gone to rest in the guest room they'd prepared for me. I hadn't meant to, but I fell asleep. When I woke up, I couldn't remember where I was at first, and when I did remember, it seemed an entire day or even two might have gone by. I lay in bed for several minutes, listening to the deserted quiet of the house, until a *clink-clink-chink* of metal against metal started up in the backyard. Uncle Enrico working, I knew that sound from years before, and in recognizing it, I was overwhelmed by a feeling I couldn't quite place; a feeling like sympathy. I got up, splashed my face with water, and went to the garden.

"I'm going out for a while," I called to Uncle. He was bent down, tying a plant to a trellis.

"See you at dinner then," he shouted back to me without looking up.

The sky that day was a transparent blue with streaks of white, the sea was still calm and streaked white too, the moon a vague outline in the west while the sun remained warm. It was one of those perfect summer afternoons that are so common in Italy and go almost unnoticed there.

I started my car and pulled out onto the gravel road toward town. The road was straight except for a ninety-degree curve that had been our challenge when we were young; each of us had fallen from our bikes on it, taking it too fast. I drove carefully this afternoon, the car jiggling along deep ruts until I exited onto the asphalt road.

The path to town followed a series of three hills, each hill a little less steep than the other, from the first you could see the water, on the second shabby condominiums blocked the view, by the third you were in the commercial area of town, the sea stretching out before you. A strip of street ran parallel to the sea for several miles, congested with cars, scooters, bicycles, and people walking slowly in wooden clogs. Alongside it, hotels and small kiosks that sold ice cream made up the facade, while on the beach itself, hotel umbrellas stretched as far as you could see, like a forest of colorful trees. I drove until the street came to a dead end. Uncle Enrico had rented the same two umbrellas from a hotel for over twenty years, at the limit of the private beaches. I pulled into a parking space and made out beach towels and pants fluttering from the umbrellas' spokes, but no Alessio.

I took off my sandals and walked down to the sea. Alessio was playing soccer in the water near massive rocks that acted as breakers. The tide was out, and the water barely reached his hips. The ball came towards him, he bent down and under it so that he could bounce it off his head. He yelled *Yes!* as the ball arched up into the air.

"Alessio," I shouted. "Alessio!"

He shaded his eyes and looked towards shore, waved at me, said something to his friends, and left the game. He hadn't changed at all since I'd been gone, I could tell as he walked towards me, even his weight must have been exactly the same.

"Bella," he said. Throwing open his arms when he was several feet from me, he hugged me tightly, stepped back, and looked me up and down.

"Bella, it's nice to see you. Really nice. But you're awfully pale. What's wrong? Where have you been this summer, Alaska?"

"Just about," I said. "They don't have a beach in Minnesota."

"Where is that exactly? Is it near New York?"

"No, it's near Chicago."

He nodded, his eyes going blank, and then he grinned, sprinted towards me, and lifted me up off the ground.

"Alessio, no, put me down!"

"Christ, but you're heavy, Bella. What have you been eating over there?"

"Alessio, put me down. I don't want to get wet, I'm serious!"

He let me go and I dropped through the shallow water as easily as a stone.

"Okay, I put you down," Alessio said, and he smiled sweetly.

"Very, very funny," I said. I couldn't help it, I was laughing like a twelve-year-old. "Could you give me a hand now?"

He helped me up, and I wrung the water out of my tee shirt, then my shorts.

"Alessio, I could kill you. The water's freezing! I'm going to go get warm."

"Okay, I'll be out soon," Alessio said.

Back near the umbrellas, I sat in a lounge chair and let the sun dry my clothes and seep into my hair, my eyes, through my toes. Alessio and his friends made their way back to shore slowly about fifteen minutes later, kicking the ball and chasing it in a pack when one of them missed it, kicking it again. Alessio introduced me to his friends when they finally got to the umbrella: Mauro and Piero and Antonello. Only Mauro stayed with us. Alessio threw himself stomach down on a towel near my feet and looked up at me, squinting.

"Hi, Bella," he said.

"Hi, Alessio," I said, and I laughed. He made me laugh for no reason, or rather for the simple reason that there was always an air of recitation to what he said, of play.

"Bella, I want you to meet my girlfriend before you go. Her name is Elisa and she's beautiful. Isn't she beautiful, Mauro?"

"They're all beautiful," Mauro said, smiling that half-condescending, half-wistful smile adults sometimes give to children. Mauro didn't have as much luck with women as Alessio did, I had a feeling. He was short, his skin was pink from the sun, his hair line was receding, and he looked like he'd be much more comfortable in several layers of clothes.

"I'm serious about Elisa. Why be sarcastic, Mauro?"

"Sorry," Mauro said, pulling a thin white towel around his shoulders protectively. I liked Mauro suddenly.

"I'm thinking of marrying Elisa. Well, not exactly. I'm thinking of thinking of marrying her, and that's a first," Alessio said happily.

Mauro sat down in one of the lounge chairs in the shade and said, "That's ridiculous."

"Mauro is my best friend," Alessio laughed.

"You're being an asshole," Mauro said.

"Mauro can call me anything, insult me, I don't mind," Alessio continued enthusiastically.

"What do you think of Elisa, Mauro?" I asked.

"I think she's very cute and young. She's sweet, but if she's ever had a thought, an idea, I haven't been around when she's expressed it."

"That's right, Mauro, you haven't been around at those times," Alessio said good-naturedly. He winked at me and then put his head down, resting it between his arms. His hair was almost dry, its dark-brown waves shining deep red in places from the sun. He was thirty, but with the curved-upwards mouth, the large blue eyes, the dimples and wide forehead of his mother, he looked like a beautiful, overgrown boy. He had always looked like this, and he had always been so talkative, with people around him at all times admiring him, no, adoring him. He didn't seem unhappy to me that afternoon, lying there tan and strong in the sun. The entire beach radiated out from him. That I might say something to Alessio to change him as Aunt Cesarina had hoped seemed both impossible and unnecessary.

"What do you do, Bella?" Mauro asked me, wiping clean his glasses with the edge of his towel, staring at them intently, the way nearsighted people do.

"I'm still in school. I'm getting a degree in American Literature. Maybe I'll teach someday."

"How interesting. Tell me, what do you think of Hemingway? He was the only American we read in high school. He's not dated?"

"No, I don't think so. He was a good writer. He's not my favorite writer, but he isn't dated. Well, maybe a little, when it comes to certain things. But what about you? What do you do?"

"I'm in medical school," Mauro said.

"That's why he's so grim, so serious," Alessio said, looking up. The sun brought out flecks of green in his eyes. "He studies sick people, disease, the most disgusting sort of diseases too. And last week he looked at cadavers. Christ, no wonder you're so unhappy, Mauro."

"I've always told Alessio that he would make a good doctor," Mauro said, turning to me as though Alessio wasn't there. "He doesn't realize it, but he has a good manner with people. And he has the intellect, he just has to apply himself."

"Oh please!" Alessio said. "I went to that one class with you, and I almost fell out of my chair from boredom."

Mauro shrugged and put on his glasses. We were quiet for a few moments. I watched the waves fall on the shore, and I felt myself relax, sink farther into the chair. I closed my eyes.

"How long are you staying here?" Mauro asked me.

"I'm staying a couple days," I said, struggling to open my eyes. I could have fallen asleep. I leaned forward in my chair to remain alert.

"You're going to stay at my parents' place a couple more days? How can you stand it?" Alessio said.

"They're nice people."

"My father's a bastard."

"That's sometimes true," I said.

"I can't stand visiting them. If I'm there five minutes, Mom starts in with, 'Alessio, do you think you know what you want to do with your life yet? I don't mean to pressure you, but is working in a hotel the best thing for you? You'll want to start a family of your own soon, and you'll need to make more money.' Money, money, money. What a pain. And a family of my own? How can she even imagine?"

"Because normally people our age start families," Mauro said.

"I'm not normal. Why should I be? My father is crazy. I bet he went on and on about his garden with you, Bella. He works there like his life depends on it." Alessio was becoming angry.

"Alessio was always a rebel," I said to Mauro. "Do you remember, Alessio, how you used to run away to that abandoned house?"

"Yes, I do," Alessio said. "I was sure I'd move there forever when I grew up."

"Where was this?" Mauro asked.

"Just down the street, oh, half a mile or so from where my aunt and uncle live. The house was totally ruined, just gaping open, and Alessio would run there when he got in fights with his father. Sometimes Uncle Enrico chased after him. Terrible scenes."

"I was a bum even then, that's what my father says," Alessio said. His voice was subdued, no longer angry. "Bella would come after me if I was gone too long."

"You scared me, Alessio. I thought you might never come back."

I would always find him sitting in the same corner, his arms wrapped around his knees. Alessio was three years older than me and I had worshipped him then, held my breath when he spoke. How proud I was when we'd walk back to his house together, as though I were bringing him back. He would brace himself like a soldier when we entered the iron gates, and I would straighten up too.

"What you need is a calling," Mauro said.

"I have a calling!" Alessio was speaking loudly. My attention had wandered, and I hadn't noticed him sit up on his knees. He was using both his hands for emphasis while he spoke.

"My calling says enjoy life, enjoy yourself. I see a pretty woman and

I'm happy all day. Yesterday I saw five pretty women. Five! Mauro, you can't look at a woman without seeing her decline, that's what you told me. As far as I'm concerned, that's hell.

"And, just last week I stayed up all night to watch the sun come up. It had been three years since I'd seen it come up, I can't wake up early, but I wanted to see it, so I stayed up all night. Is that a person without a calling? No. Living life, that's a calling. Isn't it, Bella?"

Alessio faced me and although his tone was light, something in his expression told me to answer him seriously. I hesitated too long before I said, "Yes, that's a calling."

He stood up abruptly after I answered him and brushed the sand from his legs and from his chest.

"We'll see who's better off in ten years. I'll be happy and you two will be worried. Who knows what sort of creeps you'll marry. You'll have kids who don't like you, and you won't remember the last time you had fun," he said.

"I've already become quite conventional, sort of dull," I said.

"And I've always been dull," Mauro said, smiling and giving me a sideways glance, as though we'd known each other for years, had been conspiring together for years.

"You see?" Alessio said. He smiled. His eyes matched the transparent blue sky behind him. "Now I'm going for one more swim, and then we'll get some ice cream."

He had accepted our apologies.

"Sounds good, Alessio," I said. "Don't be too long."

Alessio turned from Mauro and me. I watched him wade into the water, his muscular back catching the lengthening shadows of the sun; he dove, disappeared, and then resurfaced much farther away, only his arms, his head, and occasionally his kicking feet visible now, heading for a point beyond the rocks, some point we couldn't see. ∎

STING
Genevieve Plunkett

Helen was twenty when she met Julian. He was living above a Mexican restaurant at the time, in an apartment that was accessed through the restaurant's kitchen. Helen would follow him through, every day, avoiding the eyes of one of the line cooks, who grinned at her with a wide, roguish smile. It seemed so unsustainable to her, that grinning face, like a joke getting older and older.

What she would remember most vividly about this time with Julian was the dirty fish tank on his dresser, its only remaining inhabitants a handful of snails. She would remember his pet parrot laughing from the other room, muttering half-learned phrases to itself, like an insane man she had once encountered in a parking garage. *Yeragurgle*, it said, in what she could only guess was an attempt at "You're a good girl," even though the parrot was male. Then there were the people who laughed in the alleyway, behind the poorly fastened sheets that Julian used as curtains. She would wake up in the morning to one of the sheets having fallen, partially soaked in the furry water of the tank.

* * *

They had been living together for nearly three months when they had their first fight. It was winter. They had been at dinner when a drunken man stumbled into the restaurant and made his way toward their table. He stopped, took Julian's hand and held it to his chest. It had been such a long time, he said and he sat with them for the rest of their meal, talking too loudly, swallowing belches and looking at Helen with a sweaty, devilish face. Outside, while saying goodbye, the man tipped over, as if about to fall, and laughed at himself. He did this several more times, laughing still, a sad, moist laugh, and then, very quickly, as if swiping something off the shelf in a grocery store, he pinched Helen's breast. It seemed that the whole, strange performance had been a prelude to this vulgar action, although Helen could not find the connection between them. She put her hand in his face and the man left, hiccuping and swearing around the corner.

"What was that about?" Julian asked her. They were walking quickly over the frozen sidewalk, toward home.

"What do you mean?"

"I mean, were you trying to hit him? It seems weird to just push your palm into someone's face like that."

Helen stopped, looked ahead, twitching her leg muscles under her long coat.

"Think I'd better go back and apologize?" She watched the slow somersault of comprehension pass over Julian's features. He frowned and reached for her hand. It seemed that Julian wanted to stop everything, in the plummeting temperature, so that they could discuss this thing that had happened—discuss it down to the marrow. Helen, on the other hand, wanted to get home as soon as possible so she could pee, wanting to preserve her anger for more favorable conditions. In a way, she was grateful that he continued to paw at her, because it kept her from freezing over, made it less likely that she would throw away her resolve. And so, when they reached their block and Julian collapsed at her feet, grasping her hands, she allowed him to speak, hoping that it would only give her argument more fuel—*you restrained me, twisted my wrist!*

"Stay with me," he was saying and she tried not to look at him, but then everything that had been hard in her swelled with pity. In hindsight, it wasn't a laugh that escaped her, but more of a cooing, as when confronted with something wretched, but also sweet. A puppy without legs. *Oh God. Look at it.*

* * *

Their next fight was about the parrot. The bird had plucked out most of its feathers and Julian wondered if the bird's affliction might have something to do with Helen's tone of voice. He sometimes called her behavior "toxic," especially when she was in one of her low, obscure moods.

"Maybe if you were less condescending," he offered, in an even, helpful manner.

"To the *parrot?*" she asked.

He sighed and closed his eyes. *Yeragurgle*, the parrot muttered. It looked like a small, shirtless man.

They fought again about the parrot. The parrot had been doing poorly, so Julian brought it into the bedroom, which was so cramped that the cage had to be squeezed in between the bed and the dresser. This meant that small, dusty feathers drifted down onto the bedspread on Helen's side. The smell of the cage was sickening: a sweet, pasty smell of bird droppings and apple peels. Furthermore, the bird was in the habit of bobbing its head enthusiastically whenever they had sex, which Helen found so distracting that she finally said something about it.

"I just can't concentrate," she said.

"Since when do you have to concentrate?" Julian asked. From there it had only gotten worse.

* * *

Helen stayed with Julian despite all this. She continued to pull the curtains out of the snail water in the mornings. She listened to the parrot comfort itself in its sickly whimper. Eventually the line cook quit or was fired and his replacement did not smirk at her, or notice anything at all for that matter. She was free to move about in this not-quite-desired life without detection. A mouse under the snow.

And then her grandmother was dying. The dying came all of a sudden, although the death took almost a full year. Helen drove back home to help the old woman move her belongings into Helen's parents' dining room, which they had converted, the buffet becoming a dresser, a rolling television stand replacing the record player. Some sort of strange urn that had been there forever was moved, leaving a crater in the rug the size of a dinner plate. In the urn Helen's mother had found pennies, something that looked like a cat whisker and a note scrawled by a child that read: I STRONGLY DISLIKE YOU MOMMY. They had laughed, the three of them: Helen, her mother, her mother's mother. Framed photographs were lined up next to the bed, arranging moments from Helen's childhood in a new and binding logic. *Here she wore that hat and those suspenders. Next, the same hat, but a year later, while riding a carousel animal: a rooster. She's miserable on the rooster. Then, suddenly, she's ten, with new teeth, sidelong eyes.*

You could see how it would happen, in that room redesigned with doilies and floral tissue boxes. The mirror had been swapped with one the same size but better suited for keeping pictures in the corners and reflecting drawn curtains. Helen began to notice things like stitches in the quilt, dates in the margins of old books. She steadied her grandmother's hand around her water glass and felt something change inside her, like a grip tightened, a chrysalis beginning to turn transparent.

One evening, in the early spring, she drove back to Julian's apartment after spending the weekend at her parents' house and found Julian sleeping, red and overheating, under too many blankets, like a big, stupid heart. The perfect father.

* * *

The news of the pregnancy came just in time. Helen's grandmother frowned at the glossy printout from the ultrasound.

"What the hell am I looking at?" She pulled her glasses down her nose then pushed them up. Helen could feel the moment coming into focus, all the giddiness and uncertainty taking shape. Her grandmother harassed her about being unmarried, her father descended the stairs, carrying the little wooden chair engraved with Swiss flowers. There was a certain smell of pans becoming hot on the stove that now drove Helen out of the kitchen. Helen had created a change in the world and it was being met accordingly. Even the sentimental bits were a comfort: the mother-to-be cards from Julian's aunts, the weeping over a pair of tiny socks at Macy's. And Julian's gratitude, which he never once tried to hide out of pride. *You could have left me. And now this!*

Then one night, Helen got the call. Her grandmother had suffered a seizure and died on the way to the hospital, even though she was supposed to die at home. Helen had trouble comprehending this notion— not that her grandmother had died, but that she had done so in transit. She wondered if the ambulance had slowed down when it happened, if someone had noted a street sign or a landmark out the dark windows. She had no idea how these things worked. When it came time for the wake, the funeral director, a tall man with large, folded hands, told everyone where to go and what to do. His voice was deep and gentle and so sincere that anyone who spoke after him had the misfortune of sounding phony in comparison. He offered Helen an armchair, even though she was barely showing, and she felt as though he had seen her soul.

The days following the funeral brought disillusionment. The dining room resumed its functions, the urn rolled back into its crater. Even the mirror was taken down, like a silenced witness. Helen imagined herself bringing a new life into the world and felt very tired, as if by "starting a family" she had been asked instead to grab the hands of the dead and pull them up from their graves.

* * *

They made it two more months. In that time Helen and Julian worried about the future, about where they were going to live, how they were going to support themselves. Suddenly, everything was impossible: Helen imagined herself walking through the restaurant's kitchen carrying a car seat, hot grease flying from the pans, an infinity of line cooks sneering at her. At night, she dreamed that she put the baby to sleep in the fish tank, saw its face disappear into the murky water before she realized her mistake. And Julian had become impenetrable with devotion, full of worry and agitation. Helen found that real conversations were now out of the question; Julian was too self-conscious, too eager to please her to hear anything that she was saying. He was always promising to be better, so much better, as if it was less arduous to perform these feats of insecurity, over and over again, than to know each other.

When she ended things, Helen was surprised by Julian's lack of surprise, how he seemed to recognize her face, its new shade of calm. Helen's father was on his way to pick her up and Julian wanted to wait with her, next to her duffle bag on the sidewalk. He didn't want to talk. Helen did not understand this, but it occurred to her that she didn't have to; they were no longer responsible for getting their elbows out of the way of the future.

"I was trying to stick my fingers up his nose," Helen said, finally. And then, when Julian did not respond, she said, "Your friend, at the restaurant. I wanted to stick my fingers so far up his nose that he'd feel my nails stinging his sinuses." ■

WRITING
William Virgil Davis

In the summers
my mother would wash
the sheets and hang them out on lines
in the back yard. They would
flap in the wind, tugging
at the clotheslines strung
between posts and the corners
of the house.
                    But then,
often enough, someone
would start a fire somewhere
in the neighborhood. Black
smoke and soot would drift over
our yard and litter the clean sheets.
Then my mother would take them down,
wash them again, and again
hang them up on the lines.

THE HAMMER, THE SICKLE, AND THE HEART
Chuck Rosenthal

INVASION

Men are lazy and cruel and this is why there must be revolution, to save them from themselves. Now, the ones he'd saved had expelled him from Russia. The ones he had led watched passively or were mowed down. He, Lev Davidovich, Trotsky, was exiled. He was exiled to Soviet Central Asia, Alma-Ata, where he unified a farmers' collective. With his ideas he made friends, with his friends he went hunting and fishing. The idea of liberation wasn't dead in any human soul, in fact there was no soul at all but for the yearning for liberation, even if those who yearned for it didn't understand this. He wrote tirelessly. Too influential, even beyond the land where he once made war and saved the Russian Revolution, in the new nation he'd created with his own heart, his own fists, Stalin and the GPU had him exiled again, this time to an isolated island in the Sea of Marmara, Prinkipo. He was dangerous and immortal. Stalin was afraid to kill him.

But if he wasn't afraid to die, others were. So they betrayed him, then confessed to crimes against the party and were murdered anyway.

In Mexico, he would have preferred the invasion route of Taylor or Cortés, landing in Veracruz, not Tampico on the Norwegian tanker *Ruth*. Three weeks crawling across the Atlantic. It only took Columbus five. Their departure had been a secret. His arrivals and departures, into exile, out of one exile and into another, were always secret, less to protect him than to quell his followers, of whom there were many. Even his presence on board the *Ruth* was purportedly kept secret from the crew. In the evening when he and his wife, Natalia Sedova, dined, they dined alone with the captain and their assigned Norwegian armed policeman, Jonas Lie. The captain spoke only of the cold, the winter weather, currents, fishing, the stars, and Lie, a quiet, bulky man who ate with his pistol on the table, talked of icebergs and sinking ships. Trotsky hated him, though by now he hated the Norwegian bureaucracy top to bottom. The captain gave them no access to electronic communication, not even the wireless. The boat rocked constantly over the rough seas. They were prisoners of Norway until they reached Mexico and during the early days of the voyage, Trotsky was convinced that despite all assurances from the Norwegian government, Stalin had been tipped off and they would soon be intercepted by a Soviet gunboat, murdered, and reported lost at sea while trying to escape justice.

He and Sedova stayed in a tiny, windowless cabin, a storage room deep within the ship, with a bed, a chair and desk, a lamp. He wrote of Stalin's betrayal of the revolution. She read and fretted. She read a play that Trotsky had brought with him from Norway, Ibsen's *An Enemy of the People*, about a doctor who is vilified and stoned by his townspeople for exposing the civic and engineering corruption that has contaminated the town's water supply. Far too apropos. She was convinced, a Soviet interception aside, that this was not a deliverance, but a long ride to their last imprisonment. At night, he slipped from the room and walked the deck. Gazed out at the sea. Not to remember. Not to reminisce, but to plan.

"They'll recognize you and throw you over," Natalia said to him.

"If they recognize me, the seeds of revolution will be planted in them," he said.

"Corpses don't sow seeds."

"Revolution will spring from my corpse like grass. I'm more dangerous dead than alive." Had he read Whitman? Yes. And he believed what he said because he'd escaped death a hundred times. What indomitable will! And however great his ego, his will was greater, his dedication was greater.

This was the will that she'd fallen into the day they first met, by accident, in front of Baudelaire's tomb in Montparnasse, inseparable in revolution, the man she loved, married, fought next to, organizing women unionists into Communist cells, editing underground newspapers and journals, sneaking them into the hands of workers, for Communism, for Russia, from which they were now very far away.

"A Mexican prison if we're lucky," she said.

"Prison takes a thousand forms," he said. He spread his arms. "As you see. But inside or out, we'll fight with the pen."

So when they arrived in Mexico, she hesitated. The inevitable is often the hardest thing to face. She sat in the dim room deep inside the dark ship.

He took her hand. "Come, my love," he said. And she stood. They worked their way to the deck. Several of the deckhands saluted them as they made their way to the departure galley, but she hesitated again.

The captain rushed up to them. "You must debark!" he said. They knew enough Norwegian by then to understand.

"I must see allies, friends," Sedova said to Trotsky.

Lie stepped up, gun in hand. Trotsky stepped between him and Natalia.

"I'll kill you right here if I must," said Lie. "Debark."

"Kill me," Trotsky said.

Then a launch pulled beside the freighter and she saw American acquaintances, Max Shachtman and George Novack, both Trotskyites.

"President Cárdenas has sent his train!" shouted Shachtman.

She stepped beside Trotsky and the two headed down for the plank.

On the plank, Trotsky and Sedova were met by the famous painter Frida Kahlo, wife of the muralist Diego Rivera, who had negotiated Trotsky's amnesty with President Cárdenas. Kahlo followed Trotsky and Sedova down the plank to the waiting train of the president of Mexico. Even so, Natalia didn't trust this group. In fact, she trusted no one. Why should she? But especially not this thin beauty who limped slightly, almost coyly, beneath her colorful native dress and scarves, a single eyebrow crossing her forehead, a wisp of dark fuzz over her lip. The brow was thick and full, but it didn't completely cross over her nose. It was enhanced with black mascara.

She was honored, Kahlo said in English when she came toward the boat to greet them. "I am honored to meet the man who has changed the world."

"Lenin changed it," Trotsky said. "I only saved it."

"Maybe," said Sedova.

Trotsky laughed and then everyone else did too.

* * *

And he was prepared to keep saving it, on the Russian steppes, in Turkey, in France, in Norway, and now in Mexico, even as Stalin lay in wait to pick off his allies, his friends, and even his family, the Soviet Union was yet worth saving; the peasants and workers of the world waited too, for a crack of light to explode over them into the brilliance of their own freedom. History demanded it. No one could stop it. Not even Stalin.

Kahlo escorted them to their train car. There, as she had when they were about to leave the boat, Natalia hesitated again. She couldn't separate the link between transportation and exile, exile and imprisonment, while he welcomed each or either as if they were new opportunities. Again Trotsky held her hand.

Natalia took the window. She gazed out at the plains stretching to the foothills of the Tamaulipas Mountains like the steppes that stretched to the Urals, though this was sunbaked country, scattered with palm trees and cacti. Ahead, the mountains blazed with splendor, all of it a relief from the dismal cold winter rain of southern Norway. Though she suddenly felt more assured, she spoke softly to the windowpane.

"We won't see Russia again," she said.

He turned to her. "Things could change," he said. He touched her knee lightly with his hand. "Persevere."

As if she hadn't already persevered. She thought of her sons. Sergei, a harmless engineer, now banished to Siberia, and Lyova, running a Marxist Socialist press in Paris. You raise them. They're boys. You think it will be that way for an eternity. Though sometimes, now, she regretted the years when she hid them while she and Trotsky were on the run, years when she left Trotsky for the boys, then the boys for Trotsky, fighting to bring them all together all too briefly. Now they were men. Gone. Stalin's shadow ever advancing.

Kahlo sat at the other end of the car, alone, facing Novack and Shachtman. She looked across the way to Trotsky and Natalia, offered a relaxed smile, apparently to the both of them, but it was obvious to Sedova that her eyes were locked on Trotsky.

She was beautiful, petite, and young. So was Natalia thirty-five years ago in front of Baudelaire's tomb, in fact younger, barely twenty, and maybe more striking. Russian. In that soft, stark beauty of a young Russian woman. Even then, in the throes of love, the political world was foremost for her. And though Kahlo had faced horror, injuries and surgeries from which she could never recover, how did her martyrdom, her art, address the cause? Natalia Sedova, sitting next to Leon Trotsky, evaluated her own despair, an emotion Trotsky would never let himself feel. In that way he hadn't changed since 1902, almost manic with the fever of vision and hope in front of Baudelaire's tomb. Why there?

He'd been hungry to understand art. Devoured French novels. He even read them on the armored train as he launched his army across the plains a hundred times, thousands of miles. What had Baudelaire said? "To know, to kill, to create." Artists, like revolutionaries, perceived and portrayed realities that the masses could never understand, but could be raised up from their own ignorance against their own wills to satisfaction, to justice. Trotsky carried the copy of Ibsen's *An Enemy of the People* even now. Would Kahlo ever understand these complexities? And what of Rivera? Now their savior. Back from his dalliance with the capitalists, the Fords, the Rockefellers. Who had rejected him. And now, in Mexico, expelled by the Communist Party for backing Trotsky and not Stalin. Is that what she and Trotsky had done with the Bolsheviks? Dallied? How many of Trotsky's allies were dying now for that dalliance?

The train stopped at a small station outside Mexico City. And though they were supposed to be traveling in secret, they were greeted by a huge crowd of followers and journalists. Trotsky stood atop the train car stairs. He raised his arms and shouted in German, "Land! Bread! Peace!" The crowd roared and lunged toward him. But he loved this as much as she feared it. How many assassins were pushing through that mass? Police arrived and pushed back the crowd that parted when Kahlo appeared as the armed police led them toward waiting autos filled with more police. The crowd roared, "Trotsky! *Libertad!*"

"Police cars," Natalia said to Trotsky. Everywhere, always, police and guards. She didn't need to say "prison."

"They're here to protect you," Kahlo said. "Follow me."

And the frail woman led them to the middle automobile, a black Ford. A policeman opened the back door and Kahlo got in with them, Trotsky in the middle, Sedova to his right, Kahlo on his left. Natalia saw their legs touch. Their eyes met. For her part, Kahlo could meet the eyes, the mind, of anyone. She briefly smiled her legend into his. Natalia, to his right, couldn't watch.

"Diego will join us when we reach Coyoacán," Kahlo said, again in English, which she spoke as well as French.

Trotsky spoke French and English too, some German, but no Spanish. Natalia spoke neither Spanish nor English. Again, as in Norway and Turkey, they were in a land abuzz with alien signage and sound. But Spanish would come before they moved again, if ever they could move, and to where? He was feared everywhere, his presence a catalyst to the fears of the ruling bourgeoisie of the West because of what he meant, what he could mean, that the miracle he had performed in Russia, a miracle of hope and justice, would spread to the oppressed majority, in Mexico, in the United States yet mired in the Great Depression, with the working poor all over the world.

"I can write anywhere," Trotsky said.

Kahlo's leg again touched his. There was electricity there. She said again, "Diego will meet us."

"Rivera will meet us in Coyoacán," Trotsky said to Natalia.

The car moved through the hills, beginning to wind its way into the sky toward the Aztec capital, eight thousand feet in the air. Clouds gathered and a storm unleashed.

"This won't last," Kahlo said. "January is a dry month."

Natalia lowered her window. The air was cold, mountain air.

"A cool month," said Kahlo, "but Mexico City is never cold. The hearts of her people are too warm for that."

"Heart," mumbled Trotsky to Natalia. "*Herz*," he said to her in German, and then in Russian, "*Serdtse*."

"*Serdtse,*" Natalia repeated. The heart was trapped inside the body. You need only trap the body to trap the heart. "Everywhere we go we end up imprisoned."

"Not here," he said.

"Lev," she whispered. He would be wrong again. She reached for his bicep with her right hand and pulled him toward her breasts. She looked across him to the confident Kahlo. The young don't believe they will age. And when they look at the old, they somehow believe they were born old, never strident, never beautiful. But when Trotsky met her, back from his first Siberian exile, he was twenty-three and she only twenty, both young and strident. He was Bronstein then, Lev Davidovich Bronstein, already once divorced, with two daughters. His first wife, Aleksandra Sokolovskaya, and the daughters, Zinaida and Nina, were dead now, official word on the daughters, both Bolsheviks, tuberculosis and suicide; that's how the powerless were murdered, by the official word. Their mother, who'd remained active in the party and in touch with Trotsky, had simply disappeared.

Natalia's sons by Trotsky, Lyova, or Lev, Sedov and Sergei Sedov, were yet in Europe. Sergei, who'd married and become an engineer in Moscow, was never political, but was banished anyway. Lyova, an active Bolshevik, was constantly on the run in France. They took her name, Sedov, not his, to obscure obvious detection. Even Trotsky used Sedov on his travel documents. But it didn't keep Sergei out of Siberian prison camp for being Trotsky's son. Soon he would be dead, she knew, and Lyova too, inevitably, until Trotsky stood alone, like a stump in a cleared forest.

"Not far from the city you can hunt and fish," Kahlo said to Trotsky. "Even ride." Natalia arched an eyebrow and Kahlo spoke to her. "His reputation precedes him," she said to her, and though she didn't understand the words, she understood the tone.

Trotsky's face broke into a relaxed smile, as if he were meditating.

"Here, in Mexico, we are yet wild," Kahlo said. "Yet tribal. Nothing could change that. Not the Spanish, not the French, not the Yankee gringos." From her bag she removed a small obsidian blade. Let her thumb run its edge. As they swept north of Mexico City the sky opened into a valley, the mountains around spread out like sleeping gods. Kahlo pointed out the window, across his body, her finger almost touching Natalia's shoulder. As the car turned south she pointed to the west. "Teotihuacán," Kahlo said. "We will go there. I'll find you one of these." She opened her palm to show him the shiny black stone blade. "It was before the Aztecs, the Mexica. In its time it was bigger than Rome, bigger than London." She looked at Natalia. "Bigger than Moscow or Petrograd."

"Leningrad now," said Sedova, correcting her.

"Was a village of huts," said Kahlo.

"Does it matter now?" said Trotsky.

"Yes, it matters now," said Kahlo. "You'll learn that. We'll show you."

He could wait to be shown. He was a student of history. History, the bowels of the future, he believed. Now he was in a land west of the West, in a nation conquered again and again, living as much as any nation under the bicep of imperialism, America, which would surpass France and Germany and England, where Communism's last battle would take place.

They drove by a field where two white oxen pulled a plow. Passed oil wells and a refinery, its white silos billowing black smoke. He thought of the tractors he'd planned to be built in factories owned by the men and women who built them, fields of wheat plowed by peasants with their own tractors, sharing bread with each other and with the workers in the factories and in the cities. He thought of libraries and playgrounds and hospitals surrounding Moscow, London, Berlin, Paris.

The car slowed as it passed through a village. Boys kicked a ball in the street. Then corn fields, agaves, a pulqueria, men under sombreros, women, their arms full of babies or wood. And then Coyoacán, a barely paved avenue, a blue house surrounded by an arroyo and a field of corn. Casa Azul. ■

USA
Luke Geddes

US LANDS ON MOON
Luke Geddes

BEATLES
Luke Geddes

JUST A DREAM
Marcy Dermansky

In her dream, Meg made a U-turn much too quickly, afraid that a car would come from the opposite direction and find her blocking the road. Meg lost control of her car coming out of the U-turn and careened diagonally across the road, which was, in fact, completely empty of cars. She crashed through the guardrail, because the road was actually a bridge, a bridge over a fast-moving body of water. A river. The car sailed into the air in slow motion and then plunged downward.

In her dream, Meg thought to herself what a costly mistake she had made. Would this mean the end of her car? Or would she, in fact, die when her car went underwater? Meg was also relieved, calmly contemplating her imminent death, because somehow she knew that it was only a dream and that when she woke up, she would be in her bed. She would not die, trapped in her parents' car, underwater, gasping for breath. She would wake up first.

Which, fortunately, is what happened.

It was a disconcerting way to wake up, still. Meg was forty years old and had only just started driving again. She had gotten divorced after being married for a very long time and moved back to her parents' house in the suburbs with her four-year-old daughter.

She woke up nervous, edgy.

Driving her daughter to school that morning, she knew they were going to be late. Nothing had gone right. First Amy wouldn't get out of bed. Then, Amy wanted to get dressed herself and she put her underwear on her head and laughed and laughed. Amy proceeded to spill yogurt over her shirt and had to have her shirt changed, and then, when they went outside to get into the car, Meg realized it was raining and had to go back inside for her daughter's raincoat. Then, of course, Meg missed both traffic lights. Late. Meg drove a little too fast.

Amy's school was located on a narrow, winding road, cars allowed to drive in both directions though it was barely wide enough to accommodate the traffic. Cars were also double-parked in front of the school, blinkers blinking. It was unclear to Meg if some of these the cars were simply double-parked or, in fact, in the drop-off line. When Meg realized she was waiting behind a car that was not moving, was not on the line, she pulled back out in the road to pass it, and in doing so, she hit the parked car that she was trying to pass.

"Fuck," Meg said.

"Fuck," Amy said from the back seat.

Meg blinked. She didn't care that she had taught her daughter to curse except that sometimes her daughter repeated these words in school or in front of her friends, and even worse, her friends' parents.

"It's okay," Meg said. "Sometimes I say bad words. When the situation calls for it."

Of course, the driver was in the car, the car that Meg had just hit. He rolled down the window. He was an older black man, probably a grandfather, wearing a beret. There was no child in the car, but there was a car seat in the back. It would be better if everyone just got on the drop-off line. Sometimes, Meg just wanted to scream that. In a way, she felt that this accident was not her fault.

"Lady," the man in the car said. "You did not just do that. This is my car. You hit my car. "

"I'm so sorry," Meg said. "I couldn't tell if you were parked or not. I was trying to get by you."

"Is that an excuse? You think that makes it okay? I am going to have to call the police. This is my car. You are going to have to pay to have it fixed. You have to pay."

There was desperation mixed with anger in his voice. She had barely hit the vehicle. It was not as if he would not be able to use to his car again to get to where he wanted to go.

"I know, sir," she said. "I know. Why do you assume I won't pay? Clearly, I hit your car. Just give me a second to think. Please. I have to get my daughter to school. We are late."

It was a nondescript car, the one she had hit. Silver. It didn't look old or new. Amy started to cry, a delayed reaction. Sometimes, Amy needed that time to process events. The school's drop-off line was the short distance of three parked cars away. Meg had been that close to getting her daughter to school.

"You hit a car, Mommy. Mommy, you hit a car. We are going to be arrested."

"No," Meg said. "We won't get arrested. It was an accident. Grown-ups make mistakes."

If Meg did not get Amy onto the drop-off line and out of the car in the next sixty seconds, she would then have to park the car—there were no parking spaces and Meg couldn't parallel park anyway—and then she would have to take her daughter into the office and sign her in. At that exact moment, all Meg wanted in the world was to have her daughter at school.

She had woken up feeling shaken, knowing that all she wanted was for her daughter to be in school. Her daughter, however, was still in the back seat of the car, crying. Now she had a man angry with her. It felt a little bit too fresh, to have a man angry with her.

"I am going to be late," Amy wailed.

It probably was not that bad. This car accident. Maybe a scratch, a dent at worst. She had been driving slowly and she had taken her foot off the gas the second she heard the scraping of metal. Meg's car was more than ten years old; it belonged to her parents, who let her drive it. She did not care about a dent or a scratch.

"Look," Meg said through her rolled-down window, the rain suddenly picking up, rain coming into the car. "I am going to drop off my daughter at school and then I am going to come right back and we can figure this out."

In the back seat, Amy cried, tears running down her cheeks. "Late," she cried. "We're gonna be late.

"What about my car?" the man said. "The damage. The insurance. I am calling the police."

"Right," Meg said. "Fine. I am not going to drive off. I am going to drop my crying daughter off at school, right there, her school, and then we are going to settle this. Insurance, everything."

"I am going to have to call the police," the man said again.

"Not the police," Amy wailed from the back seat.

"Okay," Meg said. "I don't think you have to call the police but if you want to, go ahead. I have never hit a car before. I am a new driver. I don't know the protocol. I just need to drop my daughter off at school."

"He is going to call the police," Amy cried.

"I will be right back," Meg told the man.

She could not comfort her daughter from the front seat of the car. She could not wait for the car owner's permission if she still wanted to make the drop-off line. She was still determined to make the drop-off line. Meg gently pulled forward, making sure not to further hurt his car or any other car that could have appeared from nowhere.

At this point, all of the kids being dropped off had been dropped off, and there was no line. Mr. Leary, the nice man who helped her daughter from the car every day, was still there. He would still take Amy into school. In this small thing, Meg had gotten lucky.

"How are you today?" he asked Amy, like he did every day, helping Amy get out of the car. Only today, Amy was crying. Her face was red. "Oh, honey, what is it?"

He looked over to Meg. Normally, Meg pulled away at this point, always a little bit anxious but trusting that Amy would make it to her classroom. Today she was the last parent on line and her daughter was crying. Meg got out of the car and went around to help Amy put on her backpack.

"Mommy hit a car," Amy told Mr. Leary. "And the bad man is going to call the police."

"It's okay, baby," Meg said. "No one got hurt. You don't have to worry about the police. That is for Mommy to worry about. You go to school and have fun."

Lines of kids were starting to walk by. That is how it worked at Amy's school. The kids started the day in the music room, lined up by their class, and then they were taken to their classrooms.

Amy saw her class walking by.

"I am going to miss them. They are going. They are going without me."

Amy's voice was frantic. As if this was the worst thing that had ever happened to her. But Amy's teacher saw them standing by the car and motioned for Amy to join her class. She was a nice teacher. Meg was grateful Amy had a nice teacher. *Look*, she wanted to tell her ex-husband, *Amy has such a nice teacher.*

"Go away, Mommy," Amy said. "Go."

Meg didn't like this sudden rejection. She also understood it. The quicker her daughter was removed from the scene, the better. She gave her daughter a kiss on the top of the head, not caring that Amy didn't want it, grateful that her daughter would make it to her classroom today. Then she got back into her car.

"Thank you," she said to Mr. Leary.

The angry man in the beret with his dented silver car was waiting for her. Meg wished that this moment was like her dream and she could wake up again, start the day all over. Where would she wake up? Maybe in her old apartment in the city, still married, not living with her parents. Maybe she had made a big mistake. Meg didn't really think so, but in those moments, when things felt hard, that was when she doubted herself the most. Meg wanted to go back in time, if only to redo five poorly judged seconds behind the wheel. One small bad decision. She had not, at least, crashed through a guardrail and into a river.

* * *

The police did come. Meg called her mother. The area had cleared out, all of the kids in school, the double-parked cars on their way. It was a beautiful September morning. Meg had gotten Amy to school on time. These days, every day, Meg liked to make a list of things that she accomplished.

"Honestly," the police officer said, turning to the owner of the barely dented silver car, "you don't want me to call this in. I wouldn't involve the insurance companies, either."

Meg had been relieved to find the insurance papers and registration in the glove compartment of her parents' car, though it turned out the police officer didn't even want to see them. "You want to pretend I was never here" is what he told the owner of the silver car.

"This is my car," the man said. "I am unemployed. I need my car to be fixed. I keep good care of my car. I love my car."

The police officer looked at the slightly damaged vehicle. Meg had gotten out to look, too. She could see a small dent above the back tire. It was nothing. Maybe it had been there forever. She wouldn't have noticed it if she wasn't looking for it.

"What I would recommend to you is pay to have this man's car fixed and then it will be over."

"Okay," Meg said. "I will do that."

Meg had been planning on driving to Starbucks. It always felt slightly wrong to spend more than two dollars on coffee and another three dollars for a breakfast sandwich that wasn't actually very good, but she was also paying for a place to sit that was not in her parents' house. That was how Meg operated in her brain, on a dollar-to-dollar basis. She was saving her money.

"I want this fixed," the beret-wearing man said. "I want you to pay me what I am owed."

Meg understood. He had been cheated in life. Maybe his life had been hard. She certainly felt that way about her own life. She did not think that it was her job to make it up to him all the injustice he suffered.

From down the block, Meg could see her mother's silver Subaru. The situation felt slightly out of her depth. This man was angry with her and Meg did not know how to handle it. She did not have money, though she would have to pay him nevertheless. Well, she did have money, but she was saving it. For other things. For lunch at the Whole Foods. For a security deposit on her own apartment. Not a dented silver car.

Meg was looking down at her feet, her orange suede boots that looked more like high-top sneakers. They were not new anymore, though she had bought them only two weeks ago. She was disappointed in herself, how bullied she felt by this man, how she also just wanted to scream at him. *It's just a fucking dent, get the fuck over it.*

Now Meg's mother was on the scene. She was the legal owner of the car. Meg never knew how her mother would react in a situation. Her mother would get angry with Meg for not drying a dish properly before putting it into a drawer, for folding a towel incorrectly. She got angry with Meg for not making Amy sit properly in her chair at dinner.

"I own this car," Meg's mother said to the man in the beret and the police officer. "So I am going to take over here."

The police officer nodded.

"It looks like you folks have everything under control."

Meg's mother nodded. Meg nodded. The man in the beret reluctantly agreed.

"I just want to get my car fixed. I want what is owed me."

"Of course you do," Meg's mother said.

The police officer drove away. Meg wondered about Amy in school. She hoped that Amy had forgotten about the accident already. That she was busy learning the letter c and not worried that her mother had been arrested. Meg also knew better. Her daughter, unfortunately, didn't forget anything. Meg's mother took out her checkbook.

"Would two hundred dollars be adequate?" she said.

"Hell no," the man said. "This is my car."

"Exactly," my mother said. "It's just a car. It's barely a scratch."

"I want to take it to the dealership. I want to see what they say it costs to repair it."

The car, Meg noticed, was a Volvo. That, she supposed, was a good car.

"You can leave now, honey," Meg's mother said. She gently touched Meg's hand. Meg was grateful. "You don't have to feel bad. Don't think I have never hit a car before. We will fix this man's car. I know you have work to do. You can go."

Meg did have work to do. She had clients. She worked freelance writing articles and editing manuscripts. Her head was a cluttered mess. She still had that dream from the morning, lurking in the recesses of her brain.

"She hit my car," the man said.

"And I am taking responsibility," Meg's mother said. "I won't go to a dealership. They notoriously overcharge. We'll go to my mechanic. He's not far from here. He does good work."

"I want to go the dealership," the man repeated.

Meg was not sure how to feel. She noticed again the desperation of this car owner. As if having an undented silver car made him a better person. She wondered whom he had been dropping off at school and if that child was in Amy's class. She hoped not. She would not want to see him again at parent-teacher night or a school concert.

"We'll go to my mechanic," Meg's mother repeated.

Meg's mother and the distraught man stared at each other.

"Fine," he said.

Meg exhaled, overwhelmed with gratitude.

"You go," Meg's mother told her. "I am taking care of this. Go." Meg went.

She went to her local Starbucks, where she recognized the baristas but they did not recognize her. She also recognized the crazy man at the table in the corner drawing in his sketchbook. Years ago, when Meg was a teenager working at the local library, long before there was a Starbucks, this same crazy man would go the library and draw. He had once asked her out on a date. Essentially, he was harmless. He lived with his parents. Meg lived with her parents.

Meg ordered coffee and the oatmeal, even though she did not like the oatmeal. She preferred the breakfast sandwich with bacon and cheddar cheese. But the oatmeal was healthier. It had fiber. It almost tasted good with the coffee. Meg ordered the oatmeal, but she also used half-and-half instead of whole milk in her coffee. She did not see how she would ever get ahead.

* * *

Most nights, Meg ate dinner alone with Amy in the kitchen of her parents' house. When they were done, her parents would come downstairs and have their meal. This was not something that was ever actually discussed and agreed upon. It was a pattern they had fallen into. It just worked out better that way.

Meg's parents liked to watch the TV news, the volume turned up high. Meg loathed the TV news. Meg's mother did not appreciate the fact that four-year-old Amy had no patience for grown-up conversation at the dinner table. She did not like it when Amy sat on her mother's laps for meals. It was better that they ate separately. But sometimes there was overlap. Sometimes, Meg's father would find himself bored and come sit at the table and watch Meg and Amy eat their dinner. It was something that drove Meg crazy but she felt that she had no right to complain as she was living in his house.

That night, Meg's father came home with a pizza. Just a large plain pizza. No salad. Not a side of sautéed spinach or broccoli rabe that you could get at the Italian restaurant to make your dinner just a little bit healthy. Meg had suggested this to him before. It was a struggle for Meg, watching how her parents ate, almost never consuming vegetables, but she decided it was her job to take care of herself and Amy.

Still, a pizza seemed like magic. Amy would eat it and Meg would not have to expend any effort. She had not bought groceries that day. Her list of accomplishments beyond getting Amy to school was minimal. She had not crashed the car again. That was an accomplishment. Meg had been planning on giving Amy plain pasta and some slices of cucumber. That was going to be her meal as well.

Instead, pizza.

Meg set the table. Four plates. Four paper napkins. Apple juice for Amy. Three wine glasses because tonight Meg would also drink her parents' wine. She had not seen her mother since the morning. She did not know what had happened with the silver car. This had been intentional on Meg's part. The house was large enough and her parents hearing bad enough that it was easy enough to skirt around them.

At one point, later that afternoon, when Amy was home from school and they had gone upstairs to make glitter stars, Meg almost ran into her mother. Instead, Meg hid in the bathroom until her mother passed by. Meg knew, of course, that this was childish and at some point that day she would see her mother. She was pleased with herself, nevertheless, and her decision to hide.

"Five hundred dollars," her mother said now, at the table. "We actually ended up going from there to the Volvo dealership. They wanted eight hundred. Can you believe it?"

"You said Meg barely hit the guy," her father bellowed. His anger was fast, overwhelming.

"It's true," Meg said. "I just sort of sideswiped him."

"The mechanic said it was bodywork," Meg's mother said. "So that is what it cost."

"You got robbed." Meg's father's face had turned red. Meg was afraid Amy would start to cry again. That her father would have another stroke. "I bet the car was already dented before you hit him. He cheated you. You got robbed, I am telling you."

"What is done is done," Meg's mother said.

Amy ate her pizza and did not react, but she was, clearly, listening to the conversation. Meg watched her.

"Did Mommy get arrested?" she asked.

There it was: the worry. Meg patted her daughter's hand. "No, sweetie," she said. "Of course not. I spent the whole afternoon with you in the art room after school. We made glitter stars, remember? I wasn't arrested. Everything is fine."

"You used glitter?" her mother said. The instant and unmistakable anger in her voice almost matched Meg's father's. Meg's mother stood up, impotent. "You know how I feel about glitter."

"I cleaned everything up," Meg said. It was true. "I vacuumed. I used Windex on the table."

"You know how I feel about glitter," Meg's mother repeated.

"I do know how you feel about glitter," Meg said, calmly. She took a sip of wine and then another. "Which is why I made sure to clean everything up."

Amy drank her apple juice. Apple juice was mainly sugar and Meg had been too lazy to mix it with water. Now, Meg suffered a moment of conscience. She got up from the table, took the cucumber from the refrigerator, and began to cut up slices, her back to parents.

"We need a vegetable with this dinner," she said with false cheer, putting a plate of cucumbers in front of daughter.

Amy dutifully ate a slice.

"I will eat two," she said.

"Five," Meg said.

"Three," Amy said.

"Three," Meg agreed.

"There is strawberry ice cream for dessert," Meg's mother added. "And chocolate chip cookies. I bought them for you today, Amy. I made a special trip to the store just for you."

"Yummy," Amy said.

As much as Meg didn't like living with her parents, it also was not the end of the world. This was her fault, for deciding, years ago, to be a writer. For marrying a man who did not make any money. She took a bite of her pizza. It was only okay pizza, but it was good with the wine. Meg finished her glass of wine and then she refilled her glass. Amy loved strawberry ice cream and she loved chocolate chip cookies. These were her favorite desserts.

"Five hundred dollars," her father said again. "That is bullshit. That is fucking bullshit."

Meg looked over at Amy. Often, Meg did not know what her daughter was thinking. Sometimes, three days later, Amy would report back on something that had happened. She would say, "Why don't we live with Daddy?"

"It's done," her mother said. "That man was disagreeable, that is for sure. He kept acting like we were trying to cheat him."

"We weren't," Meg said.

"I bet you didn't even damage the car," her father said, his voice much too loud. Amy put her hands over her ears.

"I hit it, Dad," Meg said, quietly. "You don't have to yell. I hit the car."

"No way you did that kind of damage. That is insane."

"Don't be angry, please," Meg said. "I will pay for it."

But Meg was also surprised by her calm reaction to the situation. It was just hitting her. Five hundred dollars. So much money. Meg realized that she was upset. She was, for instance, drinking more wine than she normally did. Meg looked at the clock. In a little more than an hour, she could put her daughter to bed, and then she could close the door to her bedroom and hide. It was not that long until then. She could make it until then. But she was not sure about going to sleep that night. How would that go? She had had another bad dream the night before the dream about sailing into the river, a dream where her husband had been angry because he had tripped on one of her shoes. He had thrown the shoes across the room and one of them had hit her. It had hurt. This was something that had actually happened. The dream had been so real that Meg had woken up afraid, and then relieved, to be in her parents' house. That was something.

"You don't have to pay for it, Meg," her mother said. "It is our car. You do what you feel is right."

"I will pay," Meg said. "It was my mistake. You shouldn't have to. You already do enough."

"You got robbed," her father said.

"How about half?" her mother said. "How about that?"

"Okay," Meg agreed.

She turned her face away. Whenever her parents were kind to her, it made her want to cry. Meg did not like to cry in front of her daughter.

Meg took another slice of pizza. Amy climbed out of her chair onto Meg's lap. "Mommy, Mommy, Mommy," Amy said.

Meg could see her mother make a face.

"Your Mommy needs to eat her dinner," her mother said. "You get back into your own chair."

"You are the best Mommy ever," Amy said.

Meg put her slice of pizza down on her plate. She would not eat it anyway. She did not have to eat food she did not actually want to eat just because it was in front of her. She wrapped her arms around her daughter's waist. She put her mouth in her daughter's hair.

It was impossible to know if she had made a mistake. She had traded one bad living arrangement for another. Today, she was $250 poorer from the accident, but she had made $300 editing. She could have killed someone, from behind the wheel of a car. Herself, her daughter, somebody else's child. The man in the beret. She had gotten lucky.

She tightened her arms around her daughter's waist. Amy's hair smelled good, like shampoo. The conversation had changed. Her mother talked about the price of apples at the ShopRite, the terrible quality of their produce. Her father had bought a bag of delicious Florida grapefruit at Costco. Everything was fine. Nothing, really, was wrong.

"I love Mommy," Amy sang. "Mommy Mommy Mommy." ∎

DOES TOMORROW HAVE A RELIGION?

Waqas Khwaja

Does tomorrow have a religion?
Will it have a sun like ours?
This moon, these stars?
I am returning to you, mother.
From where I stand, I cannot tell
how near or far the waters,
how perilous the rising tides,
how troubled the sea.
A trembling note from a severed reed,
two lips perishing at its mouth.
What is real, what is not
I cannot tell.

MEMOIR
Michael Miner

My brother Peter led off the seventh with a triple. If he didn't score we'd lose and the loss would be on me. I was our team's leader and brain trust.

My eighth-grade teacher, Tom Sheppard, doubled as commissioner of the Prince Charles Elementary School intramural leagues. He'd wounded me deeply by telling me I wouldn't be playing in the senior league, for seventh and eighth graders. His reasoning, which he didn't need to spell out, was that I was two years younger than those other kids anyway and not much of an athlete to begin with. He wasn't aware of the research I'd done informing me that it wasn't only the natural athletes that reached the big leagues; some made it because they were smart and scrappy. I thought of myself that way.

"So you'll play in the junior league," said Mr. Sheppard. "But of course you'll be a team captain."

Now here we were. Going into the last inning of the junior league semifinal playoff game against Bryan Campbell's team—and one run behind. Bryan Campbell was certainly the greatest athlete ever to come through Prince Charles. He played hockey only against the bigger and older kids and he skated circles around them. Years later, when I arrived in Chicago, he was already there, centering the Blackhawks' third line. A journeyman player by NHL standards, he taught me that journeyman big-league athletes and the rest of us might as well live on different planets.

But when we played softball he was willing to share the planet. Softball was not a game anyone at Prince Charles got religious about (except me, as it was one step from hardball). The rules were not commandments.

This played into my hands.

I followed Peter to the plate. I had to get on. The pitch came in slightly inside and I made a show of twisting to get out of the way without actually moving an inch. The ball plonked me and I trotted to first, giving the umpire—my seventh-grade friend Jimmy Reesor—no time to ask himself if the Prince Charles rules even allowed for this. I immediately stole second.

My brother Clyde was up next. Nothing like myself, my twin brothers Peter and Clyde, two years younger, were two of the better athletes in the fourth grade and I felt confident putting the team's fate in their hands. Yet Clyde struck out. So now it was time for cunning measures.

I'd done a lot of reading about smart and scrappy lads who reached the bigs, and one of them was the hero of a Duane Decker baseball novel I'd studied, possibly *Good Field, No Hit*, the saga of Johnny Madigan of the Blue Sox. Any ruses that Duane Decker allowed the smart and scrappy heroes of his books passed ethical muster in my eyes, and it was time for the most brilliant of them all.

"Lemme see that ball," I yelled at the pitcher. "I think there's something on it."

The kid on the mound flipped the ball my way. I stepped aside, allowing the ball to roll into left center field, and screamed at Peter to start running. When the dust had cleared, Peter had scored, I stood on third, and the score was even.

Except that Jimmy Reesor took it into his head to rule that time had been called.

Time hadn't been called! That was the beauty of it. But Jimmy sent Peter back to third and I went back to second. Play resumed and the batter struck out.

So this was it. Two outs and the tying and winning runs in scoring position. Whoever was due up next was someone I had no confidence in. Need is the enemy of protocol. I did what had to be done.

I sent Clyde back up again.

It's amazing that Jimmy Reesor allowed this or that Bryan Campbell didn't lead his teammates off the field. Possibly everyone understood that because I was an American this was my sport—just as hockey was theirs—and my grasp of what was allowable could not be questioned.

Anyway, Clyde dug in, and I couldn't imagine him striking out a second time. Yet he took two strikes, waiting for a fat one, and then Jimmy Reesor called him out on a pitch that brushed his ankles.

We'd lost. The season was over. My captaincy was over. My dry-eyed brothers trotted off to deliver the evening newspaper and I staggered home and didn't sleep that night. This was not simply crushing defeat but defeat that was unjust and a personal insult. It could not be abided.

The next day I hung around the classroom when school ended and asked Mr. Sheppard if I could talk to him. "Sure," he said; all these years later, I can only imagine how alarmed he must have felt, staring into my anguished face. Or maybe he was thinking, *What's with him now?*

"Mr. Sheppard," I said, "I'm formally protesting yesterday's game. Time wasn't called. The umpire was wrong. I want the game replayed from that point."

Because in the bigs that's what you asked for. I understood the request was almost never granted.

He studied me. I like to think his entire life came to a point in this moment of contemplation. Mr. Sheppard was a genial but complex man. He knew my parents—he'd even acted with them in a local Little Theater production of *The Monkey's Paw*. He'd been in our home. He surely bore me no ill will. Yet about a decade earlier he'd been flying fighter planes against the Japanese. There was a rumor among the students that he'd survived a death march, a story I half believed until his obituary in 2017 made no mention of capture.

He was a man's man who'd admire a proud and defiant boy. He'd do the right thing. But an adult's understanding of the right thing often doesn't coincide with a boy's.

"No," he said. "I don't think we can do that."

"But," he went on, "I have some good news for you. You won the literature prize."

The moment in an eleven-year-old boy's life when he's told he lost the big game but won a coveted academic award can easily be construed as an important turning point. I would construe this moment that way myself, except that at eleven I still saw no reason not to have it all, both a literary destiny bestowed at birth and the one I'd achieve as a student of the horsehide game. But yes, the news exhilarated me—because I'd won, and because I'd been sure I'd lost. You see, three major literature tests were given every school year and the prize went to whoever finished the year with the highest average. (The mathematics prize operated the same way.) I consistently led the class in literature, but eighth grade had seen an anomaly. My eighty-five led the class in the first test, and an eighty-four topped everyone else in the third test. Those were typical scores for me.

But in the middle test, while I fell off slightly with an eighty-three, some of my fellow students went wild. George Jackson led everybody with a ninety-seven! And other classmates scored in the nineties. I think my best friend, Alec Leve, was even one of them, and I never considered him my intellectual equal.

So I'd come out on top of two of the three exams but I didn't have the highest average. Not even close. I felt a little like the 111-win Cleveland Indians after being swept in the most recent World Series—an excellent comparison I wish I'd made then instead of sixty-two years later.

The eighth-grade teachers had huddled and decided to administer a fourth test to George and me. A few other unlikely highflyers got to take it too, but no one pretended anyone was seriously in the running but the two of us, and when the test was over George and I left the classroom together and paced the length of the playground. Our feet crunched the gravel that made snowball fights so interesting as we compared notes. And the conversation made me despair. These tests weren't true/false and fill in the blanks. You had to think about things, and it seemed to me that George's thinking had cut a lot deeper than mine had. *He might be smarter than I am*, I thought, accepting defeat.

And now here was our teacher saying I'd won! If I won, I deserved to win. At my age, an inkling to the contrary would never have entered my mind.

The prize was awarded by the International Order of the Daughters of the Empire—the Canadian equivalent of the DAR. The night of the graduation dinner I put on a coat for what might have been the first time ever, and as the class picture was taken, Alec Leve pulled down the left sleeve of my jacket, exposing the shoulder of my plaid shirt. When my copy of the class picture arrived, I applied black ink to that shoulder and hoped no one would detect the blatant photoshopping, now to be found in a family album that I doubt anyone but myself has ever looked at.

After dinner, the scholars were honored. George Jackson was valedictorian, a status I hadn't aspired to because I couldn't spell. The math prize, which would have gone to me if I hadn't misread the first problem on the third exam, was awarded. Also the citizenship prize.

And my name was called. I came forward.

We're pleased to present, etc. etc., said the eminence from the IODE. She handed me a book. I was appalled. It was just the thing for a loser kid who collected stamps.

"Could I exchange this?" I said.

Then I abandoned the graduation dinner. The Cardinals were playing that night and Harry Caray reached Sudbury, Ontario, deep in the Canadian shield, thanks to KMOX radio's 50,000 clear-channel watts. Home was just three blocks away, and I wanted to catch the end of the game. Possibly I'd miss the dancing this way too.

When I got back to the school, my mother was fit to be tied. She said a photographer from the *Sudbury Star* had shown up to take pictures of all the award winners and no one could find me and it was too late now—he'd taken his picture and gone. Well, that was that, but not if you knew my mother. On Monday morning I took my stamp book back to Wolfe's bookstore and traded it in for the latest Groff Conklin anthology, *Science Fiction Thinking Machines*. A day or two later the picture of George, Ted, and Linda ran in the *Star*, and a day or two after that, the one of me all by myself taken once Mom got on the phone and called her friend at the *Star*.

But the memory never did sit quite right with me. Sometime after moving to Chicago in 1970, I began to seriously wonder—Chicago has a way of opening one's eyes to the world's ways—and when I returned to Sudbury on my honeymoon in 1977, I decided to clear the air.

Picturesque Thunder Bay and James Bay had delighted both of us, but Sudbury required Betsy's indulgence. Sudbury is a mining and smelting center, and there was a point, driving into the city, when not a single living thing could be seen in any direction from our car. The landscape was as desolate as the moon and was where—not completely by coincidence—NASA astronauts had trained.

Betsy brought this up to me. "It's where I was a boy," I told her. "You don't get to choose your boyhood." (As if I'd have chosen any other.)

We called on Mr. Sheppard. He'd long since left teaching, had driven a school bus for a while, and was now a bush pilot who flew sportsmen north to the lakes where the fish were. Mr. Sheppard's pontoon plane floated on a small lake adjacent to his house.

I didn't mince words. We settled in and I put it to him.

"Was the fix in?" I said.

Here's how I now saw it. George Jackson was the valedictorian. He didn't need two awards. My mother was the president of the Prince Charles Home and School Association—what they call the PTA up there. She thought I was special. I wasn't—but she certainly was. Maybe she was so special they figured an award for me would make an awkward problem go away.

I laid all this out in case Mr. Sheppard had tried to repress it. For the second time in our lives, he regarded me. He might have been trying to remember what I was talking about. I'd been eleven. Now I was thirty-three.

"You won that fair and square," he said.

"I don't know," I said, but I had to leave it there.

This wasn't my last trip to Sudbury. My daughter Joanna bought a car before her junior year at Vassar, and we drove it to Poughkeepsie from Chicago in 2001. After she unloaded, she dropped me off at Stewart Airport in Newburgh, south of Poughkeepsie, and I picked up the car I'd ordered there. I couldn't tell you the make, but it was red and the plates were from Alabama.

In that flashy rental car I set off for Toronto and then northwest to Sudbury.

When I got there I faced a problem most adult travelers who don't climb rocks have when they arrive, which is finding something to do. I had the advantage of having lived in Sudbury five years, so I could wistfully traipse around shooting video of our old haunts—the house, Bell Park, Prince Charles, which now was named something else and offered instruction in French. I even videoed myself pacing the distance from home plate to the far fence, which it seemed only kids from Poland whose dads worked in the mines could ever hit the ball over. Clyde and

I had long wondered whether those kids were that strong or were we that weak? What I discovered now was that they were bruisers. Even in my adult prime—well past—I couldn't have cleared that fence. It's never the wrong time to confront the hard truths of your existence.

Sudbury's most salient feature is its rock outcroppings, a joint product of the Canadian Shield and the sulfur dioxide that billows from the smelters. These outcroppings have never been properly exploited to lure tourists. To me they meant climbing opportunities all over town, but preadolescent boys don't write tourist brochures. Lake Ramsey, where we swam, was said to be the largest lake in the world totally contained within a single city's limits, which is to say that as small lakes go it's a big one, but as big ones go it isn't much. Today there's a science museum of repute along its shore just beyond Bell Park, but that's meager compensation for the loss of the city's supreme attraction, the slag dump. Every hour a train from the smelter west of town rolled out along a bluff and dumped fiery slag. It was an incredible sight at night and cars lined up along the foot of the bluff to watch. In seventh grade our classroom windows faced that way, and whatever Mrs. Ross was saying as hot slag tumbled down the mountain of cold slag that the tracks were laid on was lost on me.

But the slag was no longer dumped at a site visible from public land. On the other hand, near my hotel I found an excellent plate of paella. This, a Cineplex, and some impressive reforestation the town boasted about constituted the new Sudbury, but it left me turning in that night wondering what I could possibly find to do in the morning.

So I drove by the high school—I'd spent four months there before we moved back to Saint Louis—and then parked at the foot of the hill the high school stood on. On one side of the street was the new office of the *Sudbury Star*—it had become a Hollinger paper, controlled by the same Conrad Black and David Radler who then owned the *Chicago Sun-Times* (where I once worked), and I buttonholed somebody coming out of the *Star* and shared a Black/Radler joke or two. (In a few years they'd both wind up in prison as hearts leapt in two countries.) On the other side of the street was the public library, the place where I'd rented the Duane Decker novels that had served me so well. I went in there for old time's sake, and, for want of anything better to do once I'd gazed left and right, asked for the microfilm department. I had a wonderful idea. I'd find and make Xeroxes of the pictures the *Star* had published of the 1955 award-winning Prince Charles graduates.

After I did that I felt I'd pretty much exhausted the town.

I don't know why, but I had stupidly assumed that Mr. Sheppard was no longer alive. It was only after I'd packed that I thought to check the phone book. And there he was, at the very same address. I called, and no one answered. Reluctantly, I went on. Missing him had been as sloppy a misuse of time as running home to hear the radio when you could have been trying to dare to ask a girl to dance.

I drove west to Sault Ste. Marie, Ontario, and south to where the highway enters Michigan. An American customs official asked me to roll down my window.

"Passport?" he asked.

"No, I haven't. Not really required," I reminded him.

"Coming from?"

"Poughkeepsie."

"Poughkeepsie? Is this your car?"

"No," I said, "it's a rental."

"From?"

"Stewart Newburgh."

"You're going back there?"

"No, I'm turning it in in Chicago."

He grunted.

"So you're driving from New York State to Chicago," he observed. "By way of Sudbury."

"I wanted to visit Sudbury," I said.

(Nobody wants to drive hundreds of miles out of their way to visit Sudbury.)

"Really," he said. "What did you do there?"

I thought that over. "Nothing really," I said. The conversation was beginning to tickle me.

"Did you see anybody, talk to anybody?"

"No," I said.

He reviewed the information he'd received. "So, you're driving alone to Chicago by way of Sudbury in a car with Alabama plates that you rented at an airport in New York no one's ever heard of, and you intend to turn it in in Illinois."

"Yes," I said.

"Would you please get out of the car and take a seat inside?"

I cooled my heels while they tore the car apart. About half an hour went by before the far door opened and the customs guy stepped inside. He motioned me forward. Something was dangling from one hand.

When I got closer I could tell what it was. It was the Xeroxes I'd made at the Sudbury library.

He flipped them at me.

"I see you were quite the little scholar," he said.

"Get out of here." ∎

WAITING FOR MAGRITTE
Brian Allan Skinner

CLOTHES MAKE THE MAN
Brian Allan Skinner

My clothes, like me, are a little tattered and frayed at the edges. My Levi's are worn shiny on the seat and thighs. One knee is nearly out. My leather jacket is abraded, the lining long ago ripped and pulled out. My jean jacket is now the lining. I don't wash my denims unless it's inadvertent: getting caught in the rain or pushed into a pond or fountain. The soles of my biker boots are as thin as my socks. All that aside, these are my favorite clothes. I've been into Levi's and leather since I was a teenager back in Northern Ireland ten years ago. I guess it's my fetish.

Though I don't look especially shabby—certainly not by American standards—inside my clothes I feel ragged: scraped and scarred by fortune's dings and arrows. Despite coming to New York five years ago, I still have not met the man of my dreams. I've begun to think my attire is to blame, that my clothes are sending the wrong signal. It seems that, more than anyone else, young women with tattoos and piercings and wild, dyed hair are drawn to me, those my grandmother would have called "trashy trollops." I think they are attracted to my gear, not the man inside. That is why I am about to embark on an experiment to change my appearance, something I do not take lightly. My clothes are who I am.

I suppose I am desperate since even my queer mates have been unable to find me my ideal man—or even a first date that led to a second. A couple weeks back, I consulted a white-haired palm reader. Her brightly colored, billowing robes distracted me, but I wrote down as many of her utterances as I could recall upon returning to my fifth-floor apartment in The Bronx. She recommended a vintage clothing shop in Manhattan on Thirteenth Street.

I decide at the last minute to give the shop a try after work while I still have money in my pocket. I park my Harley at the curb.

They call themselves *The Vicarious Vicar*. Their painted wooden sign is sun bleached and the windows a bit grimy, but every item inside is carefully arranged upon racks by size and color. The wooden floorboards creak beneath my boots.

"Good evening, young fellow," the old man behind the counter says to me.

I didn't notice him. He closes a book he's been reading and rests his hands on the polished wood counter. All the items arranged on it seem to hark to the nineteenth century, from the carbon-copy receipt book to the brass mechanical calculator and tortoiseshell fountain pen. His gray wool suit appears to be from the same era, as does he himself, though he'd have to be much older than he looks: well over a hundred. I'd have sooner wandered up and down the narrow aisles and not have anyone breathing down my neck.

"Please feel free to browse to your contentment. All questions are free to ask," he adds, smiling.

Yeah, but how expensive are the answers? I wonder.

"It depends upon the difficulty in arriving at them," the gray-haired clerk tells me, as though he's read my mind. "I did indeed, young man," he adds. "I am Mr. Nicholas."

"I'm Fitz, short for Fitzgerald," I tell him. "Fitzgerald McGuirk. I don't see the prices on anything, Mr. Nicholas," I say, approaching the counter.

"Much goes into arriving at the proper price, Fitzgerald," the old man replies, looking down his glasses at me. "Do you intend to trade the clothes you are wearing for another outfit?"

I look at myself in the full-length mirror, liking what I see but tired of what I see at the same time. My Levi's and leather jacket have won me many chums but, so far, no lover.

"Yes, a trade-in," I tell him. "By the way, Madame Ana said to mention her name."

"Madame Ana sends us a good many of our customers."

Mr. Nicholas steps from behind the counter and circles me, looking me up and down. It makes me nervous and slightly dizzy. He jots notes in his lined receipt pad with a pencil. The pencil is short, but the eraser appears unused.

"I don't suppose the duds I'm wearing are worth much, huh?"

He continues taking notes and looks up at me when he circles round to the front again.

"Not necessarily, young man. We live in an impolite age in which slovenly appearance is considered a virtue. Forgive my outspokenness, Fitzgerald. I try to be accurate in my assessments. They affect the price. And in what outfit might you be interested?"

"Oh, I don't think I could afford it, even with a good price for the gear I've got on."

"The formal afternoon dress?" Mr. Nicholas asks.

"Yes. How did you know?"

"In my business, it pays to know what your customers want. I have had well over one-hundred years' practice reading faces. The fresher the face, the easier it is to read: fewer wrinkles getting in the way."

"I don't believe you."

"That is your choice, young man."

He goes to the rack with the black cutaway coat, walking with a hobble, and lays the suit of clothes on the counter.

"Let me look up my notes on these clothes."

Mr. Nicholas opens a wooden box in which there are index cards. He checks the number on the white tag attached to the sleeve of the formal jacket. He reads.

"Ah, yes. A Russian fellow, classically trained pianist, around your age, I'm guessing, born in Odessa. Can you read music?"

I shake my head.

"Well, no matter. You will assume his identity and have his skills, but it will still be you inside. You'll merely be putting on a suit of clothes. As the saying goes . . ." he remarks, pointing to the framed embroidered motto on the wall behind him. *Das Kleid macht den Mann.*

"I don't understand."

"It's German. I had my first tailor's shop in Buttenheim. It says, *"Clothes make the man."*

"I'm hoping they do," I tell him.

He marks more things down in his receipt book and turns the cranks of his calculator.

"The formal outfit you selected includes the gray-and-black striped trousers, white dress shirt, gray piqué waistcoat, and black calfskin shoes. Your trade-in items are more valuable as it turns out. I'll have to throw in the silver cuff links to effect an even trade."

"Really, Mr. Nicholas? That's great. I wasn't expecting that."

He attaches a white tag on a string to the cuff zipper of my leather jacket. He asks whether I intend to include the rainbow flag pin on the lapel.

"Sure. Why not?" I tell him. "Maybe it'll bring the next guy better luck than I've had."

Mr. Nicholas grins, bringing several wrinkles out of retirement. He asks my nationality, occupation, age, and birthplace, jotting my answers down on an index card.

"I'm an American now, a theater set carpenter, twenty-eight, born in County Antrim, Northern Ireland."

"Thank you. Just so the next fellow will know what he's getting into," he explains.

I smile at his wordplay. He leads me to the dressing room and helps me out of my leather jacket and jean jacket, putting them on wooden hangers. Mr. Nicholas takes them away as I tug off my boots and step out of my Levi's. I wonder what I should do about my underwear.

"Your underclothes are your own," he tells me, standing on the other side of the heavy curtain to the dressing room. "We are interested only in appearances, the part shown to the world. Perhaps you will want a white undershirt so your black T-shirt does not show through your white dress shirt," he suggests.

I take off my T-shirt. He hands the gray striped trousers to me, reaching around the curtain. They are a good fit and far less rough than the heavy denim I've been used to for so long. Next comes the white undershirt and dress shirt. I step from behind the curtain. There are no buttons on the cuffs. The long sleeves would fit an orangutan.

"They are French cuffs," Mr. Nicholas explains, "secured with the silver cuff links. Let me help you, if I may."

He folds the cuffs and attaches the ornate cuff links. I cannot imagine getting dressed in this outfit by myself.

"You will get accustomed to it the more you wear these clothes, young man. Don't be daunted by your first experience of dressing smartly. Here are the shoes, Fitzgerald."

They are spit polished and also a perfect fit. Next comes the black bow tie, which he slips around the shirt collar. He stands on a short stool and, reaching around me from behind, knots the tie as though it were a trick of legerdemain. Then comes the gray waistcoat, which he informs me is pronounced "'wess-kut." I button it down the front and think of Henry Thoreau's advice cautioning against any enterprise that requires a new suit of clothes.

"You are free to Thoreau out any counsel that does not suit you," he says, chuckling at his pun. "Here. Let's see how you look."

He leads me out to the shop and has me stand before the large mirror, tilting and adjusting it on its stand until all of me appears within its oval frame.

"What's going on?" I say. "That's not me in the mirror. Who is it? This is very strange."

"You are seeing the young Russian fellow of whom I spoke. You are wearing his clothes, so you have also put on his appearance and aspect. It will take some getting used to, but you are quite unchanged on the inside."

He takes the black cutaway coat from its hanger and, giving it a shake, holds it out for me to slide my arms into. Then he comes around the front and, pulling the lapels together, buttons the single button at the waist. He steps aside. I move my arms and turn my head in the mirror. I stick out my tongue and wink to be sure it is me. *Yes, it is me.*

"Whom else did you expect, young man?"

"I don't know. But I don't think I will ever get used to someone else staring back at me from the mirror."

I look myself up and down, squinting, admiring myself, liking what I see. Each detail is perfect. It is indeed an improvement. If this doesn't land me a boyfriend, I'm clueless what to try next.

"What do you think, Fitzgerald McGuirk?"

"It is hard to believe all I did was change clothes. My transformation is incredible, Mr. Nicholas. I even feel different."

"Very good, sir. Then you won't mind signing the voucher, the receipt."

"No, of course not. I'm completely satisfied. I can't believe it."

The odd little fellow removes the cap from his tortoiseshell pen and hands it to me. The nib scrapes across the paper like a skater's blade on fresh ice. He countersigns the receipt and its copy. Folding one in thirds, he hands it to me.

"You look quite handsome, Mr. McGuirk. Not that you were not handsome before, but your new appearance is more to my taste. I know you will be happy."

Mr. Nicholas leads me to the front door of his shop, putting his hand on my shoulder. I open the door, but turn on my heels—much easier in proper shoes than heavy boots. I meant to ask him what happens when I get undressed.

"You will naturally revert to your usual aspect, Mr. McGuirk. Beneath our clothes, we are all naked. That is when we are most ourselves. You will be yourself."

"Yes, of course. Thank you, Mr. Nicholas."

He extends his hand and I shake it. He has a powerful grip for an old codger. Oops. I forgot he's on my wavelength. *Beg your pardon, old chap,* I think.

Quite all right, he beams back at me.

I am drawn to look at my reflection in every shop window and doorway along Thirteenth Street. For the first time in five years, since I came to New York, the grimy and litter-strewn streets appall me. I used to blend in, but now I stick out.

Astride my motorcycle, I look ridiculous in my formal attire. I can't wait to get home and lay my good clothes aside, keeping them unsullied until I'm ready to meet my dream man.

* * *

Mr. Nicholas closes the book he's been reading and picks up the heavy receiver of his old-style telephone. He dials Madame Ana's number.

"Hello, Madame Ana. This is Mr. Nicholas."

"I was expecting your call. It's good to hear from you."

"I've finished the Richard Feynman book you recommended. I admit I remain a bit confused, but he makes a good case for traveling backwards and forwards in time, and for two things occurring simultaneously in the same place. It's rather like magic, don't you think?"

"I am glad you enjoyed it. Herr Einstein referred to it as 'spooky action at a distance.' Remember when you used to be his tailor?"

"I do indeed, Madame Ana. But Mr. Feynman does a better job of explaining these strange ideas. I'm just relieved to know that all the things you and I have been doing these past many years are not impossible. I've never felt comfortable doing impossible things."

"It never bothers me, but I am glad your mind has been eased. I wish you continued good fortune with your investigations, Mr. Nicholas."

"Thank you, Madame Ana. I wish you well, too. Goodbye."

Mr. Nicholas replaces the receiver and gazes out his shop window, wondering which one among the stream of passersby might be his next customer.

* * *

There it is: *The Vicarious Vicar.* The name must be a pun or some sort of wordplay. I don't understand most American puns because it is not easy to make a pun in Russian. I take the slip of paper Madame Ana gave me out of my pocket and check the number above the door.

I look at myself in the shop window, wondering whether I wish to go through with this. In my formal dress, I look out of place, but, fortunately, it is still daylight. I thought I was being followed by two women when I emerged from the subway at Fourteenth Street. They wore too much makeup. Their clothes were too tight and mismatched. My grandmother would call them *schmarovniks*—*"street sweepers"*—whether or not they were. Unfortunately, they seem to be the sort of young women my formal attire attracts.

I came immediately after my performance at the Juilliard recital hall: a small crowd of mostly old men and their wives, who wear too much perfume. But not a single young woman.

My dark-blond hair curls around my ears. I am sorely in need of a haircut. After removing my wire-rim glasses, I enter the small shop, *A Fine Men's Vintage Clothier,* as the lettering on the door announces. A bell on a coiled spring above the door jingles.

"Good afternoon, sir," a crackly voice behind me says, startling me. "I am Mr. Nicholas."

"I am Maxim Andreyevich. I'm Russian—from Odessa—a classically trained pianist."

The fellow seems ancient, but he is very smartly dressed in an old-fashioned way. In my black cutaway coat and bow tie, my attire seems just as mismatched to this rude, crude age.

My sister tells me I have to be a little bit scruffy if I'm going to catch the eye of an attractive American woman. So I am ready to become a little rough around the edges, a little less refined, at least in my appearance. I have pictures my sister Nina clipped out of American magazines folded in my trouser pocket. It makes me nervous to think of changing my appearance, but I am desperate.

"Yes, I understand completely," the old fellow says, though I haven't said a word to him. "This way, if you please, Mr. Andreyevich. Pardon me a moment," he says, taking an index card from a small wooden box on the shop counter. "And what is your age, if you don't mind?"

"I am twenty-eight, Mr. Nicholas. I began my musical education at age six, with Boris Kirin."

"That is quite impressive, Mr. Andreyevich."

He leans over the counter and scribbles a few lines on the card and returns it to the box, leaving a corner sticking up. I continue following him up and down the narrow but neatly arranged aisles.

"Here we are."

We stand before a motorcycle rider's outfit of a black leather jacket and blue jeans. Beneath them, on the floor, are black leather boots with buckles. It is exactly what my sister showed me in the photos. I turn to the old fellow, wondering how he knew what I was looking for. I reach inside my trouser pocket. The folded magazine clippings are still there.

"It is unfortunate when we must lower our standards merely to get on in life, is it not, young man?" Mr. Nicholas remarks.

He takes the items from the rack and I follow him back to the long wooden counter.

"I was sent by Madame Ana," I tell him. "She . . . uh . . . ."

"Yes, I know. She is quite an adept reader, don't you think?"

Mr. Nicholas removes the white tag on a string attached to the sleeve of the leather jacket. He writes the number on the index card and places it behind a tab in the wood box.

"This way to the dressing room, Mr. Andreyevich."

He leads me behind the front desk to a small curtained enclosure, putting the blue jeans, jean jacket, and leather jacket on a coat-tree. Then he helps me out of my cutaway coat and waistcoat, draping them carefully over wooden hangers. I take off my calfskin shoes and gray striped trousers behind the thick curtain and pass them to Mr. Nicholas.

My music teachers back in what was then still the Soviet Union denigrated anything American. Blue jeans and rock music fought for first place on their lists of things to be roundly condemned and assiduously avoided.

These blue jeans are thicker and heavier than any I've worn, but they fit me so well there is no room for them to rub and chafe me. The boots feel comfortably broken-in by their previous owner. I remove my black bow tie and white shirt and place them on the vacant hooks. Then I slip on the black T-shirt and blue-jean jacket, feeling a completely different person. The clothes make me feel sexy and masculine in a way my formal attire did not. It is all very strange.

Waiting on the other side of the burgundy curtain is the old man, holding the leather jacket open for me to slip into it. I am getting a little bit stiff inside the blue jeans in anticipation of donning the black leather motorcycle jacket.

"Let's have a look, shall we?" Mr. Nicholas says, leading me to the large oval mirror.

He tilts and adjusts it so that I can see who I've become. A strange face, a rugged, suntanned face, stares back at me, registering my surprise. Like me, he has gone a bit too long between haircuts, but his unkempt black hair suits these clothes. I run my fingers through the thick, wavy locks.

"What do you think, young man? Was this what you had in mind?"

As the old shopkeeper holds my dress trousers folded over his arm, the photos my sister gave me fall from the pocket and flutter to the floor. I bend over and pick up the clippings of men in motorcycle jackets and blue jeans.

"I'm ashamed to admit it, Mr. Nicholas, but, yes, this is the look I was hoping for."

I show him one of the photos. He glances down and adjusts his glasses.

"Quite a remarkable similarity, Mr. Andreyevich."

"Please. I think you can now call me Max. 'Mr. Andreyevich' is put up on hangers for the time being."

Mr. Nicholas smiles and puts my "old" clothes on the counter. I turn around to look at my backside in the mirror. *Not bad,* I think. *No one will recognize me.*

"You'd be surprised, Max. When you least expect it, someone knows who you are—at least that's what my customers tell me."

"Are you a mind reader, Mr. Nicholas?"

"I am not so much *reading,* Max, as merely *listening.* There are thoughts in the air all around us. I can't help but hear them. It is much harder to tune them out."

"I hear music all around me, too," I say. "It makes it hard to concentrate sometimes."

"Yes. That's a good analogy, Max."

"What does that sign up there say, Mr. Nicholas? Is it German?"

"Yes, Max. I had my first shop in a small town in Bavaria. It says, *Clothes make the man.*"

"I'm hoping they do. I'm tired of being what my sister calls a *nerd*. Am I permitted to know anything about the fellow whose clothes I am inhabiting?"

"Why, certainly, Max. Let's see."

Mr. Nicholas consults his wooden box of index cards, removing one and holding it close to his chest.

"He's a carpenter living in The Bronx, same age as you, born in County Antrim, Northern Ireland."

"And his name—just his first name?"

"I'm afraid that is not permitted, Max. I'm sure you understand."

"Yes, I suppose so," I tell him, reaching for my wallet. "Thank you for your help, Mr. Nicholas."

"It has been a pleasure, young man. Put your wallet away. I think we can say this has been an even trade. Please convey my regards to Madame Ana when next you see her."

"I will, Mr. Nicholas."

I leave *The Vicarious Vicar* and head toward the A train at Fourteenth Street. I cannot refrain from glancing in the other shop windows at myself, or, I should say, at the fellow I've become. While it may be only the higher heels of the leather biker boots, I look taller and straighter, my posture more erect, no longer hunched from leaning over a keyboard for hours and days at a time. I dawdle, wanting every young woman I encounter to look me up and down and wish I were her boyfriend.

* * *

After my Rachmaninoff recital at the Juilliard School, I go down to the locker room in the basement. I change into the Levi's and leather jacket I traded for my old black cutaway coat and gray striped trousers.

My changed appearance is not working out as I expected. Instead of catching the eye of a fetching young woman, my outfit attracts young men. Their insistence that I "must be gay" both unnerves and frustrates me. Where are the nice girls who like bad boys?

Heading south on Broadway, I walk to a strange little bar over on Ninth Avenue called The Ornery Burro. It's a tavern that seems to draw twice as many women as men, though I've not yet been successful in securing a date with any of them. At least I've had a few nice conversations and have handed my number out many times. But I never get a call. After tonight, if it doesn't work, I will be returning my "rebel" outfit to Mr. Nicholas and letting Madame Ana know I did not meet the woman of my dreams.

* * *

After work I change from my dirty Levi's, flannel work shirt, and work boots into my black cutaway coat. I head to a funky little bar over on Ninth Avenue named The Ornery Burro. After tonight, I think I'm packing it in. A couple guys there have caught *my* eye, but they never seem to return my gaze. I can't even get them into a worthwhile conversation.

The women, on the other hand, talk my ears off and are eager to tell me all about themselves. Often they buy me a drink. For the most part, they are quite smashing and intelligent. They give me their phone numbers at parting. I haven't the heart to tell them my clothes are a prop, a costume, and that I'd rather they jotted down their brothers' or their cousins' phone numbers.

I enter the pub and order an Old Curmudgeon whisky, sitting slightly sideways so I can keep an eye on the front door. I take the receipt from Mr. Nicholas from my waistcoat pocket and look over the terms of exchange. It's too bad things have not turned out as I'd hoped.

On my periphery, someone comes out of the men's room and takes the last stool at the end of the bar. I turn to look at him.

Holy crap. It's me—or, rather the guy who traded for my old boots and Levi's and leather jacket. I wonder, What if this guy is gay? That'd be some coincidence, wouldn't it?

He's still wearing my rainbow flag pin. He stands stock-still, his mouth agape.

"You've got my clothes on. You're me," he says, nearly out of breath.

"Hey, it was a fair trade. You're wearing my duds, dude. Makes us even," I tell him.

"Perhaps it does," he admits, breaking into a weak grin. "I'm Maxim Andreyevich."

"Fitzgerald McGuirk," I tell him. "What're you having?" I ask.

"Russian vodka on ice."

I signal to the bartender and order Maxim's drink. We shake hands and toast each other.

"*Sláinte,*" I say.

"*Za zdaróvye*," he replies, raising his glass. "Please call me Max. Everyone does."

"Call me Fitz," I say. "Tell me, Max. Are you happy wearing my clothes?"

Max grimaces and takes a long swallow of his vodka.

"No, not actually," he replies. "I had hoped to attract a smart, good-looking woman, but the only people interested in me are gay men. I think I'm going to return my outfit . . . *your* outfit."

I nearly choke on my whisky. I do not want to laugh at him.

"Max, you're still wearing the rainbow flag pin. Don't you know what that means?"

"Well, like unicorns and little furry creatures, things that make women smile, showing my gentler side despite my rough-and-randy exterior."

"That's *rough-and-ready*, Max. The rainbow flag is a gay symbol. That's why you were reeling in men instead of women. Wrong bait, dude."

Though I try not to, I'm unable to keep from chuckling. Max twists my face into an expression of annoyance and displeasure. At last he surrenders to a weak smile.

"I fared no better wearing your stuff, you know," I tell him. "Can I buy you another?"

Max downs the rest of his vodka. I catch Lloyd the bartender's attention and order a second whisky and a vodka.

"What was wrong with my clothes?" Max asks.

"Nothing," I say, "except that I was trying to turn a good-looking guy's head, not a woman's, though I met some very nice women."

"You mean you're gay?" Max asks, nearly sputtering. "I'm wearing your clothes."

"Don't worry. None of it rubs off. You still like women and I still like men."

He nods and laughs.

"Shall we trade?" I suggest.

"Is there nothing in the agreement we signed with Mr. Nicholas to prohibit our exchange?"

"No, I checked it. We own the clothes we are wearing, free to do whatever we like with them."

"Then shall we exchange clothes, Fitz? In the bathroom?"

"Okay," I say.

We leave our drinks on the bar and head for the men's room.

Max and I occupy adjoining stalls. We hang the items of each other's clothing over the divider. I nudge his shoes underneath it and he pushes my boots across to me. We emerge from the stalls at the same moment.

"That's much better," I say. "I feel like myself again. How about you, Max?"

"Yes, indeed. It was a foolish experiment, was it not?"

"I'm not so sure it was foolish. You found guys paying attention to you while you wore my Levi's. So why can't I?"

"And you attracted women wearing my cutaway coat, so what's wrong with me?"

We leave the restroom and return to the bar. Just as we are about to resume our places, my cousin Phaedre enters The Ornery Burro. Max stops. His eyes lock with Phaedre's.

"What're you doing here, Fitz?" she asks me.

"Probably the same thing as you, Cuz."

"Who is your friend?" she asks, her voice lilting.

"This is Maxim. He's just played at Juilliard. This is my cousin, Phaedre McGuirk," I say, introducing them.

I don't think either Max or my cousin have blinked since they laid eyes on each other.

"So what brings you to The Ornery Burro, Phaedre?"

"I'm meeting an actor for a part at Circus McGuirkus. I guess you could say this will be his audition. But I'm early."

"Circus McGuirkus is Phaedre's little performance company," I tell Max. "It's our family name. I sometimes build her stage sets."

I move to my cousin's other side and let her take the stool next to Max. They shake hands and Max nods. I don't think they noticed I was no longer sitting between them.

The front door breezes open and a Mexican fellow in snug jeans, boots, and a black T-shirt walks in, a jean jacket slung over his shoulder. His eyes are mesmerizing and his hair is as black as coal. He smiles at me and turns to my cousin.

"Phaedre McGuirk?"

"Yes," she replies. "Antonio?"

He nods while locking eyes with me again.

"Lloyd," I say, raising my hand. "A round all the way around."

The bartender nods and asks what Phaedre and Antonio are having. Phaedre is also having Old Curmudgeon and Max another vodka. Antonio orders a Dos Equis beer. He puts his jean jacket on and climbs onto the stool next to me.

"Aren't we a jolly bunch?" my cousin remarks.

Lloyd delivers our drinks and we introduce ourselves with some merriment.

"*Sláinte*," "Cheers," "*Za zdaróvye*," "*Salud*," we toast in unison, laughing and nudging one another.

"*La ropa hace al hombre,*" I tell Antonio.

"*Clothes make the man,*" he replies.

"Well, certain clothes—and certain men," I remark, turning my smile on high.

* * *

I doubt any of us expected to be at The Ornery Burro until closing. We laughed and traded stories until we were hoarse. Phaedre and Max exchanged phone numbers, as did Antonio and I.

I felt a thrill as I tucked his number into the pocket of my Levi's. Strangely, I am certain he will call me. I look forward to getting to know him.

Antonio got the part in Phaedre's production of *Lysistrata in Reverse*, in which the men withhold their sexual favors from the women. I can't wait to see the play—and his performance in it.

* * *

That same evening, Mr. Nicholas picks up the receiver of his old Bakelite rotary telephone and dials Madame Ana's number from memory. She answers on the first ring, as though she's been waiting for the call. They exchange greetings, pleasantries, and gossip before getting down to business.

"It turned out wonderfully, Madame Ana, just as you predicted. You must teach me your secret."

He holds the phone away from his ear just as she laughs her high-pitched crone's cackle.

"There are no secrets, Mr. Nicholas—certainly not from you. It is question merely of reading people who will eagerly tell you who they are. You need only figure out what they want because, surely, they do not know it themselves."

He chuckles, but it is too low for Madame Ana to hear, even with her hearing aid turned on. Her big floral turban muffles things, too.

"Perhaps I have a talent for spotting those who wish they were someone else, Nicholas, but it takes your talents to 'close the deal.' I could not do it, certainly."

"I am happy we spared them years of striving to be someone they are not," Nicholas says. "We saved two fine young men—though each in quite his own way."

"Not to mention all those around them who will be happier for their being happy," Ana reminds her old friend. "Shall we celebrate, my dear? How about the Russian Tea Room?"

"Too predictable, my dear Ana. Let's try the young people's place over on Ninth—The Ornery Burro, it's called."

"We will look painfully out of place."

"Not if we dress for the occasion. I am tempted to try the other set of Levi's and leather jacket I have on hand."

"All right, Nicky," Ana tells him, teasing. "I'll look for you. And I think I will slip into that sleek red dress you saw at my shop and commented upon so favorably. I shall wear that."

"Tomorrow at four o'clock then, my dear Ana. We'll have a jolly time. We will turn heads and give rise to comments and gossip."

"I'm looking forward to it. It has been a long time since we dressed up. Good night, Nicholas."

"Yes, it has been a very long while. Good night, Ana."

Mr. Nicholas puts down the receiver and walks among the racks of secondhand clothes, his hands behind his back. Madame Ana puts down the phone and walks over to the shiny red dress and strokes it with her fingertips, anticipating its cool silkiness on her skin.

Yes, we shall turn heads, they think simultaneously, as though still connected on the telephone. ■

THE DANGEROUS EATER
Eleanor Spiess-Ferris

"Whaaaaaa," I muffled.

The "what?" never quite got out before I felt Brother's hard kick under the table and his low-throated "Button your lips!" He took a long breath for the "button," then placed a special emphasis on "your" and then followed up with the "lips" part in almost a whisper.

Then my stepsister, Maria, did the right-handed lip twist, curling her top bow into the bottom as if a disingenuous monster had crushed a delicate flower.

They knew better how to read between Mama and Daddy's lines than I. After all, I had only ten years of experience in this family, whereas Maria had nineteen and Pain-In-My-Butt, Crown Prince, My-Father's-Star had almost sixteen years. I really believed that my brother hated me and I felt that he felt it was ALWAYS his job to CORRECT me.

From my table view, I could see them all—their grimaces, their hand movements and the way their bodies shifted in their chairs.

I had one side of the table all to myself and sat squarely in the middle with Mama on one end and Dad on the opposite end.

I was deemed a dangerous eater, being a milk spiller and all, but this gave me an audience view of the others. I might be naïve about verbal codes but I sure knew what their bodies were saying.

I knew by the tone of her voice that Mama was coding something to the big man at the head of the table that was important. She always spoke in code and I think they thought we kids were too dumb and too stupid to catch on, but I was learning and learning fast.

"Pickles," Mama said with a nod in Maria's direction.

Maria blushed.

"Yes," Dad said, "and I have made a few adjustments." Looking at us all, he went on. "The belt has to be tightened."

"Cows or chickens?" said Mama.

"As soon as possible, the dairy will have to close."

"What? WHAT!" I repeated loudly. "How could you, Dad? The cows are my friends—my only friends—my best friends. I know their names. I sing to them. I help Mr. Martinez with the milking. Milk is important. Milk helps . . ." I was in tears and my words were laced with half-swallowed milk and spring-allergy phlegm—all bubbling out of my mouth at once.

"Enough, Hanna Louise!" said Mama, pointing her crooked index finger at me.

"Sorry, Chirp." Dad did not look at me and his two words were muffled under his napkin.

"But, but, but . . .They are my minions! Blue Bird, Bossy, April Snow, Bizzy Liz, Madeline, Cinderella," I recited their Holstein names.

"What's a minion?" asked my brother to no one in particular. Then Maria gave him the stink eye as she moved awkwardly in her chair.

"Now, Chirp, some things are just not avoidable." Dad reached out his hand over the dinner table toward me as he spoke, but I quickly wiped away imaginary food crumbs from my mouth with my left hand—the hand he wanted to console.

I waved my arms in total desperation.

My glass of half-devoured milk tipped and spilled itself across the table. It streamed between the knives and forks and the dinner dishes and trickled between the leaves of the table to the wooden floor below.

Toots, my elderly black spaniel, lifted her arthritic self from her bed in the corner of the dining room near the kitchen and ambled toward the spilt milk. The lapping of my spillage seemed to be more of a duty than a pleasure now, but she did it anyway.

I could not continue eating. My stomach knotted up.

"I'm not hungry. May I please be excused?"

"No, you may not," said Mama sternly in her no-nonsense tone. "You are already too skinny."

Then Dad waved his arm in the air. I was free to go.

Mama shot eye arrows at her husband.

The stairs to the second-floor bedrooms seemed extra steep. Mama's words ran up the stairs behind me, "There will be no leftovers, so don't plan on a midnight snack!"

But it was Dad's words that left me even sadder than before. "Not to worry, she'll get over it."

By midweek the cow pastures were empty. Even the cow pies that dotted the ground had lost their color and were now just flaky brown. I had missed their departure. They had been carted away during school hours. My heart was broken and the sadness that spread over me grabbed hold like a horned toad holding on to a squirmy caterpillar. The harder I fought the feeling, the more it gripped me with its jagged, hungry teeth.

* * *

My favorite place in all the world was the wooden bridge that spanned the irrigation ditch. When the water was high in spring, I could sit and dangle my feet in the rushing water.

Sometimes I made boats out of sawed-off wood pieces. The old saddle house now stored nails, Mama's maroon paint for that single living room wall, and bags of chicken feed, as well as lumber bits and the wide selection of rusting tools that was my workshop. I stole lengths of colored yarn from my mother's knitting basket. I hammered nails into short pieces of two-by-fours. I wove the yarn around the nails, decorating each boat in a different color. I made two at a time so that I could race them in the current under the bridge.

I stood at one end of the bridge, dropping the boats into the rushing water. Then I ran to the other end of the bridge to see which one would win. Sometimes a boat got away from me and traveled down to the water spill at the end of our property, but most of the time I rescued the boats and tried it all again.

* * *

It was different now. The sounds and smells were different. My old dog did not come down to the bridge with me anymore. She no longer barked at floating objects or snapped at the rushing water. I was alone. I longed for the smell of fresh manure and the mooing of the cows, udders full, waiting to be milked.

I didn't know much about music but it was like Slim Whitman singing without his yodel or Roy Rogers without the Sons of the Pioneers. All I heard were chickens, and no moos.

Standing on the bridge, with the irrigation water rushing beneath me, I could see the old pig shed where a friend of Dad's kept his pet king snakes for a year or two until the man went off to Denver or Santa Fe or someplace. It was a dark place with several cages on newly built shelves.

Each cage housed a beautiful king—some very long but others short. The man had saved all the snakes' shed skins and had pinned them on the shed posts. I don't know where he lived, but each week he came with a box filled with live mice and once he invited me in to see his snakes.

King snakes are beautiful and not poisonous. I used to see them along the banks of the irrigation ditch. They slithered beside the water and then darted into the undergrowth. But until I looked at them in the cages, I had never seen any up close—staring right at me. There was just enough light in the shed for me to see the snakes and the man drop a mouse into each cage. At first the mouse scurried about, happy to be free. Then it realized what was there in the dark with it, barely seen. I saw the mouse freeze. I knew that it knew—and that the snake certainly knew.

The fear that stifled the air grabbed me. I felt the mouse's panic. I ran out of that shed to the safety of the bridge and never went there again. The man went away soon after that. I wondered what happened to the snakes and if he took the skins with him. I hoped the snakes were all right. I know that they, like me, had to eat, but I didn't ever want to feel that fear again.

When Dad came home in the evening, he waved at me, as he often did when he went into the house. At dinner he would ask, "Ruminating again, Chirp?"

"No," I would answer, "Just *bridge-in-ateing*."

On that bridge, some place between here and there, I liked to think and I liked to remember all kinds of stuff. On that bridge, I felt the summer's heat caressing my face. In winter, the cold would bite me and the wind would try to push me off the frozen planks.

* * *

It was from that bridge view that I first noticed that a whole bunch of stuff needed painting. My whole world was peeling. Where once the door and small windows on the adobe chicken house were painted a bright blue, I saw gray softening wood revealed. The second chicken coop was deserted and the brooder house in between was empty of the chicks that once came in peeping boxes from Sears and Roebuck. There were no chicks that spring. A sense of foreboding came over me as if a monster were reaching in and crushing the very fabric of a delicious dream.

Sitting in the middle of the bridge, I forced myself to remember everything I could about this special plot of pasture and farm buildings. My world was dissolving before my eyes.

What I would have liked most right then was to go down to the grove of big trees beyond the old railroad tracks. I had gone there once with Maria and one of her boyfriends and while they were snuggling under the plaid picnic blanket and making strange noises, I was able to run between the trees and through the tall grasses that grew there. I knew that to tell Mama anything about their "picnic" and their babysitting techniques was not a good idea. But the tall trees were off limits as being where the wild dogs roamed or where the bad people lived or some other reason given as to why I was not to go there alone.

Everyone gives me don'ts.

Dad's don'ts are: "Don't go down to the big trees." "Don't walk right behind a horse." "Do *not* walk on the top rail of the bull's pen." "Don't slide down the hay shoot."

Don't, don't, don't.

Mama's don'ts are weirder: "Don't wear your clothes inside out. It's bad luck." "Don't go near twins—double bad luck." "Don't break a mirror—really bad luck."

Brother had started dating.

His first "victim" was a girl that lived near the bend in the road. Some problem with her seemed to have led him to give me his most recent—and odd—don't.

He pulled me into Dad's car for a "talk." He said in his most serious voice: "Chirp, don't be a gold digger." I did the cross-my-heart-and-hope-to-die *X* on my chest and thought about California. I agreed that I would certainly not be a gold digger, wondering just what he meant.

Marie's don'ts were different. They were muffled into tissues and spoken with tears. They were all about her bad choices in boys. Since I did not intend to go anywhere near a boy, I really didn't listen.

On this bridge, I closed my eyes and tried to remember the names of those sold Holsteins that I loved. My memory spit them out like sugared gelatin sweets—shaking, but not totally formed.

I needed a monument—a cow monument. I needed a cemetery with the name of every cow engraved in memory stone. I feared that my companions would fade away like the paint on the outbuildings that I saw from that bridge.

* * *

I needed something to make signs with.

Light bulb time!

The old saddle house only yielded hardened paintbrushes, but I did recall Dad's Shinola Cordovan Liquid Shoe Polish with the soft sponge on a wand. That would do the trick! The quest, which led to our upstairs hall closet, yielded tins of black and brown wax polish. All were stacked neatly in a shoebox covered with leftover Christmas wrappings that I had made Dad for his forty-sixth birthday. He must have really liked the box 'cause Mama used it for all his shoe polish, although he didn't polish a lot.

After I'd found what I wanted in the shoebox, my imaginary light bulb raced me to the milking barn nestled alongside the larger all-purpose barn. There I arrived with a bottle of red shoe-polish liquid in my right hand and my inspiration huffing and puffing beside me.

A slight odor of fresh milk lingered in the air. But the milking barn was no longer spotless as it had been. Spiderwebs draped the crumbling barn walls. The cement floor was dusty and unswept. The spiders had won the battle.

How hard Mr. Martinez had fought, scrubbing, sweeping and cleaning all areas of the milking barn every day so that the milk would always be super-duper clean.

I ran my hand over the stainless steel pasteurizing machine, which had remained in place. It was cool to the touch and still shining, reflecting my face on its surface. I was surprised that it had not been sold too. I imagined the milk speeding its way around the ins and outs of the machine and, in the end, filling my little pail and then the large milk cans.

It stared up at me. I remembered my little shining galvanized bucket and my early-morning mission of filling it with the white, warm and really fresh milk. Then, lid in place, I would run down the hill to Mama waiting for fresh cream to put in Dad's coffee.

If I got to the milking shed early, I could sit on a little stool while Mr. Martinez attached the electric milkers to the cud-chewing cows. He would talk to them in low tones and rub their backs gently. Once the cows were all attached and content, he would signal to me with a tip of his worn, stained cowboy hat, and I would sing softly every verse I knew of "The Battle Hymn of the Republic" over and over again until the *señoritas*, as he called them, were done.

Now I walked to each of the empty, old stall openings with my shoe polish, wand and sponge dripping cordovan red. I reached as high as I could, and I wrote each cow's name in large capital letters while I sang "The Battle Hymn of the Republic"—my special, made-up version.

Mine eyes have seen the glory of the coming of dear Blue Bird, Bossy,
    and April Snow.
They are trampling out the vintage where the hay is neatly stored.
Bizzy Liz and Madeline have loosed their white, pure milk:
Their truth is marching on.

With tears streaming down, I sang the *Glory, glory, hallelujah* chorus three times.

I see Cinderella, White Face, and Little Wee.
I will build them in my memory in the evening dew.
No one can ever take this away from me.
Their truth is marching on.

I ended with yet another chorus of *Glory, glory, hallelujah.*
Between tears and nose drips, I sat down on the little forgotten milk

stool from where I had so often kept company with my bovine friends. I looked over the names that I had painted with dad's cordovan shoe-polish wand on the posts of the empty stalls, one name on one post—in painstaking, vertical capital letters—for each beloved cow.

Still crying, I wiped my nose on the corner of my blue striped shirt and stood up. In one last gesture, I used the liquid shoe polish to sign "Chirp" on the seat of the stool.

Then I closed the door of the milking barn behind me. I closed off the smell of fresh cow pies and sweet cow breath. I closed off the sweet mooing of my friends, back from the field where the big oak trees grew, chewing fresh grass mixed with clover bits in their cud.

I had one name yet to write. The white curly-haired bull had lived mostly between the barn and a sturdy pen alongside the barn.

"Cotton is the daddy of all the calves," Dad had said when I questioned as to why we needed a bull.

I often rested my folded arms on the fencing of the bull's pen and studied Cotton's massive head and his short, trimmed yellow horns. I loved him and I loved the calves. But the calves never stayed around long. I don't know where the calves went. One day they were gone just like their moms and their dad were gone now.

The main barn, like everything else, had turned peeling white on old gray. A sheet of the tin roof had loosened. It scraped against itself and whined as the wind bent it back and forth.

One of the barn's half doors was slightly open and I pushed it farther, stooping to enter the dark, musty building. The door swung back to the way it was as I passed through it. Mice scurried helter-skelter across the wooden floor, scampering over one another. They were alarmed at my being there in what was now their home—no longer the home of the farm animals. The mice disappeared into the cracks of the empty feed bins. They hid in the holes in the walls and the barn went silent again. I sat on the stairs to the loft, thinking about king snakes and wondering if the mice would reappear if I remained absolutely silent. ∎

AT THE PLAZA
Bob Glassman

At the plaza, a band playing Cuban music, a pleasant tropical breeze cooling the Midwestern summer evening.

People dancing together, and alone. A colorful couple, he was tall, thin, very dark-skinned, wearing pleated gray slacks, a light-colored guayabera, and alligator shoes. He looked as if he had just stepped out of 1957 Havana. His partner was Asian, wearing a short, sleeveless wine-red dress, attractive, mature. They were both likely in their late forties.

They danced salsa in a very natural way, not like entertainers, but for their own pleasure. They were at ease, creating a private world and living in it, seemingly without taking notice of the other world around them. He was leading, of course, guiding her tenderly like a whirling sculpture. She was a little rough around the edges, but she was honest and it was hard not to watch them. Of course they looked like two good stories, but speculation about their lives is best left to daydreaming.

A girl, maybe twenty-five or even younger, medium-dark skin, dark hair, dressed in a modern, loose-fitting sleeveless garment suggestive of an Indian sari, but not full-length, dancing alone, smiling, her eyes bright, moving in a way that brought to mind images of ancient temple figures. Dancing alone, happy, looking around at everyone, quickly catching some eyes but then moving on, looking at others. She was her own show, no pas de deux. Looking left, then spinning to the right and hesitating a beat while catching another pair of eyes. Then spinning left and hesitating a beat before moving right again. She was joyful, beautiful, dancing ecstatically.

An old man was sitting on a bench at the plaza. His eyes were closed, the Caribbean breeze felt good on his face. The music felt good, a sense that life was good, a relaxed vibrating trance, good vibes. When he opened his eyes, the couple was dancing close to each other, and close to him. He had been thinking about the past, the place where the best part of his life should have been. But it wasn't there.

Daydreaming about the salsa dancers. He's got to be from Cuba or the islands. Maybe he met her at another free outdoor dance, or maybe he met her at the bakery in his neighborhood. She was brought to this country from Vietnam as an infant. She's had to make ends meet by magicking something up, more than once. He lives in an efficiency apartment west of Chicago's North Side. He's lived a hardscrabble life and done a few things he won't talk about. And there are some things she would rather forget. Like long ago, when her wedding gown was hanging in the closet back at her apartment. The wedding was tomorrow, but tonight she was out with her girlfriends at her regular bar. And her old boyfriend was there too.

But on a breezy summer night, with a Cuban band playing in a public plaza, this was an opportunity to love life, and that idea was not lost on this pair. Nor was it lost on the solo dancer. When the music stopped, she stood for a long time looking at the band as they were breaking down. She was about thirty feet from them as they packed up, and then she was nearly alone in the plaza as everyone else left. Where did my ecstasy go? The old man looked at her and felt her longing as ecstasy settled back to earth.

The sun was going down. The evening light was dimming on the plaza. A noisy flock of sparrows, maybe a hundred, came down near some grass. And a member of the flock, a blue parakeet, chattered away with the rest of the sparrows as if it were a dull brown color. ■

IRENE
Harold Bordwell

I was hoping this story was going to be longer. Events, however, dictated otherwise. Because neither Irene nor I read short stories, perhaps this was life's way of tightening one of its mysterious screws on us. At some point that evening Irene said to me that she couldn't remember when she'd last read a story. I made a guess that the last time I'd read one was when I'd reread Joyce's "The Dead" in an adult education course at a community college. It was awful . . . the course, I mean. After that experience I made up my mind that I'd never take another class at a community college. And I haven't.

Irene and I met at a reading at Books by Dickens, an independent bookstore that prided itself on bringing writers in to read and discuss their books. Ray Dickens started the store, but after his death, Sally and Ted Cousins took it over, redecorating the place, jazzing up its newsletter, and producing a series of bookmarks with witty quotes. People collected them.

That night we met by mistake. We thought we were going to hear a new English writer who idolized Virginia Woolf read from her novel *Mrs. Dalloway at Eighty-Four*. We both got the date wrong and listened instead to an American humorist tell how he wrote twenty-four essays on his marriage, his children, his divorce, and the new love of his life, which turned out to be fly-fishing. The book was called *Fly-Fishing When Nothing Else Matters*. He spoke with a twangy accent and was wearing a buffalo-plaid shirt, jeans, and hiking boots.

During questions and answers I turned to Irene, who had sat down beside me, and said, "Would you have come if you had known he was reading?"

"Of course not," she said, "but it was fun, in a way. What about you?"

"I don't think so. I was looking forward to hearing Phoebe What's-Her-Name read."

"Her name is Phyllida. Mine is Irene."

I introduced myself and we sat in silence while the American humorist who had fallen in love with fly-fishing took a few questions from the audience. Someone asked him if he ever went deep-sea fishing. Somebody else asked who he thought was the best American humorist, and he said George Ade. "Who's he?" somebody nearby whispered.

"What about Twain?" someone else shouted. "And Thurber?" another voice asked quietly, twice.

I asked Irene if she'd like to have a cup of coffee.

* * *

The coffee area at Books by Dickens was small and surrounded by big leafy plants. It was often difficult to find an open table, but that night we were lucky.

"I don't know about you, but I find the commercial side of books tiresome," Irene said. "Maybe I'm getting old, but most of it seems like hype, especially the personal stuff, like those interviews in the *Paris Review*. Have you read them?"

I had to laugh, and a look of confusion came over her face.

"The thing is," I said, "I have a lifetime subscription to the *Paris Review*. George Plimpton even sent me a personal letter of thanks. And I agree with you. Who cares about your difficult childhood? Who cares if your mother was an alcoholic? Who cares if your sister married an Iranian prince? Or your father left when you were four? Or that you still use a typewriter?"

It was her turn to laugh. Since Irene looked no more than in her midthirties, I was thinking she was in no danger of getting old. She wore her hair in a pageboy style, it was dark brown, and there wasn't a wrinkle on her face. She had kept her figure and wore very good clothes. Business casual, I believe it's called. I now regretted not dressing up more. Wrinkled chinos, a worn polo shirt, and a navy-blue sweater that was beginning to ravel at the cuffs and the waistband. I was hoping that these were the kind of things she didn't care about.

"That's some reaction," she said. "I'd say you really do care about books."

The truth was, I did care about reading, but I'd often questioned myself whether literature and reading were the same thing. Somebody once said they'd read the phone book if there was nothing else around to read. I didn't feel that way exactly but it was impossible for me not to take something to read with me wherever I went.

"And you?" I asked.

"I like reading a lot. I can sit and drink a coffee with nothing to read, but I'd rather not. I was going to buy Phyllida's *Mrs. Dalloway* tonight and start reading it here and not care about anything else. But then we met."

"Do you know the owners by any chance?" I asked, not being sure what to say next.

"I was married to their son, for a while," she said. "It was literary lust at first sight. I exaggerate. I think Jim and I were just lonely, and we happened to meet. The divorce couldn't have been nicer. I think Sally and Ted still like me, but I'm not really sure. I think they like me better than they like their son. He used to complain about how cold they could be. He said they made him feel small. After he left me—he claims I left him, which is not true—I used to see Sally and Ted for lunch once a year or so, but then life intervened. I guess we knew we had nothing to say to one another. Luckily there were no children. With children it would have been a nightmare—visiting grandmother and grandfather, and so on. I think Jim lives back East. And I heard he got remarried. I didn't. At least not yet."

I felt it was my turn to be personal. I said I had never married, had my own house, and had worked off and on in educational publishing.

"You've been lucky," Irene said. "So have I. My parents are gone now and I was an only child. So there's no one to visit, really. I suppose I have a friend or two but I wouldn't bet on it. I feel they have their own lives. So do I. I'm renting now but I wish I had my own house. Jim and I had a house and a cat and a dog and a Harley, which I refused to get on. As for houses, I think I've been priced out of the market."

"Look, the humorist is leaving," I said. "He's actually waving. He must have sold a lot of copies tonight."

"Good for him," Irene said. "I'm happy for him. He can go home tonight feeling it's been a worthwhile day, that his book isn't the shit his friends say it is behind his back."

"You know," I said, "I'm tempted to buy his book. He seemed like a nice guy."

"Why don't you?"

"I will if you let me lend it to you afterwards."

"That's an offer I can't refuse," Irene said. "Your generosity is astonishing."

I got up and bought a copy. It had one of those glossy embossed dust jackets. The photograph of the author on the inside back cover flap showed him holding what looked like a rainbow trout over his head. His blurb said he had been born in Syracuse but now lived in Miami and owned an Edsel.

"So you actually bought a copy," Irene said when I got back to our table. "I thought you were going to the men's room but were too polite to say so. Good for you."

"I'm not so sure I would have bought Phyllida's novel tonight. I was debating with myself whether I want to read another English novel about class. When is she reading? Do we know?"

"I see Ted is here. I'll ask him. He's easier to talk to than Sally. She thought I was stuck up. Maybe I am. I know I am. Are you?"

"Not that I've noticed. You don't seem stuck up to me."

"Thank you for the compliment, if it is one. Maybe it's just knee-jerk insincerity on your part."

Smiling, she looked to see if she had offended me. "Take nothing I say seriously."

It was Irene's turn to get up.

"I *am* going to the ladies' first but on the way back I'll talk to Ted about *Mrs. Dalloway*."

I started paging through *Fly-Fishing* and saw that I might not get very far in it. I looked around and after a while I saw Irene and Ted talking at the register, her hand in his, with Ted showing no emotion one way or the other. She motioned toward me over her shoulder, Ted looked my way, and I waved and nodded but I couldn't tell whether he saw me or not, or cared.

"Two weeks from tonight," Irene said on coming back. "Ted says they expect the biggest crowd in a long time. The book has just won two literary prizes in England and the German translation was named the best translation of the year. He said to get here early."

"Shall we meet for the reading? I'd like that."

"Me too. He says come at least a half hour early."

We finished our coffees—mine was a lukewarm best seller by now—and we stood up to leave.

"Shall we meet here?" I asked. "I'd be glad to pick you up at your place?"

"Here would be better. This has been so nice." She brushed back her hair. "I've always trusted in the kindness of readers."

* * *

Two weeks later I got to Books by Dickens forty-five minutes before Phyllida's reading. Ted Cousins had been right. The store was filling up and I peeked in the reading room and saw that it was already half-full. I wandered around, reading dust jackets, opening one book after another, dodging customers, sidestepping two comfort animals.

At seven fifteen, I was beginning to worry that Irene might not be coming or that we might have to stand for the reading. Ted was moving around the bookstore in anticipation, going in and out of the reading room, talking to customers, talking to staff, squaring up stacks of books on tables as he passed by. I waited a few more seconds, then decided to ask him if he had seen Irene. At first he didn't seem to recognize me. He looked harried.

"You probably don't remember me, Mr. Cousins," I said. "I was here a couple of weeks ago with Irene. We were planning to meet tonight to hear the reading. But I don't see Irene anywhere. Have you seen her by any chance?"

"I take it you haven't heard. Our old daughter-in-law, Irene, was killed in an automobile accident last week. What did you say your name was?"

I told him.

"Sally and I are broken up about it. She was a lovely person but kept too much to herself. You might think this an odd thing for a bookseller to say, but she spent too much time alone reading. There was no service. She was cremated and scattered by some out-of-state relative we didn't know about. Please excuse me. I've got to run. I take it you really didn't know her well."

Out of some sort of commitment that I couldn't quite name, I stayed for the reading and then did buy a copy of *Mrs. Dalloway at Eighty-Four*. Phyllida won the crowd over with her rich laugh, literary gossip, and wild magenta hair.

"Good for her," I could hear Irene saying. ■

THE END TO CAPTIVITY
Faisal Mohyuddin

If I go walking through dawn's dewy shadows toward
the river where the carp burst through the gleaming muck

to belch air, and there, in the echoes I catch the wordless
voice of my dead father, then should the unexpected

gift of my child's embraces when I return home be like
a key? What lies buried beneath the wreckage—the solace

of my father's songs, another lost geography never meant
for me. Quietly, I ease my son back into bed, promise

him a toy truck, a rocket ride to some imagined country
in another corner of the galaxy—whatever he wants

in this age of unlimited wonder, if he would just fold himself
back into a pocket of sleep. Beside him, I will sit, listening

backwards into his slight wheezing, wondering at the hours
my father spent like this, the light of day what lessened

the strangle of his longing. Every day the child asks the same
question: when will I be older too? Along a rising flood

of worries, a bruised apple, floating alone, no tongue to taste
the perfect quiet, to protest the loneliness, the half-lit exile

that looms in the wake of a father's passing. Within,
a door locked, behind it the innocence of a skylark waiting

to be slaughtered. My son knows nothing yet of this
nightly searching for songs. To devour the bird is to taste

the night sky in summer, to commune with the bleakness
of every body. An invented memory of that first burst

of daylight at birth, of those rivers of darkness pouring
from my lungs. Paradise, a myth, a stopping place for grief,

an elsewhere for cowards. Convinced I can still breathe
under water, I plunge in, summoned by another glint of steel,

gripping my son's hand in case I need saving, or decide to
pull him under, introduce him to the hazards of time.

MEMORY—MYSTERY—MEMORY (A FRAGMENT)
Judith Aller

T he Caravelle jet landed in Oulu in early morning. The temperature was about twenty below. The yellow Mazda rental was at the ready to push up the northern route to Kuusamo. Packing my fiddle behind the seat, I threw a blanket to the pianist and drove into the blizzard.

It was February. Finnish-winter dark. Driving fast, the only light was white. Nothing but ice and snow and lumps of hills off to the right; no coffee bars, no polar bears, just whizzing silence. After an hour or so, a charging reindeer appeared like a ghost, leading her calves northbound in powdery gallops alongside my car. If there was a *Joulupukki* (Santa Claus), his village was not far. I was new to the thrill of shifting gears, so the clutch and I crunched away to the Arctic circle.

The car skated on ice and got us to Kuusamo on time. The Finnish-American Society had scheduled the violin and piano recital for 8:00 p.m., and by 7:30 p.m., the temperature was minus fifty plus the wind. As I walked up the steps to the hall, my stockings froze to my calves. Tuning, with little time to rehearse, I heard commotion coming from the crowd. And by the sound of it, the audience seemed pretty big for a town like Kuusamo. I learned later that everyone within miles was present, including members of the local Communist Party, who'd deserted their meeting for the concert (as it was told to me later, a fight had erupted within the ranks as one member tried to stop everyone from leaving). I think Finland is another world, one where music came first. And I knew I had to go there to follow a trail that reached back as far as Mongolia, where my family had lived on the run from pogroms and such. But, for me, it all began in my little room in Los Angeles, where I'm writing this now.

* * *

WHERE DOES MEMORY BEGIN?

I'm four years old, sitting on my bedroom floor, blue linoleum tiles beneath me. Through crossed legs, I see my hands holding a child's book, squarish with a faded green cover, its cloth threads frayed at the edges.

Opening the book, I see a pastel image of a boy about nine or ten years of age. The boy is Franz Peter Schubert. I put the book down for a moment and reach for two other books about Mozart and Tchaikovsky. But I am drawn to Schubert's sweetness bursting from his cheeks. He wears a bottle-green coat with worn cuffs and epaulets glinting on his trombone, pointed to heaven, while his school band marches behind him on a cobblestone street. Schubert's handwritten notes are pictured flying into the air through Vienna windows, where onlookers watch in awe. As I look at the drawing, I listen to my father playing *Marche Militaire*. Later on, my father tells me a story about Schubert's life, how he "fell" from bed each morning to write heavenly music faster than anyone else could.

I wanted to live in these stories. Schubert sang in a choir. I had no choir to sing with, so I sang in my room and next to the piano when my father played. At Christmas I walked alone through the streets nearby, caroling for neighbors, who sometimes opened a door or two with a smile as I dipped my voice to fulfill the harmonies. And all the while I dreamed I was invisible, riding with Schubert in a carriage that took him through the forest to the countryside where he taught the Esterházy girls, with their curls and fluffy dresses. On his way to the lessons, Schubert whistled tunes that he later composed at his desk. And it's true, the bouncing carriage wheels, clambering and fragile, gave much to the rhythm of his music—music only he could write. I decided then that this was my place in the world no matter what.

Destined for a life in music, I was born to the violin—it was phylogenetic. My mother, Ester Heller, was an accomplished violinist born in San Francisco. Her parents were from Poland and Hungary. Her father, Louis, whose family perished in a pogrom, was saved by a caravan of Gypsies. I've no doubt that some Gypsy was born in me, for I was always traveling in my mind, traveling with the moods, rhythms and sounds of places and peoples I felt within myself. These feelings would become my music one day. I had a father, Victor Aller, to teach me with his art as a pianist. He taught me the mysteries, the secrets of music in much the way his father, Gregory, an eminent cellist and graduate of the Moscow Conservatory, and his mother, Fannie, a piano graduate of the Warsaw Conservatory, had taught him. The lessons floated to me through centuries of learning from masters as far back as music goes. I was surrounded by the sheer joy of music my father created for Warner Brothers during the glorious *Casablanca* era. Even our home was a sanctuary of wonderment like the soundstage long ago at WB where my father assembled music from a vanishing age. The family joined in chamber music concerts and recordings for Capitol Records with Victor Aller. Among the players were my father's sister, Eleanor, a cellist, and his brother-in-law, violinist Felix Slatkin (their two sons, cousin Freddie and Lennie, also chose the music field as a career), and others in the family line, including performers of music of India. For myself, it was as if Brahms and my father and grandfather had taught: "Up to the mark or nothing." One day I would hit that mark through work with another great teacher—the violinist Jascha Heifetz—and in the landscapes of Finland and Europe, where I performed the lessons I'd learned, returning to America with no end of music in me.

My earliest training was as a listener. Because my father's work at Warner Brothers during the 1950s often kept him late, he would come home and eat a hasty supper in the kitchen, say his goodnight and then go into the studio to practice for his recordings. I would fall asleep as passages of Shostakovich's Piano Concerto thundered a room away, or wake up hours later to hear quiet passages of Franck's Piano Quintet rippling through the house. I believe these repeated experiences profoundly influenced me, molded my emotions to the feelings that are expressed in great music.

By the time I was four years old, I asked to play the violin. To me, it made the most beautiful sound of any instrument; I wanted to make that sound. I was told that I was then too young, yet I kept begging and was given my first violin at the age of five, a gift from a neighbor from Italy. Although my mother was my first teacher, I began playing the violin more or less instinctively before her instruction began. My mother showed me how to hold it with my chin. At first I struggled to reach my arm around the neck, but, the bow gripped in my hand like a little bird, I felt complete; I magicked myself into a trance. One night when we had guests, I conjured up a song as my father sat behind me playing Variations by Beethoven. His playing sounded like a revolution. I loved the beauty of it, the language, the images and sounds. At that moment, somebody snapped a photo of me.

Soon afterward, I wished to play again. The occasion was an evening rehearsal with my father and the Hollywood String Quartet. The first violinist was my uncle Felix Slatkin. It was his birthday and I wanted to play "Happy Birthday" for him. Before the group arrived, I hid and waited behind sofa cushions with my violin. The rehearsal began. And when, for a moment, the group ceased playing, I embraced the music. I was cut off by my uncle's voice. "Who's playing?" Felix shouted. I halted, and my father spoke. "That's Judy, I bet," he said with a chuckle. I stuck my arms out as proof and slipped out of the room as fast as I could. But not before I heard my uncle utter something nasty referring to me. A mystery of family enmities and resentment was unmasked with my playing, and by my father who believed in me.

My training continued with recordings I played on phonograph and radio, and by the door of my father's studio, where I stood listening for hours as he taught pupils the demands of the music. My father had a system with a metronome—electric it was; it taught me discipline, how to decipher a piece, how the notes fit together to tell a story. My father taught me the work of the great composers, he taught me the history of music theory and music structures of all kinds; he even gave me a grounding in folk music, American and European.

One afternoon while rain poured, I played a recording of Vladimir Horowitz for myself. Staring out a big window onto the street, my tears wet the glass. The great pianist played Schumann's "Traümerei," a reverie, a dream of *Scenes from Childhood*. I told my father I'd just heard what a dream sounds like. So my father played it for me again. When he saw tears in my eyes, he smiled and said, "Don't cry . . . I'll play something to make you laugh!" Suddenly elves and sprites sprang into the room from far-off woods. I danced while my father played. Then Edvard Grieg marched in; I could see him looking out his window onto green grass bridged by forests and lakes that flowed with Norwegian folktales. Next my father showed me the music for Mussorgsky's *Pictures at an Exhibition*, perhaps his favorite scene, the marvelous "Ballet of Unhatched Chicks." My God!—how it ruckused and quavered, labyrinths of pecking notes came alive, taking me to "The Great Gate of Kiev." Then came melancholy Gershwin, swaying like a lullaby. Next my father reached for a big book that opened to another world—*Fireside Book of Folk Songs*, in those days made of green cloth with red lettering on the spine and cover. The song my father played gave way to castling chords while I sang boldly as drunken sailors merged in river songs Mark Twain might've hummed to his daughter Clara, who grew up to marry a famous pianist!

Sometimes in the night when my father wasn't back from work yet, I would play a record in my room; *Said the Piano to the Harpsichord* was my favorite—a wondrous tale of piano and harpsichord conversation with music played in a grand house in the middle of night. As the story goes, both instruments act like living beings: they wake up to discuss their powers, they talk and talk themselves to a frenzy with wit and sarcasm (with very good actors!), a marvelous explication of the raison d'être of both instruments and how each was built to fit phrases to the feelings of musical humanity. Back and forth they go, scurrying over the keys, hurling words coupled with music—at times with great passion or soothing delicacy. In the end, both piano and harpsichord are triumphant, each in their own way, while the dawn comes with a blanket of dust particles settling them to sleep.

To augment my world, my father gave me a paper orchestra: like a pop-up book, but set on a base of wood built by a stage artist at Warner Brothers, a model of an orchestra for a scene in a music movie produced by WB in those glory days. Anyway, I played with my toy symphony and began to study each instrument and how they worked together through methods of orchestration. Rimsky-Korsakov was my first teacher, through his books. I must have been seven because I read a lot of books in our library: Mussorgsky, Rimsky-Korsakov, Rachmaninoff and so on as well as the best set of *Grove's Dictionary of Music and Musicians* imaginable, with photographs, pictures of paintings and drawings, and fine essays going back centuries in near stupefying detail. Page after page, I looked into a world that had disappeared—I guessed but did not know this till much later. My father knew it. His teachers knew it. Nevertheless, he guided me. God bless him.

Around that time, when everything started to fit together in my violining, my father invited my grandfather, the cellist Gregory Aller, to hear me play. I knew from the talk around me that his word was unimpeachable. I was nine years old, and Gregory, as I called him, sat down in my father's tall, curved-back, beige-leather chair. My grandfather was in his eighties, short but strongly built; his hair was thin, his face roundish, clean-shaven, olive toned; he looked Mongolian. He had beautiful hands and fingers curved at the tips like my father's, and mine too. He wore a three-piece suit and tie when he visited us, sometimes with a sweater in lieu of vest. When he came to the door to be greeted, he would step over the threshold, bend his knees and hold his face toward mine, and I would kiss his cheek in the Russian way. He wore rimless spectacles like my father's. His upper lip was full and shapely and his eyes were deep brown. He always sat at the kitchen table while visiting our home. One night I heard him say our family were "blue bloods"—and that we rode horseback from Mongolia to the steppe. Gregory's mother was a Tatar (a photograph had been taken somewhere in the steppe of the 1860s). The kitchen was close to my room, so it was easy to listen clandestinely to the detail of his stories. He spoke about literature and poetry with great love, of Pasternak—how underrated his work was; he read the *New Republic* and *Partisan Review* and argued the world. I heard unfamiliar names like Irving Howe, H. L. Mencken and others discussed. I recall Gregory's voice nearly broke when he spoke of Gogol and how one could only "feel" the depth of his work in Russian. One night I heard him memorializing Feodor Chaliapin as the greatest actor ever. Gregory had heard every great artist of that time; some with names you might not know, all part of the grand tradition that has vanished. I've kept a wooden box of his; it opens like a book. The box reads Gourmet's

Delight. Gregory's life now seems compressed within mine as I look at a mysterious photo he took someplace in Russian woods. But the greatest of his mementos are his concert programs from performances with other artists of the time, printed in Cyrillic and painted in pastel tones from a lost time.

But that day in our living room, Gregory spoke little, he just listened with his hands folded over his lap as my father and I played Mozart. As we played, I saw a large tear passing slowly down his face, and there was silence when we finished playing. He paused to clear his throat and looked at my father to say, "Victor, you are playing too loud." When he got up to leave, he said, "I wanted to teach her the cello but I'm glad she chose the violin." I didn't have that long to know him, but he made his place in my world that day forever secure. And afterward with the music he bound permanently for me—piece by piece, with heavy red and blue material, each cover inscribed with a composer's name, embellished by hand with pen and black India ink. ∎

MIDNIGHT IN THE GARDEN OF SID AND EVA
Ann Voorhees Baker

THE PARTNER GAME

S id and the half dozen others sat down along the edge of the pool and swirled their feet around in the water. Then a grumpy little white-haired woman came from behind and pushed herself into the space between Sid and the steps. She grabbed the handrail with a wrinkled iron grip and, grunting, sat herself down.

The pretty redhead in the green swimsuit standing beside them, name tag Hailey, said some gobbledegook about a water balloon. Sid waited patiently until the old guy next to him handed it over. "Pass it along!" urged the redhead. So he extended the jiggling bag to white-hair, and the little grump grabbed it with her clawlike hands and it popped.

"Ach!" she huffed, and she glared at Sid accusingly.

Redhead name tag Hailey laughed brightly. "So you two are starting the game!" she sang.

What game?

"Go ahead and get into the pool and move down to that corner," she said, pointing. "Here, let me help you, Mrs. Van den Berg."

The round little grump flashed her luminous blue eyes at name tag Hailey and snatched her arm away. "I don't need help!" Then, grumbling to herself, "And my name is *Eva.*"

Redhead smiled and stepped back. "Okay, great then!"

Sid watched as little Mrs. What-A-Bitch sank into the waist-high water.

Redhead name tag Hailey said, "Go ahead and follow, Mr. Miller!"

What? Well okay, whatever you say.

He lowered in and started to follow the round and fluffy and irritated Mrs. Van den Berg.

He said to her back, "Of all the gin joints in all the towns in all the world, she pops a balloon into mine." Then he snickered, but white-hair only squared her fatty back and raised her nose in the air and marched on, which was really only a messy slog, as that is the best you can do when you're walking in water.

GEFILTE FISH

It looked like some kind of holiday dinner and they were serving, among other things, gefilte fish.

Sid looked at his roast chicken, his matzo ball soup, his gefilte fish, his potato kugel. He was thinking that gefilte fish, let's be honest, looks like a bleached turd. If it wasn't on your plate like it was food, you'd never put it in your mouth. He decided not to eat the gefilte fish.

Little round white-hair was across from him. Sid said out loud, "Gefilte fish looks like shit."

She pursed her lips disapprovingly.

"I want a steak," said Sid.

Then he said, "Steak *smells* like shit."

She looked up. "No it doesn't."

"Yeah, it *does*. Next time you have a steak, put your nose down and smell it. Human shit, that's what steak *smells* like. Or shit smells like steak."

She tsked. He chewed his chicken.

"It *tastes* good, though," said Sid. "Go figure."

Sid kept thinking about steak; a golden edge of sizzling fat, smoky char marks.

"Umami," he said out loud.

No one paid any attention.

"*Ooh, mom*my," he said, and he laughed.

Little round white-hair shot a look at him out of the corner of her eye.

IN THE GARDEN

A bald guy was waving people out of the dining room and into the game room. Cards, board games, even coloring books.

"That's crap," said Sid to no one. He made for the door to the outside.

"Oops," said a young, slender guy with sandy hair. Name tag Matthew. "Hey there, where are *you* going?"

The words were gone. Sid wagged his hand toward the door, still shuffling.

The bald guy stepped over. Name tag Steve. "It's okay," he said to name tag Matthew. "We've got the outer gates locked already."

"Okay, then." Name tag Matthew opened the door and held it gallantly for Sid. "Enjoy!"

It was quiet outside, and cool. Maybe it even felt like fall was coming. Except nothing was right. No big red-and-orange maple trees, no vines snaking along the ground to pumpkins hiding under their own leaves. No, instead he was looking at spiky-trunked palm trees and rigid stems like green pipes coming straight out of the ground with waxy broad leaves and, here and there among them, orange-tufted bird heads as big as umbrella handles. Between it all, hard brown dirt. All wrong.

He spied white-hair behind some green knobby stalks that looked like they were from Mars. He walked over. He touched the cream-and-pink blossoms whose petals fanned out like a tiny deck of cards that had been swiped into a circle.

"It's plumeria," said Eva, sounding annoyed. She was sitting on a bench. She looked sideways at Sid with a sour face.

"Yeah, I know," he lied.

"Didn't look like you knew," said Eva.

He shrugged and laughed.

She went back to staring straight ahead.

He stepped around her and stood around for a while. Then he sat down.

"This is weird for New York," he said.

She said, like what's wrong with you: "*This* isn't New York."

He looked at her and laughed, like, good one! Like she was pulling his leg.

She frowned at him and said righteously, "It's *Pella!*"

"*Pella?*" he asked, still laughing at her joke.

Exasperated, she said sarcastically, "Pella, *Iowa?*" She huffed.

They both looked up at the sky at the same time.

Sid shrugged.

He stood up to go back in. He held out a hand to her, then remembered the redhead and this What-A-Bitch at the pool and thought maybe he'd better pull his hand back in case she bit it off. But she took his hand and pulled. Or really, she *jerked* on his arm. As she tried to haul herself up, he staggered. But he planted his legs wide like the old days on the boats, and he stood his ground, and she yanked on him until she got herself up. Her white head was just barely past his chin. "You almost fell down on top of me!" she said. "Some help *you* are!"

"Fighting tuna!" Sid cried. "You should warn me!" He took her arm and mock-jerked it.

Now they were pressing together a little. And she didn't pull away. In fact, after a couple of seconds, she pressed back a little. And then so did he.

Ooh, he felt it. It could be that this was that good thing. They stood that way for a little bit. Maybe moving a little. Testing the waters, so to speak.

Maybe she'd like it if he took it out.

She always liked that. The other she. She always chuckled when he did it.

Sid reached down to put his hand in his pants. There wasn't a zipper, just elastic, so that was easy. But there wasn't a fly in his shorts, so that was a little awkward. But his shorts were elastic too, if crinkly and therefore noisy. He slid his hand in, and there it was, and he was starting to pull the front of his pants down when all of a sudden out of nowhere a bald guy was right beside him, like poof! He looked familiar. He took hold of Sid's arm and he said, "Oh, I don't think that's a good idea, Sid."

"Yes it is," said Sid, and he laughed.

The bald guy, name tag Steve, smiled, but he didn't let go.

Sid pulled his hand out of his pants, sadly empty.

"Bye," he said to white-hair, as Steve wrapped his arm around his shoulders and turned him away.

She was looking at the sky again, frowning.

TALK SHOW

When it was pitch black outside, Sid found himself sitting on a couch. On the wall opposite was a giant rectangle of glass. And on it, two young men were talking. One was behind a desk and was wearing a suit and he looked about fourteen years old.

"Where's Johnny Carson?" Sid said to no one.

The old guy in the chair next to the couch looked over and shrugged.

On the glass was another young guy in the armchair next to the desk and he was wearing a black leather jacket and a tee shirt and jeans and his face had stubble all over it.

The guy at the desk asked, "Sooooo . . . let's quit with the *boring* chitchat about your movie and your directing and whatnot." He laughed straight at the camera. He said, "Let's ask the really *important* question . . . Are you and the gorgeous model you were seen with . . . you know . . ." and he gestured with his head, jerking it sideways, his eyebrows up and his face in a looney smile.

The guy in the chair made a face like he was confused. He tipped his head sideways. "Whaaaat?" he asked innocently.

You could hear the TV audience laughing.

The kid at the desk rocked back and forth now, smiling gleefully.

The man in the chair frowned at him. The kid at the desk kept on smiling.

Then the guy in the chair, all of a sudden his face opened up like seeing a big surprise and he threw himself backward. "OH!" he said. "OOOHHH!" Then he straightened himself up, tugged on his jacket, and put his nose in the air, just like little Mrs. White-Hair.

"Well," he said, "I consider that a rather shockingly *personal* question . . ."

The youngster at the desk laughed harder now, bouncing up and down in his chair.

Then the leather-jacket-and-stubble man blurted out, "But if you're asking, Jimmy, if you're asking have Adelaide and I made the beast with two backs?!?! Then, yes we have, Jimmy. Yes! We! Have!"

You could hear the audience howling and whistling. Jimmy at the desk rocked back and forth so hard that Sid thought he might hit his head on his desk.

"And I, for one," shouted the man in the black leather jacket, jumping up and pointing his finger in the air, "am an exceedingly happy man!"

Jimmy at the desk really bounced hard now, his wide mouth agape. Sid thought that Jimmy might pee his pants.

"Beast with two backs," Sid said to the old guy next to him. "Pretty funny." The old guy made a cackling face, but no sound came out.

SEASONS

Lying in bed that night, Sid thought about the gefilte fish and the mild breeze that evening in the garden. What the hell? It was bullshit. Jewish holiday food means fall. What happened to fall? He thought about cool and crisp October days, leaves sifting down through the air, smoke coming out of chimneys, cornstalks standing up like teepees on lawns, jack-o'-lanterns on porches. Chrysanthemums by everybody's front door.

What happened to seasons? What happened? What happened to that woman who thought he was funny whenever he took it out?

He was frowning in the dark. Pretty soon a tear rolled down his face and ran into his ear.

THE BATHTUB

"I don't want to take a shower," said Sid.

"Oh come on now," said the big friendly guy with the blue-black skin. "You know it's time."

"I want to take a bath," said Sid.

The big friendly guy, name tag Tyrone, sighed. Always the bath.

He put the mat down in the tub. He pulled the shower chair out of the shower and put it next to the bathtub. He started the water. And he started to sit in the chair.

Sid had something to say. But the words were gone again. He wagged his hand at the bathroom door.

Tyrone sighed again. He stood back up to his giant height, went out the door, pulled out the desk chair in the bedroom, and sat down out of sight of the open doorway.

Sid was still working on getting his clothes off when the tub was full. Tyrone came back in, turned off the water, got Sid's undershirt off over his head and his crinkly underpants down his legs and off his feet and he put a giant hand under Sid's stringy arm while Sid took hold of the grab bar and lowered himself slowly all the way in. Then Tyrone went back out and settled himself again in the desk chair.

Nothing feels so good as a hot soaking bath.

Except this tub was a puny excuse compared to the one he used to have. That one, oh that bathtub was a Cadillac of bathtubs, a Mercedes-Benz, a Rolls-Royce, a first-class Bentley. That tub was big, and wide, and long, and it was deep. You could fill that tub up and step over the high, straight side and slide down into it, and it was so long you could stretch your legs all the way out—*all* the way out—and your feet wouldn't even touch the faucet, and you could just lie back against the slanted end and rest your head and totally relax. The water came all the way up to your neck. The sides were so high that you had to lift your elbows up higher than your shoulders to rest your arms on the edges.

And that beautiful old tub was the color of butter.

"I used to take a bath in this great big tub," Sid said out loud.

Tyrone answered from around the doorway. "That's right, Sid," he said. "Your big yellow bathtub. That's when you lived in New York. You had that big apartment."

"Tubby Hook," said Sid, from no place in his brain.

"Mmmhmm," said Tyrone. "But they don't call it that anymore, right? They call it wood something, isn't that right?"

"Inwood Hill Park," said Sid. Also a name from the same nowhere place in his brain. "Two floors; *in* the apartment. There was a curved wall at the foot of the stairs. There were curved shelves."

"It was the most beautiful place, huh, Sid?"

Sid stared at his wavery skeletony body under the still water. His penis wagged lazily. Like a gefilte fish.

"Colleen fell down the stairs," he said. "Right from the top. I saw her face; like 'Oh shit!' but on a two-year-old. Then down, head over heels."

He wanted to catch her. He wanted it not to happen. Sid started to hold his breath. He sloshed the water with his left hand.

"Worst moment of your life," said Tyrone. "Yeah."

Sid started letting out his breath. It took a while. His chest was trembling.

"I thought her neck was gonna break." His voice pinched off into a quiet squeak. "I thought she was gonna die."

He took in a new breath and held it again. His chin quivered. He tried to let his hands float.

After a minute, he let the new breath out, and then he said in a growly voice, "I didn't catch her." Sid made a tiny hiccup. Then he was quiet.

"But turned out she was okay," said Tyrone.

Sid didn't say anything. What did that matter. He didn't catch her.

"Yeah, she went all the way down," said Tyrone, and then he chuckled. "And *you* were the one that cried like a baby."

Sid remembered grabbing Colleen up, stumbling over to the couch, holding her against him, rocking back and forth, the two of them bawling together, and he was louder.

"Uh huh," said Tyrone. "She didn't have nothin' broke. Not even a scratch. Her little baby dress wasn't even messed up."

Sid was quiet.

"That there's a miracle, Sid," said Tyrone. "A miracle. Right there."

Now Sid was crying, and his nose was running. He beat the water gently with his toes.

They were both silent.

Tyrone switched gears. "That place had a big terrace, right, Sid?" he asked.

"And a tree. In a pot. It had . . ." Sid could see the little red bobbles in the sunlight but he couldn't think of the word. Then he thought of the low planter boxes with the soft green leaves. "We grew . . ." but he had no words for that either. He waved both hands around in the air.

"A cherry tree. And you grew lettuce, and tomatoes," said Tyrone. "And you could look out and see the big river, couldn't you?"

You could. You *could*. The sun going down at the end of the day, Jesus Christ . . . He could see the wide slab of steel-colored water, the red-streaked sky.

Staring off, he said sadly, "The Hudson."

And his daughter was inside, and the other she, and the place was filled with gold evening light. Nothing was ever so beautiful.

Sid started to cry again.

Tyrone didn't say any more. He didn't say Sid's name. He didn't ask, Hey, what's going on in there? He didn't move like he was going to get up out of his chair and come in. He just stayed quiet.

THE PARTY

"Hey, what about an aloha shirt?" A short built guy with a Mexican accent, name tag Jimmy, was rooting in the closet. "It's a party. Gotta look nice, right?"

Sure, okay, an aloha shirt. Sid laughed, put his arms through the sleeves, and he buttoned some buttons.

"Huh, looks pretty good," said the built guy. "But it looks a little *torcido* to me, you know?" (Crooked.) "Let me do a coupla these buttons again, okay? Make you straight."

The guy tugged smartly on the bottom of Sid's shirt. "*¿Te pondremos guapo, sí?*" (We will make you handsome, yes?)

"*Cualquiera,*" said Sid, "*pero siempre soy guapo.*" (Whatever you want. But I'm always handsome.)

Name tag Jimmy laughed. "You always speak Spanish better than English," he said. "Guess your time as a fisherman in Peru really stuck with you, huh?"

What was this guy talking about?

The big room had tables all around and some balloons. And there was music.

And there she was, round little white-hair, at the food.

He went over beside her. She was scooping macaroni salad onto her plate. He took a plate. He scooped macaroni salad.

They sat at a table.

"I'll get you a drink," he said, and he laughed as he got up.

A pretty redhead, name tag Hailey, stood behind the table with the bottles and cans and a big bowl of ice. She looked familiar. He thought of taking her by the shoulders and kissing her right on her freckled nose. But he knew better.

Sid smiled big. "Bourbon on the rocks," he said. "With a spritz. And a Manhattan."

"Great! Sure thing," said the redhead. She picked up the apple juice and poured it into two glasses. Then she poured a little club soda in the first glass; then a little maraschino juice in the other. Then she dropped a stemmed cherry in on top.

He started to reach for the glasses but she said, "Wait!" She picked up two paper umbrellas, popped them open, and dropped them into the drinks.

"I'll be back with a big tip," said Sid.

She smiled big, and she winked at him.

Apparently, Sid was on fire tonight.

"Here," said Sid, setting the faux Manhattan down in front of Eva. "Drink it."

It felt good to order her around.

Eva picked up her paper umbrella, twirled it, then set it on the table. "I'll drink it if I feel like drinking it," she said.

Then she picked up her glass and drained it, and pulled out the cherry and bit it off the stem.

Sid looked around. He wished he really could get a bourbon on the rocks with a spritz. He didn't know why he couldn't, but he couldn't figure out who to ask.

He decided to be bossy some more with little Mrs. White-Hair. "We're going outside," he said.

They shuffled together toward the open sliding glass doors. He took her elbow and they carefully stepped over the threshold onto the patio.

There was a moon out. Or a sliver of a moon anyway.

"Feels like midnight," said Sid.

Eva said like what's wrong with you, "It's not midnight!"

"Walk," said Sid. She didn't give any smart-alecky reply, and she walked. He still had his hand on her arm, because she hadn't pulled it away.

They kept on across the patio and then gingerly stepped onto the grass.

They were walking in the moonlight. Or really, there was hardly any moonlight. "Walking in the moon-hardly-any-light," said Sid. He slid his hand around Eva's big soft waist.

A big guy with blue-black skin was leaning against a tree a ways across the grass. He looked familiar. He had his hand up to his mouth, but as Sid and Eva approached, he lowered his hand and hung his arm down, hiding something behind his leg. Sid could see a little waft of smoke floating out from behind. But whatever, who's gonna talk.

The big guy had a name tag. Tyrone. As they passed, he said, "What you up to, Sid." Saying it, not asking it. Not like stop what you're doing or I'm going to have to take you somewhere else, but like hey. Like in passing.

As Sid and Eva shuffled by, out of the corner of his eye Sid saw the big friendly guy bring his hand out from behind his leg and raise it to his mouth again, and then in a minute, he smelled such a familiar smell: good old tobacco.

He and Eva walked along, picking their way across the grass in the moon-hardly-any-light. He started to slide his hand up her back. Her flesh was loose and heavy, disorganized, all over the place; her skin was to skin as a soggy cloth is to a dry one. But it felt good.

Ahead behind a tree, he saw the corner of a bench. They went over and stood beside it. He pressed himself against her. She pressed back. Ooh, he felt it. Maybe now it was time. He reached in his pants and got hold of it; this time he pulled it right out. And after a minute, just like the other she, little white-hair chuckled.

Then she touched it.

He sucked in his breath. After a minute he took hold of the bench handle and he sat down and she did too and he mashed his hands on her big soft breasts. Everything blended together, but it all felt good. Now the little grump wasn't smart-alecky at all, and she worked her hands softly over his thing.

He reached across her and took the arm of the bench and he eased himself down on one knee and then the other. He helped her do the same. They worked their way down to the ground.

He had her underpants hooked with his fingers and he pulled down on them this way and that until finally she had a leg free. He struggled to roll on top of her.

And then she turned back into the little grump. She dug her wrinkled-iron claws into his back.

"Come on, Leonard," she hissed into his ear.

"I'm Sid," said Sid.

She dug the claws deeper. "Just do it," she said. She sounded mad, but sad too. He thought maybe she was going to cry.

"Uh," he said, struggling.

"Come on!"

"I'm trying," he said. "Jesus."

"Get over!" she said. "Get *over*!" He thought she really was going to cry.

"Left!" she said.

"I'm, wait a minute, oh," he said.

And then he said, "OH."

And then she let out her breath and she said, "*OH.*"

Now all he was looking at were her two deep-blue not-moonlit eyes and all he was feeling was what he was feeling.

Somewhere he'd heard somebody say the beast with two backs, and now they, Sid and Eva, they were that. Two silverback gorillas, making love or whatever you want to call it in the grass under the moonlight or really under the moon-but-hardly-any-light.

It wasn't pretty. But it was a beautiful thing. ■

WHITE RABBIT
Bronte Lim

I t was Katie who showed me how to remove the words. In the girls' room after Mrs. Stewart's art class, we stood in the handicapped stall together. We shoved our backpacks under the metal handrailing. The green tiles beneath our feet bore remnants of menstrual clots. A dripping sink counted us in.

She opened her mouth wide, wider, and pinched out the words, tiny pearlescent beads that she collected in her free hand. With each, she shuddered slightly. Without comment, she tipped her palm over the toilet and flushed them away. She stifled several coughs but a small one escaped, a leaping yelp. She wiped her pink lips with her sleeve, eyes closed, a ragged trail of lipstick streaking across the material.

"Now you try."

I opened my mouth as Katie had and reached into the wet darkness. I looked to her for reassurance, but she kept her eyes fixed on the door of the stall. I groped for what I thought she might have touched, tracing my hand over the dense ridges of my hard palate, the ticklish rope of tissue securing my tongue to my jaw, the soft flesh of my throat, which brought forth a gag. Saliva threatened to choke me, pooling from all sides of my mouth. I coughed when I removed my hand. I wiped its filth onto my sweater, my other across tear trails. My stomach turned.

"I can't." My words were thick in my numb mouth.

"Try harder," Katie said. Her face was pale, weak from purge. Her black eyes were opened wide, her voice assertive. "I can't keep being seen with you." Our status as the only two Asian girls in our grade led to our easy grouping by the others. Small town hadn't seen looks like ours, heard accents like ours. We had stumbled over English readings together, our tongues confused by *th* sounds and silent letters. We had shared noodles at lunch, milk candies gauzed in rice paper that clung to our molars after class. I kept the flattened white-and-blue wrappers in my locker, the cartoon rabbit ready to leap from the wax. We had spent years as best friends, by pressure, by shared circumstance and history, but when Katie found a way out, she leapt. I was desperate not to be left behind.

I kneeled over the toilet. It felt like my nightly prayers. I continued the invasion of my mouth, feeling, grasping, waiting for the chill beads to form between my fingers and the accompanying release. I didn't quite know what to expect—would it hurt? Or would it feel good? My hair hung in limp, greasy locks, at times dipping into the water in spite of my attempts to tuck it behind my ears. I retched when I pressed too vigorously, the taste of bile spilling from my mouth under Katie's gaze. When the minutes felt they could not grow any longer, I felt one. A small bubo on my tongue, hard and smooth under the ridges of taste buds that had at first tasted the salt and acid of sweat on my fingers, then only a desperate nothing. I grasped it, desperate to remove it, tiny cancer. It clung to me, connected by deep ties I could not at the time understand. It clung to me. It fought my efforts. I gasped, clapping my other hand over my mouth, as it burst free and brought with it a surprise of blood.

Pinched between my thumb and forefinger, it looked powerless. Its luster began to dull. I wondered what word it was. But now that it was out, I would never know.

"Give it here." I rubbed the mixture of pus and blood onto my skirt and handed the pearl to Katie. I felt light-headed, as though I were being rocked by the floor beneath me. My jaw tightened and loosened, positioning the bones and muscle anew.

She gave the word a look as though appraising a hangnail wrenched from a nail bed, or a piece of gravel worked out from a scab. Curiosity and contempt.

"Good." She gave the word a gentle flick with her finger and I watched it arc into the basin. It was so light it made no sound; it bobbed aimlessly on the rings of filthy fluid. "There's hope." She turned to leave the stall and shoved me back with her leg when I made a motion to follow. I was not yet presentable enough to be seen near her by the other girls.

"Rinse your mouth with mouthwash tonight. Don't speak too loudly, or too often. The bleeding will get lighter the more you get rid of them." Katie turned back to look at me. Her hair had thinned slightly from multiple bleachings and the silken white of her scalp peered at me. The rims of her eyes were smeared dark. "Prove to me this wasn't a waste of time."

Katie hadn't looked me in the eye in weeks, and meeting my gaze now, she paused. Her aloofness waned. "I don't want to have to say goodbye to you."

"I don't either," I replied. The clicking of her shoes trailed her out the bathroom.

My arms hung limply around the basin. The smell of sanitizer and urine rippled down my nose and sent waves of nausea through my gut. I vomited, blood and bile and a thin clear liquid I couldn't identify.

* * *

The moon before the bedside,
And frost upon the ground.
My face looks to its light,
My heart to thoughts of home.

Ba had booked tickets to see his other family again. He had gone out to the bar to drink and avoid us until he could put an ocean between himself and us, his failed Western experiment. I could tell by the stillness; Ma had scrubbed the house clean of his tirade. Every plate washed, dried, shelved; the coffee table had been cleared of used tissues and remotes; the glass over the dining room table bore no grease marks. The door to Ma and Ba's room was closed tightly, a red braided charm hung over its handle.

When Ma left the house to drive to the supermarket, I peeked into their room. There, she had yet to clean Ba's angry words from the bed, the closet door, the bookshelf. Black, oily smears still dripped earthwards. He had flung them at her, decrials of her growing wealth of foreign platitudes. To him, she was a coward, bowing before a strange culture. The books on raising a child by American doctors and psychologists. The American literature. The ending of my nightly homeschooling in Chinese language and culture. Ma had decided she wanted to stay here. She liked the open spaces and the ease with which Americans talked about everything and anything. She liked the clean air and mega-marts. She had begun looking forward to the times when he left.

Ba's anger promised no return; his anger said enough. He had married a woman who had betrayed him for a nation. Though we had been distantly aware that he had begun cultivating another life away from us, aware that his absences were too long and the financial returns too small for his trips to consist only of business, it was only now that he announced another wife, another daughter. And more: what began as an affair during a business trip would now be his home. We were not to be mistaken. Ma and I were the Other family, the extraneous family overseas. The anomalous, hidden past on a distant coast.

His other daughter was only a few years younger than me.

Dinner was soft food again. Over-steamed rice, silken tofu dressed in a black veil of soy sauce. Ma's teeth were falling out again; after she chipped her first last year, the rest were going quickly, as though they had decided to concede together. She passed me the bowl of English words; irregular shapes in irregular colors. Ma had chosen difficult words for me. Exams were approaching. I mixed a handful into my rice. They tasted of butter. For me, they were easy to consume and melted into my tongue, soothing the sore.

Ma told me to study, then rest. I asked to borrow her mouthwash.

* * *

Sights of the moon's light
And thoughts of frost
Stir my mind
To long for home.

Katie was right and purging became easier. We would go together during study period. She held my hair and I held hers. I began keeping a metal tin of Altoids in my back pocket, and it clicked and clacked as we walked back to our classroom. Our inside jokes began to populate in English, our old ones forgotten. Our tongues were a village, slowly freed from the old, welcoming the new.

With more room on my tongue, the English words nestled deep in my gut began threading their ropey tendrils up my esophagus, past my uvula, my soft and hard palates, and into the pink hills and valleys of my tongue. They helped rush out the old. By May speeches, I could purge two dozen words at a time, slipping them out as easily as beads on a string. In June, I was invited to go on a group outing with Katie and several girls and several boys in an upper year. It was an outdoor movie and when we begin pairing off, a boy even chose to sit with me. The field was rife with the scent of blooming weeds. Their pollen itched at my nose. I joked and laughed with the others, talking too much to follow the love story projected on the screen. In the summer darkness, I let the boy bring his hand to the hem of my skirt, the silk of my thigh. His breath warmed my neck. I leaned back, palms pressing into the soil moist with the new springings of grass.

* * *

1. *Before my bed, moonlight falls on the floor.*
2. *I thought I spied crystals of frost blooming.*
3. *Raising my head, I find the moon as a beacon before me.*
4. *To my heavy heart, it brings reflections of my hometown.*

Ba wrote me a letter, apologizing. "Ma is a witch, but not I." He asked if I would like to join him in Shanghai. "It is cosmopolitan." The international schools there meant I could study in America again for university, in a big, American city, where there would be other Chinese. There would be others like me, who had lived in many places. He described the shopping malls, the takeout restaurants, the cinemas. Bigger, better, cheaper. "*Huo po.*" Lively. I would not be lonely. I would not be an alien any longer. I would have a home.

In his next letter, he pleaded I not forget. Yet he continued to write me in English, already knowing, fearing, the distance between us. The words had been rinsed meaningless by the saltwater spray of their Pacific trek.

He asked if I still remembered the poems, the stories. The legend of the moon rabbit accompanying a goddess, pounding out the elixir of life for her to drink. A children's tale that I could no longer recall. The milky candies wrapped in rice paper that I ate as a child. I threw the candy he had placed in the letter out my window. They hurt my teeth. Ba copied his favorite poems into the letter. Ones about home and remembrance. The Chinese are always longing for what they don't have. I turned the letter over and felt the indents of the strokes. I wondered how many poems his other daughter could read.

* * *

Katie called me one summer's night before the start of senior year. I walked the familiar path to her home, past mailboxes, threading through a patch of woods, and through the back gate. The moon hung preternaturally large in the sky at an early hour. She asked if I had any left. She had gotten rid of her final word but now wanted them back. We sat on the black leather couch in her living room. Here, we had spent countless afternoons gossiping, making friendship bracelets, laughing and crying.

"I flushed every last one." I had not seen her in months. Her hair was black again, the remnants of bleached ends making her hair stringy and stiff. She looked younger and older at the same time, wearing wire-rimmed glasses and a lacy blouse.

"It's better this way," I said.

She showed me a picture of the boy she had fallen in love with. They had met during her summer internship. He was Chinese American, honest, ambitious, bilingual. His dream college was the same as hers, down in California. He had volunteered at an orphanage back in China, in Dalian. He visited his grandparents' home every summer.

"He whispered something to me, Grace. On the last night. The words sounded so sweet. They tugged at some distant part of my mind. It felt like my heart shifted in my chest. Like it moved into the correct position for the first time in my life. And then he asked me my name. The way he said it, he wanted me true name. Not the one I chose at immigration when I was six, the one that my parents agonized over for years, the one that was given by my grandma. My mouth moved to reply, and my chest felt so full, but I made a sound like I was choking.

"That was the first word I lost. My name. It was simple, it just means 'calm.' But that sounds so stupid in English. So ridiculous. Nice to meet you, I'm Calm. I'm . . . But now that I've lost it, I can't seem to . . ."

I let the silence sink over us. Distantly, the horizon claimed the last glow of sun from the summer sky, the moon still hung. I worked my fingers into the eyes of the afghan we had pulled over our knees. The round tips of my fingers looked inhuman budding from the knit.

"To grow up means to purge the worst parts of yourself, Katie. You said that to me when we were fourteen." Something in my chest twisted.

"I didn't know what it meant then to want love. To fear not having a home."

I watched my friend, curled into herself, braced in the act of longing. I ran a hand through her hair, caressed her cheek with my thumb. From my pocket, I retrieved the small plastic baggy of words I had collected before coming to her home. I fed her the words that I thought might mean "hope," "love," and "calm." They had grown hard and brittle exposed to the air, like dried peas.

With each one I gave her, I felt myself grow lighter; Katie floated closer to the earth. For the last time, I thought of the rabbit on the moon working tirelessly, pounding medicine with its mortar and pestle. I thought of the moon goddess, who was lifted by the essence of immortality to soar through the heavens. She had consumed the elixir of immortality and been flung to the heavens to protect the elixir from evil. She had been forced to abandon her beloved husband on the earth. The moon looked especially bright that night as I walked home, my feet barely touching the ground. I looked to it but in its shadows saw nothing but empty space.

* * *

My father sent a final letter that arrived on my seventeenth birthday. I wasn't sure if he had planned it that way. He must have cut his tongue licking the seal, three spots of blood, turned brown in airplane cargo, like an ellipsis along the letter's edge. I cut the short edge of the envelope off, and the folded paper sprung out. This letter was solely in Chinese I could no longer read. My eyes skirted along the lines, admiring the clusters of strokes as though admiring an abstract print. I stopped at its center. Set apart from his prose, my father had written:

床前明月光
疑是地上霜
舉頭望明月
低頭思故鄉

A poem. The first poem I had learned. The strokes wriggled on the stage, recognizing one another. They leaned on one another, grasped each other, turning merry in one another's company. Revelry. Song. A village in wild celebration. Mothers grasping fathers. Children singing songs. They burst into a chorus, a familiar tune in an unexpected space.

The moon, the frost, the longing. My tongue swelled, though I thought I had wrenched away the last of my words to give to Katie.

The poet longs for the home he cannot have. Longing for what I could not have. A home. My finger unconsciously moved in the rhythmic sweep of the word for "home." Down, down-across-and-hook—I remembered myself sitting at the dining room table with my father as I practiced writing my characters, his hand warm around mine to correct my form. I mouthed the words, holding the sound in the space of my skull, knowing that my dumb lips and tongue could no longer produce the sounds correctly; the shapes of flesh and movements of air were no longer natural. A wave of nausea clawed through me. I thought of the home my father wanted, that Ma wanted. How they consumed me to find it, to be part of it, until I had to consume myself, until I fed the substance of my words to another. Was my father apologizing? Which was the home he longed for? I wondered if this was how Katie had felt, words blooming in my chest with no way to reveal themselves.

I was on my knees, in the bathroom. Twenty words spilled out, larger and bloodier than the ones before. They were joined by a rope of tissue like the sinew of cheap pork. A ringing began in my ears and grew louder; I gritted my teeth to hold in my scream. One by one, twenty tears spilled, the same milky color as the words.

I sat by the toilet basin, leaning against it for support. I held the words in my hand, blood and pain against my teeth. The words clicked and clacked against one another. The blood began to coagulate, muting their noise. I rinsed them in the sink, pulling off the connective tissue, and dried them on my skirt. One by one, I fed them into the envelope my father had sent me. I closed it with a length of tape, then another, and another, until its entirety was embalmed, my father's blood grey under the foggy film of plastic. I tucked the letter into the drawer of my desk behind my school notes on world history.

* * *

I found that after that, no more words would fall from my tongue. No thoughts, no desires. I did not have to eat English words anymore for them to populate; they colonized my gut, my throat, my tongue through the canals of my ears or the pores of my skin. They reshaped my expressions, pulling on the muscles of my face in novel ways. They coaxed me to new people, new places, tipping *yes*es and *no*s to the right opportunities.

I examined the letter only once after that, the last night I stayed in that room. A bizarre cold snap had arrested the town in May. Ma had cried through my commencement, sobbing through my speech, though she had caught only a few words. Katie and I had gotten a picture together, her boyfriend behind the lens. Still lying in my cap and gown, I held the letter to the light to see the words:

ooooo
ooooo
ooooo
ooooo

* * *

Though the cold had begun to settle, I took the long way home. My bag hung lightly from the crook of my arm, and I tightened the belt of a jacket I had unearthed from the back of my closet that morning. The winding path of the park by the office was unoccupied. My head was abuzz with the comments from the latest project review and I felt the pieces of my report modulating in my head. The murmur of crickets in summer air beginning to chill persisted through the unending clamor of traffic. The smog made the sky red, but through its haze I spied the moon, round and full. My hand reached for my phone, feeling the fractal cracks in its screen from when I had dropped it carelessly onto the sidewalk, but when I raised it to snap a picture, I saw my camera confused by the haze, unable to focus on the beauty my eyes could feel.

I raised my head to make eye contact with the moon. A rising sensation filled my chest. I felt an irresistible compulsion to run towards it, across the empty park, and to leap. And in that leap, letting loose a guttural cry, I was sure I would soon be soaring towards the moon's welcoming gaze, bursting into a thousand shards. ∎

A SLICE OF BREAD
Elina Petrova

You haven't talked to me for thirteen years since
I blew out the candle of your last night on the earth—
let your pain leave. Last months on morphine

when we dwelled within the half-lucid, half-psychic
ward of your dreams, I still hoped, chopped onions
for sour-creamed tomatoes and my twelve-ingredient

borsht, pressed your sheets, waited for a chopper
to Kiev and, from there, for a military plane from DC
that would take you to the Bethesda Institute of Health.

Those were days of the Orange Revolution, when
more polished liars succeeded cruder ones. For two
years of our descending the staircase of cancer,

our phone rang only with calls from a former Kremlin
colonel (deserted to Maryland) who promised to help
us with a medical visa. He was not in his right mind,

but I didn't know how to discern. We waited as,
attached to me, he sent us responses to analyses
from DARPA, and we believed they were as real

as the Americans who strolled along Khreshchatyk.
One drizzly evening, when you lay—skinny
in a cotton nightdress—amidst crosswords you

fully solved even with a metastasized brain,
you had no appetite for anything and asked me
for a snack you might still enjoy. I went to

the kitchen to dry my eyes, cut a slice of white bread
and spread butter on it with the thought that I would
have died for you in any cruel way if that could help

and that I loved you even if you never taught me
how to express it. I spread butter, choking
on the unsaid, and brought it to you casually.

It has been thirteen years since then, but I can't
forget how you ate it and said, "This bread
is exceptional. I never tried one tastier."

PRESSURE COOKER
Moazzam Sheikh

A person is nothing more than a mini garbage truck, halting, moving, revving, raising a ruckus, collecting trash and mangled cardboard dreams, crunched cans of broken moments borrowed from strangers, hand-me-down words spoken, and images imagined by others. Our desires are scraps of metal and tears, our love stories junkyard lizards. I am an unoriginal thinker, more like an uninspired man, a blob, a blather, the exact opposite of what I hoped to be. Others are not any better. But the stories we tell, even to ourselves, the lies we knit . . . I am descending a morbid staircase when I spot a bus slowing down and I run for it. Breathless.

A gasp of fresh air. To step out of the apartment, like an animal allowed back into nature. Strolling down the busy street minutes ago, inhaling the scents of people, welcoming the energy of the crowd washing over me—neighborhood people out with strollers or bikes, zigzagging skateboards and swerving scooters, men happily trapped in boyhood, disheveled hair on naive faces, ears glued to smartphones, hands clutching coffee cups or eyes vacuumed by the black hole of their smartphones, wearing casual-looking designer clothes, going for the lower-middle-class look, fake rebels, spoiled brats, some with gentle souls and some with a devil's heart, the millennials, the Generation X, the gentrifiers, the motherfuckers—wait, slow down, slow down, be humble, sit down, *sit down!* What the hell, I am okay, fine, happy, almost giddy. To leave my hole today, my cozy apartment, my palace of suffocation, and I have to remind myself it's not their fault, they are not the main culprits, they are enjoying life just like I am as it snares them on the street, it's the big guy, the big-big guy, our big guy who sends in caterpillars and dumpsters and diggers to change the river's path. Who sends in the demolition man. Unfortunate folks who live close to the bank be damned! I can't get mad at these robots, apolitical zombies, not now! Not today! I want to seize happiness. Happiness, so fleeting. Happiness, so chimerical. I have the right to be happy.

Happiness is now taking a hit. I feel hot, need air, some space. Why is the bus so crowded? This is the time when people slave away at work, kids in school, night shift workers conked out in their bed, sofas, with TV on, bagels burnt in the toaster. What the hell! What's going on? The door closes and I am hemmed in on all sides by people tall and short, large and small, hyper and zoned out. I'll have to make my way to the back of the bus. Right now that's not an option. I look out the windows to feel I am not trapped. It often works. Can buses lose composure under unnecessary pressure? Can they explode under intense heat?

When I say I am happy, I am also feeling sad. It's up and down. A new life may be beginning, may be, but something I love and care for is also coming to an end. I must not mourn, I remind myself, but I can't help it sometimes. My life with Y—I'll call her Y for now—for the last two years has not been a pleasant experience, and I can't say I didn't try. We both did. I can't pin down precisely what went wrong, whose fault it is really. Easy to say that it takes two to make or break a thing, but I feel I gave my best. I am forty and Y is forty-five. She has a teenage daughter, C, from her first husband, D—his friends call him Big Dee, so do I whenever we meet—and C now lives with him because she couldn't get into one of the good high schools in San Francisco and D lives in the suburbs, Walnut Creek, where there's a high school C has grown to like. She visits us often and we like each other a lot, but I am not her father and she understands the difference. F, who I will see shortly, I believe is in her late twenties or early thirties. This is our first real date, and who knows what may happen at the end of the day. I am excited, nervous, cautious.

I can't resist thinking about my life with Y and visualizing, in slow motion, a cannonball approaching the facade of our life together. The thought plunges me into despair, yielding to sadness, even anger, and it's little consolation that I am surrounded by strangers, who have no idea what's hurting my head. But thinking about F has a calming effect on my nerves. In fact, I feel an erotic tug just by conjuring up her face, her big desert eyes, a furrow in her neck. Although she has simple features, and compared to Y her body, though much younger, shows signs of plumpness, she has a little bit extra where Y is wanting. Not that it really matters much, really, not more than idle talk. It is true that I have caught myself several times imagining F without her clothes on in all kinds of humanly possible postures, which is only natural since I have not really touched her, except placing my hands on her shoulders once when we kissed briefly, and perhaps once around her waist, where I gauged her daily carb intake. You can guess what's transpiring behind my zipper right now. God forbid, if someone accidentally bumps into my manhood! I have grown too sensitive to drawing unwanted attention in a crowded place. Thank goodness, a narrow path opens up, so I wiggle my way to the back of the bus. I breathe finally, my hardness still intact. I close my eyes for a moment to savor F's raised, celloesque behind, my tongue fondling its silky strings.

I feel as if I have been caught dead naked with my dick going limp in my grip. This can't be true. I am confused. Makes no sense. Have I boarded the wrong bus? The driver's voice announces the route number. How could I not notice when the bus turned the wrong way! The mammoth vehicle lulled me into complacency with its steady progress. And now I am on the wrong bus, barricaded by people, annoyed, lost in their own miserable world, angry beneath the mask of tranquility. Sweat erupts all over my skin. I want to move, but looking at people firmly rooted on the wrong bus, inertia takes hold. What about the Filipina-looking woman, sitting motionless, holding her purse close to her belly? Has she boarded the wrong transport? Is she, too, paralyzed? Held captive by a quiet inner commotion? And what's the story with the well-built middle-aged Latino? Is he a bullfighter or bullshitting his way through life and the bus? Why is he so shifty? What's bothering him? Every time I catch him looking at me, he looks away. If you can't hold a gaze, then why bother? If this bus is so beneath his highness, why doesn't he take a cab? Difficult to disembark? Give up the road taken wrongly? And why has the bus slowed to a crawl? I am so glad I left the house a little early.

No, not because I can't stand Y any longer.

I will get off at the next stop.

I am not a mean person, nor is she, and therein lies the sadness. If logic held sway, only when two people have irreconcilable differences does it become easier to see the twain should not meet, but when the disagreements are minor, why can't we chip away at them little by little to find some middle ground? Anyone can live with minor differences. I cook my way, she hers. We both eat each other's cooked food. But every other day we have to nag about the same things. Why do you leave the flame high if you are gonna walk away to do the dishes? And then you smell the food's starting to burn and you just stand there with a soaped-up plate in your hand and freeze and watch! She is right, though she doesn't understand the source of my inertia. She doesn't try. That hurts. Why does she have to start arguing over everything, right when we're sitting down to eat? No, I don't see this as an attack on women! Just because there's a beer commercial with seminude women during a Cowboys game, no it's not a conspiracy against your sisters. No, it's not because I am Muslim or Pakistani. Why do you waste water? Whether it is in the shower or kitchen sink! What sort of comfort do you derive from letting water run? No, it is not because Islam teaches me to respect water, no! Why don't you ever use the pressure cooker Esther gave us as a gift on your birthday? It'll save time. No, it won't burn your meat if you don't space out. No, it's not because she and I flirted once. It was wrong of me to fall into her trap. She was getting back at you for stealing her high school boyfriend. I didn't know. We were drunk. I am not trying to make you feel guilty. No, I don't feel guilty because I am Muslim but because it hurt you. No, it didn't. How could it not? It didn't. I commend your concern. No, it's not because Islam teaches me to respect women. It's because I care about you. Use the pressure cooker. It'll make the beef come out better, not overcooked and boiled. It's not the size of our little apartment. It's the countless insignificant differences we cannot manage to resolve that suffocate me. In a different life it would be so easy to fix these problems. But we have the life we have.

Should I make my way to the door? Or should I wait for the crowd to thin out? I have time. I can use this time to declutter my head. What's an extra stop! This goddamn traffic! What happened to the breeze? It was here a minute ago. Perhaps if I close my eyes, I can shut out feeling stifled. I want to imagine F getting ready to meet me, fishing for her favorite bralette and panties. Can she also be stuck in a bus? What if we both arrive late? What if she's on time and I am late? No, I have waited for this moment very patiently. I am glad that I am a patient person. I am not leaving Y in a haste. Though it has taken a heavy toll on my mental health, staying in a relationship longer than it was right, but that's my personality. I owe her that much. She's been good to me and she can still find someone better suited to her academic, activist sensibilities. I think she made a big error, and I might have played a part in it too, by maintaining the lie that I was a poet of sort. Anyone can write poetry, but not everyone is a poet. Yes, I flirted with her by using over-the-top expressions borrowed from Urdu and Punjabi—that's just courting. I am a part-time romantic. Other times, I can't decide. Sometimes I know I am spineless, but that's not true either. I can stand up for myself if I think it is important. I don't find too many things important. That's the problem. It is, I believe, a person's own pomposity that makes him view too many things in life as very important. I am just an average person trying to live an average life, without complications, without hate, without pressure.

What sort of a person chooses to stay on a wrong bus? What kind of a person have I become? I have never probed it deeply. Have you? Or how does one go about moral obligations? Sure I donate money to some causes, not out of deep conviction but more out of guilt, as a substitute for my lack of involvement with social or political causes. Like every year I donate a few dollars to a cause like fighting breast cancer, yet I have no pretensions about the fact that my dollar is a waste of money, a drop in the bucket with a hole. Perhaps one more thing that has come between Y and I is that I don't have a single activist bone left in me. I don't want to be an activist. I just want to be an okay person. Y disagrees. To be good, she lectures me, is to be an activist, to be active and alert and engaged with the world, with the issues of humanity impacting all. I stress "okay," not "good," but she doesn't hear me. I hate her sloganeering, especially when she succumbs to cliches like *Injury to one is injury to all!* I could not disagree more. She is too involved with the Palestinians' struggle for independence and has posters describing Israel as an apartheid state. My lack of concern irritates her. I can't pretend, change myself. I have gone to a few marches with her and that doesn't satisfy her. My concerns lie somewhere else. She cannot understand that being a Muslim (not practicing) and a brown person from a third world country do not make me want to be political and join an anti-colonial struggle. You might think I am a cynical person, but I assure you that's not accurate. Where I am willing to meet you halfway is that I might not have strong values. Having granted that, I insist that a person is inconsequential. That realization controls my behavior.

I don't want to sound ungrateful but I can't help being sucked into a downward spiral, regretful of the time when I could've made a different decision, the day I met Y, when my life could have taken a different turn. I remember the woman I courted at the party and I remember that I went home with Y instead. I can't remember her name—it started with K—though I can still recall her face, her light-brown eyes. Funny, I have never run into her all these years despite the fact she was one of those very few native San Franciscans. She was sarcastic yet sweet, a tough cookie because she liked asking tough questions.

"Where are you from?" I remember asking her.

"Why should that matter for us to talk?" she had said with a smile, which disarmed me.

"I am curious," I replied, swiveling my drink with ice and a cherry in it.

"Shouldn't you be asking me my name?"

"I am probably nervous," I said.

"Or you could offer to get me a drink!"

"Can I get you a drink?"

It is when I went to get a beer for her that I noticed a pair of eyes panning along my profile. And when I walked back with a beer in my hand, I noticed Y, as she listened to a tall guy, her eyes locking with mine, and just as I was about to disappear from her view, she rolled her eyes faintly, signaling she was with a bore. The hard liquor had already colored my judgment by then.

As I handed K her beer, she asked me if I really wanted to know where she came from or was it just a ploy to get a conversation going. I was tipsy. K and I flirted with each other. She said she was born in San Francisco, her folks originally from Mississippi. At some point the crowd shifted and Y and I established an eye contact. I don't know why

K suddenly asked me if I had experienced any incidents recently that might be construed as bigoted or discriminatory. Drunk and distracted, it took me a moment to register the jolt K had given me. I just stared at her, baffled, slowly realizing the terror implicit in her question. I wondered why she had suddenly shifted gears. If memory serves me right, we were talking about sex and sexuality and American films and commercials in general. I shook my head, unable to recall a clear incident where I might have felt attacked or insulted. But I was made aware of the oppressiveness I had been harboring, and now I felt even more bottled up for not being able to express it. My feet began to feel warmer. "What made you ask that?" I didn't recall having told her that I was Muslim raised in Pakistan by a mildly conservative father and a reluctantly open-minded mother.

"Because of your brown skin, my dear!"

"My brown what?"

"You don't exactly look Latino or Italian."

"No . . . but . . ."

"Well, look around. How many dark-skinned people do you see here?"

I took a quick survey and shrugged, then sipped my drink, trying to relax again, as alcohol calmed my nerves. "Not many. I see another man over there, but he . . ."

"And when you entered the room, you came straight over to me. To another dark-skinned person."

"I am sorry. I can be clumsy sometimes." My armpits were warm pools already.

"Oh, no need to be sorry. I didn't mean to put you on the spot. I saw you enter, grab a drink and get away from the crowd fast. That's when you saw me.

She laughed a deep laugh coming from her guts.

"Yes, I did feel nervous entering alone. I still haven't spotted my friend who invited me to this party."

"I know one of the roommates, but before you showed up I'd been standing alone waiting for you," she teased. "For quite some time actually." Her tone changed to sarcasm, then she added, "I am enjoying speaking with you. Aren't you? Why be grumpy!"

"Instead of being sad and depressed."

"There you go!" She laughed.

I remember nodding.

"I am a nursing student in my final year at USF. And I can't wait to finish. So you've been okay? With all the wars we've been waging. Bindibustings! Islamophobia, attacking Sikhs."

My skin was set afire. My body crammed inside a cauldron. I looked at her lips, feeling drained of sexual desire, as her mouth sculpted air. I blinked. Pieces began to fall into place. Incidents that had happened to me over the last several years resurfaced. I felt exhausted. I wanted to hear her, but I gawked, numb, noting there wasn't much to say. I'd have to meet this woman somewhere outside, like on a date. I took another sip. The clatter of the party crashed against my eardrums. I noticed she was silent.

I laughed sheepishly, pretending to have been following every word of her. "I normally don't like parties," I said, "especially big parties. I don't function well . . ."

"Neither do I," she blushed. Did she suggest that we cut the party?

"I don't have an accent, so to speak. What made you ask that question?"

I began incoherently, "It's been hard. It's a tough place. It used to be different. I remember friends joked about Arabs and Muslims, pure jest, influenced by the action movies with bad Arabs. But not malicious. There was a time you could joke about many people. It was okay. Jokes were jokes. Or perhaps I was oblivious, naive. But now even educated, smart people feel free to make all kinds of assumptions and I don't know where to start, how to counter them without making them feel slighted or angry. It is sometimes easier to listen to their bullshit and swallow it. It is not smart to anger those in power. I guess it makes one meek. It tenses me up. It turns the insides into sticky noodles. They acknowledge I am good. Not necessarily a good person. Just cool. They don't realize what they are saying, that I am different from my own people. Unlike my family and friends I left behind, I am modern. I can fit in. We can get along and that's why we can meet and hang out and I can be invited to the party. Despite the mess we have heaped on the rest of the world, the reason the world is fucked up and poor, the reason men like me leave, so many here still believe in the bullshit about them being more civilized. I am sorry I am ranting. Let's . . ."

"I am listening. I wanna hear. Go on!"

"You want to hear something real funny?"

She nodded as if a hand were dribbling her head. I exhaled and guffawed. I wanted to release the tension that had balled up. "Not too long ago, a good friend of mine broke down sitting by my feet after she showed up at my apartment looking a bit haggard and I am thinking she's here to screw me. It's happened to friends, to one of my roommates. Okay so I am saying that it's a brown man's fantasy come true. You with me so far?"

She nodded again, with the dribbling gone, a quizzical look on her face, jealous?

"She says she's been meaning to tell me something. I am thinking I shouldn't raise my hopes up, perhaps she's killed someone. I'm looking into her eyes and they are bereft of lust. I'm saying I am misreading the signs, this is a sure fuck-fuck situation, remain calm, whenever she wants. My heart's pounding, my throat's dry, groin's on fire. You wanna guess what she spits out?"

"Have no idea. Tell me. I am hooked." She exaggerates her interest, widening her eyes.

"You won't believe it!"

"Try it."

"'I am terrified of Islam.' I can't believe my ears. For a moment I guess she's talking about another colleague of hers, this guy from the tech department, a Muslim guy from Fiji, Saleem, but that's not what she means. I have to stifle an urge to call her a stupid white bitch and slap her face. Instead I am filled with compassion because she is exposing her inner self to me. I could've called her all kinds of names and she would have forgiven me. I too made equally terrible assumptions when I came here. I notice we both are weeping, and my erection is gone. All I hear from her small mouth is that she knows it's not true, it's the media and how it dumbs down already dumb Americans and I am thinking, But you live in San Francisco, yet I can't say anything, not a wrong word . . . she is not here to stab me in the back or tell me to go back to my country, no, none of that, in fact just the opposite, recognizing something is wrong with this country. We hold each other's hands, as I lift her up and make her sit next to me. I am not upset anymore. We both exhale. I make tea and we chitchat. She'd like to acclimatize to the Muslim world. I promise to dig up a few titles. After she is gone, I am wondering if other friends, too, hide their true feelings. Is everyone stuck in *Raiders of the Lost Ark*?"

K tapped my arm a few times and I sensed steam escaping my skin like when you nudge the metal weight atop the pressure cooker lid.

"Quite a story!" said she while looking deep into my eyes. I didn't realize that Y, the long-haired man, and another man had crawled closer to us. My prime audience saw me getting distracted by the presence of an intruder. She wasn't a fool. Though I tried to recover, belatedly, she'd seen the enslaved man, withdrawing gracefully with an excuse to visit the restroom. She slipped through my fingers. Had I persisted, perhaps, I might have been a different person. I had boarded the wrong bus then and couldn't do anything about it.

I have zoned out again. For a minute I have no idea where the bus is. Has the bus been idling away at this spot or lurching like a slug? I want to panic, but my body feels like it's been drugged. I have to admit there's a certain pleasure I take when I zone out. I have never had the courage to tell Y. Like it frees me from the grind, from reasoning, even from caring. From the nightmares of my previous dreams. Even now someone else in my shoes would make an effort to get down. Instead, I make a hasty calculation, convinced that time is still on my side, allowing me to daydream. I can afford to stay a little longer on the wrong bus. F won't mind. I detest myself slipping into lethargy. I see an empty seat beckoning to me. I have no idea who got up and where that person went. Was it the heavyset woman with a shopping bag? She must have bumped into me before slithering past me. Did I have mushrooms for breakfast? I hear Y's voice, in fact several voices of hers, berating me, instructing to turn down the flame, turn off the faucet, not to forget the keys and lock myself out, to sit down when I pee *please*! In my mind, on my way to zoning out again, I ask her, several times, because I can't remember, if I should add more salt or less!

Something irritating has blocked my entry into my private little world. A washed-up young dolt, his neck and arms covered with tattoos, engages invisible demons in a monologue. Too young to have been a hippie himself, his clothes suggest he's mourning a bygone era. I want to feel sorry for him but his clatter is chipping away at my inner peace. I want to block off his gibberish, the catchy poetic rhythm. I can't deny my attraction to what I am hearing despite his repulsive features and overall appearance, while I can't tell if he's cursing his mother or a friend or the system, all rolled into one it feels.

I am trying to decode his accent, which he really doesn't have, but there's a flirtation, a tease beyond my grasp and if I lend it too much thought it'll drive me nuts. I can't tell if he's of Middle Eastern extraction, or part black and part white, a bit of Latino, definitely not Native American but maybe yes, certainly not East Asian, yet, then again, who knows. He could be part Indian or Pakistani, although I have my doubts. I didn't use to think that men from Indian or Muslim background could slip through the cracks in the US but experience has corrected my erroneous assumption. Nobody else seems to give a damn about him. He's driving me up the wall. The more I try to block him off, the more I feel the itch to tell him to shut up, something I won't do out of nervousness, that feeling of being naked despite being fully clothed, the state of nascent terror that I detect within. The last thing I want to do is to give another person the chance to put me in my place, to awaken me to the probability that I am somehow out of place, unaligned, that I don't belong here, the US, or the bus, a permanent outsider on a temporary welcome. Unlike him I have not learned the art of camouflaging myself. He could be Maoro, Martin, Manuel, Manny, Maajid, Maaz, even Marcelo for all I know. This decoy will protect him. I am without one. I can be made out, in a flash, an outsider. My innate nerviness works as my sixth sense in anger-ridden situations and guides me to take a step back, back off, or back away. Experience has showed me that if there's a heated argument among narcissists, the owner of a bruised ego might just pick on me to assuage his wounded pride . . . *You want me to wipe that grin off your face?* Or *Why the fuck are you laughing, you little shit?* I usually make my exit, I can't rely on someone to stand up for me or ignore my humiliation; there are occasions when a retreat is not allowed, and whether someone stands up for you or not, both action and inaction reduce your self-confidence to a pile of turds.

I had blocked Y out but Y had staged a coup d'état. It is possible, generally speaking, that I have been attracted to older women, but that sort of desire was probably influenced more by watching *Summer of '42* and *The Graduate* than having lusted after older cousins and neighborhood aunties—the fact that Y was very blonde, her very Nordic looks notwithstanding, is besides the point. One of the two men, the one with long hair, attracted to my protestations, misunderstood me, and though he let me know how irritated he was by my slight of Americans, he also let me know that he was one of the hosts of the party to which I had been invited by a friend, who couldn't be found anywhere, but he was obligated by his sense of hospitality to assure me a good time here. The other man seemed sympathetic, perhaps because his parents or grandparents were migrants from some European country and he had heard accounts of their struggle shaping their earlier years in the harsh yet welcoming new climate. When I told the men that it was the kindness of strangers that the most vulnerable often need, it prompted Y to ask me if I was a poet. The men withdrew. I lied carefully when I said with fake reluctance, "Perhaps! How did you know?" She said she could tell when she saw one. I forgot K for the rest of the party.

Y and I ended up in a room where people squatted on the floor in small groups taking occasional swigs from their drinks and smoking pot. The couch was empty and Y inquired if I'd like to sit down. But we had barely plunged into the soft comfort of the couch when the same man who'd taken offense to my earlier takedown entered the room, peered, squinting as if in a mock spy act, then blurted aloud, "Hey, who told you guys you could smoke in here? Out, out, this is my room." Bewildered, the men and women got up, grabbed their drinks. Before Y and I could figure out what was happening, he reached for my collar, pulling me up, my tense body following the command of his rude hand. Y sprang from the couch and stood up for me and told him calmly, "David, he is not your boy!" He might have said something to her. "Let go off his collar. He's not a dog, you realize?" I was ashamed of being there and though my eyes were riveted by the cool anger of Y's eyes beholding the man in contempt, I felt the man's hand retreat. He seemed drunk and confused, mumbling. Y wanted to know if I'd like to leave.

We left the party and began seeing each other as a couple soon after and now I was in the wrong bus running away from the very woman who'd stood up for me. It was Y who had said that we were both runaways. I had run away from Pakistan, though I had not thought of that departure in those terms. She had run away from her *situation* in Boston. For her it was more literal, running away from her stepbrother, who had repeatedly molested her while her alcoholic mother turned a blind eye. She said she had written about it in several articles. Now as I sit in this bus with a torn heart, I can't be certain if I am taking the right step. The thought brings me back to the realization that I am on the wrong bus and unless I make a quick decision and get my ass off the seat, I won't make it in time to meet F. I snap out of my reverie. Only to be stunned out of my wits.

And I don't believe what I see. I want to rub my eyelids. The bus is completely devoid of its passengers, except the driver, who's looking at me, motioning to me, hollering, "Out of the bus, man, out, out!" I try not to panic. I try but I can't get up. I sense extreme disrespect in his tone, and though he hasn't called me a name, I hear myself telling him in a calm voice that I am not his Paki boy. I want to ask what's happened! I feel paralysis squeezing my balls. This time I am not zoning out. I want to speak to him, explain that despite the effort, I can't get my butt off the seat. I don't think I have ever been in an empty bus before. I believe it's this thought that has stunted me. I am trying, I am trying. But I am frozen. My limbs refuse to listen. My own body parts have gone in a rebellious mode. I am acutely aware of the situation that doesn't seem right. While I zoned out something terrible must have happened but without noise, otherwise I would have, like others in the bus, reacted.

What sort of a bus is it that doesn't have any passengers in it? Is it even a bus? I should've been outside the bus. I am who didn't want to be in this bus, shouldn't have taken this bus to begin with, now can't seem to get up. I am feeling hot, engulfed by perspiration. I must have blinked. The driver is not there. When did he leave? He must be a ghost. Another person has entered the front door, leaning in, with one foot still on the step. The temperature inside the bus has risen. I wish someone would open the windows a bit, letting out the steam that's suffocating me. A cop. Is he going to arrest me? Please, officer, would you tell me what's happening here? Why am I the only one on this bus? Will he shoot me because I can't move? I holler, Let me go! *But how?* Help me! I can't move! My voice hasn't reached them. My glance slides from his hand to my feet as I attempt to wiggle my toes, catching in the process a glint from something shiny, metallic, on the floor, near the back door three yards from my legs. Recognition registers and panic explodes. Why is a pressure cooker left down there? Is it . . . It's beginning to make sense. Click! *Oh fuck! Oh shit!* Don't shoot me. I have nothing to do with this thing! No, no, he's reaching for his gun. Is he? My eyes can't focus . . . I can't see. He is stiff. He goes out of focus. He is speaking into his walkie-talkie. I scream . . . *What we have here is* . . . Despite the panic, I can use my eyes. I spot former bus riders and passersby . . . *a failure* . . . gathered beyond the sidewalk and I note police cars with flashing lights and cops moving about . . . *failure to communicate* . . . "Don't move, you retard!" I must have moved. That's a good sign, though I didn't feel any stir within. My mind is making up words. Is it all in my head? That's a mixed signal. To move or not to move! I wish Y were here. She'd protect me. But she is not here. Instead she'll get a call, "*We regret to inform* . . ." I am relieved it won't be my mother receiving the call. The cop has the gun in his grip, but it's not pointed at me. Not yet. Is he going to shoot at the pressure cooker? What if the bullet bounces off? If she were here right now, she'd tell the cop to put that nasty thing back. She is not here. Nor is K. Or C. Or D. Or F. Just me and him inside a bus going nowhere. Not now. For now it's just the gun. I am inconsequential yet I . . . try to communicate . . . god knows what . . . god knows why . . . imagining the pressure cooker as a deal broker, a hostage. Am I inside a nightmare? Is this for real? Can you intervene on my behalf? How badly I want to point out his assumption, that I have nothing to do with this goddamn pressure cooker. *Mine is inside my head! You have a solution for that, officer?* ■

IN THE COLD
Robert Kerwin

After failing in the saloon business, my father couldn't find another job, so there we were once again—on the outside looking in.

"There's nowhere else to go," my mother said. "Who wants us? Nobody."

The only thing to do was pile in on the old folks and see what happens.

My grandparents were in their late seventies and lived on the second floor of a two-flat on Ada Street. They rented the downstairs to a couple who had a son my mother said "wasn't right."

When Grandma saw the six of us in her doorway, she pulled back, then stood rigid, frowning, her arms akimbo.

My mother, who was carrying our new baby brother, said, "Hello, Mom." My father tipped his hat.

We hauled our stuff through their parlor and down their dingy hallway. We'd brought our small stuff only. Our big stuff—our couch, my father's chair, our dining room set—we'd put into storage until it came time to move to the next place, wherever the hell that would be.

Grandma and Grandpa gave their bedroom to my mother and father and the baby, and took the small guest bedroom for themselves. My sister, my brother, and I got the "sleeping porch," a spare frame structure that was attached to the rear of the flat and used mainly for storage.

My mother worried about it being too cold for us out there. "One of you is liable to catch your death," she said. But I didn't mind: the sleeping porch was nice and private, and—for now, anyway—it was *ours*. Nobody could throw us into the street. Set on top of an old sewing machine was a statue of the Blessed Virgin, dressed in a blue cape and a white *babushka*. I liked that. The Virgin Mary watching over us day and night, with eyes that never closed.

* * *

My mother's relatives didn't appreciate us piling in on Grandma and Grandpa. Regularly I overheard my aunts telling my mother how they felt.

"When is that hopeless husband of yours going to get a job?"

"Isn't there some other place you could go?"

"Ma and Pa are too old for this."

I'd never done any wrong to relatives on my mother's side. On the contrary: I'd always harbored the kindest feelings about them. Actually *loved* some of them dearly. So, when I overheard them talking about us the way they talked, it sickened me.

I felt like we were outsiders. Our whole family treading around every day like zombies.

Whenever I asked Grandma where Grandpa was, she gave me a dirty look and said, "Down below." So I'd go into the basement, and there he'd be, by himself in the coal bin, sitting on the broken stool he'd found in the alley.

Some days my mother set our baby brother, Donald, on the floor of the sun parlor and asked Grandma to keep an eye on him. It wouldn't be long until we heard, "Go wan out of that now, ye filthy little pup ye. Don't come near." We'd rush in, and there'd be Grandma aiming a mean, squinty-eyed kick at Donald. He'd bitten her again or had smacked her bad leg.

"Don't mind him," we said. "He didn't mean it, he's only playing."

"Only playing, me arse."

We left them by themselves, and minutes later, hearing Grandma's rocker creak aggressively, we hurried in again, and there she was—with a grim, determined mouth on her—tossing and lurching, her arms urging the chair in tugs and jumps to where Donald was playing on the carpet. With a cruel joyful look to her face, she went into a final swift lurch and rocked the runner onto Donald's foot.

Grandma listened to *The Goldbergs*, *Maxwell House Coffee Time*, and *Wieboldt's Your Neighbor Invites You Over*, but her favorite radio program was *The Irish Hour*. When *The Irish Hour* was on, she sat softly tapping her foot to the music. Sometimes she hummed along with an almost contented, *happy* look on her. In fact, the only time I ever saw Grandma smile was when she was listening to *The Irish Hour*. I used to peek in at her, feeling pleased to see her looking so happy and content.

Some evenings, if I promised to stay quiet and not disturb her, I was allowed listen to *The Irish Hour*, too. One evening I was tapping my foot to the music, the same as she was, and a warm, knowing smile came over her. "And what's that you're tapping to," she said, "do ye know?"

"'Garryowen.'"

She seemed delighted that I knew "Garryowen," and as we tapped to it together, Grandma looked as if she genuinely cared for me, *liked* me.

She patted the cushion of her chair: "Come sit by me."

Jesus, that was a new one. I couldn't believe what was happening, but I climbed onto her chair anyway and squeezed in beside her. Then she actually put her arm around me.

When the program was coming to an end, Grandma pulled me in closer and said, "You don't have nothing to be ashamed of for not going to the Catholic school. You're not to be embarrassed because you go to the public. I know many a good person who went to the public school. So just because your father don't make enough and can't afford to send you to the Catholic school where all your cousins go is no disgrace at all, and you're not to be ashamed of yourself, do you hear me? You're just as good as they are, you're just as good as anybody, whatever school you go to don't make any difference."

* * *

One morning I woke up to a man's crying.

I crouched behind our bed and peeked into the dining room. Mister Sweeney from downstairs was on his knees, with his head in Grandma's lap, she looming above him stone-faced.

"Mother McCarthy," he cried. "Please, Mother McCarthy, I'm on my knees to you."

With a look of bitter disgust, Grandma said: "Get up out of that now, you. Stand on your two feet. I want to tell you something." Mister Sweeney stopped crying.

With her crooked finger, Grandma tapped her knee for emphasis, and said, "You'll have the rent in my hand first thing Monday morning, or you and your family be out in the cold." We'd been thrown into the street a few times ourselves, and I didn't like hearing that ultimatum issued to anybody—even somebody like Mister Sweeney, who everybody in the parish said sketched from the collection box that he passed every Sunday at Saint Sabina's.

When Monday came around and the rent wasn't in Grandma's hand, she threw the Sweeneys out into the cold.

It was February, the temperature nearly zero in the street, and as Grandma and I looked out through the lace curtains of the sun parlor window, the Sweeneys were huddled by the curb next to their meager assortment of furniture. Huddled with them was their retarded son—big oversized head on him going in all different directions.

Grandma gave me the keys to the Sweeneys' flat. "Go downstairs now, you," she said. "See if they've left the place in good order."

The Sweeneys' flat looked pretty empty and had a creepy, echoey feel to it.

Grandma called down over the bannister rail: "Mind you look in the bathroom, too, see they left it nice and clean."

A horrible stink was coming out of the bathroom. I went in, breathing through my mouth, and there, laid out in front of me, were seven shits: two of them behind the toilet, two out in the open next to the tub, one looking up at me from the middle of the floor, and the remaining pair tucked beneath the radiator in the corner.

"Jesus Mary," I cried out.

Grandma shouted down the stairs: "What is it? What in hell's goin' on down there?"

I pretended I didn't hear.

* * *

As soon as the Sweeneys were gone, our family moved into their flat, and Grandma and Grandpa went back to living their normal life up above.

But my mother's relatives didn't go for that arrangement, especially when we were getting the downstairs flat rent-free. I thought that letting us have the flat for nothing was generous of my grandma.

Certain conditions came with the new living arrangement, however: one was that we were to look after Grandma and Grandpa—we were to do *all* the looking after—so that the relatives wouldn't have to travel to Grandma's three times a week with groceries and wouldn't have to make daily meals for the old folks anymore, or do their laundry, or change their bedclothes, or anything else. As long as we were getting free rent, all household chores belonged to us.

The routine we worked out was this: my father would look after the upstairs, and my mother would take care of down below.

My father went up to Grandma's three or four times every day. Sometimes he brought me with. We knocked, waited, and soon from the other side of the door we'd hear: "Who is it? What is it ye want?"

"It's us, from down below," said my father. "We came to see if everything is all right."

"Of course everything is all right," Grandma would say crossly. "Why wouldn't everything be all right? How else do ye think it'd be?"

Then the door opened a crack, and Grandma, wearing a wrinkled gray nightgown, peeked out, looking half asleep, and angry, as if we'd just woken her up. She looked like a specter, or ghost; it scared the shit out of me.

My father said, "We were thinking—"

Grandma opened the door all the way. "We're well able to take care of ourselves," she said with a dirty look, "whether some people realize it or not."

"We've brought your supper."

In the dining room, my father nodded a hello to Grandpa, who sat meekly in his corner, smoking his pipe.

My father set the table, arranged their supper dishes; then, as usual, he looked around for things to be picked up off the floor and put where they belonged.

Seeing my father serving Grandma and Grandpa their meal was bad enough, but watching him as he stood at the kitchen sink—his sleeves rolled up, doing their dishes—was even worse. Then to see him putting their old ketchup and mustard jars back into the icebox. Jesus Christ! When he gave a slipshod mopping to their kitchen lino was the worst of all.

My father went to the store for them, too. And made their bed. One day while he was at it, Grandma pushed him aside. "Mind you get out of my way now," she said, and attempted to make the bed herself, but did a sloppy job of it, leaving wrinkled sheets and comforters hanging down onto the floor, my father having to make the bed all over again.

Once a week my father went from room to room in Grandma's flat, collecting dirty laundry, stuffing it into a cloth bag, and humping it into the basement for a wash. This is not my father, I thought, as I watched him, sleeves rolled, leaning over the laundry tubs. This is not the kind of father I want.

One day, after we'd been installed there for a month or so, Grandma made her creaky way down the stairs and offered us her rug. "So's the child have a nice warm carpet to play on," she said.

My mother protested, but Grandma insisted. Next, the Persian rug was rolled out on our living room floor. As soon as the relatives heard about that, they scheduled the famous meeting.

* * *

My cousin Jack and I waited until they were all inside the meeting room, then we crouched outside, listening. What concerned me most was the effect that the famous meeting would have on us, on our family, on our future, which was now in the hands of the relatives who were sitting around Grandma's dining room table.

As the meeting progressed, two of my aunts became hotly involved, you could hear their shouting all over the flat.

Jeez, I was thinking, my poor mother and father sitting in there at that table, surrounded, taking it, saying nothing during the entire proceedings.

To me it sounded as if the relatives had leagued up and an ultimatum had been determined in advance; the repetitive demand I kept hearing was "Move."

Aunt Agnes, as if reading from a script, was laying out the strict conditions under which we could continue to stay. Each condition was followed with "Or if you don't want to do that, you can move."

"If these don't suit your fancy," said Aunt Ida, "then what you do is move."

After the first dozen or so "Moves," my cousin Jack took me by the shoulder and walked me away.

* * *

Our family stayed in the downstairs flat for a while longer, but nobody went upstairs anymore to look after Grandma and Grandpa, no more of my father mopping and cleaning around, changing bedsheets and the rest.

After the famous meeting, the only contact we had with my mother's relatives was when one of them came to deliver the supper. Our doorbell would ring, I'd step down to the vestibule and let in whoever it was—an aunt, uncle, or cousin—and sometimes they'd say hello to me, at other times they just brushed past, looking at me as if everything was all my fault. Then whoever it was went up the stairs hefting the cloth-covered tray or wicker basket containing the hot meal.

I wondered: Who is doing Grandma and Grandpa's dishes nowadays? Probably Grandma, because many evenings, around suppertime, we heard dishes crash and shatter up above.

Whenever my mother answered the suppertime doorbell, she gave a disgusted look to whoever was making the delivery. Usually she received no response, but sometimes she was told, "Please get out of my way." One aunt said to my mother: "Oh, are you still here? I thought you lot had gone by now."

Aunt Agnes, my mother's eldest sister, showed up one evening with the hot meal. With a wicker basket over her arm, she burst into our flat without even knocking, took hold of the Persian rug, and yanked it off the floor.

"I'm taking the oriental," she said, rolling up the rug as we watched; then at the window she shouted to whoever was waiting for her outside: "Come and help." The last I saw, Aunt Agnes and Uncle Pierre were dragging our rug across the sidewalk and stuffing it into the trunk of their car.

Right after that, we moved. ∎

THE GLASS LADDER
Deni Ellis Béchard

W e saw her come down this road, past the birch growing out of the foundation of the old spring house, and she may have paused briefly, there, in the shadow, thin as it is. What she wanted none of us could imagine, but that face of hers, those Normand eyes bright under the hood of rags, passed over us. She followed the road like a beggar, as if to call out for leftovers or coins, but continued silently, her feet bleeding and her body wrapped in a tattered sheet. She dragged her gaze over everything—our farms, our house.

Maybe she was destined for her trials since birth. She'd been granted too many hardships, and though we have all known difficulties, hers were not honest labor, the rearing of children, or the hand on the plow, but the result of pride, and not just her own. A girl raised by a fool and a harlot, in a house half-brothel, half-convent—as divided as a Hebrew temple—she'd never had a true place. It was as if she'd been chosen—sanctified through tribulation—though we and, in truth, everyone in this village has been tried like Job and purified through suffering in smaller ways. Still, we should have taken her in, or offered her something. We have never been wanting.

The least we could have done was make the boys leave her alone. They followed her to see what had become of her—madness, we were calling it then.

Emelisse, they shouted. None dared throw rocks. Then we'd have said something. But her eyes, they hadn't changed, and if anything, pain had made her more striking, had given her the look of a terrified bride, one who, perhaps, had yet to meet her groom.

Emelisse, the boys taunted, and when she at last flinched and gave them the gaze they wanted, they paled and backed away. Maybe they saw death in her eyes and couldn't hate her as they'd hoped, though she did look hateful, clutching the sheet over her rags, careful to cover that body of hers, when once you could have paid the price of a bonbon to see it. Well, no doubt the price wasn't so cheap. But she'd never had a chance to start right, brought up by only two mothers, each crazy in a different fashion.

It's an odd story, and there are a couple ways about it, though it basically ends up the same. Some parts never change and others are always different, so you know what to expect and yet look forward to hearing it again.

* * *

One of Emelisse's mothers was Félicité, daughter of Albert Dubé. She was tall and pale, the source of those Normand eyes, and had had another daughter with a drunkard postman years before. That child was conceived out of wedlock, a week before the two were supposed to marry. A few of the old timers recalled that the father had the same eyes, and a story made its way among us that he'd been Félicité's estranged brother, separated at birth, and had fled after their union, realizing the nature of their sin. Félicité gave her daughter an odd name, Riva, and raised her in isolation, the illegitimate's religious education being the mother's penitence—in a small house on her father's farm, with a high view on the sea.

The girl grew up awkward, so lonely on that coast she married the first man who paid her any attention. That was Gilles Boulay—a typical Boulay, lanky and hardworking. Family broods were so large none of us clearly recall which one he was. She was sixteen, and she lived in town with Gilles for two years, but she failed to give him a child. Then he went to *la Nouvelle Angleterre*, for a job in a shoe mill in Nashua. He said he'd send for her but never did, and a year later, she went and found him, newly married with a pregnant wife. She stayed on as if to be a second wife, working as a hotel maid and living in a rooming house, accepting his visits. We knew this from relatives who emigrated.

It was madness, we told ourselves, an acceptance of immorality, and no doubt in her blood, in light of what happened next to Félicité.

* * *

Emelisse's second mother was Bibianne Miouse, granddaughter of Donald MacNeil, who, during *la drave*, when the men ran timber downriver, could pull out the corner of a logjam by himself and get things moving. She took after him, a squarish woman who wore her apron everywhere, except to church, and walked with kicking strides, swinging her arms like an angry child.

It was as if Emelisse's life were planned and the lives of others were sacrificed to bring her into this world. Whereas in the years after Riva left, Félicité had the earnest attention of every village man but unnaturally never grew ripe, Bibianne repeatedly miscarried with the exception of a baby boy, a tortured thing whose body twisted on itself until he died. Her husband and the dead boy's father was Arthur Miouse, *un vrai innocent*. He was handsome but foolish, pompous and without a trade, living on the graces of his father, a clothes merchant. Before his marriage to Bibianne, Arthur cuckolded many men, all the while courting little Lise Marceau, a beauty and not too brilliant herself. We'd been sure the two would make a couple until the day Bibianne announced that Arthur had gotten her pregnant. When he denied it—and *bon Dieu*, he denied it—she gave him a thrashing in front of the courthouse. He wasn't a small man either. We all enjoyed that.

So Arthur and Bibianne married, and to prove his son's worth, Arthur's father built them the biggest house in town, an ugly affair with columned porches that gathered snow and so many windows that heating the rooms must have been impossible.

Arthur and Bibianne came to church every Sunday, for she was so devout that if she'd let Arthur bed her out of wedlock, it was as near to a miracle as we'd seen. Had the Holy Virgin been as piously prude as Bibianne, and the Good Lord in his carnal form less seductive than Arthur, there would have been no immaculate conception, and we would all still be pagans. But in the pews, Bibianne held Arthur's arm and squeezed it, not with affection but with wincing pressure each time his eye strayed to Lise Marceau or the narrow shoulders of another village girl. But though Bibianne kept a leash on him, she lost all her children, and, once, she grew in size until we were sure there were twins, but then—and we can all swear by this—she mysteriously became smaller, until her size was normal, stomping out chores and swinging her arms above great broad steps through town.

All the while, Félicité lived alone in that little house above the sea. Her sisters and her daughter had moved away, and then her father died, and we began calling her *la veuve*—the widow. We didn't know who started that, but it suited her. Some of the old timers have even gone so far as to say she briefly had a husband who died and who has since been forgotten, but that seems unlikely. Age has fogged their memories, and they must merely be recalling the death of her father who'd been a private, aloof man and the only person to assure her well-being.

But the strangest thing about Félicité was that she didn't age. Her beauty didn't dim. If anything, it grew. Unlike most of our women, who'd had a dozen or so children, she'd had just one and kept her figure. Her solitude had always seemed a sin, taking what God intended for matrimony and wasting it on seclusion. In her house that buckled beneath the snow and leaned away from the sea wind, she accepted a widow's fate, surviving on what men brought her during their secret nightly visits.

There was even a traveling salesman, a gaunt figure with some Jew blood who stopped in on his trips. And, of course, there was Arthur.

On a July afternoon, Bibianne was coming down from the high fields up past Félicité's land. She'd been picking wild strawberries, and as she passed the house, she saw the bright green door on it. We all knew that a bear had broken into Arthur's new car garage—his father having bought him a Ford—and had stolen off with the leather seat cover. Arthur replaced the garage's side door, which the bear had cracked, and then installed it in Félicité's house, since, though cracked, it was better than the rotten one she'd had. It was a door we would have recognized on a passing barge—banded, with a small square window, and paint as green as July.

The first time Bibianne saw the door on the house, she'd stood in the road, staring and trembling. Germain Dugas, who was returning home with a sack of freshly-shot grouse, saw her, saw the basket of berries spill onto the dirt, and her face become as red as a wound.

She said something then, about a harlot, and went up the porch and knocked open the door. Sure enough, Arthur ran out naked. Bibianne wasn't fast enough to grab him, so she dragged Félicité out by her hair, shaking her so that it's a wonder her neck didn't snap. She'd meant to carry the sinner into town and strip her camisole—which was all Félicité had had time to get on—and beat her in front of everyone, but Félicité said—and Germain Dugas heard this—that she was pregnant and it was Arthur's.

So Bibianne carried her back inside and put her to bed, told her to stay put, as if that wasn't already where she spent most of her time. Then Bibianne went home, gathered her possessions, and returned to take care of Félicité. Right up until the birth of Emelisse, the two of them lived in that house.

Arthur wasn't seen again, though Onésime's cousin, down working the mills in Hartford, said he'd read about his death in the paper. Arthur had been in Manhattan, dressed in pinstripes with a boutonnière of tiny pink roses—*that* was in the paper, Onésime told us. As Arthur came around a corner, he almost stepped on a skunk, right there, on *l'Avenue du Parc*. It sprayed him and he jumped out of the way, into the street, and a taxi hit him. That's why it was in the paper, because it was a silly death and nobody had claimed the body. The police knew his name from the papers in his wallet.

Bibianne was generally accepted as a widow after that. Arthur had left with his money and car, but she sold the rest, even their parcel of land, though she had their house moved, board by board, and rebuilt next to Félicité's small, rotting home, so that she and Félicité could live together. Isolated from town, set on those empty hills above the sea, the immodesty of the house was clear—an extravagance, the exaggeration of qualities that should be kept to oneself.

* * *

We should have known from Emelisse's life, the odd events that might be read as signs, that she would be special. Curé Félix was running the parish then, and he hated Félicité, but what he did to Emelisse—even if she was the fruit of sin—was too cruel for a man of the cloth and had to be a test delivered from the divine hand which casts affliction and catastrophe.

The first we heard of Emelisse was from passers-by on the road who saw Bibianne on the porch with a baby, but none heard the child cry, making us wonder if she hadn't gone mad and was carrying about a doll, or worse—another stillborn. A few years later, when we passed on the road, a dark-haired girl watched us from the brambly garden or from behind the pillars of the porch. Not long after, Bibianne began parading her through town, showing off the small girl—a startling pretty creature with the blackest hair braided with such intricacy we didn't doubt the vanity in that home. Already then, the girl stared out with the awed eyes of a creature who never expected to see a world like ours. She didn't touch anything or speak, and in church, we watched her as the curé gave his sermon. Those eyes didn't seem to blink.

The world must have appeared strange to her after her isolation in that house, and her life was unimaginable to us. Our days were the same: the fields and the hunt, the steady readying for winter and the logging camps when the earth froze. Our children had lain in the same cradle that we had, been rocked on the same floor, heard the old stories and felt them on their own lips—the voices of uncles and grandfathers, nephews and sons.

But to have grown up in that house on the coast, to be fed by the lust of men who came at night, we could not imagine. The garden returned to forest. Branches scarred the house's walls when the sea wind blew. Stories of life inside came from Félicité's furtive lovers. Clément Singelais told us that men brought firewood and that when this ran low, Bibianne pulled boards off the small home Félicité had previously lived in, so that it disappeared slowly, devoured by the big house. A bedroom turned into a chicken coop, stocked with the hens men used as pay. A sitting room filled with poorly mended household goods cast off by village wives and brought by husbands. There was even a stained glass window, made and brought by the same artisan who fashioned the new one for the church, and it hung where a storm blew out a grid of panes, above Félicité's bed.

We would pass in the road and see Bibianne reading to Emelisse from the bible, each few words staggered with pauses, since she'd never been quick. Félicité still didn't age, enduring the way hermits do in their solitude, her beauty enlivened by her absence from our lives since we pictured her from stories but never saw her up close. Maybe nothing could impede her desire after so long without a husband, but why Bibianne didn't throw the men out, we weren't sure. She'd understood something about the hand of God, or she simply couldn't hate anything about Félicité, not after she'd given her the child she'd so desired.

Emelisse became tall and slender, with eyes like sunlit water, and though she was pious, attending every mass, we saw what she did in the fields above the sea. All of us observed it sooner or later. It might have been dancing. We'd witnessed nothing like it. She hopped and turned in the tall grass like an injured bird, her arms extended. She pranced on wide, flat ridges of stone, silhouetted against the curving sea—she'd spun, twisted, and leaped, moving her arms in strange shapes. We could attach no meaning to her motions. No one here could have taught her this. We understood why the curé hated her.

As she grew, she spent more time performing her mad rituals, even in the snow. We began to see who her real mother was from the sway of her hips, how she smoothed her skirt to her thighs before sitting, or even how she carried her gaze over and past men, as if they weren't there, but so that they could look upon her face. She wore a simple necklace, a silver chain, and when she neared workers on the road or young men by a splitting stump, she moved her fingers past her throat and lifted the simple cross from between her breasts. Some said she'd been too isolated to understand. Bibianne had guarded her, stepped in front of people who tried to speak with her, and even struck Onésime's golden spaniel dead when it growled at Emelisse in the street.

After killing the dog, Bibianne lost sensation in her fingers. Her hand curled into a permanent fist and withered. Not long after, she began to tremble, her jaw shaking and her hair going gray.

One dawn, a grave appeared on the hillside above the sea. We tried to imagine Félicité and Emelisse digging that hole in the unsanctified earth, though we saw neither do so—only Emelisse performing her vexing dance around it. Soon after, we were shocked to see Bibianne shuffling along the road, her good hand bandaged from the shovel. Félicité's soul had fled to the source of her passions. We couldn't imagine how, though some speculated that her soul had aged cruelly and died even though her body persisted with its tawdry charms.

* * *

As a young woman, Emelisse didn't speak to anyone in town or even pray, as we do, kneeling in the pews, hoping that winter will be gentle or the wheat too high to see the elderberry at the fence lines. We have argued over this late at the table, until the meat turned cold and clotted in our throats, even though we had to wake soon, to feed pigs and cows, carry the plow into the pastures, or burn out stumps and vines. Cutting back weeds, we have all been alone with our memories of what she became at the end of her life—that barefoot wretch, leaving prints of blood on the dusty road, shapeless beneath her sheet but for the stories the men told of how she danced herself to shame in the city, for money, under colored lights. We've had to ask if our own suffering could do what hers eventually did—crack a church foundation or bring snow out of an August sun.

One source of her confusion, we understood, was that everything had been new to her. The village was as bustling and overwhelming to her as Montréal would be in the eyes of a farm boy. Since Bibianne had kept her from us, Emelisse didn't even know the other children. She stared on their games as if they were the rituals and intrigues of courtly society. We saw this, but we didn't know the power of her estrangement until the autumn that she met Magloire Fortin.

Magloire—this is how his father, Onésime, tells it—idealized her, had seen her sitting on her faraway porch, back against a cracked pillar, reading, or in her trance of wild, provoking movements in the field. As is to be expected of a boy in the heat of his teenage years—he'd imagined a profound, lonely, and inventive girl—had, in short, imagined her. Magloire was handsome, much as Onésime had been—tall and broad shouldered—but unlike his father, he was dreamy. He wrote poetry and told people openly how the church had hidden great works of art.

Onésime, being the mayor at that time, warned him to keep opinions private, not for fear of trouble—there's no real trouble to be had in opinions—but out of respect and the sharp tongue of Curé Félix. The worst thing that could happen to any of us was to have the curé deliver a sermon about something we'd done or failed to do. But Magloire claimed, back then at least, that he was guided by his heart. Since Bibianne was now unable to leave the house, Emelisse went alone to the store once a week and spoke only the single words that identified each of the items she needed. Magloire walked up to her, cavalier in plain sight of the men gathered at Anctil's store, and asked her to the harvest dance.

Onésime, who saw the whole thing from the oak bench on the store's porch, said she held Magloire's face with those unblinking eyes. The wind didn't move her hair or ripple her clothes, though the sign above Anctil's doorway creaked on its chains. Other than this and the wind itself, the silence was complete.

According to the others on the porch, Magloire blushed at the show he'd given the village men and was turning away when she said, Yes. But Réjean Fournier, who'd also been on the porch, said Emelisse was the one who blushed and drew her hands up to her chin, her arms over her breasts.

What? she asked and then, Why? as if Magloire's proposal were inconceivable.

The harvest dance, he repeated, pleased, according to Réjean, by her timidity. He took the opportunity to step close, his face an inch from hers, and spoke quietly toward her lips—words nobody heard because of Gérald Coulombe's almost incessant blathering about the hockey game he'd heard on the radio the day before. It was only when she left and Onésime asked Magloire that they all found out she'd agreed to go.

At first, Onésime forbade the match. Magloire said a rose can't be blamed for growing among briars. Onésime invoked common sense, madness, inheritance, and then simply shouted, No! so loudly that he startled the baby next door into a fit of crying.

For all of Magloire's dreaminess, he was as hardheaded as his father. Onésime found endless tasks for his son on the family's land and in the courthouse. To make sure that Magloire didn't scamper off, Onésime worked side by side with him, pausing only to ask him if he could abandon his ideas of the girl though Magloire refused to respond. Only after having reinforced the sagging rafters of the barn, rebuilt stone fences where frost heaves had broken them, and sanded and varnished the courtroom floor, did Onésime relent. He let Magloire sleep the two days before the dance.

Onésime drove to Campbellton, in Nouveau-Brunswick, to the house of Adélard Carrier. Onésime was frank, as he had little time. He showed papers relating to the family legacy and presented his friend with a leather pouch of bank notes. The deal was made. Adelard's daughter Brigitte was a known beauty and also intelligent. Though Adélard had worked out a way for her to be schooled near Boston, in a place called Wellesley, Onésime sold his friend on her new future. Of course, Réjean Fournier, who had family in Campbellton, told us that American schooling was simply one of her fantasies and that her father was in fact pressuring her to marry Patrick Gordon, an aging, well-to-do Scots merchant. Onésime arrived just in time, and since she had fond memories of playing hide-and-seek with Magloire on a visit years before, she agreed to the match.

Onésime returned with Brigitte at dawn, well before Magloire awoke from his long adolescent sleep. She waited among the trees at the edge of a field until Onésime, as a signal, swept the porch and stairs. She came up the road. The hem of her skirt was wet from crossing the field, her hands and face flush with cold. She knocked.

Get that, Onésime called, and Magloire, having just come downstairs, opened the door on an apparition of beauty and despair.

My parents, she said, and then held back a sob, they've drowned.

She fell into his arms. He later realized that she was a friend of the family, that they shared childhood memories of hiding in a cornfield and of chaste kisses under a purpling, stormy dusk. He learned that her parents had gone down in a ship just outside the port of Dalhousie. Later, when she was calm and they sat together on the couch, she confided in him—as Onésime had schooled her to do—that the most beautiful works of art were surely kept hidden by the church.

Brigitte had a fair complexion and was pleasantly confident, so that walking the road or at work in the house, she appeared at ease. That harvest dance, we chose her as queen, and she was a joyous one, as she'd discovered that her parents weren't dead, but that another ship had capsized and the reports had been confused. She'd told Magloire that her pain had been as real as if they'd died and his kindness had healed her.

As the fiddlers played, she danced in and out of Magloire's arms. A warm wind blew up from the south, pushing the cold out to sea, and new clouds covered the moon. Briefly, in the shift of climates, flurries fell, the snow almost warm, catching in our hair and melting before it touched the ground. The bonfire's sparks trailed into the sky. More than one child was conceived that night, and a few marriages ensued. Even the confessional and Curé Félix seemed welcoming. We all looked to Brigitte as she moved among us, snow melting on her cheeks.

Her smile faltered only when Emelisse came to the edge of the circle. The musicians stopped. She wore a black dress with cutaway shoulders and flaps below the arms. She must have made it from an obsolete garment, inspired by a magazine clipping. It was sepulchral and yet obscene, a dress that might have been worn for a dead matriarch's vigil but refashioned for a nightwalker. Even worse was how she entered the circle. She moved the way she did in the fields, her arms lifted as she turned in strange, prancing steps.

In the old stories, it is the devil who interrupts the dance and takes the village's prettiest daughter into his arms as the instruments leap involuntarily to life in the musicians' hands. He holds his palm to her back and it burns itself there as they dance, faster and faster, until he lets her drop with a wound that will never heal. We must have all shared this thought as she encroached. Red-faced, she stopped her dance, sensing our fear or hearing muffled gasps and laughter. Her eyes reflected the firelight, as empty as those of a frightened horse.

Brigitte took Magloire's hand and stepped forward and said loudly, Go away!

A baby began to cry, and Roger Chouinard, a barrel-chested and already balding country boy who was soon to take charge of his ailing father's potato farm, said, Wait. Dance with me.

She looked past him, at Magloire, and then ran clumsily away, into the shadow ringing the fire. The folds of cloth below her arms flapped like wings.

* * *

It wasn't long afterward that Emelisse spoke with the curé and told him, in a soft, disjointed voice, that she'd decided to become a nun.

Curé Félix had always disliked the women on that farm, even Bibianne. They were the town's scandal—a sign that he hadn't fully conquered his parish. He'd long had the habit of spitting into his handkerchief. In public, when faced with someone he didn't like—village boys who smoked at the maple shacks or men who bought whiskey from passing ships—he pulled the handkerchief from his pocket, snapped it open, and held it before him, directly in front of the person's face. With the two corners pinched in his fingers, he spat into it, the wad of phlegm striking the thin cloth.

Clouds had brought evening early that day. Edouarde Labrie was on his way to pray for his youngest, who suffered fits. As he opened the church door, he heard the shouts—the curé's voice distended, breathless with anger, like wind hissing through the rocks and tall grass along the shore.

Standing penitent, Emelisse endured the old curé's rage until he spat into his handkerchief. Then she spun and ran past Edouarde, pushed open the heavy door, clutching her shawl at her throat. The curé fled himself, into his quarters so quickly that Edouarde was left alone, squinting into the musty dark. No candles burned in the nave. We all noticed, at the next mass, the fissure rising between the hewn stones, though a few claimed the foundation had been washing out for years.

Edouarde—and he is an honest, hardworking man—told us what he'd seen: her thin, startled figure below the sudden dark of clouds, her slim arms and shins as she ran, her shawl snapped from her grip and twisted up along the wind, and the church door, a slab of engraved oak that, in the gusting silence of her flight, fell shut behind her.

* * *

Perhaps, we said, God made us reject her so she could come to her trial and suffer gloriously. It seemed we had hated her, yet we couldn't say we'd known her. She was an empty glass, ready to receive what the world put into it.

Early next Sunday—how this happened none of us understands—a cream-colored Chevy Impala drove into town. The driver was a young man named Jack Beetle, an American, he said, and he told us in good French that he'd come for Emelisse. He was pale, in a pink shirt that might have been silk, and his hair and eyes and suit shone black like the polished leather of a whip. Some said that no exhaust came from the muffler of his Impala. Clément Singelais swore that the air from inside was as cold as winter.

While we made our way to church, the Impala drove through town and disappeared up the road to the farms along the coast.

That evening, Bibianne came into town raving. She smashed a bench and tore up a hitching post, and when men tried to calm her, she threw them down. According to Laurent Pelletier, the men followed her shouts into the woods and after many struggles fixed up a sort of halter that they used to drag her back to her house. They said that when they brought her into those empty rooms, she collapsed. It seems now that was also the night Onésime had his stroke, though he survived. The next day, Curé Félix consented to burying Bibianne in the church plot, since, of those women, she'd been the only one without sin. During the mass, he was haggard, coughing, his handkerchief in his fist.

At first, we wondered what happened to Emelisse. Some said she had, in fact, gone to a convent, but Réjean Fournier's boy, who is rumored to own a few books forbidden by the Index, said—and he said this in public, right in front of Anctil's store—that she'd gotten the hell out of this town and who could blame her? We heard about that from the pulpit, three Sundays running. But more quietly, we wondered if there was something we could have done, if we'd been too harsh, and it did seem, when word finally got around that she was dancing in the cabarets, that we were relieved not to have been wrong about her.

It must have been two or three months after she left that Samuel Boudreau brought a load of soapstone down from Montréal. He swore he'd seen a girl in a cabaret who looked like Emelisse, though she had a different name. She was dancing on a stage in that way of hers—he recognized it from the field—or, when others danced, she was sitting next to Jack Beetle—at least, it sounded like him—his black-gloved hand on her thigh.

It was around that time that Edgar Chassé, a childhood friend of Magloire's, returned from France—one of the few men we knew who'd gone and survived Normandy. He'd arrived in Montreal with fellow soldiers. They were celebrating the end of the war and their return home, and he invited Magloire to join them. Brigitte was furious with his sudden trip, what with the chores to be done since the birth of their son, but already then, even before the accident, Magloire was changing.

Magloire was the one to tell Edgar about Emelisse, and of course Edgar remembered her and had to see what she'd become with his own eyes. During his nights celebrating in the city, he met a fellow in show business who knew where she danced. She was going by the name Anastasie Angélique. Edgar and Magloire later told us what happened next but in their own ways, which is normal, since Magloire came back blind and Edgar took to the bottle and moved south to *les States.*

The two friends had waited outside the club with the former soldiers. Magloire told them about Emelisse—her strangeness and beauty, her harlot mother, her isolation on that coastal farm—until soon they all felt they'd known her. But when she arrived with Jack Beetle, her city garments almost made her unfamiliar again. She moved with confidence. The wind molded her blouse as if of her own will.

They followed her inside. The other girls in the club appeared distant and mysterious under the lights, but the soldiers, having heard stories of Emelisse, felt she was one of theirs. Edgar told the club owner he'd grown up with her and when Jack Beetle came out, they paid him so they could be alone with her in a room. Our boys wanted to celebrate the victory for which they'd risked their lives, and, as for Emelisse, she'd chosen a certain role, not so different from that of Félicité. We have since forgiven our men who took the night road to her farm.

Edgar said that the party was all in good humor. They wanted her to dance the way she had in the field, and she did—brashly, nothing of the shy girl left. She gave them a show, taunting them with the movement of her shoulders or moving her thigh through the slit in her dress. They wanted her best trick and pooled their money.

What she did was almost humble and awkward, Edgar said, and Magloire agreed. She dropped her gaze and slipped her arms from the straps of her dress. She held her chest and knelt, and then lowered her palms as if with an offering, or in penitence.

Edgar said he would have paid for that alone. When asked, Magloire grunted his assent. But the soldiers wanted more. They'd been to France and Germany, corrupted by the desperate acts of hopeless women. No one recalls how she ended up doing the trick. The idea must have been her own. It was something involving two bottles. She pulled off her dress. The men fell silent. Not even they expected this—a performance with two long-neck beer bottles that she took from the men's hands and emptied onto the floor. They all noticed how she wasn't looking at them but staring at the back of the room, to where Jack Beetle sat, as if she were doing this for him. He just watched, a cigarette in his fingers, his pale face dressed in smoke.

Edgar swears that he looked away as she turned her back to them and put the bottles partway into her body, one and then the other. When she released them, they hung there. Then, for the soldiers' amusement, she jerked her hips, and the bottles knocked together, clanking. Their round bottoms faced the men, not quite like eyes. Their scuffed ends were as dull as nail heads.

Edgar did get cut that night. He'd survived Germany without a scratch only to be gashed along the side of his neck—a pale mark, not yet faded in the days before he went south. But it was Magloire whose eyes received the shards. He had been at the edge of the stage, staring up at her thighs and back, which he might have experienced as a husband, when she jerked her hips even more violently—as if, as some of the men said, she were experiencing the only intimacy she'd ever known. Magloire saw the bottles come together—and then the splintering air.

If Edgar is to be believed, Magloire leapt back in pain, his eyes bleeding as he swung his fists blindly, attacking everyone in the bar. He tried, he grudgingly admitted on one of his nights when he'd had too much to drink, to kill Jack Beetle who'd brought this curse upon all of us. In his agony he accidently struck another soldier, and a small tussle broke out—nothing unusual for soldiers, playful, in fact, Edgar had said. But somehow she was knocked from the stage, and with those shards in her. That's the only way the men could explain what happened next. In the high spirit of their victory in Europe, they hadn't realized she'd been luring them into a moment that would harm so many lives.

We have since seen Magloire weep on his porch, blind to those who pass as he recalls the shards falling into his eyes like tears denied for so long that, condensed and resilient, they came to possess the cutting obstinacy of diamonds. Edgar told us that, in the moment before she fell from the stage, she stood like a naked child, bleeding like a woman, her face transpierced with passion: sunlight through stained glass. And when she came through town, that dirt-stained sheet covering her rags, she paused sometimes. In those places, there was blood, gathered along the insides of her feet, the half prints more like a forgotten scriptural mark than the trace of a passing woman.

Magloire rarely speaks about all this. His children are grown and do not visit him, and Brigitte died young. They have said that he beat them like no other parent in our town. When he was angered, he reached about him frantically and caught one of them by the hair or shirt and then struck them with clumsy blows to the face and chest until he exhausted himself. It was the blindness that changed him.

* * *

When Emelisse returned that August, we first mistook her for one of the beggars who goes village to village, door to door. Some claimed it wasn't even her, but others saw her face—those eyes—and remembered her. She never stopped, not after night fell, not even as she passed her old house above the sea.

Clément Singelais, who'd been caring for the abandoned land, saw her on the road. She was muttering to herself in the way of people who have lost their minds or have been alone for too long, though she spoke of a dream—a narrow ladder of glass that tore at her flesh and led to a garden. Each night, before she reached it, she grew weak from loss of blood and slipped from the rungs and woke.

When she came through the village, Eude Pelletier, drunk as usual, followed her, as did a few boys. When Clément told the story of the ladder, Eude said this was what he'd overheard her mumbling—how each night she danced around a garden spring where she saw someone from the village drinking: Magloire to heal his eyes, Curé Félix to soothe his lungs that made climbing to the pulpit a struggle, and others, even Eude himself. The last time she had the dream, after climbing those lacerating rungs, she found herself in a garden where a shepherd gave her of the milk he took from a sheep. She awoke with sweetness on her lips, knowing she had only to wear out her days here—never sleeping again, never climbing in her dreams. As she spoke those words to herself, she passed here, on this road, right there, through the thin shadow of that birch tree.

The boys said that, when she left the coast, a path opened in a dense forest between mountains and closed upon them as they followed, so that they were lost for a day and a night. We searched for them from the road to where the land meets the sea and into the mountains on the other side, all this with the help of the constable. All that night, the hounds of Germain Dugas brayed, and in the mornings, birds wheeled above treetops—large, dark shapes slow against the wind. A hunter dozed in the woods and dreamed her with a crown of shards.

In the forest, a shrine appeared—a lean-to of sticks, hung with rags, the rocks around it decorated with smashed beer bottles. Some say it was a schoolboy prank, others that it is dedicated to the Fair Penitent. There has been discussion among us about which day Emelisse disappeared—in August or rather in July, on the day of the Magdalene.

When we tell her story now, we nod, but the grandchildren do not understand. They have been to the city. They disdain the stony fields, the compulsion of sun and season, or have simply never known it, eager as they are for easy work.

Among us, there are still some who dream glassy air suspended like a ladder. The boys who followed her have grown but they tell us that when she lay down in the forest, on the stones, crystal snow fell from the warm sky like the blossoms of a shaken tree. ■

SHOW TIME!
Chuck Kramer

BLONDES HAVE MORE FUN
Chuck Kramer

LATE NIGHT DOG RUN
Chuck Kramer

SISTERHOOD
Chuck Kramer

TOPSPIN
John Blades

My name is Melanie and I'm a tennis player. I wanted to be a professional once, actually not so long ago. But all my motivation, my dreams, were destroyed the night my father attacked my mother with a tennis racquet. She was just lucky he used her racquet and not his own. He had a pro graphene model that could have done a lot of damage. But Dad was so hyper that night, and so high, that he didn't stop to think about what he was doing. He just grabbed the nearest racquet, which happened to be Mom's antique aluminum model, and started swinging. He's got a deadly forehand slice but the oversize sweet spot probably saved her life since her head made contact with the strings and not the frame. It also kept my dad out of serious trouble, maybe out of jail. I'll never say another bad word about oversize racquets.

Anyway my dad was really broken up right after he bounced that racquet off her head. I don't honestly think he knew what he'd done until he saw Mom on the floor with blood from that cut above her eye dripping all over the carpet. I was holding his arm then so he couldn't take another shot at her head, scratching him with my free hand and kicking him in the leg, but I was wearing my Reeboks and with my ankle already swollen to twice the normal size, I was hurting myself a lot more than I was hurting him. Anyway he finally just seemed to come to his senses and stop. He dropped her Prince and the next thing I knew he was down on the floor himself, kneeling beside her and crying and apologizing and trying to stop the bleeding with his wristband but that wasn't doing a lot of good because it was still sweaty from the match he'd played that day. I don't think I ever saw him cry before, or her so much. Even after they got the blood stopped and came back from the emergency room with her head bandaged, they were still crying and they kept on and on, practically cried the whole night, and I know because I thought I'd never get to sleep.

What a Fourth of July this turned out to be! I never even made it to the fireworks show and I didn't feel like I missed a thing. Afterwards my dad blamed the whole thing on me, just like I knew he would, like he always does. I was counting on it. This time it was partly my fault, I'll admit, but never to him. If I'd played in that family mixed doubles final instead of her, he never would've flipped his stack about her blowing the match to the Gallaghers. If it hadn't been for my trouble with a certain person the night before, we would've won for sure, no sweat but no big deal either—we would've just had one more trophy to put on the shelf with all the others we'd won at Fourth of July and Labor Day and Memorial Day tournaments, so many I've lost track, but my dad would've been real happy, higher than an aerial bomb, and he wouldn't have needed a single drink.

So that much he can blame on me and I won't make a case out of it. But he can't hang what he did to Mom on me. That's one guilt trip I won't take. Also, he's got a lot more than that to answer for himself because that whole scene was what totally turned me off to tennis, totally destroyed my concentration, totally spoiled everything, so my heart wasn't in the game anymore. I could've been a contender. No joke. I really could have. Look at the numbers. My sophomore year I was number one varsity singles player. I finished third in our region that year and would've gone to state my junior year if it hadn't been for my shoulder injury.

But I'm getting way ahead of myself here so let me backpedal just a little, go back to the beginning. We weren't always a tennis family, we started out as pretty average people really. I don't even think my dad or mom had ever picked up a tennis racquet till after we were born. But then they started playing with their friends.

It was the social thing to do, you know, like their parents used to play bridge or cribbage or backgammon when they were my mom and dad's age. At first they only played on weekends, then they joined a club, started playing nights, signed up for lessons, entered tournaments, started buying only the right clothes and equipment, doing the whole scene, in other words. I don't think my mom bought it as much as my dad did. She used to complain about him being gone all the time and the house falling apart because all he ever did was play tennis but then she went along just to keep the peace, especially after he joined the club, and so did my brother, Kevin, and I but that was because we didn't have much choice.

They would drag us along to the courts and we caused such bad scenes, fighting and yelling and running onto the court, breaking up their games and embarrassing them, that they finally signed us up for lessons just so we'd stay out of their hair, figuring it'd be cheaper than hiring a sitter. But actually I don't think we caused any worse scenes than they did, screaming at each other, mostly him screaming at her for not hustling enough, for complaining about the sun, headaches, sweat in her eyes, stopping to get a drink after every shot, stuff like that.

But anyway you can probably guess the rest. Me and my brother got to be pretty sweet players, much better than them, and before too long my dad was more interested in our game than he was in his own. Actually he was more interested in my brother's, since he was a lot better than me and he would've been a high school star too, with an even better shot at turning pro except he wasn't tough enough mentally. He freaked out early and now he's living with my aunt and uncle out in California but that's another story and a sad one. He was a real pain while he was here and I was jealous of him but now that he's gone I miss him. Last I heard he was doing a lot better.

I never had any trouble being tough on the court myself, it was off the court where I had problems, social problems. By the time I got into high school, tennis was important—I made the team when I was a freshman and all that—but it wasn't my number one priority. Boys were. The problem was, I wasn't a very high priority with boys since I still had a lot of baby fat then, a regular Miss Piggy, or that's how Daddy Dearest liked to refer to me. The only dates I had were on the tennis courts and I knew that was only because I was this awesome ball machine. I mean, even though I was a little on the plump side then, I could really move around the court and return anything hit to me and the boys would usually get a good workout, sometimes too good since I could usually wipe them out and that didn't help improve my ranking socially either.

My best friend, Cheryl, was on the freshman team too and she wasn't half the player I was but she weighed maybe half as much. That's a slight exaggeration of course but she did have so many boys calling her that her parents had to get her a phone of her own. So I started taking out all my frustrations and hostilities on the court and that paid off after a while. I got to be the best player in the school of either sex and best of all I lost all my excess body fat, got to be a regular Maria Sharapova clone, and before long I was getting more calls than Cheryl, from boys who wanted to play games besides tennis.

So I was feeling just terrific, physically, mentally and socially tough for the first time in my life and then that's when I really started having trouble with my dad. First off it was the shoulder, which he took harder than I did, I think, and he kept telling me I ought to go ahead and play, that the exercise would be good for it, it'd loosen up, and not to pay any attention to the trainer, who wouldn't have been working at a high school if he knew his stuff. But it was too sore to play and I missed the whole season and he never got over it, just moped around and acted like I'd let him down personally, like this was more painful for him than it was for me.

But the shoulder got better after I rested it for a while and by the summer I was in peak condition again, actually better than I'd ever been before. I had my rhythm down and I was graceful as a ballerina, doing my little dance step on the court, one, two, three, step, bounce, smash, and I had all this power and confidence going for me. I was hitting balls for a couple of hours every day and I won singles, doubles, and family doubles in the Memorial Day tournament. In fact it was so easy that the other players—kids and parents both—were ranking on me for even being in the tournament and saying that I was just too good, practically a pro, and they were right but I wasn't about to drop out because of them.

My dad wasn't unhappy about all this of course, just so long as they couldn't actually keep me off the courts, because he was my doubles partner. But he sure was giving me a lot of grief about my social life, saying that it was taking too much time away from my tennis game. But it was only one part of my social life that he was worried about and that was Jean-Pierre and he wouldn't have thought twice about that if Jean-Pierre had been white instead of black. Actually I don't consider him black myself. Jean-Pierre is from Jamaica and he's sort of coffee colored. Or at least that's how I put it when my dad and I had our big blowup over me going to the junior prom with Jean-Pierre.

"He's not black, Dad, he's mocha," I told him. "Think of him like that and it won't make you so hyper."

"I'm not hyper," he said, "and I'm not prejudiced either. He could be vanilla—an albino even!—and I still wouldn't like you spending so much time with him. You should be hitting tennis balls."

I might've halfway believed him if he hadn't started ranting then that no matter how light skinned Jean-Pierre was, he was going to look a lot darker in the picture of the junior prom court and their dates. "Black as a black cat in a coal mine at midnight" was how he put it and that's what really let the cat out of the bag for me, no joke. He said the picture would be in the local paper and all our friends and neighbors would see it. Not that he cared what they thought—oh sure, Daddy!—but how could he send a copy of the picture to my grandparents, who were from a different era and weren't open-minded like him and my mom were?

Well, he had no choice but to be Mr. Open-Minded this time because I was madly in love with Jean-Pierre and if I wasn't going to the prom with him, I was going with nobody and that's exactly what I told my dad. In that case my dad couldn't not let me go because then all his friends and neighbors would've known what a bigot he was. But he didn't give up without a fight and a lot of grief and for a week or so before the dance I would hear him prowling around the house late at night. First he'd be stomping around outside my door, making sure I was awake, then he'd go downstairs and stomp around the kitchen for a while, opening and closing the fridge, popping the tops off beer cans. When I'd come downstairs in the morning, he'd be asleep on the couch in the TV room, the set turned on to ESPN. I'll bet he didn't sleep more than two hours a night that whole week.

I was expecting a real hassle the day of the prom but all of a sudden everything was cool and he didn't say any more about it, I guess because my mom had convinced him it was a lost cause and he might as well not lose his head over anything so hopeless. As for my mom, she didn't have much to say on the subject of Jean-Pierre, not to me anyway, which was just like her. But it would've been hard for her to say much of anything anyway with my dad yelling at me and slamming doors and acting like such a big baby. I knew that deep down she was just as grossed out as he was but I think she thought that if she just ignored the problem it would go away. That shows how much she knew. I mean, when I went through that rough time in my freshman and sophomore years, with all that baby fat, she knew enough to keep quiet about it, unlike Daddy Dearest, who kept making these rude and insensitive remarks about Miss Piggy and how if I gained any more weight I'd have to quit tennis and join the sumo wrestling team.

So anyway, on the night of the prom they made it a point not to be home when Jean-Pierre came by to pick me up, figuring out of sight, out of mind, and it ended up that we had a terrific time. I was a little uptight when the picture came out in the paper but my dad just pretended to be this real liberal and everything around our neighbors and I thought that was real funny, knowing all the time what a prize hypocrite he really was.

Then it was summer and things got hotter than ever between me and Jean-Pierre—if my dad had known just how hot I think he would've committed me to a convent for the rest of my unnatural life. But he didn't even know that I was still seeing Jean-Pierre. As far as he knew that was all over the night of the prom and that's what I wanted him to think. It wasn't like I was afraid of him or anything like that, I just thought it would be better for him not to know, just for the sake of peace and quiet around the house, my own mostly, I'll admit, but it was starting to get to my mom too and she always seemed to be ready to get hysterical herself. I was playing tennis every day again, hitting balls for a couple of hours, working on my serve, my overheads, my whole bag of shots, and my dad was real happy. But he wouldn't have been so happy if he'd known that I wasn't spending all day on the courts, that me and Jean-Pierre would go off for hours, to the beach, to movies, parties, even over to his house when his mother and his brothers and sisters weren't home.

My dad might have been happy about me playing so much tennis but Jean-Pierre wasn't all that thrilled about it. He was quite the jock himself—soccer, basketball, track, a natural at everything he did. But the one sport he refused to play was tennis. He called it a game for rich white plantation owners. Now I know he said that just to get me mad because he knew for sure I wasn't a bigot, especially not where he was concerned, and we for sure weren't rich either—my dad was forever telling me how he had to take out a second mortgage on our house, just so he could afford the club and my tennis lessons. Now all that left was white and Jean-Pierre didn't have a case there either because I had this fantastic tan that made his mocha skin look pale next to mine, so for the summer anyway he was actually whiter than I was! I think Jean-Pierre was just using this as an excuse because he was afraid to play tennis with me. He knew how competitive I was and that I could easily blow him off the court and humiliate him. Of course when it came to Jean-Pierre I wouldn't have been all that aggressive and I would have at least let him win a couple of points, maybe even a game or two. But anyway, that didn't make life with Jean-Pierre any easier that summer.

Meantime, life with father was no picnic either.

Against my better judgment I'd let him talk me into playing mixed doubles with him in the Fourth of July tournament. There was no fun and no glory for me but it meant a whole lot to Daddy. With me as his partner we were sure winners and he needed a win—and bad. He'd turned fifty a couple of years ago and was going downhill pretty fast. Gray hair, turkey chin, beer gut: he had it all. What he didn't have was any natural athletic skills, especially not at tennis. He had won a couple of doubles tournaments without me but only because his partners had all the speed and the right moves. Forget singles. He was lucky to make it to the quarterfinals.

It wasn't only his tennis game or mine that was causing him to act like such an overgrown brat. It was the whole midlife crisis thing. He was so cranky and miserable to me and my mom that when I came home from practice, I spent all my time in my room with my door shut and my music turned so loud I wouldn't have to listen to them shouting and arguing. And this was supposed to be their happy hour!

So it was up to me to singlehandedly give his ego a boost, the dutiful daughter bit, and what else could I do but go along? Isn't that one of the commandments: humor your parents? That way you make it easier on everybody, most especially yourself, right? Except it wasn't as easy as I'd thought because I didn't realize how much he'd slowed down. I mean, I had to cover almost all his half too, so it was like playing singles on the whole court. By the time we got to the finals, I was beat, really beat. But we still could've won the tournament without too much sweat if it wasn't for that unfortunate accident the night before the Fourth.

You really have to spend a Fourth of July where we live to know what they're like, just how terrible they are. At least I think they're terrible and so do most of my friends. But that's not an opinion shared by a lot of people, particularly not my mom and dad. Every summer I always say never again, I'd rather be away at fat camp or almost anywhere but here. But my mom and dad wouldn't be anywhere else. So that doesn't leave me with much choice unless I go my brother's route and that's what I was afraid would eventually happen. The tennis tournament's the main thing but that's not all: there's a bunch of other activities, the parade, the wine tasting, the pita throw, the pasta-eating contest and then the glorious fireworks show where they set off more explosives in one night than they did in the whole Iraq War.

But that's just a warm-up for the real fireworks, the party at our house where my mom and dad and all their friends come over for the postgame tennis highlights. It was bad enough when we just had to listen to them but we have to watch them too, a replay of the whole boring tournament with stop-action and slow motion and all the video special effects.

Then after they've had enough gin and tonic and beer, the fun really starts. That's when they start running the video backwards. Anyway the Fourth of July always seems to last about a week and when it's over I feel lucky that I survived.

This year my luck ran out. But like I said, my problem wasn't actually on the Fourth but the night before. As usual, Mom and Dad were going over to the Gallaghers to watch *Yankee Doodle Dandy* on TV but I couldn't go anywhere. I was grounded. Daddy's orders, of course. He wanted me in super shape the next morning. It didn't matter how late he stayed out because all he had to do was show up on the court, hit a couple of balls, and pick up our trophy for us. I could take care of the rest.

But that isn't quite how it worked out. As soon as they left, Jean-Pierre came by on his Honda and we took off for the Jamaican solidarity picnic. Now that was a real celebration, except for the barbecued goat, which was totally gross. They had this reggae band, this huge barrel of Jamaican punch, and we were doing the limbo, the samba, the mambo, all kinds of down and dirty dancing, when all of a sudden I was on the ground, screaming and twisting in pain, and everybody was clapping and cheering me on, like I'd invented this new dance move or something. When Jean-Pierre finally figured out that I wasn't just freaking out over the music, that I'd hurt my ankle and was really screaming in agony, he got me out of there as fast as he could, a good thing too because lying on the ground like that I was about to get trampled. He wanted to take me to the hospital but I said no, my ankle'd be okay if I could just get home and put some ice on it. It was a good thing I didn't go to the emergency room as it turned out because two of us from the same family in twenty-four hours would've looked a little weird.

Well, the ice didn't help at all and by the time my dad and mom got home, my ankle looked like a grapefruit, a purple grapefruit. When he came in I could tell my dad was feeling no pain, then he saw my ankle and from the way he moaned and carried on you'd have thought that he was the one who'd gotten hurt and not me. Anyway I'd gone to all this trouble to dream up an excuse, about how I was so keyed up for the match that I couldn't sleep and how I was doing aerobics on the living room carpet when I slipped but I don't think he was worried about how it happened at that point, only that it had happened. "Just don't put any weight on it, it'll be okay in the morning, you'll be able to play." He kept saying this over and over but I knew better and so did my mom. But she made the mistake of saying so and he really blew his lid then, saying how she was always so negative, why couldn't she be more positive like he was, that was why she was such a loser at tennis, and carrying on like that for hours.

It was hard enough to sleep with my ankle throbbing so much but he didn't make it any easier by talking to himself and banging around the house all night. The sun wasn't even up when he was in my room, wanting to know if it was any better, if the swelling had gone down. "Try to stand up," he said, "that way you'll get the blood circulating." But it killed just to put any weight on it and you didn't have to be a doctor to tell that I could barely walk, much less play tennis. Well, it took a while but when he finally got that through his head he just got this stoned look on his face and walked out of my room without another word. Thinking back on it, he was a lot more scary when he was quiet like that than when he was hyper but I was too tired to think about anything but going back to sleep. When I got up, I could hobble around some but that was about all. I wasn't about to go anywhere anyway. It was the middle of the afternoon and hotter than a toaster oven. Besides, the parade was almost over and probably the tennis matches too, especially since the big match of the day hadn't even been played.

Or that's what I thought. Jean-Pierre came by to see how I was but I couldn't let him hang around for long. He was the last person I wanted Mom and Dad to find when they came home with all their friends. But it turned out he could've stayed all day because they didn't get back till almost dark and they were by themselves, though you would've thought from all the noise that they'd brought the whole parade and half the town with them. They were having this big fight and they went straight for the refrigerator and got out the ice and made themselves drinks, yelling at each other all the time. I knew better than to go downstairs. I didn't even come out of my room but they were so loud it sounded like they were right outside my door and it didn't take me long to figure out what'd happened. Mom had subbed for me in the match. But I knew he'd forced her to do it because she'd sworn she'd never play with him again after the last match they'd played, when he didn't just blame her for her own errors but his too, saying she got him so rattled it threw off his game. From what I could tell they hadn't even finished the match. He'd gotten so twisted out of shape that she walked off the court, pretending to have a heat stroke. He accused her of being a quitter. He forced her to quit because of his tantrums. She humiliated him. He humiliated her. That was the way it went, back and forth, like a tennis match with ugly words instead of balls. I'd heard it all before so it got to be very boring and I finally fell asleep. But not for long because pretty soon I heard furniture moving, walls shaking, windows rattling, and I knew it'd gotten physical and that's when I ran down to help, nearly breaking my own neck on the stairs because of my bad ankle.

So that was the end of that, the end of my dream anyway. For a long time I thought it was the end of my life but I can see farther than that now. I'm not such a big lollipop that I'd say it was all for the best but I do think some good came out of it, that it was a learning experience. And my mom did get a new carpet for the living room. Anyway, I swore off tennis that very night. I'll admit I've had moments of weakness ever since, when I'd break out in a cold sweat and feel light in the head and my hands would start shaking, but I haven't cracked and I think the worst is about over. That's why I'm so thankful for this support group. I couldn't have done it without your help. I don't think my mom needs any help. She'll be happy if she never sees another tennis racquet, or ever puts her hands on one again. But I'm still a little worried about my dad. He did take the pledge and I do have to give him credit. So far he hasn't given in to temptation. He hasn't once picked up a racquet or set foot on a court that I know of. I never thought he'd ever go cold turkey like that. But every once in a while I can see that crazy, faraway look in his eyes and I can tell he's not out of the woods yet. But I've been working on him and I'm hopeful that my greatest wish will come true, that one of these days he'll be standing up here too, right next to me. ■

THE GREAT UNKNOWN: ME AND JOHN FOWLES
Syed Afzal Haider

My desire to visit Lyme Regis began in October 1982 with a black-and-white image of Barbra Streisand wearing a black hat and looking directly at the camera on the cover of *Esquire*. The magazine arrived faithfully in the mail courtesy of my deceased wife, *forever absent, forever sought*. That issue carried an article on the reclusive John Fowles by Donald Hall. Titled "John Fowles's Garden," Hall's essay described how he entrained from London to Southampton, hired a mini, drove southwest from Dorchester to find Fowles at Belmont House, his residence in Lyme Regis, where he'd lived since 1965. And how since 1978, Fowles had devoted a great deal of his time and activity working at the Lyme Regis Museum as an honorary curator. Hall captured his subject and the "lost domain" in a very accessible way.

Fantasy, illusions, and delusions grew as I read the Hall story. I imagined arriving in Lyme Regis, finding Fowles in his third-floor office in the museum, where I presumed he'd faithfully arrive at 11:00 a.m. and work diligently until 1:00 p.m. For the first few days I would sit two desks away from his office and watch him work through a window, but on the third day someone would take the chair where he usually sat, and he would walk over and sit down at a desk opposite mine. He would smile awkwardly. I would stand up, lean over and ask if he knew French. He would smile his awkward smile again and say yes. I would then present a piece of paper and recite:

"*Je m'en vais chercher un grand peut-être.*"

Fowles would get up, lean over and read from the paper I was holding and translate for my benefit.

"I'm off to seek the great unknown."

While he translated, I would stay still, quiet and polite, like I did not know who he was. Then I would graciously nod, almost bow, but not speak a word, and he would smile encouragingly like a teacher and would become very busy fidgeting at his desk. As immobile as I would be, I'd leave him alone to his chores and walk out.

Back in 1982, I was forty-two, a widower and a single parent of a three-year-old boy. John Fowles was fifty-six. His new book, *Mantissa*, came out to mostly negative reviews, while the film of *The French Lieutenant's Woman*, based on his novel, was nominated for an Academy Award. A TV production of *The Ebony Tower* with Sir Laurence Olivier as Henry Breasley had been shot in France. So a lot was going on in the life of Mr. Fowles, a writer I had read and so admired since reading *The Collector*, his debut novel, the story of an inhibited young butterfly specialist who kidnaps a girl and adds her to his collection. One has to wonder if it would get published in 2019.

By the 1980s, Fowles had sold millions of copies of his books, to mention a few: *The Collector* (1963), *The Aristos* (1964), *The Magus* (1966), *The French Lieutenant's Woman* (1969), *The Ebony Tower* (1974), *Shipwreck* (1974), *Daniel Martin* (1977), *The Enigma of Stonehenge* (1980), *A Short History of Lyme Regis* (1982), and *Mantissa* (1982). Success brings fame and notoriety. Fowles avoided it in Lyme Regis. Despite his international literary stature and superhero status, he remained humble, kind, courteous, and to those who sought him, accessible. As Hall said, "With the reputation of a recluse, he seemed not so much reclusive as far away—his distance not cold but alien, as if mere human contact required from him the concentration people usually reserve for speaking foreign languages."

* * *

By 1989, I had accumulated my share of losses and made a major decision to escape to writing. "I don't think of myself as giving up work to be a writer. I'm giving up work to, at last, *be*," Fowles had said. But I lacked the tools. I needed to learn how to write and be a writer, show something for my existence. John Fowles, master of writing, gave me a conceptual understanding, whereby "loss is essential for the novelist," as he put it, and "immensely fertile for his books, however painful to his private being." He says, "Loss has given me a voice. What is entirely lost demand to be endlessly named: there is a mania to call lost things until it returns. Without loss there would be no literature."

My friend Lisa McKenzie—a writer and fellow editor at *Chicago Quarterly Review*—told me that it's finding the right voice that's most important to her. Another friend, Jory Post, says writing is fictography— autobiography, biography and fiction. How much really and actually happened? How much came from the imagination?

A verse by Urdu poet Ghalib says:

These thoughts are sent from beyond,
Your pen, Ghalib, scribbles the voice of source unknown.

John Fowles's fiction flows through a domain, a lost domain forever absent, forever sought. "Novelists," says Fowles, "are like conjurors, always expert at misleading."

Someone asked poet Donald Hall, "What do you write about anyway?"

"Love, death and New Hampshire," Hall replied.

I believe in true love and I truly believe in death. And love's death I know I can't forget, hence dying for love is worth writing about and worth dying for. Your love losses show in everything you say and do. They are shadows of death that show on your face, in everything you write, the life you knew ended on that day your love passed away.

The news is rather sad,
the prognosis is unfavorable,
hope and hopelessness are ahead.
If premonition is tendered, rendered, foretold,
it is tried, tested and troubled.
Go ahead . . . be sad, be bad, be mad.
Jump off a cliff in an alien world.
Forgetting where you may belong.
Being is neither humanly nor Godly,
No one forgets or forgives.
Give peace no chance.
While is at still;
Relic of time, fossil, vestige, remnant will remain.

Writing is rewriting, layering and relayering.

In *The Pillar of Salt*, Albert Memmi's semiautobiographical novel about a young boy growing up in French-colonized Tunisia, the young hero and narrator Alexandre Mordekhai Benillouche believes only exile and writing fiction—"mastering . . . life by recreating it"—may avert despair. I, an Indian/Paki/American, a total alien in any land, do live in exile and do try to write fiction, or fictography. In the hope it may avert despair.

The silver ray of brightness in the transition from here to there can lose its brilliance. Wherever *there* is, which is *nowhere*, and that is disheartening. For believers die happy with smiles on their faces as if they are only sleeping and dreaming of getting there. But for me sleep doesn't come easy.

The writer's heart is a cheating heart. He falls in love with all good writing—his writing, her writing, writing in any language. And he tests his love for them. He could, if he would, rob them, cheat on them. He could, if he would, consciously or subconsciously use and steal from everyone, from all encounters. As T.S. Eliot said, "Immature poets imitate; mature poets steal." True, it is as self-serving as it is ambitious to steal what you write. We all have a tendency to assume a view that is, if we are honest, unknown to us, to slip into a familiar narrative as if that is how it has happened. But do we not all have a right to our own thoughts and beliefs? Have we no choice but to remain silent and not express them? Maybe I've nothing to say. Maybe I'm babbling incomprehensible mumbo jumbo. And maybe what the writer takes for new is not new to the reader.

* * *

Now in 2019 I was writing the preface to my second novel, *Life of Ganesh*, about finding the path of the story and getting there. The novel went through the loss of a handwritten manuscript that itself became a lost domain, something I was able to touch, so many blank pages scribbled with an almond-green Walter A. Sheaffer fountain pen in Pelikan 4001 ink, Brilliant-Braun, that I brought along to write my travel journal. Forever lost, forever sought.

In John Fowles's *Wormholes*, a collection of essays and occasional writings, he describes, "All my life . . . I have kept a diary . . . But to say that all the essays here 'are not really me' is sort of shamefaced excuse I do not seek. I do believe everything that is said here, and I know it is absurd to say I wish it had been expressed better."

Sleep does not come easily for me. All my life I have lived in the shadow of doubt, haunted by a bleak view of existence and the human condition. Despite doubt, or maybe because of it, I may pretend otherwise and believe myself to be better than I really am. I still do that. So I know that everything that is expressed here, regardless of how well written and how good I may feel about it, could have been said better.

Others before me, no doubt, have traveled this way and chronicled their journeys, with their own story angles. But to tell one's story, one must remain centered and free of diversions—lest the splendor of the surrounding landscape seduce one off the road.

* * *

Moving fast backward, in 1989 I was forty-nine, my motherless child eleven. I'd married again and had another son, a three-month-old. Now, I can't believe that in August that year I traveled to India, the land of my birth, with my elder sister and my eleven-year-old son while leaving my three-month-old son in his mother's care. But then India was my lost domain, and two weeks later, I was able to meet my wife and our infant son in London, from there to visit John Fowles in Lyme Regis. The comfort of that travel was that John Fowles was back living in Belmont House.

Following Hall's path, we rented a Volkswagen Golf at Dorchester train station and arrived late on a Sunday afternoon at our bed and breakfast on Coombe Street, a short walk from the museum. I still had hope of seeing the man walking to the museum. If not, at least I'd be sharing the air, the sunrise, the sunset. And, of course, there was the Belmont House, where Fowles lived. All I had to do was ring the doorbell and announce my arrival.

Over the next three days, I vowed to wake up early, have breakfast at the B&B and walk over to the main street—leaving my wife to care for the children. An Indian/Paki, sitting in a public place, was not a total alien, only an outsider. A curry joint sat two doors down from a fish-and-chips place on the main drag, crisscross from the museum, where Fowles was said to still volunteer, his health permitting, as honorary archivist. Every day around 12:30 or 1:00 p.m., I'd return to our B&B, John Fowles still not seen.

But on the fourth day, Fowles was sighted in Lyme Regis, a town with a single timed traffic light. It was shortly after 11:00 a.m. on a cool Thursday, the day before we, my family, were to leave the city. I saw a big, bulky man in a plaid shirt limping slightly toward the museum. I jaywalked across the street from the fish-and-chips place, where I had been enjoying a cup of tea. And because of his slow gait, I easily reached the museum entrance before he did. It was there that I waited—casually, mind you, looking away from the object of my fascination. I observed the cracks on the sidewalk. I looked at the other side of street, acted like I was waiting for a friend. Finally, when Mr. Fowles arrived at the entrance, I took a deep breath and casually opened the door for him. The courtesy and politeness of one stranger to another—open the door and hold it open until the person behind you enters in first. I waited another moment holding the door open, exhaled quietly, but instead of following him, I let the door close. Mission accomplished. Perhaps the man was just another Brit who looked like an unmade bed. But I knew the man was John Fowles. And I walked back to the B&B, feeling content—happy to have held the door open for John Fowles and to have let him go.

Now it is 2019, and John Fowles, writer of my obscure persuasion, died November 5, 2005. Donald Hall, the instigator, who led me on my journey to Lyme Regis, died on June 23, 2018. I'm seventy-nine, biding my time, and writing about my travels to Lyme Regis in late August of

1989. *It don't come easy* to write a memoir when the memory of things that happened gets caught in the haze of gray. It is like the memory of a perfectly good vacation, when all you can remember is the lost umbrella. Storytelling is fictography: autobiography, biography and fiction. A writer scribbles the voice of a source unknown. Which flows through a domain, a lost domain forever absent, forever sought. And only I can tell my story. What I don't know remains unknowable or maybe I just don't want to know it.

Writers who greatly influenced me are few, partly because I've only read so many authors in detail. R. K. Narayan has shown me the simplest way of telling my story, text and expression. And Albert Camus has shown me the human disconnect that says: You are never home, always an outsider from within. The origin and the heart of a story evolve from a lost domain, forever sought, forever lost. Like Fowles I always fall in love with my heroine—often being unfaithful to my wife—which is the flight of my fantasy.

Now it is all in the past, not just in the past tense. RIP, dear John Fowles. I will keep a candle burning. ∎

This essay is an extension of the introduction to my novel *Life of Ganesh*.

AUDITION
Gary Houston

I entered the room, far too big for its present purpose, with a familiar foreboding. Two women sat behind a metal folding table, before them a disordered mass of audition sides. The one on the left wore glasses with dark frames. Her hair was black and cut short. Her older colleague wore an authoritative expression under a canopy of brown hair trending gray; she made me think of the U.S. Representative for Illinois's Ninth Congressional District, Jan Schakowsky.

They declined the headshot and resume clutched in my hand because, said Jan, they had what they needed "on file."

"We want you to know," Jan said, "we are only interested in seeing to it that all who audition succeed, succeed in the sense that whether or not you ultimately get the job, you'll be able to leave here knowing you did your very best." She smiled.

The one with the glasses spoke next: "Let us start with the category of popular song."

Suddenly each held a sheet of paper without particularly caring to look at it. Instead they looked at me.

They whispered an eight count and took a joint breath.

"There's a spark of magic in your eyes," said Glasses. "Candyland appears each time you smile. Never thought that fairy tales came true. But they come true, when I'm near you. You're a genie in disguise. Full of wonder and surprise, and . . ."

Then Rep. Schakowsky joined in:

"Betcha by golly, wow. You're the one that I've been waiting for forever. And ever will my love for you keep growin' strong, keep growin' strong."

I realized a bit tardily I had been hearing singing, not speaking, just before Glasses resumed her solo—"If I could I'd catch a falling star to shine on you so I'd know where you are . . ." She somehow found a moment to whisper to her colleague something I could not hear. Jan, looking downward, nodded with a tight smile.

They spent a long time after they finished staring at me in something like astonishment.

"Well," said Glasses, sharing looks between me and her partner, "I don't mind saying that was amazing. We have seen about a dozen people all day"—it was now two in the afternoon—"and I think this is the first time," she looked to Representative Schakowsky for confirmation, which was rendered with a quick yes, "that it all came alive to me, perhaps more importantly it all made sense to me, and it was perfectly, just stunningly delivered."

"All right," said Jan, "we don't want to get ahead of ourselves, but Amy here is right. It was . . ." I could see she was determined to be prudent. ". . . very good."

I swelled inside that Amy appeared to be in my corner, but I had to be careful. I didn't want to look cocky.

"I had a good time, myself," I said.

They laughed lightly, as though as a rule they would not have but for now some sort of disapproval had been deferred or overruled.

"Uh-huh, okay, let's move on," said Jan as she flipped through the sheets in front of her. "Now we are most interested in hearing some vintage Alka-Seltzer copy." She searched a stack, then another. "I'm looking for a specific spot with Speedy."

She looked up and studied me.

"Do you remember Speedy Alka-Seltzer?"

"I sure do," I said, immediately aware I was being boastful.

"Well," said Jan after a pause, "that remains to be seen. This spot is titled 'For Relief.' Do you know it?"

I said, "I'm not sure."

"Well, you see, that's what I mean. One shouldn't pretend to know what one does not. Should one?"

It took a moment to grasp that she expected me to say something.

"No," I said finally.

"No," she averred, pinning me with a look.

Amy held up a piece of copy.

"Found it."

"Good," said Jan, still with the look. "Then we may begin."

The next thirty seconds were a blur. I was smothered in shame, I confess. I just recall one read the announcer and the other read Speedy. I was so out of it I didn't notice who was reading which. I didn't know how long they had been looking at me after they had finished.

"Speedy was spot-on," said Amy.

"The announcer could have had a tad more personality," said Jan.

"But then so could most announcers," they said together.

They stood and extended their hands.

"It was a pleasure," said Amy. "Pleasure," said Jan.

"Me too," I said. I think I shook their hands but questioned in the next moment whether I had.

I turned to the door and opened it. But I could not go through. They had wanted me to leave knowing I had done my very best, and I could not escape the sensation that I had not done it. Somewhere in the air I grabbed an idea and turned back to them.

"I . . ."

"Yes?" inquired Jan, surprised.

"I guess this is unusual, but can we try one more thing?"

They consulted their watches.

"Yes?" said one of them as I sought to collect myself.

"Well, an old commercial from when I was little came to me just now . . ."

"TV?"

"Yes, TV. It was for a product called Lite Diet Bread. It must be long off the shelves now, but I can remember two housewives in a kitchen looking at a TV set that seemed to be rigged to a wall above the refrigerator. Is that possible?"

From their stare they might at that moment have taken me for a fool, or a madman.

"Well, I may have the refrigerator part wrong. It was so long ago it seems like I am just recounting a dream."

"Yes?"

"Sorry. Anyway, they sang a jingle to the tune of what only many years later I realized was 'Tit Willow' from Gilbert and Sullivan's *The Mikado*. And—"

But already they had pounced upon their stacks. "Lite Diet," they both repeated in an accelerating frenzy.

"It might not have been a national spot," I said. "It might have been local."

"Which market? Eastern? Central? California?"

"I guess central."

"You guess?"

Jan had again lost patience. But again Amy came to the rescue.

"Found it!"

"Very well," said Jan. "But this had better be good because we are going into time that belongs to the next person."

They shared a sheet.

"I'll do the housewives," said Jan to Amy. "You do the man on TV."

They whispered an eight count and inhaled together.

"Did you hear what he said?" asked Jan. "He said, 'Lite Diet Bread.'"

"Lite Diet, Lite Diet, Lite Diet," said Amy.

"Did you listen to him?" asked Jan. "It will help you stay slim."

Amy said, "Lite Diet, Lite Diet, Lite Diet."

And she went on to say, "Oh, the texture is fine, and the flavor is great. It's the best-tasting bread that you ever ate. And with Lite Diet Bread you will never gain weight."

Then together they said, "Lite Diet, Lite Diet, Lite Diet."

Except they were singing.

Again as if there had been no transition, they were looking at me, this time speechless, this time quite incapable of speech.

At that moment, I knew. I was booked. ■

A LIFE'S WORK
Elizabeth McKenzie

Have I earned this? One could argue an award is overdue, but as yet I am unable to see anything remarkable about my work here. For that reason, I may feel something of an imposter going up to accept it, but it will happen, I will soon be smiling and thanking people, at least one of whom will be thinking that I don't deserve it. It's Leanne P. who will be thinking this, and I must make sure not to make eye contact with her when the moment comes. Fortunately, the lights are so bright that from the podium you can see very little, and my strategy is this: I will pretend to be someone else at that moment who completely and categorically believes she deserves the award and hears no dissenting voices in her head. I have a knack for this kind of concentration. According to my mother I used to play with unusual intensity as a child, finding it difficult to transition from imaginary scenarios back to real life.

That's rather funny to imagine now, as I am so reactive and accommodating. I should also take into consideration the likelihood that most people attending the gala have no reason to be suspicious and therefore will accept me as the recipient of the award with no trouble at all, and possibly with some envy and admiration. It is highly unlikely too that Leanne P. will cry foul, for that would show disrespect to the governing body and reflect badly on her, though I've heard rumors she may believe the governing body is old and ossified and needs toppling. To that end, she may begin a campaign as soon as the ceremony is over, fully owning her disdain not just for me but for the entire institution. This may depend on a number of factors, such as her apperception of the general mood and previous canvassing she may have done, not necessarily about me but about the direction we've been taking as a whole. Should she have a sense that the momentum is there to be tapped, she may well use the recognition I'm about to receive as a touchstone for everything she is unhappy with, with me as a symbol of the old ways. All of this is worth considering as I sit here listening to our director describe the achievements of our department since our last gathering.

We've had a very good year, and there are a lot of achievements to mention. I believe this serves me well; the applause for each milestone is growing, revealing a receptive audience and a general sense of goodwill towards the establishment. Really, the entire unit has been giddy with good news and profits. We have been hearing reports that make us burn with pride, and the bonuses we have received quarterly have borne out the good news. I am surrounded by a flotilla of heads, mouths opening and closing as the members of our workforce lift their forks and spoons, tasting the fancy meal they have earned through their hard work and company allegiance. Through thick and thin, we like to say.

But it's within the thin zone perhaps I've failed. I've always had a hunch that Leanne P.'s dislike of me stemmed from an incident that occurred nearly twelve years ago, shortly after she was hired. At some point during her first days here, she paraded from office to office, placing little plates of cookies on each and every desk, accompanied by Post-it notes saying how happy she was to be joining us. When I saw this, I burst out laughing. I had nothing against Leanne P. joining the company, though her resume wasn't the strongest, I'd felt, but the wobbly paper plate with the four hard, dry cookies on it actually repulsed me. I tossed them in the trash, and I'm not one to waste food. Also, I saw in the gesture an unseemly desire to please; that the cookies were ugly and unappetizing seemed to portend a misplaced arrogance on her part. That we would be endeared to her because she went to the trouble to make the cookies, despite not having gone to the trouble of making genuinely tasty cookies, seemed to have been her plan. So that in a way, she would be dominating us, forcing us to gag down her gesture without giving us any real pleasure. I never thanked her or responded. There were about eighty of us working for the company at that time, and I somehow doubt that everybody showered her with thanks. I did ask Greta about it later, but Greta said something typically Greta, such as, "Oh yes, that was really sweet." I smiled and nodded to disguise my sour take on the matter. After all, it was possible that Leanne P.'s standards for cookies were simply different, that she'd been raised making those cookies and thought them perfectly adequate. Still, I could not bring myself to thank her, because more or less I took the whole thing as a singular act of aggression.

From then on, our interactions were mixed. I always responded to any of her questions or requests promptly and professionally. When, eventually, others at the company formed collegial friendships with her, I wondered why but tried not to dwell. About five years ago, I learned that she'd organized a dinner party for many of the people in our department and didn't invite me. Initially, I felt relief. Remembering her cookies, I shuddered imagining the menu. And yet perhaps I was fooling myself, because I believe now that I did feel hurt, and I began to reexamine the whole way we'd gotten off on the wrong foot. I still felt, five years ago, that there was no possible way she could have interpreted my lack of response to her cookies as the rejection it, in fact, was, that it would have been almost paranoid and insane of her to interpret it that way, despite the truth of it.

Nevertheless, I started to make an effort towards Leanne P. She wasn't going away anytime soon. I even allowed myself a brief pang of regret. I thought how petty I'd been. Couldn't a perfectly nice person make an awkward gesture, simply to break the ice? Was I merely jealous that an unremarkable person like this could nose their way in so effortlessly? I remember spending the greater part of a weekend composing a note, in which I admitted I hadn't acknowledged her cookies and yet trying to come up with an excuse to explain why. My mother had been ill, I thought of telling her. And I'd been depressed at the time. I considered saying that I had meant to respond but had forgotten until just now, but seeing as it was years after the fact that seemed a bit far-fetched. Finally, I convinced myself that it was egocentric of me to think she'd even noticed or cared, and gave up. But how else to explain her unfriendliness?

And so began my campaign. I started to say hello to her, using her name. I asked her questions about her children one day in the elevator. When she was carrying some recyclables out to the bin I asked if I could help. And yet—my efforts got me nowhere. There was no crack in the ice, no sudden recognition of points in common. I continued to see her being friendly with others at the company, but there was nothing there for me.

At first I blamed no one but myself, but her indifference or possible hatred of me began to gnaw. I felt indignant that she'd rejected my overtures and began to dislike her more than ever. And because I have greater seniority and the ear of the top people here, I saw myself start to marginalize her, bit by bit. When asked for lists of names of people for upcoming projects, I wouldn't include her. If ever I was asked why, I'd shrug and say, gently, that those I'd put forward were the powerhouses of the department, the best choices. I never said anything about her directly.

I have always tried to hold myself to high standards. I have always felt that there were very definite ways one had to behave, partly because my parents were strict and partly because I have a strong fear of being shunned or disliked. There were many cases of this in my family, so my fears were not ungrounded. My grandmother had historically made very bad impressions in social situations, causing my mother extreme isolation and shame. Then I observed my mother's foibles around the clock while growing up. There seemed to be countless ways to end up friendless and alone, I concluded, and I didn't want this to happen to me.

And so I've done everything I can to be different from my models, even if it costs me a lot in stress: I've hosted parties, never yelled at children who come to the house, said hello to people and tried to be helpful if anybody was in need. But somewhere along the way, something must have caught up, some rumor about my family or what I was made of, because somehow Leanne P. had identified me as someone she did not care to know, and all at once I came to realize that I was considered a very disagreeable person. Literally! One horrible day, two women from another department were dropping off empty bags for a food drive and didn't know I was staying late. Just as a bag came sliding under my door, I heard one of them say, "This is Emma Flynn's office. She's a very disagreeable person."

I knew the voice; it was Meredith S. I'd never said a rude word to her, I'd said good morning to her for years, I'd even bought damned raffle tickets from her kid to raise money for his school. My mother would never have done any of that, not even close.

And so, I came to understand, maybe there was nothing I could have done, or not done, to undo the impression of being disagreeable. Maybe it was in my DNA. I had been born a disagreeable person, and there was absolutely nothing I could do to change it.

This realization caused me severe anguish. For several weeks I was dead to the world. I took long-overdue vacation time and could barely get out of bed in the morning and go through the motions. I was at a loss. I had no guidelines now for how to behave, as I did not know who I was without my previous understanding of what it meant to be a good person. I wanted to believe that I could go on as before, but how?

* * *

Our director has now come to the awards presentation. It's almost my time. I am starting to wish, come to think of it, that no award were coming my way. By being recognized, I'll stir up the ill will of everybody who's thought badly of me in the company, all at once, in concentrated form. It will come at me like a blast, it may knock me off my feet if I'm not ready for it. I am actually quaking a little. I'm suddenly having the strange premonition that Leanne P. will be called up to the podium to present the awards, having insinuated herself so she can finally wreak her revenge. When she calls my name and I approach, she surprises me with a plate of her cookies. *The cookies are the award!* As I gasp in horror, she shoves one of the jaw breakers into my mouth and I choke, but everybody just thinks I'm faking it in order to be disagreeable. There's a chunk stuck in my larynx. I can't breathe. I fall to the ground, and the last things I see are the gleaming eyes of Leanne P.!

Instead, I get up from my table, start to weave around the other tables and guests to find my way to the exit. An award is an award, whether you walk into the spotlight or not. I'm escaping sudden death, and once outside, I'll take a deep breath of night air. Maybe I'll get an ice cream cone before I drive home.With each happy lick the scoop will shrink, shrink, shrink. How in the world do you hold on to happiness?

"Emma Flynn!" The voice rings like a knell. "Would you please come up and be recognized?" ■

THE OTHER SIDE OF THE DOG'S HEAD
Signe Ratcliff

Though she hadn't been told as much by an official on the subject, Josie believed her strange new pastime was a gift, a thing rare and odd, like being able to move an ashtray with your mind or count the number of brushstrokes in a Picasso—only better, because being able to mentally revise this new street until it looked exactly like her old street was something far more useful than moving ashtrays.

From the front steps of her new house, Josie gazed down Leavitt Street to where it met Devon Avenue and transformed the figures that passed by into those of her old neighbors, adding a mustache here, a ponytail there, dressing them in the hand-me-downs of her old, faraway block. Where there was a birdbath, she put a birdhouse. She swapped daffodils for petunias, cardinals for pigeons, aluminum siding for the stone and brick of an older side of town. She interrupted the quiet of Leavitt Street with her carefree, early-morning greetings:

"Hi!"

"How are *you* today?"

"Looking good!"

"Nice scarf!"

"Cute dog!"

Josie was ignored. Mostly.

She'd begun transforming the street shortly after they moved here to the North Side from 18th and Loomis. This was after Ma let the dog chew her Barbies into mangled chunks while she was at school and Josie discovered that make-believing the street was far more interesting. She also discovered that here, in this revised world, she could nearly see her father zigzag down the sidewalk in his boyish, distracted way, headed home as if nothing had happened. Her father had told her she had a great imagination, a thing, Josie was sure, she got from him and not Ma—his eyes were often caught helplessly by a bird in flight or the glint from a glass, so that he'd walk straight into things and Ma would tap his elbow just enough to set him straight.

These were the sorts of ways they talked—in gestures, in looks—though Ma didn't know that Josie had noticed. Ma didn't know the many things that Josie noticed, because Ma thought that to be eleven was the same as being ten, but in fact they were different. To be ten years old was to be encased between something hard and soft: a one, a zero; a mother, a father. But eleven was to be stuck between two bars, two straight lines, two hard places—a grieving mother and the cold, solid feel of her father's absence.

* * *

If Ma were a Barbie, Josie would dress her in a vermillion cotton dress, an A-line with a bit of ruffle at the bottom, because this was what she wore before and because she was so like a girl in her heart, much more of a girl than Josie. Now, Ma sat in a green chair, her back facing the street. As the day wore on, Josie would be able to tell the time from how far her mother was slumped; like a setting sun she inched down over the horizon of her chair, and by six o'clock just the dark hemisphere of the top of her head was visible, soon to disappear altogether.

Standing next to one another, her mother looked more the eleven-year-old than Josie—Ma was small, prone to staring up at her daughter, her large eyes seeking direction. Josie was more like her mother's loudmouthed babysitter who at times found a way to make her smile. The effort in doing so, however, was draining, and in the morning she felt the weariness of someone like a baker, the goods produced from her hands all used up, and now she must start over from scratch, hoping, as with a bowl of dough, that Ma's spirits might rise.

"Good morning! Love your dress! Yellow is your color!"

Another old woman in a sari. Josie imagined the sari as a dated floral dress, her sandals as flip flops. The woman looked up, shook her head and walked on.

Today, like most days, she was getting the Strange Look. Josie was well-acquainted with the Strange Look, especially from Pyotyr, who was in her gym class at the new school and who dazzled Josie *to death* with his peaked green cap that looked like it came from another country. Pyotyr refused to remove his hat for gym class, all glary-eyed and snarly, he was and Josie cheered him on with her big, dumb toothy smile that Pyotyr Strange-Look-ed her for. In any case though, it was best not to think of Pyotyr, because it was very unlikely Pyotyr would ever love a girl as big as Josie. He was so sharp-nosed and angular, so small, so swift—as tiny as Josie was large. Plus, Josie's ears stuck out and Pyotyr's did not.

Josie got the Strange Look, too, from the teachers at school, who often didn't appreciate her questions (Do birds dream?) or her answers to their questions. Like the time Mrs. Munch asked, What are clouds?

and Josie raised her hand to say the clouds are the sky's thoughts and she said this knowing it was the wrong answer but it was important to say it out loud—she *knew* it wasn't true, but still she *had* to say it: The clouds are the sky's thoughts. It was a statement her father would have agreed with, at times his gaze fixed so intently on the sky it seemed the clouds were speaking to him. And Munch gave her the Strange Look as the other students laughed, and then gave her a look that said: You Should Know Better Than That. And yes, at times many teachers seemed to think there were things she should know that she did not.

For instance, for a very long time she refused to believe that there was a whole other part of the city beyond her side of the dog's head. The dog's head was what she called the Sears Tower when she was ten, because that's what it looked like and so that's what it was. The head of a black dog, upturned to the sky, emitting a long, haunted howl. It was a belief she carried long past the point at which she knew better, needing to pretend that the world ended at the dog's head and she and her mother and father were intact, alive, happy together on their little street and had no need to venture any farther.

But then, she turned eleven, was crammed between those two spears of a sudden new age. Suddenly, she and Ma were headed up Lake Shore Drive in a borrowed van, north of the dog's head, far to its other side, where, it was said, things were safe. Josie then felt she'd grown a whole year in the length of two harbors and ten stoplights, a tennis court and zoo.

Now, she was pretty much old. She would know much more than the teachers now, had seen and felt and heard the things you wouldn't learn in school, not unless there was a special assembly with a counselor present.

Yes, Josie had become old, very old, and risked the Strange Look from Ma when she told her this new street looked like a broken zipper from afar, its rows of two-flats with their jutting porches were like zipper teeth struggling to close the gulf between them. But Ma did not Strange-Look her. Instead, Ma set the dog down on the empty floor and dragged the green chair to its center, settled in, and said: "You are right, Josefina. This street is a broken zipper."

* * *

Now, Josie regretted giving voice to that particular observation as it seemed to have led to Ma thinking the street really *was* a broken zipper, whereas Josie had only meant that was what it *looked* like, at that moment, in that light, and she really ought to try and keep these thoughts from spilling out, but it was too late. The street was a broken zipper. It wasn't worth looking at, it was gone to her before it even started: this new life, this new place, all the hope of beginnings dashed through the carelessness of Josie's words.

* * *

By the look of Ma's head, Josie decided it must be about half-past seven, nearly the time her regulars would be out.

It was hard work, getting people to like her. It was possible they all thought she was too loud, her ideas stupid, her appearance oversized and grotesque. Josie worried the street would cheer and clap if she were to move out. They would spill from the doorways and dance. Even the name of the street, Leavitt, was unwelcoming and should be a warning to any newcomers (Leave It! the street signs scolded) and at times Josie wanted to slink back to the other side of Ma's chair and beg to be taken back to her side of the dog's head.

Josie kept her eyes steady, saw hints of her father in twisted glints of light bouncing off cars, heard his steps in the thumps of children jumping rope a block away. He was so close, she *felt* him, but still he failed to materialize from all the elements she had gathered in her imagination and thrown to chance

* * *

Leavitt Street was an odd place, deserving of a Strange Look of its own, there being so many types of people, their paths well-worn, but their movements past Josie's porch mostly silent. They knew Josie well, they knew each other well, yet they didn't. Neighbors, but not. This was very different from Josie's old street, where everyone was always talking, and on summer nights lingering conversations between neighbors filtered through the window as she fell asleep. Josie's old house was bright red and had a green door, was built by Czechs, her father had said, all the way back in the 1800s. He had been a math teacher, but knew all about history too, and told her once that if you try very hard you can feel the soul of a street, of the hands that built its buildings, the stories of its many lives. But when Josie put her hand on the same bricks, she'd only felt a generous remnant of her father's hand, and here, in these new bricks, she couldn't feel anything at all.

"How are *you* today?" Josie called out to a small family passing by.

For this effort, she got nothing more than the Strange Look from the mother and father, who herded their children on. The children smiled at her, though, coy and secretive under their thick mops of hair. It seemed they had misunderstood. It seemed they didn't speak English. It was like one of those "communication problems" talked about by Munch when she complained about Josie forgetting to tell Ma about the conferences and meetings because Josie did not speak the language of conferences and meetings. Munch told Josie that she and Ma needed to work on their communication problems or they may need to start an ODR, which stood for Official Disciplinary Report, and Josie trudged home thinking of how these school people had a terrifying way with words. They kept little phrases like *ODR* at their sides like attack dogs, making the commonplace seem dire, and if Munch had understood she might have kept her little attack dog at bay and instead sent Josie away with a smile and a pat to the shoulder, because, really, how was she supposed to communicate with someone so far away—or rather, someone so unreachable, as if Ma were not only stuck at the bottom of the ocean, but stuck inside an ocean vent where glow-in-the-dark, eyeless sea creatures floated about, and Josie at the surface, only able to communicate via some sort of expensive sonar equipment.

Josie, thinking of ODRs, hunched over her knees and nearly missed the girl in the giant green pantsuit.

Of all the neighbors, the green bean was the most mysterious, the most worried looking and Josie decided she'd be happier in a smart pair of slacks paired with a bright orange blouse. But even with the new outfit Josie dressed her in, she still looked anxious. What was she so worried about? Had someone died? Because Josie knew about that, she knew about death and the need to do strange things like sit on the floor for hours poking holes into sheets of paper with a ballpoint pen. And what about now? Was sitting on the porch calling out to strangers, was that one of the strange things? Maybe one day she'd look back and determine it was, and this was a strange thing all by itself because, at the moment, it did not seem strange at all.

The green bean drifted by, offering just a slight nod.

Josie sighed, planted her cheek in the palm of her hand, fully discouraged, just as the humungous Chinese man dashed by for his millionth run of the day.

This one she called the Champ, and at first Josie thought he was training for a marathon, out five, six times a day, his pace and expression the same, as if he were a prerecorded loop you sometimes saw in the background of old movies. Oh wow, Josie had thought, he's going to be in the Olympics, but then she began to note the strangeness of his running clothes: the eighties headband, the sloppy sweats, the polo shirts stamped with peeling logos from a local junior high. His Nikes were so battered he'd recently stuck some black duct tape where his pinkie toes had poked through and were suspensefully exposed as he dashed by, just *asking* to be stubbed by the sidewalk's uneven pavement. He was no Olympian; they would have special outfits—Josie was sure of it. And lately, it appeared he was running *from* something, and Josie felt a dark ball form in her throat each time he dashed by, that look on his face: anxious, like there was something behind him he just couldn't wait to get away from. Like no matter what he did, there it was, that *thing*; he just couldn't run fast enough, and this was the type of problem Josie understood.

Sort like the day after her father's funeral, feeling like she would never, ever sleep again, she'd walked around the block twenty-eight times and didn't even want any of the supermarket sandwiches or Bundt cakes that kept arriving in giant plastic clamshell containers that made a horrible sound when you pulled them apart. She couldn't eat any of it because it wasn't real food, they weren't the sardine and mayonnaise sandwiches they'd eaten together late on an autumn night back when Ma still graded papers.

"Morning!" Josie shouted to Champ, though something in her voice broke, she sounded feeble. Champ stared straight ahead, didn't seem to hear her or want to hear her, or heard her but didn't want to respond, and Josie breathed deep, said, quietly, mostly to herself, mostly in a way that was kind of like a prayer, she said: "Looking good!" He didn't respond, and it wasn't quite his fault anyway because she'd made her voice so soft, and anyway, she understood it wasn't Champ's fault that something was chasing him and he had to get away fast. It was the sort of thing you didn't have to explain to Josie.

Now that the Champ had sped by, she craned her head, expecting his wife to soon make her queenly appearance, her swishy, sweeping walk past Josie's field of vision. This was the part of the morning she most looked forward to because Mrs. Champ was *spectacular* and Josie had recently made inroads with her. Last Wednesday she got a nod; Thursday a tiny smile; and by Friday, when Josie bellowed her *Good Morning!* from the porch steps, Mrs. Champ said "Good Morning" back. Also, she'd very nearly looked Josie in the eye, hesitated a bit, as if there was something she wanted to ask, but reconsidered, sweeping away in a vision of embroidered scarves, leaving Josie to call excitedly after her: *Talk to you later! Have a good day!* And now Josie felt this was the day, this *had* to be the day that Mrs. Champ would say what was on her mind.

Josie had never seen someone like Mrs. Champ on the her side of the dog's head, except for maybe certain types of bag ladies seen on the CTA, which sounded like an insult, but what Josie meant was she was kind of strange, and, to use this week's vocab word, *unabashedly* strange, her wardrobe full of quirks and madness, her hair a bright neon orange, her stature tall, her posture perfect, her gait grand. Josie felt no need to change her.

What was it like, Josie wondered, to be married to Champ? Did he ever laugh at her outfits? Did she ask him why he ran so much? Sometimes, it looked like he was running away from her, especially on the days in which his dash past Josie's steps was immediately followed by Mrs. Champ's slow and deliberate gait, as if she were some sort of stately Godzilla that chased him from their house, and this thought made Josie laugh just a little. But Josie waited and waited and still there was no sign of Mrs. Champ. She turned around and checked the time: a little past nine o' clock by the look of Ma's head. Mrs. Champ was late. Josie began to worry. Did something bad happen?

Two birds landed in front of Josie and drank from water that had collected in an empty parking space and she tried to focus on them, her stomach queasy like in the days of the Bundt cakes. The birds peeked at Josie, hopped around, flew up into the trees, drawing her gaze into the sky. It was the sort of sky she liked: Barbie-eye blue, with slow drifting clouds that hung around, not rushing off, not ignoring, not keeping secrets. The clouds were the sky's thoughts, and today the sky was thinking of Josie. Here's you Josie, eating sardine and mayonnaise sandwiches with your father. Here's Pyotyr offering you a stick of gum. Here's you, up there all on your own, in massive puffy curves, drifting along, and the entire world is waving to you…

Josie's gaze snapped back to earth. Somehow, she'd missed the squad car pulling up into the empty space where the birds searched for water. Another car pulled up, spilling more blue light onto the street and she felt her heart begin to thump. On Josie's old block there had been so much blue light it was like they lived in a separate blue-tinted atmosphere. Cozy on their side of the dog's head, they'd watched their happy street slowly turn blue, like a person running out of air, and Josie hadn't expected the blue air to follow her. She remembered the sickly churning of police lights, the unrolling of yellow tape, the distant cries, the choppers above. She remembered trying very hard to think of stray bullets as just stray dogs and cats: from unknown origins, circling the city aimlessly, following her father on his way home from the train and landing in the exact wrong spot purely by chance. She remembered thinking, for a cold, very lonely moment, that she was only pretending. That someone had pulled a trigger.

A lady cop stood at the bottom of the steps, her hips encircled by a garland of weaponry. Josie imagined the sagging belt as a grass skirt. She tried to turn the street into the grassy hills overlooking the ocean that Ma had once shown her from a travel book and struggled to transform the lady cop into a hula dancer. A champion hula dancer. The Guinness World Record champion hula dancer. Yet, she was staring straight at Josie, not moving at all.

Josie cleared her throat. "How are you today?"

The lady cop leaned forward, her eyes amused, her voice quiet. "I got a call," she said. "A woman yelling at people on the street. That's not you, is it?"

"I'm not a woman. I'm eleven," said Josie.

Josie's hula dancer nodded. A small smile formed at her lips. Josie would paint her lips a cotton-candy pink and do her eyes up with some dark liner to accentuate her bright button-like eyes.

Two large men emerged from the squad car, but Josie's hula dancer waved them away. They stood bathed in the blue light of their cars, their hands shoved into sides of their vests, their faces amused, bored. Josie gave them ukuleles and hoped for the best, but she kept seeing the blue light, the yellow tape, the helicopters above. She looked back to check on Ma. *Don't turn around.*

"Good morning. What's going on here?" Mrs. Champ had floated by in her scarves of lavender and mustard and teal, the contrasting colors of Josie's old street. She sat beside Josie and patted her hand, smiled up at the hula dancer as if they were best friends. Josie looked down at her shoes.

The lady cop smiled. "A misunderstanding ma'am. We get a lot of dumb calls. You okay young lady?"

Josie was hunched over her knees, trying hard to catch her breath as it rushed in, rushed out. She nodded and slowly looked up, taking in Leavitt Street, seeing its cardinals, its daffodils, the brightness of Mrs. Champ's scarves. The lady cop waved goodbye, a smile on her face, and all three left. Josie breathed and looked up at Mrs. Champ.

"So," Mrs. Champ said. "How are *you* today?"

Josie smiled but couldn't speak. Instead, she looked up and just then saw that the sky was thinking of her father. She blinked and watched her father's cloud move beyond the sun. The sky was thinking hard, clearing its thoughts, leading Josie's father to the horizon, the cloud growing smaller, thinner and thinner still. And then he vanished into the blue air.

"I'm good." ■

LIVE FAST
James Stacey

In the fall of '83, Dave went back to the Coq d'Or in Chicago's Drake Hotel for the first time in more than a year. The room was undisturbed by time. There were the same tables here, banquettes there, and the polished bar dead ahead. Dave took his place and ordered a gin martini straight up with a twist. On his right were two world-weary women.

"So what did you tell him?" one asked the other.

"I told him it was time to begin understanding the meaning of 'no.'"

"And what did he say?"

"He said he never takes no for an answer . . ."

Their voices drifted on, discussing the many deficiencies of the singles scene.

"David Hoffman. As I live and breathe."

Dave turned and saw Sidney Gabel sitting beside him and offering his hand with a smile. Of all the members from the old group, Sidney was the only one Dave truly liked. Everyone called him the "arbiter of taste," an accolade he accepted with a detached sense of humor. He once allowed that if he cut everyone for a breach of decorum, he soon would be spending every evening alone.

The bartender came over and, with a bow and smile, said, "Champagne cocktail, Mr. Gabel?"

"But of course. You've read my mind once again."

Sidney had Hollywood-handsome good looks. With his trim suit, colorful tie, and deep tan, his appearance suggested someone like Cary Grant. The women to Dave's right noticed. Dave could almost feel them stirring on their stools. At last both he and Sidney made a full turn to face them.

"What a lovely tan," one woman said. "Where did you get it?"

"My dear, I got this tan walking past the cosmetics counter at Bonwit Teller."

"Oh."

Their smiles faded, and they now spoke in whispers.

"How have you been?" Sidney asked. "Still traveling, still writing?"

"Yep, still doing the same old stuff."

"I saw your piece in the *Tribune*, the one about the death-penalty insanity plea. I thought it was awfully good."

"Thanks," Dave said, as the bartender set Sidney's drink before him. "But how is everyone? How is Kixie?"

"Still impossible. She's managed to get rid of another man."

"And Betty and Bob?"

"They finally made up and moved to California."

"To California?"

"Yes. Everyone's going California these days. So boring of them."

"And the boys?"

"The boys will be boys. A.J. continues cruising. Donald is cheating, as always, and Peter, as always, forgives him."

After a pause, Dave asked, "And Cindy? How is Cindy?"

Sidney blanched, as if at a stab of pain.

"You haven't heard?" he said at last. "Cindy's dead. She died months ago."

"Cindy's dead?" Dave said, shaking his head. "Dead. It's hard to believe. She was so full of life. Never stopped talking. What a shock. The last thing I would expect to hear."

"So sad, always so charming, always chatting away."

Dave remembered their first night together. She opened the door, took one look at him, and kicked off her high-heeled shoes, saying, "You're short. I didn't notice last week. We were sitting down at the reception. Does it make you uncomfortable? Should I wear flats? Would it make you feel better?" And he said, no, he wasn't bothered by heights.

"Come, let me take your coat. My, but it's heavy, but you have to bundle up, don't you? You don't have a car, poor thing. You have to travel by el and trudge through snowbanks and such. Come, let's fix you a drink. You like gin martinis, you said. I've got a fresh bottle in kitchen, along with vermouth. It may not make you warmer, but it should make you happier."

The short hallway led to the main room, a long expanse with sofas on the left, a glass cocktail table in the center, and a dining area on the right, separated from the rest of the room by a bench that served as an implied wall. The walls right and left were plastered with posters, oil paintings, etchings, chalks, and watercolors.

"There are thousands of dollars in art on the walls. They represent years of collecting. One of my friends has a gallery and studio in the Tree Building. It's filled with artists, a veritable sanctuary. My oils are from there. The posters are classics. They're priceless. But I'm going on about this when you need a drink. Here's the kitchen." She passed through an open doorway to the right. One wall in this room was filled with antique tools, wrought iron chisels, pliers, hacksaws, and wrenches.

"I used to go antiquing with a friend around Galena, New Glarus, and Spring Green. It' a whole other world, where people made things with their hands. So primitive and appealing."

After drinks, they went to the basement garage, and she got behind the wheel of her car and raced along ice-covered streets, sliding past stop signs and parking in front of a fireplug steps away from the restaurant entrance. She pronounced the place "Charming, gemütlichkeit" and added, "You know, you have all the makings of a leaf kicker, the way you talk, the way you move."

"A leaf kicker?" he said.

"He's the kind who takes you for a walk through Lincoln Park on a Sunday afternoon. After a while you wind up at the zoo, and he buys you a hot dog and soda. One week later he takes you for a walk along the lakeshore and you end up watching a softball game in Grant Park. On the following week he takes you to his apartment, fills you with wine, cheese, and crackers, and takes you to bed. Then he bids you goodbye and never sees you again."

At a loss for words, Dave took a sip from his drink, knowing leaf kicking had nothing to do with him. After dinner, they went back to her place and into her room, where he put to bed any suspicions of kicking leaves, leaving them both pleased and breathless.

Turning toward Sidney, Dave asked, "How did it happen? Were there pills, something like that?"

"No, nothing like that. They found her alone in her bed, as if she'd worn herself out, died from exhaustion."

"How did she look? I mean, did she look like herself?"

"Yes. Lovely as ever."

"That was her wish," Dave said. "She used to say, 'Live fast, die young, and leave a good-looking corpse.' She was only forty-five."

"Willard Motley made a lot of mischief for impressionable young readers."

"She did read, too. Crammed that into her fast-moving life. The light would be on as I drifted off, and she would be out of bed when I woke up, in the kitchen, grinding beans for coffee, cracking eggs for omelets, popping bread from toasters. So lively. I only wish . . ."

"I was sorry things didn't work out for you two," Sidney said. "It looked good for a while."

"It was. I was hoping to see her today. We used to meet here. She would come in that door, wearing a white dress, blond hair down to her shoulders, perfect makeup. She looked like a movie star. Then she would walk the line, and men seemed to wobble on their barstools when she passed by, but she was coming to me, only me."

"What went wrong?" Sidney asked.

"I wasn't enough," Dave said, looking down at his drink. At last he raised the glass to his lips for a sip. "But tell me about Kixie. I always liked her. She was something like Cindy." He was sure that Kixie and Sidney loved one another, by turns enchanted and chagrined. They looked made for one another, both tall and straight-backed. At cocktail parties, they looked like a pair. But it was not to be. She was straight, and he was not.

"Remember the time she told us she had a way into the Sardine Bar, where Bobby Short was performing?"

"Another folly," Sidney said.

The two of them stood in the hallway, waiting for Kixie and watching a parade of people open the door and enter the bar, counting their blessings that Kixie had a special entrance. When she arrived, Sidney said, "Where's our way in?"

"Right there," she said, pointing to the passage used by scores of others while they waited. "Follow me."

A mass of people filled the room, jammed together right up to the doorway. Kixie plunged in, twisting this way and that on her way to a narrow bandstand. Sidney and Dave followed, feeling something like lemmings. At the appointed place, Kixie stopped and addressed a waiter who was holding a tray above his head.

"Cuba libre," she said.

"Gin and tonic for me," said Dave.

Sidney shook his head and after the waiter left, he said to the others, "I'm leaving. This is entirely too much fun for me."

Off he went, twisting and turning on his way out. Not long after, Bobby Short arrived, twisting and turning like the rest of them. Stopping beside Kixie and Dave, he said, "Kixie. Where's Sidney?"

"He left. He said this was entirely too much fun for him."

That was how Dave learned Sidney hosted dinners for people like Bobby Short. Once Short asked if he could bring a friend to the party. Sidney said, "Of course," and Short showed up with Leontyne Price. But no matter who was invited, or who showed up, Kixie always was there.

"You know, I saw Kixie just the other day. I was waiting in the reception area for my shrink, when who should walk out of his office but Kixie herself. We looked at one another in absolute shock. Later she telephoned and asked, 'Did you talk about me?' I said, 'Certainly not,' but that's all I talked about the whole hour."

They both laughed about that. Then Sidney said, "Well, I must leave. Good to see you again."

As he reached for his wallet, Dave said, "No, no. This one's on me."

"No, it's my pleasure."

They both were standing, wallets in hand.

The waiter came over and said, "Why don't you just take care of your own?"

They looked at one another and nodded. Then they looked to the right, where the world-weary women were looking at them, wearing a mask of marked disapproval. ∎

A FUNNY THING HAPPENED ON THE WAY TO THE COLUMBARIUM
Umberto Tosi

"In three-tenths of a mile, slight left."

Almost in sync, the girl in the back seat—a tall twelve, but looking older in the simple, black Betsey Johnson puff-sleeved scuba dress that her mother had bought her for the memorial—pinched her nose and mimicked the GPS in a nasal voice:

"In three tenths of a mile, slight fart." She grinned, flashing her braces. She brushed bagel crumbs off her black skirt and left a pale white smear from the cream cheese still on her fingers. The stain looked like the wispy cirrus clouds high in the chill December sky that morning.

"Stop it, DeeDee!" Carol, the girl's mother, glanced back from the passenger seat. "We can't hear the directions. And I told you not to bring that breakfast bagel in the car!"

DeLia had a habit of eating in her father's aging sedan from the days when her parents were still together and he would drive her to school. The sweet, slightly rancid odor of old peanut butter cereal bars lingered in the back seat from when she was eight years old—a time that seemed as remote as the Jurassic to her now.

"S'all right." Her father shrugged from behind the wheel, which he held with two fingers of one hand while he fished for the phone vibrating in his shirt pocket. Vincent slipped the sedan into the right lane, which veered gradually onto another freeway. The phone stopped vibrating.

Carol shot him a furious look. "Don't undermine me," she hissed at him under her breath. "Let's just get through this," she added, keeping her voice low.

"I was just practicing my German for class," DeLia piped from the back seat. "There's a test tomorrow. F-A-H-R-T!" she spelled out. "It means 'journey' in German."

Vincent smirked. "Nice to know we're getting our money's worth from that school of yours," he said.

"Dies ist eine Fahrt in das Land der Toten," DeLia exaggerated the Teutonic syllables like a German character in a Hollywood war movie. "Ist eine journey to the land of the dead," she translated. "Toten!" She passed a finger across her throat and stuck out her tongue sideways.

"Don't joke about your grandmother's memorial, DeeDee," Carol shook her head.

"Grandma Flora would have," said DeLia. "She would have wanted us to dress up in skeleton masks. She used to say, 'I want you all to party when I die.'"

"Mom never left the stage, even after she retired," Vincent said. "I loved her, but she was always dramatizing and dispensing guilt," he added. He glanced back at DeLia. The car strayed out of its lane and cut off a truck before Vincent righted it. He shuddered, imagining that his dead mother had just tugged at the wheel to give him a scare.

"Keep your eyes on the road, Vincent," said Carol.

DeLia tapped her side window. "Look, the sign says Emeryville ¼ Mile. Shouldn't we be crossing the Bay Bridge?"

Just then the dulcet GPS voice piped up:

"In two-tenths of a mile, slight right at next exit."

"Oh shit," said Vincent.

DeLia twisted in her seat to look out the rear window. "Look!" She said with unconcealed glee. "The rest of the funeral cars are right behind us. They got it wrong too."

Vincent checked the rear view mirror and saw a half dozen cars following them with their headlights on. He could see the FUNERAL on the dashboard through the windshield of the SUV directly behind them. "Lemmings!" Vincent blew air through his lips and shook he head as he edged the car into the right lane of the I-580. The cars behind them followed.

Carol glanced back. "They're all going to be late now too, because of us."

"Don't they have GPS? They didn't have to follow us."

"They probably had theirs turned off," Carol fumed. "Why did you have to have yours on, instead of just following the procession like everyone else?"

"'Like everyone else' is not me," Vincent said.

Carol raised her voice. "The GPS said 'slight left' back there. I heard her, Vin, that was to the ramp that leads onto the Bay Bridge, not all the way to the left lane. You know that! How many times have you crossed the bridge to San Francisco? Lots!"

Vincent white-knuckled the wheel with both hands now. "Well, if you had quit with the hammering for a minute so I could have concentrated . . ." He glared over to her.

"This was all a mistake," said Carol. "I never should have gone along with this charade!"

"It was all your idea, Carol," he replied. "Because of your dad and your sister, and all."

"That's it, blame everything on me, as usual," said Carol.

"You're the one who slept with my brother." Vincent honked at a pickup that cut in front of them. "Asshole!" He let the window down and yelled in vain as the truck pulled away.

"Shh . . ." Carol jerked her head. "DeeDee shouldn't hear this."

"She knows about everything," Vincent muttered.

DeLia wiped more crumbs off her dress. "I know everything," she mocked them. She scowled. "I know what you did last summer!" She raised a hand and made a claw, and did her impression of an evil laugh. Then she smirked and returned to her normal voice: "I also know that you just passed your turnoff!" She laughed and pointed behind her. "The green sign back there said Emeryville Exit!"

"Shit! Shit! Shit" Vincent pounded the steering wheel.

Carol flipped down her visor on the passenger side. "Don't yell, Vincent! You'll get us in a wreck!" She aligned the visor's vanity mirror to look out the back window. "Looks like we lost the other funeral cars behind us. I don't see their headlights anymore."

"Take next right . . ." the mellow GPS voice said.

Vincent pounded the dashboard and pressed buttons. "Shut the fuck up! How do I turn this damn thing off?"

"I think you just did, or broke it," said DeeDee, who leaned forward in her shoulder belt. She wiped bagel crumbs off her mouth with the back of her hand as she swallowed the last bite of it. "Can I have a tissue and some lipstick, Mom? Please."

"Might as well keep going now—up to the Richmond–San Rafael Bridge and cross the bay there," said Carol. "Why didn't you keep up with the procession?" she asked. "And why did you let your brother Robbie and your cousin Alice drive ahead of us?"

"Why didn't you go with Robbie, then?" Vincent growled to himself just loud enough for Carol to hear him.

"Now you're being a jerk again," she said. "We've been all over that. You and I were broken up already, and it was just that one time when he brought the Persian rug back from being cleaned."

"Sounds like a porno plot," he muttered.

Carol tossed a quick look back towards DeLia, signaling Vincent to be discreet.

"You know what I mean," he said,

"No, I don't know anything of the sort. You were the one who spilled red wine all over that rug, and threw up on it too. It was my father's from Iran, an antique. You knew what it meant to me."

Vincent nodded sheepishly. "I wasn't thinking much at the time," he said, almost in a whisper. "I was drinking then. I did a lot of things. I've got to say, it was hard on you—and on my mother too."

"Your mother was a true matriarch," said Carol, "even to me."

"Controlling, is what she was," said Vincent. "Don't forget she directed shows, not just acted in them."

"Well, she was a fixer," said Carol.

"Put her nose in everything, bless her," said Vincent.

"And what a great nose it was," said Carol. She drew a breath. "And your brother Robbie got me through a lot during that time. He sure got you out of a jam with the accident and helped me get you to a hospital, and finally . . . You're lucky he's a good lawyer."

"Yeah, lucky. I know. I know," said Vincent, slouching down as he drove. He edged the car into the left lane of the freeway that led to the San Rafael turnoff.

"I was vulnerable," she continued, keeping her voice low.

"You and he didn't have to tell me—like you were rubbing it in," he said. "You never let me forget. And neither does Robbie, with his superior attitude."

"Come on, Vincent. Your ragging on Robbie all the time is just your way of shifting blame when you should be looking at yourself," Carol said. "I thought you were supposed to take responsibility in your program and all that."

"I do. I do take responsibility." Vincent's voice grew irritable. "Goddamn responsibility is my middle name," he said. "What a sham all of this is. You and I riding to mom's memorial acting like we're back together, one big happy family, like nothing ever happened . . ."

"This show was your idea," she said.

"Just for dad. He doesn't have that long."

"Or do you mean, just to show your brother. I'm supposed to be the trophy in your endless sibling pissing match."

"Is that what you think?" Vincent shrugged. "I'm sorry. Maybe so, but I looked at it differently. I thought maybe . . . you and I still have a chance . . . I don't know." Vincent looked over at her with his big, soft brown eyes that had always seemed to charm her.

"Keep your eyes on the road," she said. "There!" She pointed. "There's the sign for San Rafael."

"I saw it," he said.

"It shouldn't take long to cross to San Rafael, if I remember right," she continued. "Then go south and we'll be on our way back."

"Then we'll be in goddamned Marin County," said Vincent, hearing his own voice go sarcastic again. He tried to soften the edge with details.

"We'll have to swing south across the goddamned Golden Gate." He shook his head.

"So then you'll have to drive all the way down Nineteenth Avenue through traffic to get to the freeway and Colma?" Carol lamented. "We're going to be sooooo late for the burial."

"It's not a burial. It's called an interment," Vincent reminded her. "And it's not in Colma, it's the San Francisco Columbarium, just north of Golden Gate Park. You might remember it from when we lived in the city, out near Ocean Beach—that Greco-Roman building with the greenish bronze dome—looks like a miniature of city hall. I thought we visited there once. Mom's family owns a crypt there."

"I remember you took me there, Daddy!" DeLia spoke up. "It was spooky and so beautiful inside."

"A fine outing," said Carol.

"She asked about it every time we'd see the dome from Geary when I would drive her to school." Vincent turned his head halfway around towards his daughter. "DeeDee! I'm surprised you remember that. You were pretty little then."

"I remember it was cool. We saw where that actor's ashes were kept—the one that was in the old Planet of the Apes movie, the one they play on the old movie channel," DeLia said.

"Roddy McDowall," said Vincent.

"And Harvey Milk," DeLia added. "I remember the name because I thought it was a kind of milk, or maybe ice cream. I kept looking for it at the store. Who was he now?"

"The San Francisco gay rights hero who was assassinated back in the 1970s," said Vincent.

"Mom! The lipstick, please!" DeLia changed the subject.

Carol fished tissue, a compact mirror and a stick of lip gloss from her purse and handed them back to DeLia. "Just wipe and don't try to put on the lip gloss until we stop," she said.

"Mom. I can handle it," DeLia said. She flipped the compact open and examined her magnified reflection in his mirror. She had applied some of her mother's foundation makeup before leaving that morning, which gave her complexion a ghostly white patina. She parted her full lips and smiled widely, exposing her braces. The slanting morning sunlight glinted off her coppery hair and the metallic braces. It gave her a demon-vampire look. She took a breath. She liked it. "If I can't be beautiful, I'll be scary," she said under her breath.

"What did you say?" Carol strained around to see her daughter more fully.

"Nothing!" DeLia said.

"This is sooooo embarrassing!" Carol glared at Vincent. "I could never stand your chronic lateness when we were married. I had to suffer the embarrassment, while you would be just la-di-da."

"It's MY mother's funeral," Vincent said, "and mostly my relatives and friends."

Carol punched his arm.

Vincent leaned away. "Watch it, Carol. You'll make us crash."

"You asshole! They always blamed me for whatever bullshit you pulled, never their fair-haired boy wonder."

"That's not true," said Vincent. "In fact they still like you more than me!"

"Well, I feel bad for your mother. We need to say our goodbye to her, respectfully. What would she think?" Carol folded her arms and stared out the passenger window, no longer paying attention to where they were going.

Preoccupied, Vincent had slowed the car way down. Traffic went around them. A couple of drivers blasted their horns as they passed. One gave them the finger as he passed and yelled something inaudible.

Vincent gave him the finger back. "Screw you," he yelled through his closed window. "Story of my goddamned life," he muttered. "Wrong turns, wrong turns and wrong turns. Shit."

"Story of your sorry-ass whining," said Carol. "Story of your wouldas and shouldas, ifs and buts, and how you're sorry you married me and we had DeeDee . . ."

Vincent glared at her and shook his head. "That's your line, Carol!"

"I'm right back here," DeLia shouted. "Don't talk about me like I'm not here," she said. DeLia whispered into the air, as if saying a prayer to her dead grandma, "They're already worse now with you gone, Grandma. You're my refuge. I was sad when Dad moved out, but now I don't know if I would want him to come back."

"Let's all drop it. Okay?" Vincent said. "Let me concentrate on my driving."

"Yeah. Like you have been," said Carol.

"I'll get us there. Don't worry." he added, suddenly resolute. "They won't start without us. I'm paying the goddamned priest."

"You don't pay priests," Carol said.

"I made a so-called donation," he snapped back. "Same thing. You think they don't dip into the poor box?"

He drove on a few minutes in silence, then added: "My mother would have wanted us there—and especially DeeDee." He glanced back at DeLia in the rear view mirror.

DeLia caught his eye and shook her head. "No," she said. "Grandma would rather just keep going to the wine country," she smiled merrily. "She told me."

"When?" Carol turned back to her daughter.

"Just now," said DeLia, and she looked to her left. "Grandma is back here with me right now." DeLia pointed at the empty back seat next to her. "Just tell them, Grandma."

Carol rolled her eyes.

"Grandma doesn't want to be put in a tomb—in that columbarium or whatever you call it, sealed up all in marble and stone," said DeLia. "She wants to go to the wine country."

"She's right," a voice came out of nowhere.

Carol craned her neck to the back seat again, but saw no one except DeLia. "Who was that?" She asked.

Vincent slapped the dashboard again. "I think it was the goddamn GPS saying next right." He mimicked the breathy voice of the GPS. "I must not have turned the goddamned thing off."

"Your mother always loved the wine country. Remember when we all spent that Fourth of July week in Calistoga?" said Carol absently.

"I remember that," DeLia volunteered.

"That's how they get rid of you," said the voice, but this time Carol and Vincent didn't hear it. "They put you in a box or in a jar and bury you or toss you into the ocean or put you in a crypt and they're done with you, DeeDee. It's for them, not you."

DeLia sniffled. "I don't want them to put grandma in an awful jar." She wailed.

Vincent didn't miss the turnoff this time and negotiated connecting ramps westward onto the double-decked, five-mile-long, cantilever San Rafael span.

DeLia could see her Grandma Flora next to her more sharply now, as the light shifted with the change of direction. Flora reached towards the front seat and tapped Vincent on the shoulder of his black dress jacket.

"When you get across the north bay to San Rafael, go north on the 101, not south towards San Francisco, if you please," she implored him and Carol in a clear voice. The two of them paid her no attention. Vincent brushed off his shoulder but otherwise didn't respond.

"They're not listening, Grandma," said DeLia.

She smiled sadly at her granddaughter.

"Who are you talking to back there?" Carol asked. "No phone calls this morning please."

"Can I text at least?" DeLia blew impatiently. "I just want to answer a friend. Don't want to be rude," she said.

"Well, all right," said Carol. Then she turned to Vincent. "I'm going to phone your brother Sam and tell him we've been detoured."

"Any excuse," Vincent said. His face reddened.

Carol didn't take the bait. She took her mobile out of her purse and scrolled to Sam's number.

"I see you've got him on speed dial," said Vincent, and he tightened his grip on the wheel. "Sam! It's Carol." She paused, listening, and nodded her head. "Yes, your brother. We missed the ramp. We're fine. Are you there yet?" She listened and nodded again.

"Tell him to go ahead and we'll get there," said Vincent. Then he mumbled, "I'll bet he's gloating about his idiot brother now."

"Thank you, Sam," said Carol. She paused, listening to him on the other end. "You're a darling . . . yes . . . probably an hour or less . . . Okay, don't worry. We'll see you there, darling . . . Thanks. Hugs to you too . . . and Sadie," Carol added quickly, glancing at her ex-husband fuming behind the wheel.

Vincent did a mincing voice. "Darling? Hugs?"

Carol clicked off her phone and did her best to ignore his jibes. "Sam says they've put off the ceremony for another hour. That gives us plenty of time—if you don't lose your way again."

Vincent shot back: "I didn't 'lose my way'! I missed the ramp with you talking . . ."

"Well, shut my mouth!" Carol tossed her phone back into her purse. "Why don't *you* shut *your* mouth, Vinny?"

"Let's not argue more in front of DeeDee," said Vincent, hunching down. He could see Point San Quentin ahead to their right as they drove high up over the second span of the bridge. "There but for the grace of I-don't-know-who . . ." he whispered to himself, thinking of his drinking days, and he fell silent.

"Hi Grandma. ♥ Can you read this?" DeLia texted Grandma Flora's mobile number, which fortunately still functioned. She showed her iPhone screen to Grandma Flora, who remained seated next to her.

Flora was wearing a silky black nightgown and Japanese floral silk robe, with embroidered black, green, yellow, and red dragon slippers. Her thick white hair fell to her shoulders on both sides, framing her olive-complected, still severely beautiful aquiline visage like a painter's imagined Greek oracle. Flora held a cigarette in a long silver holder. DeLia smelled its white wisp of tobacco smoke mixed with her grandmother's lavender perfume.

Carol thought she smelled it too, and glanced back at DeeDee. "Are you smoking back there?"

"Mom!" DeLia rolled her eyes.

Carol looked at Vincent, who shrugged and kept driving. "Must be from the old days," he said. Carol cracked the passenger-side window.

". . . You talk." DeLia texted and showed her grandma Flora the screen again, then pointed to her parents up front. "They can't see you—won't hear you."

Flora grinned at this new game and nodded. "You don't have to show me your screen, dear. I can see your messages in my head," she said, "just like you can hear me in yours."

DeLia's eyes widened. She texted: "In your head?" She didn't show Flora the screen this time, but Flora smiled and nodded a yes.

"Are you dead?"

Flora shrugged.

DeLia texted again—her fingers flying over the pad. "Mom said the Neptune Society is going to cremate your body after the ceremony this morning. Better get out of there."

Flora shuddered a little. "If I can wake up from this dream . . . I take it this is a dream, right?"

DeLia gave her a wide-eyed look and hunched her shoulders. "Beats me," she texted. Then, "Whose dream? Yours or mine?"

"I don't know, DeeDee honey. I just want to go to Calistoga and have a glass of Pinot Noir and have me a hot-springs mineral water soak. Then everything will be all right—even if it is the off-season."

DeLia texted. "I'll try to get Dad to blow off the columbarium thing, or whatever, and turn north."

"What are you doing back there, DeeDee?" Carol squinted back towards DeLia and then straight at where Grandma Flora was sitting, as if she had caught sight of her late ex-mother-in-law—or a facsimile thereof.

Carol slumped in her seat. "This was a horrible idea," she said again, and she glared over at Vincent. "I should have taken DeeDee and driven in my own car—and left you to your own devices, Vincent." She turned her head and stared straight ahead. "All we've done is argue. It's all we've ever done."

Vincent shook his head, suddenly shaking off tears. "Well, that's not all we ever did. We had some sweet times . . . admit it."

"You ruined it all," Carol said.

"I could say the same of you," Vincent responded softly, "but I won't argue the point."

"This reminds me of another dream I had," Flora said.

DeLia texted: "Are we in das Land der Toten, Grandma?"

Flora's image shimmered for a few seconds. "I don't think so. Maybe that's in Calistoga, or . . . the columbarium. I remember now we have

a small family crypt there that my father bought years ago right after
he emigrated from Athens. He said he wanted to live and die in San
Francisco, but he sold too soon and lost his money in the crash."

The car had cleared the central span of the bridge and was closing
in on the Marin shore now. "Go north! Go north!" DeLia shouted to her
father. "What are you talking about, DeeDee?" Vincent craned his neck
around to her. The car began to drift out of its lane.

Carol grabbed the wheel to right and but oversteered it rightward.
A pickup truck just behind them to the right blasted its horn. Vincent
grabbed the wheel harder and took control of the steering again.
"We're all gonna die!" Carol yelled. "Are you sure you haven't been
drinking?"

"Goddammit, Carol. You know that's not true!"

"Well I'm glad, but pay attention!" Carol turned back at DeLia
again. "And you stop yammering back there, DeeDee!"

"Heil, Herrin Hitler!" DeLia made a mock Nazi salute.

"You shouldn't talk to your mother that way, DeeDee," said Flora.
"She's been through a lot."

"She's a tyrant!" DeLia put her iPhone on her lap and slouched
back in her seat.

"I'm right here," Carol said. "You don't have to talk about me in
the third person."

"I'm speaking to Grandma," said DeLia. "She's the only one who
ever listened to me."

"Now I'm in the past tense?" Flora asked.

"Sorry, Grandma," DeLia said.

Flora reached over to pat DeLia's hand but passed right through it.
"Now I know this is a nightmare," Flora said.

"This is a nightmare!" Carol complained at the same moment.

"Goddammit! Goddammit! Goddammit!" Vincent yelled, and he
pounded the steering wheel, nearly sending the car out of control again
as it sped along a curving ramp onto the massive 101 freeway. "101
NORTH!" Vincent shouted. "Wrong way again! This is a trip to hell!"

Grandma Flora sat up, beaming! "No, it's a trip to Calistoga," she
said. "And it's heaven to finally have your attention and be off to float
in that warm mineral water pool at the hotel where we always stayed."

"You tell 'em, Grandma!" DeLia said. "Did you hear that?" She
shouted at her parents in the front seat.

"Hear what?" Carol collapsed in her seat like a cloth doll with
the stuffing knocked out of her. She rubbed her forearms, which had
gone to gooseflesh. "Do you have the air conditioner on?" she asked
Vincent.

Vincent checked the dash controls. "No," he said. "But I feel a chill too."

"Maybe we're all dead," said DeLia, gleefully. "Das Land der Toten! It's not so bad after all," she said.

Grandma Flora tried in vain to pat her granddaughter's hand again. "Don't fret, DeeDee. It's my dream and I'll wake up soon."

"Or not," said DeLia.

"I'm seeing it more clearly now," said Flora. "We're on this road until you kids all get this right. Then I can go on to whatever awaits!" She smiled. All three of them heard her this time. Vincent saw her appear in his rearview mirror and Carol gasped and let out a strangled squeal as she turned and caught sight of Flora as well. ∎

WHEN THE SLACK CHAIN TIGHTENS
Jake Young

When the slack chain tightens,
the pedals spin, and the gears crank;
the rubber tires go bald
against the asphalt, and the air sings
past my ears. I let go of all
regret. When I'm suspended
above the saddle, riding high
in the stirrups, leaning forward
over the black handlebar,
it's the speed I can't resist.
I am flush, even in winter, racing home
from work, two pints deep
after scrubbing down the bar,
dreaming of dinner, feeling light
as the mist that speckles my glasses.
At the top of the last hill,
I hit the downshift, and coast.
I could almost believe
this body, this sack of organs,
tendon and bone, was meant to fly.

NOTES ON CONTRIBUTORS

JUDITH ALLER is an American-born virtuoso violinist, a product of a vanishing musical tradition. Guided by her father, the late Victor Aller, (a Capitol recording artist also known for his chamber music recordings with the Hollywood String Quartet) and her teacher, violinist Jascha Heifetz, she has become and remains a completely individual artist. There is no other like her on the scene today. She is capable of re-establishing that grand tradition of which Heifetz, Kreisler, and Piatigorsky, and so many great composers from Brahms to Bloch are a part. For years, during the 70s, she maintained a successful solo career in Scandinavia and throughout Europe generally, operating (by an accident of marriage) from a base in Finland. She has received recognition both there and here in America and has an established audience for her work. After remarrying, she moved to Paris with her husband Bruce Cook, a novelist known in both continents. Many of her recordings can be heard on her website judithaller.com. After her husband's death, she began writing and helped to complete his last books. In Los Angeles, where she lives, Judith Aller gives concerts in libraries that feature "The Secrets of the Classical Music Golden Age."

CHRISTOPHER TODD ANDERSON is Associate Professor of English at Pittsburg State University in Kansas, where he teaches courses in American literature, poetry, environmental literature and film, and popular culture. A 2018 Pushcart Prize recipient, Anderson has published poetry in numerous national literary magazines, including *River Styx, Crab Orchard Review, Prairie Schooner, Wisconsin Review, Tar River Poetry, The Main Street Rag*, and *Greensboro Review*, among others. Anderson has also published academic articles on images of garbage and waste in American poetry and on the film *WALL-E*.

A native of Greensboro, North Carolina, **BILLY BAITES** is a classically trained pianist whose career in arts management spans four decades. After positions with two leading New York classical music arts management companies, he managed the performing arts series at Emory University and served as executive director of the Rialto Center for the Performing Arts, both in Atlanta. For three years he held the position of Cultural Affairs Manager for the City of Miami Beach before returning to his hometown to tend to family matters in 2006. In 2019 he will complete a debut collection of short stories, *Billy Is That You?*, which recounts the outrageous adventures of a gay southerner and celebrates a cast of colorful characters who have paraded proudly through his life. *Hilda's Work Camp* is one of the stories included in the collection. Another one of the stories in the collection, *Daddy Don't Go*, was published in the 2018 winter edition of *Catamaran Literary Reader*. "Tar Heel Sissy," another story from the book, was published in July 2018 in *Chelsea Station*.

During college, **ANN VOORHEES BAKER** submitted three short stories to *The New Yorker* and one to *Ladies' Home Journal*. The former returned three rejections, each a hand-written editor's note with encouragement and a request for more. The latter sent a letter of rejection, in which an editor critiqued her story and asked to see another. Here's the thinking of a twenty-something: Four rejections! *Quelle tragédie!* Ann decreed her writing career a failure and turned to other pursuits; enforcement attorney for the United States Environmental Protection Agency, student at the Joffrey Ballet, mother, parenting magazine publisher, divorcée, online marketing specialist, web designer, ghostwriter. Forty years later, she decided to return to her real passion, writing. She's written several short stories and a first novel, which she is spending an inordinate amount of time editing. Ann lives in Southern California with her husband Brad in a house near the ocean. She takes yoga classes on the beach and ballet classes at the Lauridsen School. Her two adult daughters continually amaze and delight her but live very far away. She hopes they will follow their passions much sooner in life than she did. This is her second published work of fiction.

DENI ELLIS BÉCHARD is the author of *Vandal Love* (Commonwealth Writers' Prize for Best First Book); *Of Bonobos and Men: A Journey to the Heart of the Congo* (Nautilus Book Award for investigative journalism and Grand Prize winner); *Cures for Hunger*, a memoir about his bank-robber father (an IndieNext pick and an Amazon.ca best memoirs of 2012); *Into the Sun*, a novel about the civilian surge in Afghanistan (Midwest Book Award for literary fiction and chosen by CBC/Radio Canada as one of the most important books of 2017 to be read by Canada's political leaders); *Kuei, My Friend: a Conversation on Race and Reconciliation*, an epistolary book of YA nonfiction coauthored with Innu poet Natasha Kanapé-Fontaine; *White*, a novel exploring the legacy of colonialism and the impact of neocolonialism in the Congo and in Canada; and *A Song from Faraway*, a short story collection forthcoming in 2020. He has reported from India, Cuba, Rwanda, Colombia, Iraq, the Congo, and Afghanistan. He has been a finalist for a Canadian National Magazine Award and has been featured in *Best Canadian Essays 2017*. His writing has appeared in the *LA Times*, *Salon*, *The Walrus*, *Pacific Standard*, *The Huffington Post*, *The Harvard Review*, *The National Post*, and *Foreign Policy*.

MAX BERWALD is a writer from San Diego, California. He is pursuing an MA in cinema and media studies at the University of Southern California. His fiction has appeared in *Spittoon*, *Potluck*, *Third Point Press*, *Blackbird*, the *Shanghai Literary Review*, the *Massachusetts Review*, as a part of *Tin House*'s online flash fiction series, and elsewhere.

JOHN BLADES has been the fiction editor of *CQR* for eight years. He's the author of the novels *Small Game* (Holt, 1992) and *Common Criminals* (awaiting publication). His stories have appeared in *Catamaran*, *Printers Row*, *TriQuarterly*, *Chicago Works*, and other literary magazines. As a journalist, he has worked for the *Miami Herald*, the *Chicago Sun-Times*, and the *Chicago Tribune*, where he spent twenty-eight years as magazine editor and writer, book editor and critic, and cultural reporter. His nonfiction has also appeared in the *Washington Post*, *Publishers Weekly*, and dozens of other publications.

HAROLD BORDWELL has had poetry and prose published in *The Yankee*, *Commonweal*, *The Chicago Review*, *The Carleton Miscellany*, *Light* and other magazines. He was born in Corning, New York, and grew up in Pennsylvania and Ohio. After working and living in Silicon Valley for more than ten years, he now lives in the Chicago area.

STEVEN CARRELLI is a visual artist and writer living in Chicago, where he teaches in the Department of Art, Media and Design at DePaul University. He earned an MFA in Painting from Northwestern University and a BA in Studio Art from Wheaton College. His awards include a Fulbright Grant, as well as grants from the Chicago Department of Cultural Affairs and Special Events, the Ruth and Harold Chenven Foundation, and the Union League of Chicago. Carrelli's paintings and drawings have been exhibited nationally in numerous solo and group exhibitions and have appeared in many publications, including the *Chicago Sun-Times*, the *Chicago Reader*, and *New American Paintings*. His work is included in the collections of the Illinois State Museum, Elmhurst College, Northwestern University, DePaul University, and the City of Chicago, among others. His paintings are represented by Addington Gallery in Chicago, and his writing has appeared previously in *Chicago Quarterly Review* and *Crab Creek Review*.

MICHAEL COLLIER's most recent book, *My Bishop and Other Poems*, was published in 2018. He is a professor of English at the University of Maryland and a director emeritus of the Bread Loaf Writers' Conferences.

GERARDO SÁMANO CÓRDOVA is a writer from Mexico City. He holds an MFA from the University of Michigan. "Pencil Werewolf" won a Hopwood Graduate Short Fiction Award at the University of Michigan in 2018.

WILLIAM VIRGIL DAVIS's most recent book of poetry is *Dismantlements of Silence: Poems Selected and New*. He has published five other books of poetry: *The Bones Poems*; *Landscape and Journey*, which won the New Criterion Poetry Prize and the Helen C. Smith Memorial Award for Poetry; *Winter Light*; *The Dark Hours*, which won the Calliope Press Chapbook Prize; *One Way to Reconstruct the Scene*, which won the Yale Series of Younger Poets Prize. His poems have appeared in most of the major periodicals, here and abroad, including *Agenda, Agni, The Atlantic Monthly, The Gettysburg Review, The Georgia Review, The Harvard Review, The Hopkins Review, Hotel Amerika, The Hudson Review The Nation, The Malahat Review, The New Criterion, PN Review, Poetry, The Sewanee Review, Southwest Review, The Southern Review, TriQuarterly*, and *The Yale Review*, among many others.

MICHAEL DAY is a traveler, writer, and translator from Chinese and Japanese based in Mexico City, though originally from the American Midwest. He received an MA degree in East Asian Languages and Cultures from the University of Southern California with a thesis focusing on Kurahashi's fiction. His work has appeared in the *Los Angeles Review of Books China Channel, Words Without Borders, Structo, Pathlight, Paper Republic, Saint Ann's Review*, and the English PEN website.

MARCY DERMANSKY is the author of the critically acclaimed novels *Very Nice, The Red Car, Bad Marie* and *Twins*. For more information about Marcy, go to her website www.marcydermansky.com or follow her on Twitter and Instagram at @mdermansky.

REGINA DIPERNA is the author of the chapbook *A Map of Veins*. Her poetry has been published in *Boston Review, Missouri Review, Passages North, Gulf Coast, Cincinnati Review, 32 Poems* and others. She lives and works in New York City.

CHRISTINA DRILL's fiction has been published in *The Florida Review* and *Chicago Quarterly Review* and is forthcoming in *Hobart*. She is currently an MFA candidate in fiction and Michener fellow at the University of Miami, and the former production editor of *The Miami Rail*. She was raised in New Jersey and is currently based in South Florida. (Online: @stidrill)

PATRICIA ENGEL is the author of *Vida* (Grove Atlantic, 2010), which was a finalist for the PEN/Hemingway and Young Lions Fiction Awards, a *New York Times* Notable Book of the Year and winner of Colombia's national prize in literature, the Premio Biblioteca de Narrativa Colombiana; *It's Not Love, It's Just Paris* (Grove Atlantic, 2013), which won the International Latino Book Award; and *The Veins of the Ocean* (Grove Atlantic, 2016), winner of the Dayton Literary Peace Prize and named a *San Francisco Chronicle* Best Book of the Year. She has received fellowships from the Guggenheim Foundation and the National Endowment for the Arts, among others. Her books have been translated into many languages and her stories have been published widely as well as anthologized in the *O. Henry Prize Stories, The Best American Short Stories, The Best American Mystery Stories*, and elsewhere.

PETER FERRY's stories have appeared in *McSweeney's, Fiction, OR, Chicago Quarterly Review, StoryQuarterly*, and *Fifth Wednesday Journal*; he is the winner of an Illinois Arts Council Award for Short Fiction. He is a contributor to the travel pages of *The Chicago Tribune* and to *WorldHum*. He has written two novels, *Travel Writing*, which was published in 2008, and *Old Heart*, which was published in 2015 and won the Chicago Writers Association Novel of the Year award. His short story *Ike, Sharon and Me* was selected to appear in *The Best American Mystery Stories 2017*. He lives in Evanston, Illinois and Van Buren County, Michigan with his wife Carolyn.

ROBERT LONG FOREMAN's first novel, *Weird Pig*, comes out in late 2020 from SEMO Press. His collection of essays, *Among Other Things*, is available from Pleiades Press. He has won a Pushcart Prize, and his work appears in magazines like *Agni, Kenyon Review Online, Willow Springs*, and *Crazyhorse*. He lives in Kansas City.

LUKE GEDDES is a writer and collage artist living in Cincinnati, Ohio. His novel *Heart of Junk* will be published by Simon & Schuster in Janauary 2020. For more information and to purchase art, go to lukegeddes.com.

BOB GLASSMAN writes fiction and nonfiction, and makes books by hand. His novella-length prose poem, *Abscission Layer*, was featured in the Best American Poetry Blog in July 2014. An excerpt was published in *Fifth Wednesday Journal*. He produced about fifty hand bound, hardback copies for friends and acquaintants. The story "At the Plaza," published in this journal, is part of a second book, a collection of stories entitled *Caught Dead in Glenview*, again hand bound, about thirty so far. Another story in the book, "Broken Lifeline," received honorable mention in *Glimmer Train*'s final story contest. He lives and works in Evanston, Illinois.

SYED AFZAL HAIDER, author of two novels, *To Be With Her* and *Life of Ganesh,* is Senior Editor and founder of the *Chicago Quarterly Review.* His stories have appeared in many literary magazines. Oxford University Press, Milkweed Editions, Penguin Books, and Longman Literature have anthologized Haider. sahaider@sbcglobal.net

LIAM HENEGHAN, a professor of environmental science at DePaul University, is author of *Beasts at Bedtime: Revealing the Environmental Wisdom in Children's Literature* (University of Chicago Press, 2018). He is currently writing a novel set in 1st Century Ireland. He tweets @DublinSoil

CHARLES HOOD lives and teaches in the Mojave Desert, and cites two April snowfalls in one week as proof that Wisconsin in uninhabitable. He does though recommend fried cheese curds and the housing prices anywhere north of Chicago. In the past year Charles has spoken at the Getty Museum, photographed bats in Arizona, looked for snow leopards in Mongolia, received four speeding tickets, and has published two and a half books. One is a field guide to mammals of California, one is a guide to the urban nature of Los Angeles, and the third project is an essay about aerial photographer Michael Light. He is currently working on a field guide to desert reptiles and a poetry book about dead people.

GARY HOUSTON of the *CQR* staff was an editor and writer for the University of Chicago-based *Chicago Literary Review* and the *Chicago Sun-Times* before attempting a full-time acting career. He was the original Roger, "King of the Mooners," in the world premiere of *Grease* at Chicago's Kingston Mines Theater and later on various stages he portrayed

Nelson Algren, Saul Alinsky, Ring Lardner, William Blake, Samuel In-
sull, George M. Pullman, Robert S. Strauss and Presidents John Adams
and Ulysses S. Grant. He was also in *The Blues Brothers, Fargo, Watchmen,
Proof, The Astronaut Farmer* and a modest number of other appearances
on film and television.

HUGH IGLARSH is a Chicago-based writer and editor. (Well, more
or less. He lives in the proudly hipster-free suburb of Skokie, IL, with
his daughter Rosa and two cats.) He graduated long ago from Oberlin
College in Ohio and the University of Michigan, with a specialty in
English. His theater and book reviews, essays, satires and feature stories
have appeared in a variety of publications, including *Newcity, Counter-
Punch, Bridge, Apparatus Magazine* and *Chicago Jewish News.* He has also
given numerous presentations on topics historical, cultural and political
at venues ranging from the vaguely raffish (e.g., Bughouse Square in
Chicago) to the supposedly respectable (e.g., Penn State University). He
is a member of the Nelson Algren Committee (www.nelsonalgren.org),
sponsor of the annual Nelson Algren Birthday Party. His travels to the
Philippines, which inspired "Divers' Paradise," occurred some years ago;
these are his subjective impressions of one small place at one particular
point in time.

CHERYL COLLINS ISAAC emigrated to the United States in 1996
from Liberia, West Africa, where she was born, raised, and as a teenager,
survived six years of the Liberian Civil War. Her nonfiction, fiction, and
poetry have appeared in *Hawaii Pacific Review, Ocean State Review, South
Writ Large, Cosmonauts Avenue, Forbes,* and others. She has been a writing
resident at Tin House and Disquiet International workshops.

ROBERT KERWIN's celebrity profiles, essays, short stories, and travel
and op-ed pieces have appeared in *Playboy, Cosmopolitan, Travel & Leisure, Ellipsis, Chicago Quarterly Review, Catamaran, The New York Times, The
Washington Post, Chicago Tribune Magazine,* and *Los Angeles Times Calendar,*
among others. Born in Chicago, he received a BS in Journalism from
the University of Illinois, and later attended University College Dublin,
Ireland, as a graduate student reading English Literature. He now lives
in northern California, and most recently has been working on a memoir, *Another World, Another Time.*

WAQAS KHWAJA is Professor of English at Agnes Scott College. He
teaches postcolonial literature, 18th and 19th century British literature,
and creative writing. He has published four collections of poetry, a lit-

erary travelogue about his experiences with the International Writing Program at the University of Iowa, and several edited anthologies of Pakistani literature in translation.

CHUCK KRAMER is a Chicago-based freelance photographer and writer. His photo-journalism has appeared in the *Windy City Times*, *Nightspots*, *InChicago*, *Show*, and *Knack* magazines. He's also shot book covers, album covers, and author portraits. His fine art photos have appeared in gallery shows and online at various sites. More of his photography is available at Chuck Kramer Photography on Facebook and chuckkramerphotography.smugmug.com. He has been working with *CQR* since 2015. Poetry at *Eclectica Magazine*, *Write City Magazine*, and *Third Wednesday*. Fiction in *Every Day Fiction*, *Off the Rocks*, and *Hypertext*.

YUMIKO KURAHASHI, a Japanese author whose works of fantastic, mythical, genre-bending experimental fiction consistently question literary and social norms, was born in 1935 in Kōchi, Shikoku. Without her parents' knowledge or consent, she applied and was admitted to the French department at Meiji University, where she wrote her graduation thesis on Jean-Paul Sartre's *Being and Nothingness*. Kurahashi's short story "Partei" [*"Parutai"*] was nominated for the prestigious Akutagawa Prize in 1960, while she was still a student. Though she did not win, the exposure made Kurahashi famous. She went on to win the *Meiji Daigaku gakuchō shō* [Meiji University President's Prize] in 1960, the *Joryū bungaku shō* [Women's Literature Prize] in 1961, the *Tamura Toshiko shō* [Tamura Toshiko Memorial Prize] in 1987, and the *Tokubetsu kōrō shō* [Lifetime Achievement Award], which was awarded to her posthumously by Meiji University in 2006. She continued to write prolifically until her death in 2005.

LOUISE LEBOURGEOIS is a painter and writer living in Chicago. She earned her BFA from the School of the Art Institute of Chicago, an MFA in Painting from Northwestern University, and an MFA in Creative Writing-Nonfiction from Columbia College Chicago. LeBourgeois has exhibited her work throughout the United States and in Italy, Japan, and the Netherlands. Her work is included in the collections of the City of Chicago, Fermilab, the University of Chicago Hospitals, Ampersand Art Supply, and others. She was commissioned from The Chicago Department of Cultural Affairs to create a permanent public work for the city's 17th District Police Station. She is a recipient of an Artadia grant and an Illinois Arts Council grant, and participated in residencies at the BAU Institute in Otranto, Italy, and the Ragdale Foundation. Her paintings have been featured in the *Catamaran Literary Reader* and the *Jung Journal: Culture and Psyche*. Her essays have been published in the *Chicago Quarterly Review* and *The Rumpus*. LeBourgeois swims in Lake Michigan from May until October. Her open water swimming provides her with visual and kinesthetic memories that inform her paintings.

DAVID LEHMAN is a poet, writer, and editor. The most recent of his ten books of poetry are *Playlist* (2019) and *Poems in the Manner Of* (2017). He is the author of nine nonfiction books, most recently *One Hundred Autobiographies: A Memoir* (2019). *A Fine Romance: Jewish Songwriters, America Songs* won the Deems Taylor Award from ASCAP in 2010. Lehman is the editor of *The Oxford Book of American Poetry* and *Great American Prose Poems*. He initiated *The Best American Poetry* series in 1988 and continues as the general editor of this distinguished anthology series. He has received a Guggenheim Fellowship and an award in literature from the American Academy of Arts and Letters.

BRONTE LIM was born and raised in Burnaby, British Columbia, to Chinese immigrant parents who accidentally gave her a literary name— thus, no umlaut. She graduated with a BA from Harvard College, where she majored in English and minored in Chemistry, performed improv comedy, and spent summers abroad in Paris, Beijing, and Boston for study and research. For her creative short fiction thesis, a collection of stories exploring Chinese immigrant identity and bodily autonomy titled *White Rabbit*, she received high honors. When not writing, she is cycling, watercolor painting, or bird-watching. She currently works as a documentary researcher and lives in Somerville, Massachusetts. This is her second published story.

KATHLEEN MCGOOKEY's most recent book is *Heart in a Jar* (White Pine Press). Her book *Instructions for My Imposter* is forthcoming from Press 53 and her chapbook *Nineteen Letters* is forthcoming from BatCat Press. Her work has appeared in journals including *Crazyhorse, Denver Quarterly, Epoch, Field, Indiana Review, Ploughshares, The Prose Poem: An International Journal, Prairie Schooner, Quarterly West, Rhino, Seneca Review,* and *West Branch*. She has also published two other books of poems, two chapbooks and a book of translations of French poet Georges Godeau's prose poems.

ELIZABETH MCKENZIE is the author of *Stop That Girl, MacGregor Tells the World*, and *The Portable Veblen*. A former staff editor at *The Atlantic*, she has been with the *Chicago Quarterly Review* since 2003.

MICHAEL MINER was raised in Canada and suburban St. Louis, educated in journalism at the University of Missouri, spent a couple of years in the navy (he published a couple of poems in his ship's newspaper), and came to Chicago in 1970 to work for the *Sun-Times*. He's been a staff writer for the *Reader* since 1979.

FAISAL MOHYUDDIN is the author of *The Displaced Children of Displaced Children* (Eyewear 2018), which won the 2017 Sexton Prize for Poetry, was selected as a Summer 2018 Recommendation of the Poetry Book Society, and was named a "highly commended" collection of 2018 by the Forward Arts Foundation. Also the author of the chapbook *The Riddle of Longing* (Backbone 2017), Faisal's work has appeared in *Chicago Quarterly Review*, *Prairie Schooner*, the *Missouri Review*, *Catamaran*, *RHINO*, and elsewhere. He serves as an educator adviser to the global not-for-profit Narrative 4 and teaches English at Highland Park High School in Illinois.

ROBERTA MONTGOMERY is a former editor at *The Atlantic* and wrote and produced many TV game shows including "Liars," and "Family Feud." She currently lives in Sag Harbor, New York.

DIPIKA MUKHERJEE is the author of the novels *Shambala Junction*, which won the UK Virginia Prize for Fiction, and *Ode to Broken Things*, which was longlisted for the Man Asia Literary Prize. Her short story collection is *Rules of Desire* (Fixi, 2015) and she has two poetry collections, The *Third Glass of Wine* (Writer's Workshop, 2015), and *The Palimpsest of Exile* (Rubicon Press, 2009). Her work is included in *The Best Small Fictions 2019* and she frequently writes for *World Literature Today*, *Asia Literary Review* and *Chicago Quarterly Review* as well as a literary column for *The Edge* in Malaysia. She is core faculty at StoryStudio Chicago, teaches at the Graham School at University of Chicago, and is affiliated to the Buffet Institute for Global Affairs at Northwestern University. www.dipikamukherjee.com

GREGG MURRAY is Associate Professor of English at Georgia State University's Perimeter College and Editor-in-Chief of *Muse/A Journal*. His essays appear regularly in *The Huffington Post* and *The Fanzine*. Gregg has new creative nonfiction in *Pleiades* and *The Doctor T.J. Eckleburg Review*. He also writes poetry and throws elaborate art parties.

SCOTT NADELSON grew up in northern New Jersey before escaping to Oregon, where he has lived for the past twenty-two years. He is the author of a novel, *Between You and Me*; a memoir, *The Next Scott Nadelson: A Life in Progress*; and four collections of short fiction, the most recent of which, *The Fourth Corner of the World*, was named a 2019 Association of Jewish Libraries (AJL) Jewish Fiction Award Honor Book. His stories and essays have appeared in *AGNI*, *Ploughshares*, *Harvard Review*, *Glimmer Train*, *Alaska Quarterly Review*, *New England Review*, and *Prairie Schooner*, and they have been cited as notable in both *The Best American Short Stories* and *The Best American Essays*. A winner of the Reform Judaism Fiction Prize, the Great Lakes Colleges Association New Writers Award, and an Oregon Book Award, he teaches at Willamette University and in the Rainier Writing Workshop MFA Program at Pacific Lutheran University.

NATALIA NEBEL is a Pushcart Prize nominated writer whose work has been published in literary journals that include *Fifth Wednesday Review*, *Burnside Review*, *Free Verse*, *Prague Review* and *Seems*. In 2017 and 2018, Northwestern's MFA program nominated her for the AWP First Journal award in the essay and short story categories. She is co-curator for Sunday Salon Chicago, a literary reading series that was named one of 2019's Top 50 Chicago literary organizations.

NAOMI SHIHAB NYE is the Young People's Poet Laureate of the Poetry Foundation of Chicago for 2019-2021. Her most recent books are *The Tiny Journalist*, *Voices in the Air: Poems for Listeners*, *The Turtle of Oman* (a novel for children, named as the Little Read selection of Lenoir-Rhyne University, Hickory, North Carolina, in 2019), and *Transfer*.

HARRY MARK PETRAKIS is a novelist and short story writer with twenty-four published books. He has been nominated twice for the National Book Award in fiction. In addition to writing, Petrakis has been teacher and storyteller, in the old Bardic tradition, appearing at colleges and clubs to read his stories. Now in his mid-nineties, and still writing stories, Petrakis and his wife Diana have been married for seventy-three years. They have three sons, four grandchildren and a great-granddaughter.

Until 2007, **ELINA PETROVA** lived in Ukraine and worked in engineering management. She has many publication credits and a book of poems in Russian. Her English-language books of poetry are *Aching Miracle* (2015) and *Desert Candles* (2019). Elina's poetry has been published in *Texas Review, Texas Poetry Calendar, FreeFall* (Canada), *Ocotillo Review, Voices de la Luna, Melancholy Hyperbole, Illya's Honey, Panoply, Poetry of the American Southwest* series by Dos Gatos Press, various anthologies by Mutabilis Press, *Echoes of the Cordillera* (Sul Ross State University), *Selfhood* (India), several anthologies of the Houston, Austin and Waco poetry festivals, and an upcoming Bosch and Bruegel Anthology. Elina, a frequent Pushcart Prize nominee, won top honors in the 2018 Ekphrastic Poetry Contest of the Friendswood Library, and was a finalist for the post of Houston Poet.

GENEVIEVE PLUNKETT's fiction has appeared in *The O. Henry Prize Stories* and journals such as *New England Review, Southern Review, Colorado Review, Crazyhorse,* and *West Branch,* among others. A 2017 recipient of the St. Botolph Foundation Award for Emerging Artists, she lives in Vermont.

JORY POST lives in Santa Cruz, California, where he and his wife make handmade books and broadsides as JoKa Press. His work has been published in *82 Review, Chicago Quarterly Review, Red Wheelbarrow, Porter Gulch Review, Catamaran Literary Reader,* and the upcoming issue of *The Sun.* His first book of poems, *The Extra Year,* will be released by *Anaphora Literary Press* on October 1. Post is the editor and founder of *phren-Z* online literary magazine, dedicated to showcasing the work of Santa Cruz County writers since 2011.

SIGNE RATCLIFF is Contributing Editor of *Chicago Quarterly Review.* Her short fiction has appeared in *Chicago Quarterly Review* and *Conclave Journal.* Her work was selected as a finalist entry for the James Jones First Novel Fellowship. She lives in Chicago.

ALYSSA RIPLEY is a student at the University of Missouri where she will graduate with a bachelor's degree in English. Her work is published in *SAND Journal* and has also appeared in *Sky Island Journal* and *Levee Magazine.* She also works at a small daycare with kids who make her life exceptionally bright.

CHUCK ROSENTHAL is the author of eleven novels, among them *The Loop Trilogy; Elena of the Stars; My Mistress, Humanity; The Heart of Mars; Ten Thousand Heavens;* and *The Legend of La Diosa.* Rosenthal has published a memoir of childhood molestation, *Never Let Me Go;* a travel book, *Are We Not There Yet? Travels in Nepal, North India, and Bhutan;* a book of narrative essays, *West of Eden: A Life in 21st Century Los Angeles;* and two books of experimental poetry with Gail Wronsky. His book on animal cognition, *How the Animals Around You Think*, is forthcoming in October 2019. He's published in numerous magazines and read and lectured to live audiences and on television and radio throughout the U.S. as well as in Mexico, Argentina, England, and India. His work has been translated into German, Italian, Spanish, Swedish, and Korean. His fiction and nonfiction have been nominated for the PEN West Literary Award, the National Book Award, the National Book Critics Circle Award, and Best American Nonfiction. "Invasion" is an excerpt from his forthcoming novel *The Hammer, the Sickle, and the Heart, Trotsky and Kahlo in Mexico*. He has traveled and researched extensively in Mexico City and throughout Mexico.

R. CRAIG SAUTTER is author, coauthor, and editor of ten books including *Expresslanes Through The Inevitable City* (poems, december press). For nearly four decades, he has taught courses in philosophy, politics, history, literature, and creative writing at DePaul University. This is his third story published by *CQR*.

EMILY SCHULTEN is the author of *Rest in Black Haw*. Her work has appeared in *Prairie Schooner, The Missouri Review, Barrow Street,* and *Tin House,* among others. She is a professor of English and creative writing at The College of the Florida Keys.

Born and raised in Lahore, Pakistan, **MOAZZAM SHEIKH** came to the US to earn an undergrad in Cinema and a Masters in Library Science. He has made his home in San Francisco since 1985. Librarian by profession, he is the author two short story collections: *The Idol Lover and Other Stories,* and *Cafe Le Whore and Other Stories.* He is the editor and translator of *Circle and Other Stories* by Intizar Husain, which was also published in India as *Intizar Husain Stories.* In 2004, he edited *A Letter from India: Contemporary Short Stories from Pakistan.* He is the guest-editor of the special issue on South Asian American writing by *Chicago Quarterly Review* (2017). He has finished a novel recently, and lives with his wife and two sons.

BRIAN ALLAN SKINNER has written and published more than 120 short stories which appeared in small press and literary magazines, as well as anthologies, in the United States, Canada, and Ireland. He is a former poetry and nonfiction reviewer for *Kirkus Reviews* and a production artist for *Scientific American Newsletters* in New York City. His two most recent collections of illustrated short fiction are *Shoot Me, Jesus: Tales of the Old & New Southwest* and *The Magic of Kindness: A Novel in Short Stories.* In 2015, Brian moved to Taos, New Mexico, which he first visited with his grandmother on a cross-country train trip aboard the Santa Fe Chief in 1960. He quickly settled into the thriving artistic and literary communities of Taos where he draws sustenance and inspiration from his many artist and writer friends.

CHRISTINE SNEED is the author of the novels *Paris, He Said* and *Little Known Facts,* and the story collections *Portraits of a Few of the People I've Made Cry* and *The Virginity of Famous Men*. Her work has been included in *The Best American Short Stories, O. Henry Prize Stories, New York Times, Chicago Tribune, New England Review, The Southern Review, Ploughshares, Glimmer Train,* and *O Magazine*. She lives in southern California and teaches for Northwestern University's and Regis University's graduate creative writing programs.

ELEANOR SPIESS-FERRIS is a visual artist and only recently turned to writing, blending childhood memories of her native New Mexico into short stories. She is cited as a significant American surrealist and is known for her narrative and feminist iconography. A retrospective of her visual art will open at the end of October at the Illinois State museum in Springfield and move to the Evanston Art Center in Evanston, Illinois in early spring of 2020. A one-person exhibition of new works will open in May 2020 at Hofheimer Gallery, Chicago. Eleanor has been involved with the *Chicago Quarterly Review* for close to seven years.

JAMES STACEY is the author and co-author of two nonfiction books on health policy. He also has written feature-length articles for the *Washington Post, Chicago Tribune, Chicago Sun-Times* and other publications, and served as a reporter for Fairchild Publications, *Business Week,* and *American Medical News*. He has been an editor at *Chicago Quarterly Review* since 2012.

A lecturer at Smith College, **PATRICIA STACEY** has written, taught, and published widely on the subject of love and desire. Her creative nonfiction on the subject has appeared in *The New York Times* "Modern Love" column, *O, The Oprah Magazine, Cosmopolitan* and *Brain, Child*. A recipient of the Massachusetts Cultural Council Award for creative nonfiction and fiction, she has also published in *The Atlantic* and other publications. Her first book, *The Boy Who Loved Windows,* joined *The Life of Pi* and *The Curious Incident of the Dog in the Night-time* as one of BookBrowse's Favorite Books of the Year by Debut Authors.

UMBERTO TOSI is the author of *Sometimes Ridiculous, Ophelia Rising,* and *Milagro on 34th Street*. His short stories have appeared various journals, including *Catamaran Literary Reader* and *Chicago Quarterly Review,* where he has been a contributing editor since 2013. He was managing editor for pioneering online book publisher MightyWords, Inc., from 1999-2002 and was a contributing writer to *Forbes* covering high tech culture. Prior to that, he was an editor and staff writer for the *Los Angeles Times* (for eleven years) and managing editor of its Sunday magazine, *West.* He also served as editor of *San Francisco Magazine.* He has written more than 300 feature articles for newspapers and magazines, online and in print. His writing bends towards magic realism on its own. He has been a contributing member of the indie writer-publisher group, Authors Electric, since 2015 and has contributed to several of its anthologies, including *Another Flash in the Pen* and *One More Flash in the Pen.* He has four adult children—Alicia Sammons, Kara Towe, Cristina Sheppard and Zoë Tosi—nine grandchildren, and three great grandchildren. He resides in Chicago. (Contact: Umberto3000@gmail.com)

ALVARO VILLANUEVA received a creative writing degree from California State University at Long Beach, and promptly disregarded it to become a book designer instead. He publishes much more apace with books for various publishers than he ever would have as a novelist, though he can sometimes be found late at night writing killer email. He runs a small design studio in Oakland, California, and teaches in the Graphic Design department at California College of the Arts in San Francisco. His portfolio is online at bookishdesign.com

JAKE YOUNG received his MFA from North Carolina State University, and currently attends the PhD program in creative writing at the University of Missouri–Columbia. His first collection of poems is *American Oak* (Main Street Rag, 2018). He has published in numerous journals and anthologies, and his most recent work appears or is forthcoming in *Miramar, Askew, Cloudbank,* and *The Hudson Review.* In 2014, Jake attended the Djerassi Resident Artists Program. He also serves as the poetry editor for the *Chicago Quarterly Review.*

INVISIBLE

A STAGE PLAY about the

1920s Women's Ku Klux Klan Movement.
Just in time to see history repeat itself.
Name your 'ISM'. Join! "All the best people do."

Written by Mary Bonnett
Directed by Cecilie Keenan

OCTOBER 3 - NOVEMBER 3, 2019

THURSDAY - SATURDAY 7:30PM   SUNDAYS 3:00PM

At STAGE 773   1225 W. BELMONT AVE. CHICAGO, IL

TICKETS: stage773.com

Information Group Rates: HerStoryTheater.org 312-835-1410

Sponsored by The Oppenheimer Family Foundation

The Extra Year
by Jory Post

"These poems, written in a burst of productivity following a diagnosis, are smart, merciless missives sent from the edge of time. Poems that reveal a mind that wants to know all; about the nest of a hooded oriole, the behavior of humans on the oncology ward, the powers of the linear accelerator. Here is a heart brave enough to grieve all it has ever loved. And a speaker who takes the time to sift through the dirt, find riches, and lay them out for us, one gem at a time." - Danusha Laméris

"Rainier Maria Rilke said that for a poet there are two kinds of poems: the ones a poet writes and the ones a poet has to write. In The Extra Year, Jory Post has given us those necessary, significant poems. Mortality and the imminence of dying is the window that frames the vision of this astonishing book. With candor, wit, and a deep humanity, he details a reverence for life out of the ordinary and commonplace of our days. He beholds the world with wonder, graciousness, and gratitude. This is a book you can return to again and again. I know of no other work quite like it." - Joe Stroud

"Bracingly honest and beautifully wrought, Jory Post's The Extra Year explores mortality as well as the business of living. His wife's snoring sounds like "…percussive inhaling, cello and bass on the exhale, an occasional hint of tuba…" A playful humor runs through many of the poems, both belying and intensifying the subjects. With an extraordinary scope, Post shares with us his fear of "the hot eye of death," his love of the art of Joseph Cornell, and above all, his family and friends. He shares the story of a life well lived, told movingly and poignantly." - Ellen Bass

"In his marvelous book of prose poems, Jory Post asks, "What would I do if I was given an extra year?" This is not idle speculation. We learn early on that Post is writing in the shadow of a terminal cancer diagnosis, though he is determined "not to fuss about it too much." In that spirit, he has written a book not about dying, but about living. The Extra Year also celebrates the writing life, and it's clear that Post lives to write, and writes to live. His collection reminds us that life is both a gift, and a challenge to embrace it as deeply as we can." - Gary Young

Anaphora Literary Press
https://anaphoraliterary.com
October 1 Release date

The Stuart Brent Children's Book Club

TODAY A READER,

www.stuartbrent.com

Share your passion.

The

Nelson Algren
Committee

On the Make
Since 1989

nelsonalgren.org

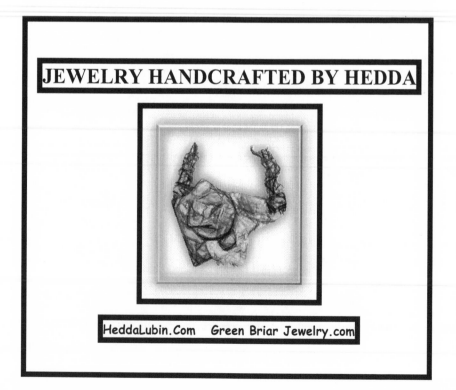

THE BOOK STALL

811 Elm St. Winneka, Il 60093 / 847-446-8880 / www.thebookstall.com

The Book Stall is a full-service bookstore located in Winnetka, Illinois. Our selection has something for every type of reader: from history to fiction, philosophy to graphic novels, and more. We stock a wide variety of greeting cards, stationery, puzzles, and other great gift items.

The Book Stall is known for its many special events for kids and adults alike. We host reading groups, poetry sessions, and a regular story-telling time for children.

the Celtic Knot
PUBLIC HOUSE

Open for Lunch, Brunch and Dinner
Live Music • Storytelling

"your home away from home"
626 Church St. | Evanston | 847-864-1679
www.celticknotpub.com

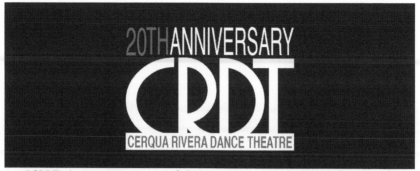

20TH ANNIVERSARY
CRDT
CERQUA RIVERA DANCE THEATRE

"CRDT pieces engage some of the most pressing questions of our time."

"The company has never looked better."

"Cerqua Rivera Dance Theatre has been growing like a wildflower."

Cerqua Rivera Dance Theatre uses dance and music to nourish
the mind and the soul. The company unites artists and
audiences to explore themes that shape our community.
more on Facebook, Instagram, and www.cerquarivera.org

L i f e   o f   G a n e s h

a novel by Syed Afzal Haider

A beautiful meditation on the cheating heart, the broken heart. Original and memorable.

— **Karen Joy Fowler**

*In **Life of Ganesh**, Syed Afzal Haider has given his readers a sensual and lyrical meditation on love, family, loss, and desire. This is a beautiful, sexy novel by a wise and gifted writer.*

— **Christine Sneed**

***Life of Ganesh** is an unforgettable novel of vision and wisdom, laughter and tears. Haider writes beautifully about love and longing.*

— **Elizabeth McKenzie**

$17.95 ISBN: 978-0-9843776-4-0

Small Press Distribution

WEAVERS PRESS, SF

Weaverspresssf@gmail.com

PROP THTR

Writers Aloud

Reading of new works
Fiction, non fiction, poetry

3502 N Elston
First Sundays (usually)
3-5pm

No reservations needed; just come. Want to read
your writing? Contact: karen.o.fort@gmail.com

THE PHANTOM COLLECTIVE
& DAVENPORT'S PRESENT

REBECCA TOON IN

Reckless Daughter
The Music
of Joni Mitchell

Monday, November 4, 2019, 8 pm
Davenport's Piano Bar
1383 N. Milwaukee Ave. 773.278.1830
www.davenportspianobar.com
$15 cover charge / two-drink minimum
Christopher Pazdernik, *Director*
Ryan Brewster, *Musical Director*

2018
In The
Margins Book
Award

2018
Paterson Prize
Honor Book
For Books For
Young People

AHGOTTAHANDLEONIT

Donovan Mixon...

is one of those ambidextrous, crossover artists. He has been a faculty member of Berklee College of Music, won an NEA grant for jazz composition and taught and performed abroad in jazz festivals and schools in Istanbul, Budapest, Shanghai and Singapore. Mixon has released four recordings that feature prominent musicians from Boston to Milan to Istanbul, including the great alto saxophonist Lee Konitz – and meanwhile also became a writer. Ahgottahandleonit is his just-out Young Adult novel. A graphic novel, "Race for Next to Last Place," is now in the works.

"A NATIVE SON for a new generation"–
John Wright, Professor Emeritus of Classics at Northwestern University

"GIVE TO FANS Of Daniel Keyes's Flowers For Algernon Or Sapphire's Push."
2017 School Library Journal Review

"AN EXISTENTIAL examination of the CYCLE OF VIOLENCE."
Kirkus Reviews

Cinco Puntos Press cincopuntos.com

DONOVANMIXONWRITER.COM

Best Books of 2018

"A stunning debut memoir..."
KIRKUS REVIEWS

Best Book—Indie Nonfiction 2018
CHICAGO WRITERS ASSOCIATION

2020 RIVER STYX MICROFICTION CONTEST

500 words max per story, up to three stories per entry fee

$10 entry fee: a copy of issue 104 (with winning stories)
$20 entry fee: a one-year subscription

1st, 2nd, and 3rd place will be published in Issue 104
All stories considered for publication
See website for guidelines:
http://www.riverstyx.org/submit/microfiction-contest/

prize of
$1,500 and
publication in River Styx

enter online via
Submittable

deadline
December 31, 2019

www.riverstyx.org

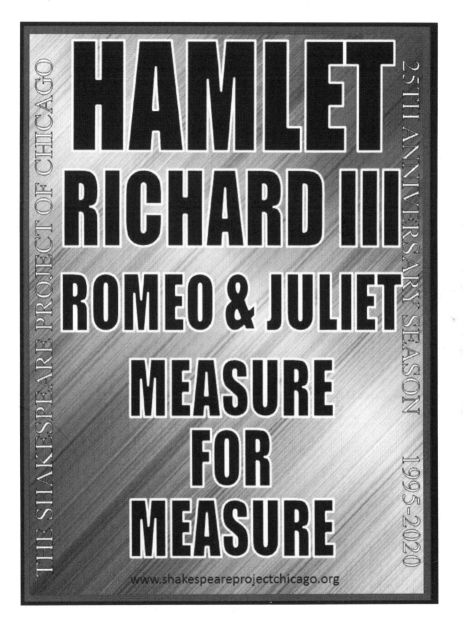

SUNDAY SALON CHICAGO
IS A READING SERIES
THAT TAKES PLACE EVERY OTHER MONTH

OPEN TO ALL
FOR OVER TEN YEARS
THE SALON SERIES HAS BROUGHT WORD POWER TO
NEW YORK CITY, NAIROBI, MIAMI AND CHICAGO
MAKING OUR BEST LOCAL AND NATIONAL WRITERS AVAILABLE
TO A LARGER COMMUNITY

WE MEET AT
THE REVELER
3403 N Damen Ave., in Chicago
FROM 7PM TO 8PM ON THE LAST SUNDAY OF EVERY OTHER MONTH

EAT, DRINK YOUR FAVORITE DRINKS, MAKE NEW FRIENDS
AND ENJOY EXCELLENT READINGS WITH US!

OUR EVENTS ARE ALWAYS FREE

Find us at https://sundaysalon-chicago.com
https://www.facebook.com/Sunday.Salon.Chicago/

Made in the
USA
Columbia, SC

79545297R00269